S0-FIY-472

EAST TIMOR

EAST TIMOR

Nationalism & Colonialism

Jill Jolliffe

University of Queensland Press

Typeset by Academy Press Pty Ltd, Brisbane
Printed and bound by Silex Enterprise & Printing Co., Hong Kong

Distributed in the United Kingdom, Europe, the Middle East Africa and the Caribbean by Prentice-Hall International, International Book Distributors Ltd, 66 Wood Lane End, Hemel Hempstead, Herts. England

National Library of Australia
Cataloguing-in-Publication data

Jolliffe, Jill, 1945–.
East Timor.

ISBN 0 7022 1480 9
ISBN 0 7022 1481 7 Paperback

1. East Timor–History. I. Title.

959.86

Contents

Illustrations

Preface

This book was written with several aims. One is to trace the historical roots of modern Timorese nationalism and, in so doing, to outline the problems of writing an adequate history of the people of East Timor. The core of the book is the product of three months spent in East Timor as a journalist, from 11 September 1975, soon after the UDT coup, to 2 December, five days before the Indonesian assault on Dili. It records the initiation of a de facto administration by FRETILIN, the political movement which emerged victorious from the civil war of 10–28 August and the re-establishment of peace in the territory, contrary to reports then being published and accepted outside East Timor. It also documents escalating Indonesian incursions into East Timor, which I witnessed at Batugadé in late September and at Atabae in the closing weeks of November 1975, which led to FRETILIN's unilateral declaration of independence on 28 November and eventually to the full-scale invasion of East Timor on 7 December.

I have also endeavoured to answer the question: 'what sort of government would an independent East Timor have?' For this reason the book is largely a history of the development of FRETILIN, as Basil Davidson's history of Angolan nationalism, *In the Eye of the Storm*, is principally the story of the MPLA. It is apparent from the recent history of East Timor that, given political regroupments which may occur between Timorese nationalists of all shades inside or outside East Timor, FRETILIN (itself subject to change) would be the major component of the government of an independent East Timor.

The book attempts to present events in the period September-December 1975 as they unfolded in East Timor itself and to explain developments as I think they appeared to politically conscious Timorese. On this first principle, material dealing with the death of the five journalists at Balibó has been spread over several chapters. The material in Balibó and Beyond (Chapter 7) describes what was known in East Timor at the time of the attack on Balibó, and later, from those who came from the area—in particular, the Portuguese television crew and the FRETILIN soldiers who retreated from the town. Material dealing with contemporary investigations by the Foreign Affairs Department in Australia is reserved for Australia's Role (Chapter 10) and later information from Timorese who entered Balibó with Indonesian forces, and who subsequently defected, is dealt with in the last chapter, which spans events since 7 December 1975.

Place name spellings have been taken from the Portuguese government map of East Timor, although these frequently vary from local usage. The range of different spellings in use (for example, Liquiçá is spelt variously Liquissa, Liquiçé and Likisa) necessitates use of the Portuguese standard. The one exception to this is Dili, which has been spelt in conformity with international usage rather than the Portuguese form Díli.

At the time of writing, Indonesia's war against East Timor continues unabated, behind the information cordon thrown round the territory on 7 December 1975. The response of the international community to the invasion of East Timor, in which charges of wholesale killing of civilians have been levelled against the Indonesian Republic, has been slow. Isolation is the traditional enemy of the East Timorese: it was so during the harshest years of Portuguese colonial rule described in The Colonial Impact (Chapter 2) and today, under Indonesian occupation, the old enemy has returned. No physical contact has been made with FRETILIN leaders in East Timor since December 1975. *East Timor* is written in the hope that the information it presents may lead to international action not only to break the silence but to subject Indonesia's role to the scrutiny of the world community.

Acknowledgments

Thanks are due to Helen Hill for the use of her notes, Cristóvão Santos of the Democratic Republic of East Timor Information Office in Melbourne for patiently answering many queries, Michael Harrington for criticism and assistance, Jim Brady for proofreading, Kevin Sherlock for access to bibliographical material, Gavin Quinn and Julie Jordan for general assistance, Pat Bonnice for typing, Dr John Whitehall for access to his Timor diary and to Grant Evans for use of material produced in Appendix A. Thanks also to many friends who assisted with time, money and advice, and to the Australian Performing Group collective for the use of their facilities and for financial assistance, before a New Writers Fellowship from the Literature Board of the Australia Council made full-time writing possible. Above all, thanks are due to the generous assistance of East Timorese with whom I worked during three months in East Timor, including the FRETILIN administration for their co-operative dealings with the press.

Prologue: "Peace and Stability"

The day, not yet dawned, was 7 December 1975 in Dili, capital of tiny East Timor, 620 kilometres northwest of Australia. The town slept, tensely. Military transports moved around the streets, no lights showing. Behind their iron-shuttered shop doors some of the city's several thousand remaining Chinese played mah jong.

Nine days before, the first national Timorese government in the history of the territory had been declared. Five days before, the Australians had left, or rather, all but one. Medical aid workers, Red Cross officials, a couple of journalists and an eccentric old-age pensioner had flown out to Darwin following a cable from the Australian government. Some Red Cross workers had continued their clinic in Dili, commuting on the five minute air trip from the neighbouring island of Ataúro. They had left at 5 pm the evening before. As they flew over Dili they noted three grey forms sliding down the coast past the town of Liquiçá.

Because the capital was on full military alert no lights showed. The foreshore lay flat and exposed—the Hotel Turismo, the Bishop of Dili's house, the Museum and the fashionable Farol district, now empty of the Portuguese officers who had desported themselves there.

About two hours after midnight the night erupted. The black was broken by a series of flashes out to sea, the silence by the unearthly boom of naval bombardment. Children cried, the memory of fighting following a coup the previous August freshly scarred on their minds. Screaming filled the air as shells pounded the city. Planes came too, swooping and bombing, swooping and bombing. Those who could, ran towards the hospital at the rear of town or were transported by the few FRETILIN[1] vehicles still operating. For days the hospital had been the tacitly-agreed centre in the event of the feared Indonesian attack.

The Australian who remained, journalist Roger East, regretted his decision to stay at the Hotel Turismo. The day before, the diminutive President Xavier do Amaral had invited him to move to his pink stucco house at the rear of the city. East had declined; his stomach was upset and he felt more comfortable staying where he was—he had been in war zones before but the Turismo was on the foreshore, isolated from the rest of the city and a difficult place from which to retreat.

For three or four hours the bombardment continued. The airport at the eastern end of town was pounded, as were the western suburbs—the hills behind Fatocama beach where the Indonesians knew there to be a gun emplacement. Chinese huddled in the Taiwanese consulate on the foreshore, but soon the shells ploughed into it too. FRETILIN soldiers positioned themselves around the town, especially in the airport area, where a landing was expected. At dawn the soldiers came. Six or seven Invader bombers and DC3s dived over the town dropping not bombs but paratroops.

Just west of the Comoro river mouth, past the airport, Japanese marines had swarmed ashore a little over thirty years before. Now Indonesians used the same landing place, where the land falls into the sea like a sheer underwater cliff and no coral reefs obstruct. They landed, like their predecessors, at a place where they thought they might have some local assistance, near the predominantly pro Indonesian Moslem quarter. But the area was staked out by front-line Timorese soldiers who fought the landing troops like people possessed. By now, dawn was breaking and the sky was ablaze with fires at all points of the city. The Indonesian marines pushed forward, taking heavy losses. They aimed to proceed along the course of the Comoro river to behind the city where they could cut off retreat. In Dili bay, too, landing barges bouyant on the high tide skimmed the coral reefs packed with marines.

At around eight o'clock a Minister of the newly-proclaimed Democratic Republic of East Timor made radio contact with Darwin. He was Alarico Fernandes, who had been to Australia shortly before, vainly appealing to Australians to act against the possibility of what was happening now.

Soon after the bombardment began, Alarico had gone to Roger East, to collect him in preparation for the retreat from Dili. But East wouldn't come. Perhaps he mentally froze at the prospect of going into the streets where the Indonesians were shooting anyone they saw, or maybe he held some hope of getting a message through to Darwin via the Marconi telecommunications post in the centre of town. So Alarico went to Carmo, his vice-Minister in the government. Fernando Carmo had been under fire on many occasions and had a cool head. He was trained in Angola by the Portuguese army. After FRETILIN came to power in August he commanded the border zone. Everyone felt safe when the gentle Carmo was around: he exuded responsibility and was wary of expressions of fanaticism.

Now he tried to get back to Roger East to insist that he leave. With a group of soldiers he took a jeep and tried to edge his way through the streets, turning and taking another course when he saw groups of Indonesians ahead. The city was alight and mortars and grenades crumped all around. Round a corner, in the cemetery suburb of Santa Cruz, he turned into a group of Indonesians. Before the fatal mistake could register he was cut down by automatic fire. Too late, the soldiers with him returned the fire. A number of paratroopers fell: three ran away. Carmo was already dead. Leaving the car, one of the escort, Fernando, led a group which made its way towards where Roger East had been. He had met Carmo's fate. Almost a month later Fernando was to rejoin Alarico and tell him of the ill-fated expedition. Now he just had to get out of Dili and into the hills.[2]

In Darwin a group of journalists clustered anxiously around the Red Cross radio. They heard the desperate pleas of Alarico Fernandes whom some of them had left only a few days before:

> Indonesian forces have been landed in Dili by sea, by sea ... They are flying over Dili dropping out paratroopers ... Aircraft are dropping out more and more paratroopers ... A lot of people have been killed indiscriminately ... Women and children are going to be killed by Indonesian forces ... we are going to be killed! SOS, we call for your help, this is an urgent call ...

Fernandes was appealing to the Australian government to take action. He may as well have addressed his appeals to Iceland. Just three days before, ex-Labor Prime Minister Gough Whitlam had said that his government would have taken no action in the event of an Indonesian invasion.[3] Perhaps the few members of the party's parliamentary caucus who had championed the rights of the Timorese may have been able to change his position. Whitlam had come to the leadership of the Labor party in the mid-sixties on a policy of moderating his predecessor Arthur Calwell's unpopular but unyielding stance on the Vietnam war. The burgeoning anti-war movement had demonstrated against the betrayal then. By 1972 mounting pressure from Labor party branches and the development of a massive extra-parliamentary anti-war movement had moved Whitlam to a more principled position. Given time, the same may have been true for Timor. But the dissidents were few and the Timorese didn't have time on their side.

In early November the Labor government was ousted in an amazing sequence of events and the Liberal-National Country Party government of Malcolm Fraser took power. Fraser had earlier denounced FRETILIN as "Communists". One week before an election which was to confirm Fraser's caretaker government in power, the mood of the Australian people was inward-turning. Consumed with domestic questions, the labour movement had no intention of fighting the election on foreign policy. Apart from other factors, to do so would involve self-criticism. In December 1975 the Australian labour movement once again expressed its traditionally ambivalent attitude to the peoples of Asia. Perhaps if Europeans had never come to Australia and the Aborigines had been in power they might have heeded the radio plea from a Timorese brother. They shared some common points in history. The Portuguese had used them as slaves, too. In their *caravels* they had come to Melville Island and carried off Aboriginal people.

Dawn revealed six or seven warships in the harbour. The Indonesians were killing in a crazed manner, including each other. In the main streets they entered the Chinese shops, breaking the locks on the iron shutters, sweeping commodities off shelves, dragging women away and answering resistance with bayonets or a burst of fire from their Akai 47s. When the first soldiers came, a group of Chinese from the Tropical Hotel apartments in the main street came out with gifts for the invading forces. They were executed en masse.

One of the first targets was the Marconi centre. Equipment was smashed and torn from its installations. The Indonesians were in a city where the population spoke a different language and no communication could be trusted.

By now they controlled most of the foreshore area. Tanks, landed from the warships, patrolled the shorefront. Their tracks were later detected by a keen-eyed Australian journalist who accompanied Indonesian Foreign Minister Adam Malik into Dili in early January. From the centre of town the paratroopers pushed towards the FRETILIN military command in the suburb of Taibesse. They piled the rewards of their pillaging on to landing barges and ferried them out to the warships. They were also dragging women on to them. One woman wouldn't go. She was Muki, secretary of the Popular Organization of Timorese Women.

Rosa Muki Bonaparte returned to Timor from her studies in Portugal early in 1975. She came back enthused with ideas and quickly established herself in the leadership structure of FRETILIN. She participated in talks initiated by the Portuguese Decolonisation Commission in Dili in May 1975. Small, intense, very Timorese, the Portuguese had called her 'the petite revolutionary' and 'Rosa Luxemburg' for her contribution to the talks. When she resisted the Indonesians she was shot on the wharf and her body thrown into the harbour.

Borja died that day too. Francisco Borja da Costa wrote poetry in the classical form, in the Tetum language. Its images were of all the beautiful things of Timor: of the spiralling mountain peaks, of the chickens in the *knuas* (villages), of the rivers which divide and re-unite endlessly. He used to come to my hotel to talk. Shy and earnest, he would huddle over a glass of beer. In mutually broken English and Portuguese we would discuss Australian foreign policy. Timor, his country, was very tiny, he used to say. It was too small for the superpowers to care about. Their policies were based on expediency, but it was not expedient to offend Indonesia for the sake of a small country. Timorese would surely have to fight for themselves. It was clear Australia would not help; illusions were dangerous.

Smother my revolts
  With the point of your bayonet
Torture my body
  In the chains of your empire
Subjugate my soul
  In the faith of your religion ...

he had written. Now they did. The voice of a poet is always dangerous. The message later transmitted to Darwin read: 'The Javanese killed Borja with barbarities, because they said he was a Communist'.

The fighting raged all of the day of the seventh. Between 4,000, and 6,000 troops were landed, near a 1:1 ratio for the civilian population of Dili at that time. Paratroopers and marines, operating together for the first time under a new command structure, fought each other as they landed. Paratroopers dropped on the airfield clashed with marines disembarking near the Arab quarter. From Ataúro that end of the capital appeared to be all ablaze. The confrontation between the sectors sharpened the edge of the invaders' aggression; the civilian population was their next target.

When the walls of the Taiwanese consulate threatened to cave in under the bombardment the consular staff fled into the streets in search of a new sanctuary. The consul's wife fell with bullet wounds. Elsewhere the Chinese cowered in their houses in fear of the pillaging raids of the invaders. A Catholic priest later lodged an official complaint with Adam Malik against the entry of troops into private homes.

Months later a letter smuggled from the territory told something of the horror:

> ... everything around us has been death and destruction. I cannot tell you all in detail, you understand; but when everything is death, destruction and suffering, the best thing is to keep silent. A part of the house was bombed by the Indonesian aviation and destroyed and the rest was "taken away by the wind"; we have saved our lives, only because our time had not arrived yet, but I saw death before my eyes and thought my last moment was arriving ... I've prayed so much in these moments of peril that I can hardly pray ...

Early on the seventh Nicolau Lobato tried to make his way through the streets to his home, where his wife Isabel, sister-in-law Olímpia, and brother-in-law José Gonçalves were trapped, along with his child, two and a half year old José, or 'Ze, as he was usually called. This was the second occasion within months that their lives had been endangered. Just fifteen minutes before the UDT[4] coup of 11 August, Olímpia, Isabel and tiny 'Ze had escaped on foot from Dili with other members of the Lobato family. For two days they walked through the mountains, sleeping out, until they linked up with other FRETILIN people heading for Aileu. On that occasion José Gonçalves stayed behind. He suffered from heart disease and would not last long in the mountains.

Gonçalves was the son of the *liurai* of Atsabe, a leader of the pro-integrationist APODETI[5] party. His brother Tomás was the APODETI military commander and had been in Indonesian Timor since early 1975. He worked under Indonesian command at a military camp near Kupang, training East Timorese who had crossed the border. A few days before the Dili landing, José Gonçalves had been sworn into office as a Minister of the new republic. He had studied abroad for sixteen years and continually stressed to journalists that he worked with the FRETILIN administration as a technical adviser. With his poor health, his family connections and his insistence that he was apolitical, he seemed a weak link in the government.

Lobato never reached the house. Every street he turned into was filled with advancing paratroopers. Misery in his heart, he retreated. Already, in the cruel sequence of events since 11 August, he had lost a brother, sixteen year old Domingos, president of UNETIM, the National Union of Timorese Students. Domingos's mutilated body was found on a beach off the hamlet of Bi Susu on the south coast, along with ten others. His death had reinforced Nicolau's steely strength. Newly sworn in as Prime Minister of the republic, it was obvious to observers that this Timorese nationalist above all had the strength to lead his people in a fight to the end.

The Indonesian troops were led to the Lobato house by a betrayer. When they reached it they asked for Gonçalves by name. He stepped forward. One section of the paratroopers escorted him to the government radio where he called for surrender to the TNI, the armed forces of the Republic of Indonesia. Another section remained at the house, over which they hoisted the red and white flag of the republic.

Isabel Lobato met Muki's fate. They dragged her, in her floral print dress, to the harbour area where she was executed and her body dumped in the sea. They wanted to take the baby too, but Olímpia managed to save him.

On the night of the seventh the seminary at Dare was bombed. In run after run the bombers dropped their load on the small mountainside village. Most of the Timorese nationalists had been educated at this pacific mountain retreat. Now it was ripped and twisted by the bombardment. Somewhere among the rubble was a photo album of historic moment to Timor. It recorded the passage of Xavier do Amaral, Nicolau Lobato, Rogério Lobato, Abílio de Araújo, Hermenegildo Alves, Domingos de Oliveira and Francisco Lopes da Cruz through the seminary.

On Ataúro an amazing farce took place on 8 December. It provided an ironic final commentary on the Portuguese presence in East Timor. Ataúro had been the seat of nominal Portuguese power since the administration's panicked retreat from the capital in late August. Under the old régime the island was a place of exile for political undesirables from the mainland.

The International Red Cross team joined the Portuguese during their last days on Ataúro. From 3 December until the eve of the invasion the team flew into Dili each day. Two Portuguese corvettes, the *João Roby* and the *Afonso Cerquiera* were also at anchor off Ataúro.

The bombardment of Dili was clearly visible from the start. When it began the captain of the *João Roby* turned on the ship's radar; Indonesian military movements were thus monitored until the ship sailed the next evening. Dili could also be seen with the naked eye from Ataúro.

For the second time within four months the Portuguese made a decision to evacuate their seat of government. When the invasion began, Lisbon was notified through the ship's radio. But the final decision to evacuate was taken on Ataúro at midday, before a reply from Lisbon gave the order. The evacuation was planned for 6.30am on the eighth. With Dili burning in the background, the captain of the *João Roby* was unable to raise the ship's anchors. Somehow they had become tangled.

For twelve hours every conceivable means was used to free them. The Timorese sub-lieutenant deputed to remain in charge of the army unit on Ataúro sailed out on a barge and attempted to use its bow to raise the stubborn anchors. Two Portuguese divers plunged into the Ombai-Wetar Straits but hastily surfaced on the appearance of several hungry-looking sharks. Captain Carlos da Costa Pecorelli shunted the corvette to and fro to manoeuvre the anchors free. The Red Cross doctors watched with apprehension as they drew closer to an Indonesian warship. In desperation Pecorelli ordered the anchor chains to be cut with a hacksaw. At 6.30pm on 8 December the *João Roby* sailed for Darwin, marking the last significant physical involvement of the Portuguese with East Timor.

In all this time the bombardment of Dili was visible to those on board the corvette, who later recounted what they saw. First indications of the attack came early on the Sunday morning when what appeared to be soft thunder and lightning broke their sleep. Everybody gathered on the beach from where army officers had walkie-talkie contact with the *João Roby*. The ship's radar detected aircraft over Dili and six or seven ships in the harbour. With no sign of the bombardment relenting, at midday the decision to evacuate next morning was taken and stores and people were loaded on the corvette. That evening after dinner there was a more dramatic view of the bombardment, from the *João Roby*'s bridge:

> The radar picked up seven planes. They appeared to be to the left, directly behind Dili, though it could have been Aileu. It was the same lighting of the sky that we saw the previous night, but this time we could see the flashes ... We watched for about half an hour, but then went down. It was too depressing. It was lighting up the hills behind Dili. The flashes themselves were beyond the hills, illuminating the intervening range at the rate of three or four flashes per minute.

It was only the next day that they noticed fires, at around 3pm. At first they saw just smoke, but then flame was discernable in the sky over Dili:

Dili burning, 8 December 1975, seen from Ataúro island.

> At one stage we saw a bright burning mass which lasted for about forty-five minutes. We had good binoculars and could see the flame, but it was clearly visible with the naked eye from 30 kms away. The smoke was going up in columns and covering all Dili. The sky was stained with smoke for about 2–3kms around ... It continued until we couldn't see any more. We left at 6.30pm.

As they watched the burning they listened to Radio Australia at hourly intervals. The newscasts were quoting Jakarta government statements saying that peace and stability had been restored in Dili.

The two corvettes were sparkling new. The Portuguese had taken delivery of them only nine months before. They were capable of outpacing and outranging the World War II vintage Russian escort destroyers which shelled Dili. But the Portuguese navy was an anachronism in 1975. The corvettes were crewed by long-haired sailors who didn't want to fight any more. In Portuguese the word *exploração* expresses what are two separate words in English: exploration and exploitation. Two years after Lisbon's "flower revolution" brought new hope to a war-weary people it had merely compounded the centuries-old misery of the Timorese people. What Henry the Navigator began, the Armed Forces Movement completed. *Exploração* bred a nation of soldiers and sailors sickened of fighting foreign wars but trapped in the ideology of a military caste.

When the Portuguese left East Timor on 8 December, hundreds of Timorese lay dead in the streets of Dili. The Indonesian invasion had begun.

1

The Colonial Impact

The island of Timor is located at the eastern extremity of the Indonesian archipelago, in the Lesser Sunda group. It is about 480 kilometres long and 100 across at its widest point. The nearest major land mass east of Timor is New Guinea (the western half of which has been under Indonesian rule since 1963), south it is Australia.

At the beginning of 1974 the Portuguese province of East Timor covered an area of approximately 14,953 square kilometres. Its territory consisted of the eastern half of the island, including the offshore islands of Ataúro and Jaco, and an enclave, Oecusse on the north coast of Indonesian-administered west Timor. Its population stood at around 650,000 of whom a large proportion were concentrated in a swathe from either side of Dili to the south coast, contrasting with the sparsely-populated eastern region.

The crocodile-shaped island is dominated by a great cordillera stretching along its centre. This mountainous spine has tempered Timorese economic, political and cultural life for centuries, and has been a major factor in creating conditions of life which make Timor exceptional in its region.

On 12 June 1789 after forty-one days cast adrift in an open boat by the mutineers of the *Bounty*, Captain William Bligh and his crew sighted the coast of Timor at 3 o'clock in the morning. When dawn broke this is what they saw:

> The day gave us a most agreeable prospect of the land, which was interspersed with woods and lawns; the interior part mountainous, but the shore low. Towards noon, the coast became higher, with some remarkable headlands. We were greatly delighted with the general look of the country, which exhibited many cultivated spots and beautiful situations; but we could only see a few small huts, whence I concluded that no European

> resided in that part of the island ... I saw several great smokes where the inhabitants were clearing and cultivating their ground.[1]

Although Bligh's perceptions may well have been heightened by his plight, two centuries later the first appearance of Timor can still catch the traveller's breath. From the air the same "smokes" with which the Timorese have cleared the ground for centuries are visible. Low-lying jungle thicket alternates with expanses of eucalypt-dotted savannah; along the coast the white sand and blue glitter of the South Seas is intersected by river estuaries choked with mud carried from the mountains by tropical rains. And above all, the mountains: twisting and turning up towards Tatamailau, or Ramelau, 3000 metres high in the rugged interior centre south-west of Dili. The plane's shadow crosses clusters of grass huts from which coils the smoke of domestic fires and between which a few animals move: pigs, goats, a dog or so. Occasionally herds of *kuda*, the sturdy Timorese pony, can be seen. Buffalos loll in water holes.

Village settlements occupy even the most extreme tips of the terrain, nestling in the crags of apparently wildly inaccessible mountains. The English naturalist H.O. Forbes complained in 1882:

> I encountered only pinacles and ridges and precipitous valleys and wishing for geodetic purposes to obtain a base line of about two hundred yards, I could not find that amount of flat land anywhere![2]

The rocky outcrops (*fatus*) which everywhere jut from the landscape have a special place in Timorese folklore. But their historical function has been more practical than mystical:

> Towering above the surrounding countryside and almost inaccessible, in Timor's past they provided a natural refuge for the mountain folk. There the people built their fortified mountain villages; there they lay in wait for the enemy. Even the reports of the former Royal Netherlands Indies Army speak on occasion of stubborn fighting against these mountain people, barricaded as they were in these strongholds.[3]

Forbes also noted the function of the *fatus* during war:

> Being really of a very cowardly spirit, they never fight in the open, but from behind trees and crags.

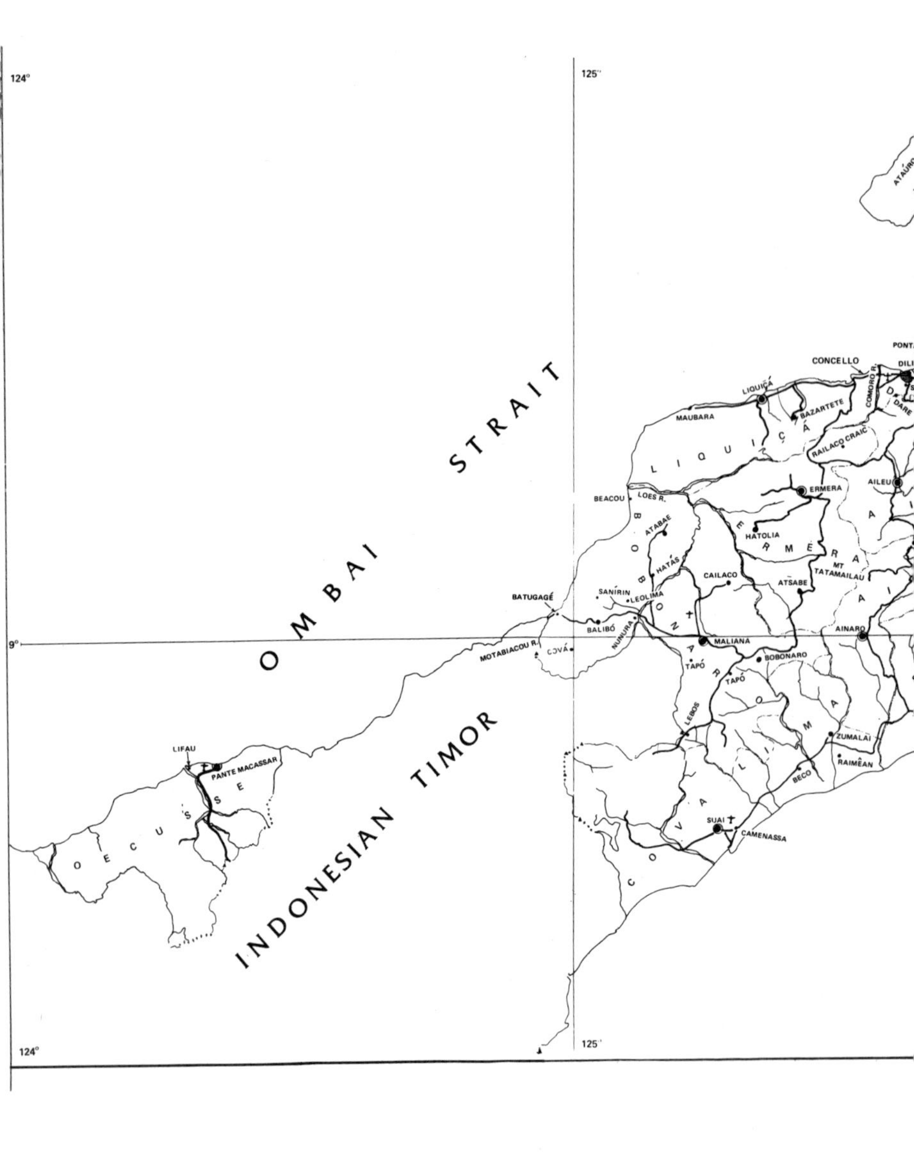

124°
125°
9°
OMBAI STRAIT
INDONESIAN TIMOR
OECUSSE
LIFAU
PANTE MACASSAR
ATAURO
PONTA
CONCELLO
DILI
COMORO R.
DARE
LIQUIÇÁ
MAUBARA
BAZARTETE
RAILACO CRAIC
AILEU
ERMERA
HATOLIA
BEACOU
LOES R.
ATABAE
BOBONARO
HATÁS
CAILACO
ATSABE
MT TATAMAILAU
SANÍRIN
LEOLIMA
BATUGAGÉ
BALIBÓ
NUNURA
MALIANA
BOBONARO
AINARO
MOTABIACOU R.
COVÁ
TAPÓ
TAPÓ
LEBOS
ZUMALAI
RAIMÊAN
BECO
COVALIMA
SUAI
CAMENASSA

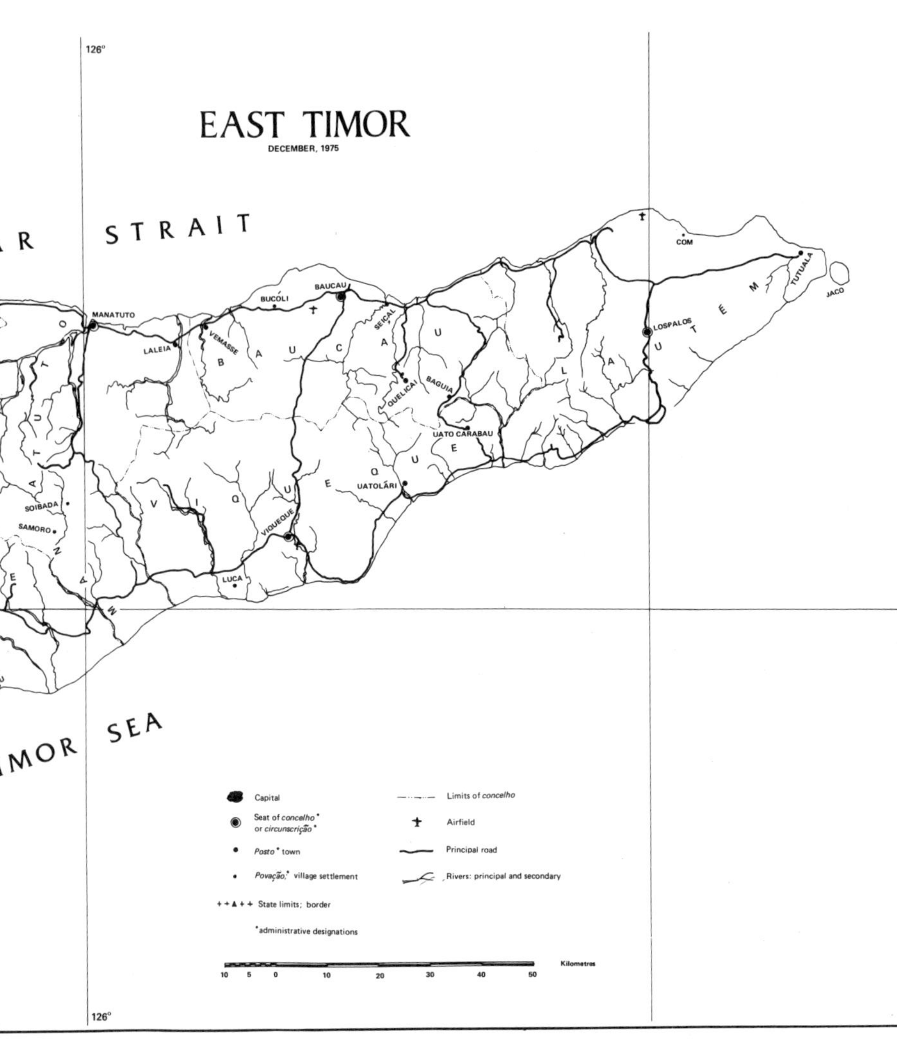

126°
EAST TIMOR
DECEMBER, 1975
STRAIT
MANATUTO
BUCOLI
BAUCAU
SEIÇAL
LALEIA
VEMASSE
QUELICAI
BAGUIA
UATO CARABAU
UATOLARI
VIQUEQUE
LUCA
SOIBADA
SAMORO
LOSPALOS
COM
TUTUALA
JACO
TIMOR SEA
Capital
Seat of concelho*
or circunscrição*
Posto* town
Povação;* village settlement
State limits; border
*administrative designations
Limits of concelho
Airfield
Principal road
Rivers: principal and secondary
Kilometres
10 5 0 10 20 30 40 50

The flat, whitewashed settlement of Dili is fringed by suburbs of traditional houses and is sited on one of the island's few natural harbours. In 1974 its population was around 20,000 and most of its buildings were recent, the capital having been destroyed by Allied bombardment during the second world war.

One hundred and thirty kilometres to the east along the north coast road is craggy Baucau. The drive to Baucau along East Timor's execrable main highway may take almost a day if the rivers between the two towns are running high. In 1974 Baucau's international-standard airstrip one kilometre from the township provided the territory's main link with the outside world. Tourist aircraft landing on the modern bitumen strip taxied in alongside produce-laden Timorese peasants trudging to the nearest market.

The Catholic Church claims nearly 200,000 adherents of the population of 650,000. There were also some 2,400 Protestants and 910 Moslems, mainly descendants of Arab traders who had settled on the north coast. The traditional religion of Timor is animist. Each village community has its own *uma lulik* or *lulik* house (or, less commonly, *pomali* house) attended by the community priest, the *dato-lulik* or *rai-lulik*. Every major event of Timorese life in peace or war is accompanied by ritual sacrifices and tributes presided over by the *dato-lulik*—each important phase of the agricultural cycle, initiation of warriors, and declarations of war and peace. Relics relating to the tribe's history, especially in battle, are kept in the *uma lulik*. Among the most common of these relics are ancient Portuguese flags. Thses venerated *lulik* flags are often centuries old and in some cases are kept with letters of presentation or old prayer books. The practice of head-hunting is long-standing and it is only in the twentieth century that Portuguese intervention has curbed it. The *pomali* is a prohibition on a property or place marked by the posting of some sign: a few palm leaves stuck outside a garden, stones or bones tied to a tree, a clump of broken twigs. Both Forbes and Lord Alfred Russel Wallace, a colleague of Darwin's who visited Timor twenty years before him, believed the *pomali* to be of Pacific origin, akin to the *tabu* applied by islanders.

The island of Timor is something of a racial meeting-point, a place populated by successive waves of migrants, predominantly Malay and Melanesian. Arab, Chinese and African faces are also part of the Timorese crowd (the Africans were brought as slaves or conscript soldiers by the Portuguese); some faces also bear features strikingly similar to those of the Australian Aborigine. Timor has been described as 'a Babel, resulting from the convergence of more varied ethnic groups, or an inextricable melting-pot of ethnic groups'.[4]

The Atoni ('people of the dry land'), who have inhabited the central highlands of the island for centuries, are believed to have been the original inhabitants of Timor. They speak a language known as Timorese or Vaiqueno.[5] The Tetum-speaking Belu are more recent intruders. The Atoni occupy most of what is now Indonesian Timor. The Belu people are located on the rich southern coastal plain which extends either side of the border, although their greater number is concentrated in the east. The migrations of both Atoni and Belu occurred many centuries ago, so that a distinct Timorese culture existed well before European colonisation. Indeed the Tetum word 'malai', meaning foreigner, has become a concept important to all Timorese and the theme of the Timorese united against the *malai* is deeply embedded in Timorese history. Overall, the dominant racial groups are Proto-Malay with an admixture of Papuan and Melanesian types, largely in the interior of East Timor. The frizzy hair of many of the Atoni points to Melanesian descent, while most Belu people have wavy to straight hair, similar to the Malays.

Before the sixteenth century the people of these two main language groups constituted one kingdom, the powerful realm of Waiwiku-Wehale, located on the South Belu plain, in 'one ritual, dual monarchy'. Waiwiku-Wehale had three subordinate governors: the *liurai* of South Belu, the *liurai* of Suai-Camenassa (the Belu area in East Timor) and *Sonba'i*, the ritual ruler of most of the Atoni area.[6] With time and the encroachment of the colonising powers the kingdom was divided along language lines into two major spheres of influence, so that by the early eighteenth century Timor was said to be inhabited by the tribes of 'Bellos' and 'Servião':

> The island was then, and for long afterwards, divided into two

Timorese tribesmen, Dili, 1974 (Grant Evans).

Timorese women, Maubisse, 1974 (Grant Evans).

> roughly equal districts, the eastern being called Bellos (*Belum*) and the western Servião (*Survian*) ... [7]

They were also described as 'Belus' and 'Vaiquenos':

> who differ a great deal from each other, making up as it were two provinces and two peoples, the eastern part being inhabited by the Belu, who live in the province dominated by the Belu, and the western part by the Vaiquenos in the province called Servião ... These two provinces were divided into kingdoms or *reinos*. The province of Belu comprised 46 kingdoms of varying power, but they were all free and independent, one of the other ... The province of Servião consists of 16 kingdoms, all of which recognize Sonba'i as their supreme ruler. He bears the title of emperor (*imperator*) and is king of the kingdom of Servião, whence the province derives its name.[8]

The Belu kingdoms lay in the sphere of influence of Dili, while the sixteen predominantly Vaiqueno-speaking kingdoms owed allegiance to Servião in west Timor. This traditional division roughly corresponded to the final border agreement made between the Dutch and Portuguese colonial administrations in 1910. The eastern kings have generally retained the title of *liurai*, while those of west Timor have taken on the Indonesian title of *raja*.

The 'Bellos' sphere of influence was divided into a greater number of kingdoms and was therefore not as politically cohesive as the west. But the east also encompasses groupings which, although they may have paid tribute to 'Bellos' in immediate pre-colonial days, were of different, probably Papuan, racial origin. Thus East Timor covers a complex range of languages and dialects. On the whole island there are probably twelve to eighteen languages drawn from both the Austronesian (Indonesian) and Papuan language families and subdivided into various dialects. The Papuan languages are mainly confined to the mountainous interior of East Timor. The closest to a lingua franca is Tetum, which is spoken in two forms—the corrupted Dili Tetum and the 'high' Tetum of the south coast, Tetum Terik. Portuguese is spoken in the urban centres and by some people in the larger villages.

Timor is the only part of the Indonesian archipelago subject to tropical cyclones. Various cyclone reports stretch through Timorese history: 1674, 1843, 1882, 1939, the late 1960s. But the incidence of cyclones is an extreme expression of Timor's problematic geography, to which F.J. Ormeling has devoted a whole study, based on field work in west Timor.

Conditions within the island vary enormously, largely due to the influence of the mountain chain on winds and rainfall. The island has the longest dry season in South-East Asia, but rainfall distribution is the crucial factor. Ormeling divided Timor into four rainfall zones: *the south coast and immediate hinterland*, which shows a fairly favourable rainfall due to the eastern monsoon rain which blows in from the Australian continent and gives two wet seasons on the south coast; *the central depression behind this area*, which has a severe dry season; *the northerly mountain districts* with a favourable rainfall distribution, and *the north coast* which has a severe dry season. Because the south coast areas catch the eastern monsoon, two harvests are possible here (in East Timor the Suai and Viqueque areas particularly benefit) while there is only one on the north coast. Although this means that the agricultural economy is generally richer in the south, the third zone, the northerly mountain district, is potentially exceptional in that temperate zone crops can be cultivated at this height, such as wheat, corn, potatoes and legumes. Lord Wallace noted:

> The fact that potatoes and wheat of excellent quality are grown in abundance at from 3,000 to 3,500 feet elevation, shows what the climate and soil are capable of if properly cultivated. From one to two thousand feet high, coffee would thrive; and there are hundreds of square miles of country, over which all the varied products which requires climates between those of coffee and wheat would flourish ...

He also spoke of the harshness of the dry season on the north coast:

> The drought of the hot season is so severe that most of the streams dry up in the plains before they reach the sea; everything becomes burnt up, and the leaves of the larger trees fall as completely as in our winter. On the mountains from two to four thousand feet elevation there is a much moister atmosphere, so that potatoes and other European products can be grown all the year round.[9]

H.O. Forbes spent forty days of his six month visit in 1882 on a journey to the interior, where he stayed for some time in the kingdom of Bibiçuçu. Here he drew up a calendar of the agricultural cycle in the kingdom, including a description of the effects of the eastern monsoon. The month of May he described as the 'month of fogs and heavy rains from the sea'. In June there was 'less rain; little possible to be done these two months'.

Manatuto on the north coast represents the opposite extreme of this meteorological spectrum. It has as little as one month of rain in a year and has been compared to Alice Springs in its aridity.

The climate, then, is not tropical monsoon typical to South-East Asia, but a savannah climate which resembles desert in the dry, and in the wet has the characteristics of tropical rain country. The landscape is parched bare and fissured in the dry, and scoured by water erosion in the wet. The rains flood down the mountain slopes, carrying soil and vegetation before them. The courses of the rivers are unpredictable, and when they enter the coastal plains their levels rise and fall rapidly.

In such a hazardous climate the subsistence farmer is victim to the vagaries of nature. By the 1970s the backwardness of Portuguese colonial rule had combined with the harshness of nature to impoverish the Timorese peasant. Staple crops were corn and rice, the latter grown by both the wet (sawah) system in the lowlands and the dry (swidden) system in the highlands. Tapioca, sweet potatoes, pumpkins, peppers, citrus and some tropical fruits are also grown. The digging stick is the main implement of cultivation. Coffee was introduced in the hills behind Dili in the mid-nineteenth century, to become the territory's only important export. Some rubber and tobacco were also introduced. The buffalo, which is highly prized in traditional society and used for bridewealth, is not generally cultivated for its meat or used as a draft animal, although its use to trample and break the soil for wet rice cultivation is unique to Timor. The peasant economy is supplemented by food-gathering and hunting, a mode the Timorese can fall back on in times of scarcity.

When in April 1974 democratic army officers seized the reins of power in Portugal and initiated decolonisation of the country's overseas possessions as part of their programme, the Portuguese had been in the Lesser Sunda islands for over 400 years.

The history of Timor before their presence is not consistently documented and the history after colonisation (by both the Dutch and Portuguese) is largely a coastal history, expanded as the respective powers commenced penetration of the hinterland. In the Dutch case this occurred from the middle of the eighteenth century, in the Portuguese (who only established themselves east of the centre of the island in 1769), it was a century later.

Colonisation was marked by two phases: the mercantile phase in which the colonisers exercised power only through coastal contact and small trading posts, relying on political treaties with local (and often rival) coastal *liurais* to maintain a balance of power in the interior, and the settler phase when penetration and direct force against interior kingdoms became necessary to assert supremacy. The first was an overtly political method, the second military, but there were points at which the two overlapped as, for example, in 1642 when a Portuguese expedition marched across Timor and razed the centre of its most powerful kingdom. The political impact of this act was sufficient to ensure Portuguese monopoly of the coastal trade in the coming period without the need for further inland ventures.

When coastal power was established at strategic points Portugal, formerly the leading mercantile colonial power, was under strong challenge from the Dutch. The first European settlement in the Sundas was in 1566. The Dutch East India Company was formed in 1602, seven years after a Dutchman smuggled the route to the Indies out of Lisbon. In the following century the Portuguese mercantilists were to be driven further east in South-East Asia as various centres of their power fell to the Dutch.

Chinese and Moslem traders were already acquainted with various coastal trading points in Timor. The principle of paying tribute through gifts to a coastal chief who then exercised his political power to have sandalwood and other products brought to the coast, was established before either the Dutch or Portuguese had contact with Timor. A seventeenth century Dutch commander described this pre-established system:

> The Timorese are a people whom one should treat with the utmost patience. When one arrives there to trade one is required to offer a few gifts ... to the kings and their nobles, as is the custom of old. Then one has to negotiate with them as to the amount of ... toll ... and ... anchorage dues, and other such things, that has to be paid to the king. With regard to this, it is customary for it to be given to him first before any of his subjects are allowed to bring wood. The latter are then given his consent to sell this on the beach. They sell it at ridiculously low prices, so that they are hardly compensated for their toil. All other profits are for the king and his most prominent nobles.[10]

The first recorded European settlers were Portuguese Dominican friars from Malacca who settled on the island of Solor in 1566. There they built a stone fort to protect against Moslem raiders the Christian converts they had won in Flores and Solor. Around this fort grew a community of lawless, buccaneering *mestiço* Timorese, Portuguese soldiers and sailors, and sandalwood traders from Macau and Malacca. C.R. Boxer described this community as 'a kind of Alsatia, largely populated by vagabond European and Eurasian cutthroats with their native consorts'.[11] Its members became known as Topasses or Black Portuguese or, later, *Larantuqueiros*.

In 1613 the Dutch sent a force to Timor to win control of the sandalwood trade. They attacked and seized the Solor fort from the Dominicans. The friars and their Topass followers then evacuated to Larantuka, on the eastern tip of nearby Flores, from whence they derived their third title. Their strength at the time of this flight was over 1,000, of whom thirty were Portuguese or Eurasians and seven were Dominicans.

In the next thirty years control of Solor passed to and fro between the Dutch and Portuguese. On one such occasion, in 1629, it reverted to the Dominicans when the Dutch commander Jan de Hornay, forbear of a long line of Topasses, defected to Larantuka. Despite Dutch-Portuguese conflict the ships of both powers continued to ply a trade from the Timor coast, the main products of which were sandalwood, beeswax, Timor ponies and slaves.

Both Dutch and Portuguese carried on a flourishing slave trade from Timor until well into the nineteenth century:

> Apparently the Timor archipelago, like Sumba, was one of In-

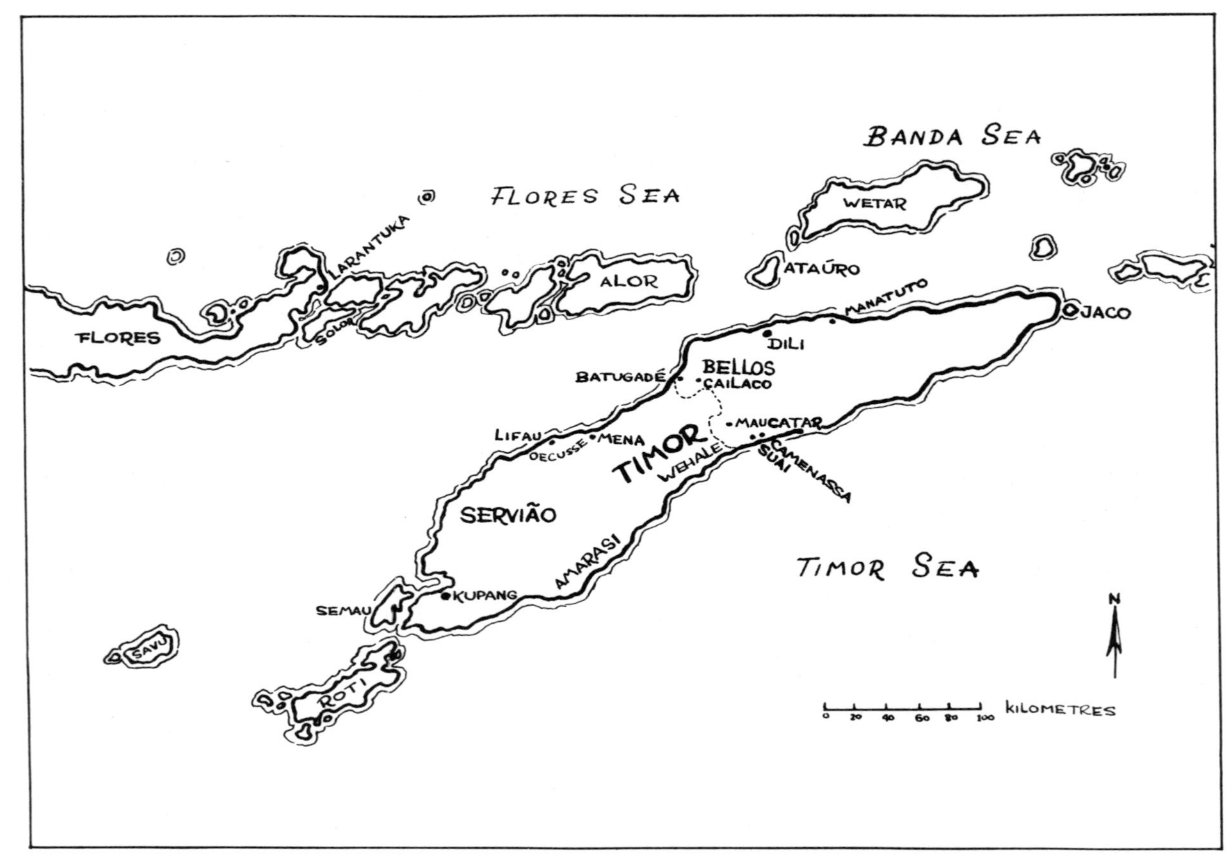
BANDA SEA
FLORES SEA
TIMOR SEA
WETAR
ATAÚRO
ALOR
LARANTUKA
SOLOR
FLORES
JACO
MANATUTO
DILI
BELLOS
BATUGADÉ
CAILACO
MAUCATAR
LIFAU
OECUSSE
MENA
TIMOR
WEHALE
SUAI
CAMENASSA
SERVIÃO
AMARASI
KUPANG
SEMAU
SAVU
ROTI
N
0 20 40 60 80 100 KILOMETRES

> donesia's slave reservoirs, and Timorese of reproducing age have been deported as slaves for several centuries. "Timor"—as Huyser (1792) says—"provides good-natured slaves for household purposes. They are also used on Banda to collect nutmeg and mace" ... practically every ship arriving at Batavia from Timor carried slaves. Generally they numbered tens, but sometimes a hundred or more.[12]

Slavery was customary in traditional society, but the concept was somewhat different: *liurais* and *datos* (nobles) kept retinues of slaves who in some areas took on the social rank of their overlord when he died. These slaves were initially obtained in wars between kingdoms. In colonial times they were captured during Dutch and Portuguese excursions against traditional kingdoms, in some cases being awarded as spoil to local allies, in others being shipped abroad. The Portuguese are also thought to have taken Australian Aborigines from north coast islands into slavery:

> When Captain King first visited Melville Island ... the natives appeared on the beach and called out to our voyager, *'Ven aca,'* the Portuguese term for 'Come here.' From this, coupled with many circumstances that came under his observation during his stay at Melville Island, Major Campbell ... states it to be his opinion that the Portuguese sometimes touch here and carry off the natives as slaves.[13]

In 1641 the loss of Malacca to the Dutch led the Portuguese to concentrate on the eastern region of the archipelago. They now made Macassar, an important entrepôt for the Timor trade, their key post. The Moslem Macassarese had until this time held some influence in the Lesser Sundas, especially Flores and Solor (they regularly sailed south to trepang fishing bases, including Darwin). Now, in the mid-seventeenth century, they vied with the Dominicans for influence in Timor, attacking towns which converted to Christianity. The Dominican mission on the mainland began with the conversion of coastal *liurais*, including those of Lifau (in present-day Oecusse) and Mena (near Atapupu in Indonesian Timor) and the construction of a fort at Kupang in 1640. Threatened by this European encroachment, the ruler of Waiwiku-Wehale became Moslem and thus an ally of Macassar, so in 1642 the Portuguese mounted a punitive expedition against the Wehale kingdom. An expedition led by a

Solorese Captain-Major embarked from Solor and, with the support of local *liurais*, marched across Timor,

> Laying waste the regions through which he marched with his troops, the captain major held out in the face of pursuit by the enemy up to the place where [Wehale] had his residence; after reducing everything to ashes there he withdrew to Batimao.
>
> The news of the destruction of the mighty potentate of Belos spread rapidly through the other kingdoms in the neighbourhood.[14]

Wehale's defeat marked the beginning of a concerted attack on Timorese society. Many *liurais* were baptised soon after.

Traditional Timorese rulers adapted their tactics to the changed situation and henceforth tried to survive by balancing the several groups which threatened them—Dutch, Portuguese and Topasses—against each other. The Topasses in particular were an ascendant power. Ironically, it was largely through their supremacy in Timor and their nominal loyalty to the Portuguese flag that Portugal retained Timor at a time when its other Asian strongholds were falling, yet the Viceroy in Goa was incapable of controlling them.

Their power was firmly established in a major battle at south coast Amarasi following Dutch seizure of the Kupang fort in 1653. The Topasses had killed the two previous Dutch commanders and the Dutch now vowed to break their power. They appointed for the task Arnold de Vlaming van Oudshoorn who had recently put down an uprising in Ambon.[15] In an expedition reminiscent of the Portuguese march on Wehale, de Vlaming led a force to Amarasi where Topass commanders Matteus da Costa and António de Hornay (son of Jan de Hornay) lay in wait with their forces. He had to march twice against them, on the first occasion driven back by heavy rain before he was able to engage the enemy. The second time he was decisively defeated.

De Vlaming's brisk prose description of the furious assault of the Topasses on his retreating troops is an outstanding document of Timor's fighting tradition:

> We had to walk in single file if we wished to escape uninjured; this put us at a disadvantage, which the enemy turned to his own advantage, and after sending down a shower of assegais [spears] on

> us assaulted us like lightning, stabbing some of us in the back. This gave rise to a great deal of shouting and commotion, one man trampling another underfoot in his bewilderment. The lieutenant captain, who had been struck down by his own men, almost lost his life but for one of the soldiers kicking over the black who was already sitting astride him, his assegai poised to strike the final blow, so that Keler escaped with his life. The enemy, seeing that some of our men were incapable of properly handling a rifle, were goaded on to unheard audacity, furiously flinging themselves at them with no more fear than if the rifles had been mere hemp-poles, seizing now this man's now that man's rifle from his shoulder or out of his hands, transfixing their bodies with assegais as though they were helpless sheep. Nay, what is more, they carried off by force ensign Gerrit Gerritsen from the midst of his company, with banner and all, and seized the drummer's drum, and there was nothing we could do to stop them. As the bewilderment of our men lessened somewhat, the assaulter was forced to take to his heels.

De Vlaming's losses were heavy and he immediately embarked for Batavia (Jakarta), ordering the evacuation of the Solor fort on the way.[16]

From 1673 António de Hornay ruled Timor virtually as an independent king, paying tribute to Portugal through generous contributions of gold dust to the Crown coffers. The Portuguese thought of replacing the Dominicans (whose free-living activities were as uncontrollable as the Topasses) with Jesuits, but were met with stubborn defiance by the Topasses, who declared they would only allow Dominicans on Timor:

> These are they who formerly taught our ancestors and forefathers, and who at present teach us. We were brought up by them, and it is not right that we should abandon them and turn to others.[17]

The Dutch appear to have been besieged at Kupang from this time (thirty years later the Portuguese bluntly informed them that their influence in Timor was limited to the range of the cannons at the Kupang fort). It is not surprising, then, that when William Dampier sailed into the harbour in 1699 he was met with hostility by the Dutch, who initially refused to let him take on water. They had recently been attacked by 'pirates', they said. They suspected him of being a pirate for reasons other than his reputation, and disbelieved his claim to carry a British commission. Dampier then sailed along the north coast to Lifau, where he viewed the Topasses with some astonishment:

> The Inhabitants of the Town, are chiefly a sort of Indians, of a Copper-colour, with black lank Hair: They speak Portugueze, and are of the Romish Religion; but they take the Liberty to eat Flesh when they please. They value themselves on the account of their Religion and descent from the Portugueze; and would be very angry if a Man should say they are not Portugueze: Yet I saw but three White Men here, two of which were Padres.[18]

In 1702 the Portuguese Viceroy sent a carefully-selected representative to be the new Governor of Timor. The previous candidate had been ignominiously expelled by a popular uprising led by the Topasses. António Coelho Guerreiro moved the seat of government from Larantuka to Lifau. For two years he was besieged by Domingos da Costa, son of Matteus, until in 1704 he slipped out of Lifau in disguise, on the ship of the English captain Alexander Hamilton. His governorship nevertheless left a permanent mark. He initiated the process of creating new élites among traditional power-holders by conferring ranks on co-operative *liurais* and executives of their realm. The permanent effect of this practice was to undermine the power of the *liurais* through the elevation of this secondary layer, the *datos*, and in later times, through the appointment of Portuguese-sponsored *liurais*.[19]

Hamilton's view of the Topasses was similar to Dampier's, except that he noted their rebellious disposition, perhaps imparted to him by Coelho Guerreiro, who travelled as 'Captain Alexander Pinto':

> The natives acknowledge the King of Portugal their Sovereign, and have embraced the Romish Religion. They permitted the Portuguese ... to build a Fort ... which they called *Leifew*, and the Dutch a Factory called *Coupang*, but would never suffer either to interfere with the Government of their country. The Portuguese of *Macao* drove a very advantageous trade to Timor for many years, and finding the natives to be passive Catholics, tried by fair means to get the whole government of the country into the Churches' hands, but could not beguile them that way, therefore they tried force, and commenced a war, but to their Cost they found that the Timoreans would not lose their liberty for fear of the loss of Blood.[20]

But the early conflicts were minor compared with what was to come. An island-wide revolt was brewing. In 1719 a number of *liurais* met in a secret assembly to make the Camenassa Pact. They swore a blood oath (*pax consangue*) not to rest until the white Portuguese were driven from Timor. To this end they intended to ally first with the Topasses but later to drive them out also. The Topass Francisco de Hornay led the revolt and for the next fifty years Timor was in a state of open warfare. The potential force of the traditional rulers is described by Boxer:

> The tribes of Bellos could muster about 40,000 warriors, of whom only 3,000 were musketeers, the remainder being armed with swords, spears, bows and arrows. The warriors of Servião numbered about 25,000 of whom a couple of thousand were equipped with firearms.[21]

In 1726 the Portuguese attacked the rebels in their headquarters on the crags of Mt Cailaco, assisted by two columns of loyalist Timorese. Like de Vlaming, they were driven back by monsoonal rains.[22]

In 1729 a new Governor arrived determined to crush the revolt. Colonel Pedro de Mello was able to bring with him from Macau only 50 supporting troops. The rebels were now entrenched in Dili where de Mello vainly attempted to dislodge them. He was subsequently besieged at Manatuto. For 85 days his forces were reduced to eating 'the leaves of trees, powdered horse-bones and vermin' until in January 1731 he rallied his forces in a desperate but successful bid to break out. The enemy retreated with some loss and a number of petty chiefs submitted themselves to Portuguese authority.[23]

In 1749 the Topasses took advantage of a lull in the fighting to turn on the Dutch at Penfui, outside Kupang. On 18 October a local *liurai* reported to the Kupang fort that his subjects in the highlands had spotted an advancing army, of at least '2,800 rifles besides those of the Amarasi'. A later report claimed that the force was 50,000 strong. It was led by Topass Lieutenant-General Gaspar da Costa and a number of *liurais*, including some from the Belu tribes. The appearance of this enormous army on the plains of Kupang must have struck fear into the heart of its defenders. Their Rotinese and Savunese allies were on the point of fleeing, but the Dutch kept them there by 'handsome promises', not to mention the fact that they turned the fort's cannons on their ships in the harbour and sank them, cutting off escape. After some inconclusive skirmishes, the Dutch decided to launch an attack, using available forces, which numbered only several hundred. The Topasses had constructed trenches. Fighting hand to hand the Dutch forces drove the Topass army back to its last trench:

> our Timorese, who had until then stood immobile, now gathered courage and assaulted them in an almost complete circle and committed such a dreadful massacre among them that the field was instantaneously covered with dead bodies.

Gaspar da Costa was killed in the attack:

> struck down by a Timorese with an assegai and immediately beheaded like all those killed before him. Though it is difficult to estimate their number it is at any rate certain that that very evening our Timorese carried off in triumph approximately a thousand heads and at least as many again in the course of the next two days, while they were still relentlessly pursuing the enemy.[24]

Dutch victory at Penfui represented a crucial stemming of the tide of Topass power in Timor, but perhaps more importantly, it marked the establishment of Dutch power, for the battle was a prelude to a series of Dutch attacks on various Timorese centres. In 1752 and 1758 they attacked Amarasi and Noimuti. The *liurai* of Amarasi stabbed himself to death in full view of the thousands-strong advancing army rather than submit. A German-born commander named von Pluskow led the Noimuti expedition. Noimuti was a Topass stronghold and after its defeat allied kingdoms declared fealty to the Dutch, who then stationed permanent detachments in the interior.

Seven years later von Pluskow was assassinated in Lifau by the Topasses. Such was the Dutch government's attitude to Timorese affairs by this time that they expressly forbade reprisals and initiated a Timor policy of strict non-interference in the affairs of either the Portuguese or the Topasses. They resigned themselves to a holding operation and it was only at the end of the nineteenth century that they moved to finally assert their power on the island.[25]

The Portuguese, too, resigned themselves to limited power after dealing with fifty years of Timorese-Topass rebellion. In

1769, after two years of a fresh siege of Lifau, Governor António José Telles de Menezes took the decision to abandon Lifau in favour of Dili. He had no hope of relief from Goa or Macau and a garrison of only 15 Portuguese, plus responsibility for a civilian population of 1,200. On the night of 11/12 August 1769 he loaded what he could on to available shipping in Lifau harbour, set fire to what remained on shore and proceeded to Dili, via Batugadé.

The Topasses offered Lifau to the Dutch but, having learnt from the Portuguese experience, they declined. The Topasses continued to fly the Portuguese flag but to rule the area (which eventually became the enclave of Oecusse) themselves, alternating the leadership between a da Costa and a de Hornay.[26]

Over a century after the destruction of Wehale the Portuguese now faced the prospect of holding their position at a new site, this time in the east. There appears to have been little interior penetration beyond those areas of the Belu kingdoms which extended into East Timor, for the Portuguese lacked either the physical or political resources for the task.

The beginning of the nineteenth century saw the conclusion of the Napoleonic wars in Europe, the rise of independence movements in the declining Spanish and Portuguese empires and in Timor the stagnation of Dutch and Portuguese activity. The British occupied west Timor between 1811 and 1816. Until 1814 the Iberian peninsular was a theatre of the Napoleonic wars and the Portuguese royal family were forced to flee to Brazil, leaving the other colonies effectively severed from the metropolis. Exploiting the disarray, the Brazilians soon after fought the first successful independence campaign in a Portuguese colony, under the slogan 'independence or death', proclaiming their sovereignty in 1822.

When a Dutch lieutenant visited Timor in the course of a voyage of inspection of outlying areas of Dutch empire following the Napoleonic wars, he found the Portuguese settlement at Dili squalid, demoralised and in a state of half-siege. Chauvinism may have played a part in Lieutenant D.H. Kolff's view of Dili. He spoke, for example, in shocked tones of the slave trade although a contemporary account of the Kupang settlement describes the Dutch as having 1,200 slaves there. Nevertheless, his outrage seemed soundly based:

> The Governor of the Portuguese possessions in the north coast of Timor usually resides at Dilli, and pays himself and the other officials out of revenue derived from the trade. They are all engaged in mercantile pursuits. Their pay, indeed, is extremely small ... Their dwellings are miserable, dirty, and poor ... The Governor appeared to be much pleased on finding that I was in want of some cattle and various articles, with which he offered to supply me ... Slaves were frequently offered to me on sale, the Commandant, among others, wishing me to purchase two children of seven or eight years of age, who were loaded with heavy irons. The usual price of an adult male slave is forty guilders, that of a woman or a child being from twenty-five to thirty. These unfortunate people are kidnapped in the interior, and brought to Dilli for sale, the Governor readily providing the vender with certificates under his hand and seal ...

Kolff reported that these abuses were a source of widespread discontent: 'many of the inhabitants of Dilli, both natives and Chinese, expressed to me their strong desire to be freed from the hateful yoke of the Portuguese'. Kolff wished to speak to the 'chief of the native inhabitants' who resided a short distance inland to the south-west', but did not when the Governor expressed displeasure at his suggestion. He noted what appeared to be 'a large gallows' to the east of the settlement. The Portuguese showed no signs of activity and 'appear to have given themselves up to an indolent mode of life, all their actions being redolent of laziness and apathy'. He concluded:

> The land would produce abundantly were the indolent Portuguese to turn their attention to agriculture, or to encourage the natives to do so; but they prefer seeing the innocent natives carried off from their peaceful homes in the hills, that they may profit by their sale, to allowing them to better their condition by their labour and agricultural skills.[27]

Despite their limited authority, Holland and Portugal were now the uncontested claimants to colonial power in Timor and in this period negotiations began towards a border settlement. In 1834 the Portuguese expelled all missionaries from Timor, removing, for the next forty years, a source of perpetual irritation to them.[28]

Lord Alfred Russel Wallace visited Timor between 1857 and 1861, spending a few weeks in Kupang and four months in Dili. He described himself as 'a travelling naturalist of limited means'. Like Kolff, Wallace was singularly unimpressed with Dili:

> ... a most miserable place compared with even the poorest of the Dutch towns. The houses are all of mud and thatch; the fort is only a mud inclosure; and the custom-house and church are built of the same mean materials, with no attempts at decoration or even neatness.

He was also outspokenly critical of the administration:

> The Portuguese government in Timor is a most miserable one. Nobody seems to care the least about the improvement of the country, and ... after three hundred years of occupation there has not been a mile of road made beyond the town, and there is not a solitary European resident anywhere in the interior. All the Government officials oppress and rob the natives as much as they can, and yet there is no care taken to render the town defensible should the Timorese attempt to attack it ... during an insurrection of the natives (while I was at Delli) the officer who expected to be sent against the insurgents was instantly taken ill! ... it is much to be feared that Timor will for many years to come remain in its present state of chronic insurrection and mis-government.[29]

In 1882 H.O. Forbes followed in Wallace's footsteps. He travelled to the archipelago on the same ship as a Major da Franca, the newly-appointed Governor, who invited him to Timor and offered to facilitate a trip to the interior. Forbes observed that there were then 47 kingdoms 'under certain chiefs called Rajas or Leoreis, each of whom is independent and absolute in his own kingdom', although some kingdoms held a vassalage relationship to others. His view of the Portuguese is more positive than Wallace's, perhaps influenced by the fact that his host was the Governor. Wallace later footnoted *The Malay Archipelago* with the observation that Forbes's description suggested that things had improved since 1861, but events soon proved otherwise: one of da Franca's successors was assassinated soon after. If contemporary East Timorese accounts of the anti-colonial war led by the *liurai* Dom Boaventura of Manufahi are reliable, it began 3 or 4 years after Forbes's visit. Forbes spent some time of his 40-day expedition to the interior in the kingdom of Bibiçuçu, adjoining (and later allied with) Manufahi, but there is no hint of the impending storm.

That the *liurais* of the original 'Bellos' grouping were still independent and absolute in 1882 is attested by the fact that Forbes was met at the border of each kingdom by 'an officer belonging to it, who assumed all responsibility for my safety and baggage'. There is no evidence in his report of any permanent European post in the interior. Responsibility for his safety had apparently been relegated by the Portuguese from Dili: 'during our stay in the interior the rajas were ordered to see us supplied with all necessaries'. At one point of his journey Forbes accidentally shot a pig belonging to a *liurai* and had to treat with officers of the kingdom over the matter: there is no question of Portuguese interdiction. He does make one hearsay reference to a district 'commandant' in the Matabia Mountains (near the present centre of Baguia) but in the course of his journey, which took him as far north-west as Balibó, south-west as Cová and Suai, to Luca on the south-east coast, and Vemasse on the north-east coast he makes no mention of contact with Portuguese.

Forbes provided rare descriptions of traditional life, of social organisation at the village level, the functions of the *lulik* house, the taking of slaves, agricultural practices and a valuable detailed description of rituals preceding war between kingdoms. He listed languages and dialects and outlined the agricultural calendar of two south coast realms, Saluki and Samoro.[30]

By the late nineteenth century Portuguese and Dutch colonial possessions were under challenge from the newer colonial powers—Britain, Germany and France. In Africa, as in Asia, although the Portuguese had graduated from non-resident, mercantile colonisers to coastal settlers, they had barely seen many inland areas of their overseas possessions by 1850. In Angola, for example, there were only six whites resident in 1846 and some eastern kingdoms remained intact until 1920.[31] In Dutch Timor the kingdom of Insana did not come under colonial rule until 1915.[32] Forbes's 1882 account suggests the situation was similar in the east. Pressure from other world powers in the last half of the century forced both colonisers to consolidate or abdicate. The Berlin West Africa Conference of 1884–5 considerably reduced Portuguese power in Africa:

> The dream had been of a Portuguese empire in Southern Africa stretching in a bold sweep from the Atlantic to the Indian Ocean. But it was already too late. The Congress of Berlin divided the continent between the greater powers, and Portugal was left with three African enclaves only ... Restricted to these areas, only now did Portugal begin her colonisation in earnest. Traders and military forces infiltrated, and some white settlers too.[33]

A flurry of colonial legislation followed in Portugal to provide instruments of pacification—tax laws, contract labour laws—and the rebellion which began in Timor in the late 1880s and continued until 1912 was paralleled in most of Portuguese Africa.[34]

It was only in this period that steps were taken to restrict the wide availability of arms. From the time of de Vlaming's expedition against Matteus da Costa in 1656 the Timorese seem to have been equipped with muskets and Wallace was amazed to see Lombok natives manufacturing their own firearms. In some areas of the Indonesian archipelago cannons had been locally cast and rifles bored for centuries. The rifles Wallace saw were similar to those in use on Timor, decorated with ornate silver butts. Forbes also noted the pride taken in rifles. 'By his side [the Timorese] always has a knife or a short sword', he wrote ' ... and is rarely without a gun, flintlock or percussion'. Elegantly decorated buffalo-hide ammunition pouches had long been a part of ceremonial dress.[35] In 1889 Portugal imposed an embargo on imports and exports of modern firearms.[36] Two years previously the newly-appointed Governor, Lacerda Maia, had been assassinated in Dili, in response to his oppressive treatment of the local population, especially his use of the whip.[37]

The assassination signalled a new general uprising. Once again the *liurais* of Timor entered into a blood pact to resist the Portuguese, this time under the leadership of Dom Boaventura of Manufahi (present-day Same). The rebellion was only defeated in 1912 after a desperate plea to Macau for assistance brought troopships of Mozambicans. As well, by applying divide and rule policies, the Portuguese won the defection of certain of the *liurais*.[38]

In January 1912 the cannonship *Pátria* arrived from Macau. The *Pátria* bombarded Boaventura's forces in their south coast stronghold from Betano. The Portuguese by this time had infantry forces encircling Boaventura, with the result that when the rebel government finally fell under the *Pátria*'s guns the Portuguese took thousands of prisoners of war.

The campaign was recorded in detail by Jaime do Inso, a second-lieutenant aboard the *Pátria*, who described the causes of the revolt as 'complex and not well understood':

> The first must reside, probably, in the warlike and proud character of the Timorese, who, for the same reasons that we, when a stranger enters our house by force, do not readily accept interference in their house.
>
> This would be the remote cause, aggravated with time and with other more immediate causes.
>
> Of these, I have heard say, one of the principal was the proposed augmentation of the head tax from one pataca to two patacas, ten avos.
>
> I heard, too, that in the first battles of the people of Manufai they said to our representatives: 'come and get the two patacas, if you can!'
>
> Besides these, other causes were pointed to: the prohibition of the cutting of sandalwood before a certain age, the imposition of a tax of two patacas for every tree cut, the registration of coconut-trees and livestock, the creation of a new tax, apparently of 5 patacas on the slaughter of animals for festive occasions.

Inso also heard it said that the change of the design of the Portuguese flag with the advent of a republic in 1910 had been resented by the Timorese, to whom it had long been a *lulik* object.

The *Pátria* fought, too, against rebels in Oecusse, Baucau and in support of an expeditionary force at Quelicai, demonstrating the breadth of the rebellion.[39]

The Melbourne *Argus* reported the revolt and its suppression in 1912, with the anxious note that 'Port Dilly, the scene of the outrages is closer to Darwin than Hobart is to Melbourne'. On 19 February 1912 it reported that Government House in Dili had been looted by members of the Raimêa tribe, who had also decapitated Portuguese officers and paraded their heads on poles through the capital. The next report came on 26 August, telling of the rebels' defeat. A 'startling message' had been received in Lisbon, it said, telling of a great battle in which 3,000 of the rebels were killed and 4,000 captured. It concluded

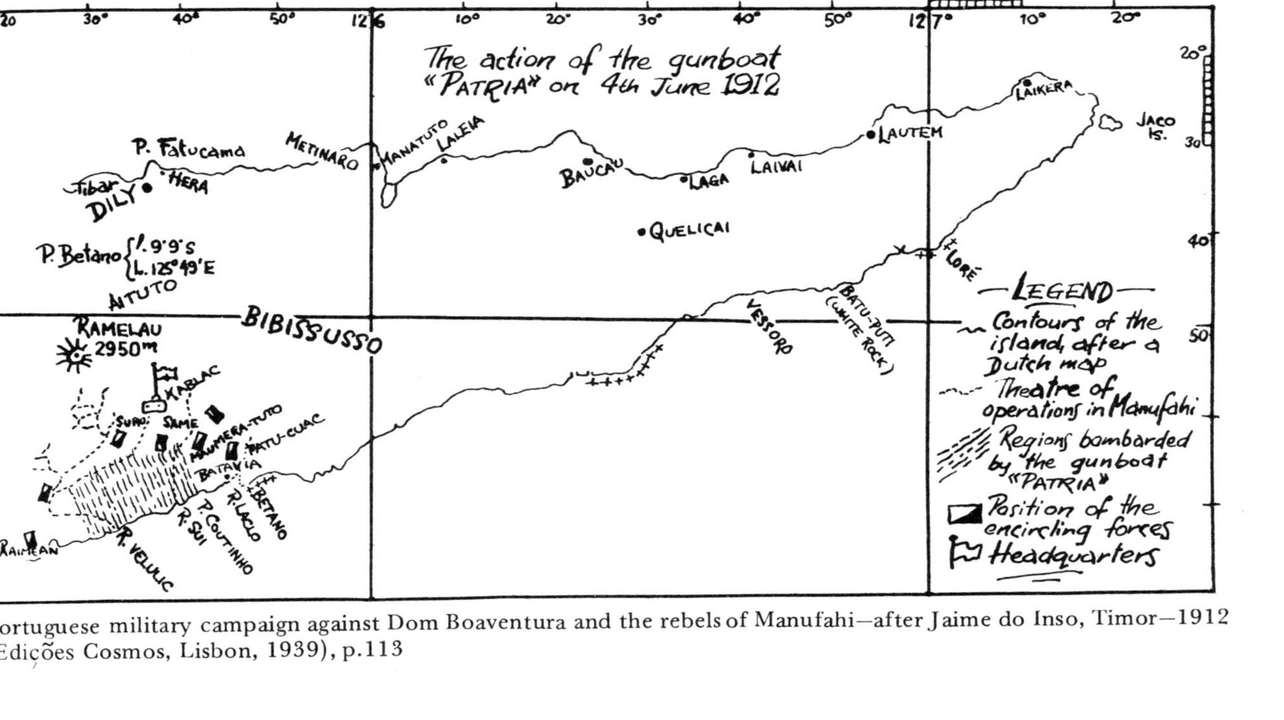

Portuguese military campaign against Dom Boaventura and the rebels of Manufahi—after Jaime do Inso, Timor—1912 (Edições Cosmos, Lisbon, 1939), p.113

BERLIN, Feb. 18.

rought in the German egent Luitpold, was Saturday, in the pre-

IN PERSIA.

ussia Back.

LONDON, Feb. 17.

ary (Sir Edward Grey) ortant questions in the t the Manchester Re-

agreement with re- e spheres of influence had produced a good the two powers, and thority of the Persian hout the agreement of an internal revolu- o Teheran, the capital, uld then be compelled ian frontiers against

tain and Russia agreed to limit the spheres interests in Persia to s adjoining the Rus- e one hand and the the other. The two integrity and indepen- at the same time con- e necessity of financial y with the principles When Russia demanded ne Persian Treasurer- n Shuster), and occu- he demand was met, d compliance, because o have two great na- the actions of any in- d his intentions might offence was that his gendarmerie meant the ropeans who would n the Russian sphere. as attacked, and bit- s of the Persia Com- or assisting Russia in y held, would destroy a had secured after ution.]

The Earl of Selborne, formerly Governor of the Transvaal and High Commissioner for South Africa, said at Cambridge on Friday that he did not suppose that the Asquith Ministry had the desire to introduce the system of spoils to the conqueror, but it was true that they had made wholesale appointments to the civil service. He also deprecated conferring honours on men whose only merit was that of donating largely to party funds. This tended to render public life corrupt, and to bring honours into contempt.

REVOLT IN TIMOR.

GOVERNMENT-HOUSE LOOTED.

LISBON, Feb. 17.

Reports of the insurrection in Timor, in the Malay Archipelago, show that the revolt is general. Ramea tribesmen have raided the port of Dilly. Many residents were murdered, and buildings burnt.

During the street fighting, Major Ingley and Lieutenant Silva, of the Portuguese Defence Force, and several soldiers, were killed. Their heads were cut off and stuck on poles.

Government-house has been entered by the natives and looted.

[Several days ago it was announced that negotiations were in progress for the sale to Germany of the Portuguese portion of Timor, with the territory of Ambeno and the neighbouring isle of Pulo Cambing. This report was afterwards denied by Portuguese officials. Port Dilly, the scene of the outrages, is closer to Port Darwin than Hobart is to Melbourne.]

FATE OF PALMYRA.

PACIFIC ISLAND'S OWNER.

WASHINGTON, Feb. 17.

The State department admits that a United States warship is now heading for

MISS

MINE MA

A Government in September t stances connect worth of gold tary Gold-minin was alleged to treatment of ma was believed to mission reporte loss, but that t was due to the in the calculati

Mr. Petheric mine, is now a the amount o mine in the f with having sta from milling, ing, and theref

CARRIED

MEN FIG

Four men, w the murder of were hanged t On the previo were Poles, g bursts, and fie warders, by overpowered. demned men f

The whole P to secure the trymen, but f

The men we semi-conscious

REAI

Melbourne *Argus*, 19 February 1912.

with a brief 'history of the trouble':

> Early in February it was reported that a rebellion had broken out among the natives and the Governor telegraphed to the Portuguese authorities, asking for a warship to be despatched. About the middle of the month reinforcements of 100 Europeans and 200 natives were sent to the island from Mozambique. The gunboat *Patria* was also despatched, and the Government made a statement that they considered these forces would be sufficient to re-establish order. In this the authorities were mistaken, for a few days later they had to send instructions to Mozambique to despatch another full company of troops to Timor. It was announced in Lisbon about this time that a special fund was being established to defray the expense of stamping out the rebellion. In spite of all the efforts of the authorities they were unable to properly quell the disturbances. In April the Portuguese Minister for the Colonies received a telegram from Timor, stating that the situation there had grown worse. Fighting took place between the rebels and the Portuguese forces, but, aided by the guns of the *Patria*, the troops put the enemy to flight. Early in May further troops were despatched from Mozambique and from Lisbon, and towards the end of that month desultory fighting took place. Although the authorities realised the situation was serious, no one anticipated that an engagement anything like that reported in today's cable would take place.

The memory of 1912 is still strong in the territory. At the end of 1975 one of Dom Boaventura's wives was still alive in Same, and there are others who remember the Great Rebellion, as it was known.

So East Timor came into the twentieth century. Originally administered from Goa and then Macau, in 1896 Timor was separated from Macau to become a separate administrative unit. After 1912 the Portuguese established an administration throughout the interior. The smallest administrative unit was the *povoação* (village cluster), the largest the *concelho* or *circunscrição* as it has been known at various times. In 1974 there were thirteen *concelhos*, each with a central seat of administration and a number of *postos*, smaller administrative posts.

The 'pacification' was accompanied by other processes of Portuguese consolidation, which contrasted with those of the Dutch. Whereas the Portuguese enhanced the power of

N ON THE JOB.

BOUR CRITICISED.

'AIR DAY'S WORK."

LONDON, Aug. 24.

ppears in the "Economist" ut the revelations made in to the failure of the day- in Australia to give an ade- r money expended. correspondent of the "Eco- that it is doubtful whether hich Mr. Griffith, the New Minister for Public Works, public enterprises will ever iate return. labourers," says the corre- doing as little as they can. anything like a fair day's appears to be no check on extravagance, however, and revenue continues buoyant hich really pulls the strings, and means of keeping up the

FROM ADMIRERS.

VE SIGNATURES.

us" of August 3 a letter was m a correspondent to the the ratepayers of Toorak, asion to use motors and would offer up a prayer when the work of under- phone lines in Toorak-road It was complained that it of impossibility to squeeze the by-streets, as the space so narrow. The writer added drays loaded with earth from not seem to care where they es and vehicles. They were n the centre of the already- way. The writer concluded t the tired feeling displayed was a disgrace. A depart- was held into the allega- Acting Postmaster-General ey) on Saturday morning the following report from postmaster-general (Mr.

nce to the recent criticisms d in 'The Argus' in connec- uit works being carried out road, I beg to inform you r has been carefully investi- m quite satisfied that there n for the adverse criticism. ible officers in charge of the bmitted written statements ey are unanimous in saying gress is being made. The concerned considers that he ucted body of men under his

has been taken to prevent erference with either pedes- lar traffic, but where exten- ation has to be carried out, of conduit-laying, a portion ust be fenced off and closed in every case the greatest

GREAT ISLAND BATTLE.

Timor Rebels Defeated.

Killed Number 3,000.

LISBON, Aug. 25.

For several months past there has been unrest in the Portuguese portion of the Island of Timor, in the Malay Archipelago. At various times a fresh outbreak of rebellion has been reported, and troops and warships have been despatched to quell the disturbances.

A startling message was received in Lisbon yesterday. It contained a brief report of a great battle between the troops and the rebels.

Very heavy loss of life occurred. The rebels were defeated, leaving 3,000 dead. Four thousand of the rebels were captured.

The losses sustained by the Government troops are not reported.

HISTORY OF THE TROUBLE.

The trouble in Timor is interesting to Australians, seeing that the island is only about 400 miles to the north-west of Port Darwin. It comprises 12,000 square miles, and has a population of about 400,000. The south-western portion of the island belongs to the Dutch, the capital being Kupang, while Portugal owns the north-eastern part of the island. Deli, on the north coast, is the capital of the Portuguese territory. Early in February it was reported that a rebellion had broken out among the natives, and the Governor telegraphed to the Portuguese authorities, asking for a warship to be despatched. About the middle of that month reinforcements of 100 Europeans and 200 natives were sent to the island from Mozambique. The gunboat Patria was also despatched, and the Government made a statement that they considered these forces would be sufficient to re-establish order. In this the authorities were mistaken, for a few days later they had to send instructions to Mozambique to despatch another full company of troops to Timor. It was announced in Lisbon about this time that a special fund was being established to defray the expense of stamping out the rebellion. In spite of all the efforts of the authorities they were unable to properly quell the disturbances. In April the Portuguese Minister for the Colonies received a telegram from Timor, stating that the situation there had grown worse. Fighting took place between the rebels and the Portuguese forces, but, aided by the guns of the Patria, the troops put the enemy to flight. Early in May further troops were despatched from Mozambique and from Lisbon, and towards the end of that month desultory fighting took place. Although the authorities realised that the position was becoming serious, no one anticipated that an engagement anything like that reported in to-day's cable message would take place.

IMPERIAL CRICKET.

IMPERIAL POLITICS.

SMALLER LIBERAL MAJORITY.

LONDON, Aug. 23.

The election contest for the East Carmarthen seat rendered vacant by the death of Mr. Abel Thomas, the Liberal member, was held yesterday. The candidates were:—Rev. Towyn Jones, Liberal; Mr. Mervyn L. Peel, Unionist; and Dr. J. W. Williams, Labour. Mr. Peel fought the 1910 and 1911 elections unsuccessfully against Mr. Thomas.

The Liberals retained the seat, but their majority has suffered a decrease. The returns were:—

Rev. T. Jones (Liberal) 6,082
Mr. Mervyn L. Peel (Unionist) 3,354
Dr. J. W. Williams (Labour) 1,089

The returns at the general election of 1911 were:—Thomas (Liberal), 5,925; Peel (Unionist), 2,315; Williams (Labour), 1,176. The Unionist vote has thus risen from 2,315 to 3,354, and the Liberal only increased by 257.

Mr. Keir Hardie, M.P., in an article in the Merthyr "Pioneer," says it will be almost a miracle if the Government can be kept together for two more years.

RUBBER SCANDALS.

CLERGYMAN'S CHARGES.

DIRECTORS DEMAND REDRESS.

LONDON, Aug. 24.

Strong exception has been taken to remarks made by the Rev. Herbert Hensley Henson, canon of Westminster Abbey and rector of St. Margarets, regarding the Peruvian rubber atrocities. Canon Henson delivered a sermon in Westminster Abbey denouncing certain people connected with the company which controlled the rubber industry.

A firm of solicitors representing three English directors of the Peruvian-Amazon Company has now written to Canon Henson complaining that his sermon contained baseless charges. The principal remark objected to is that the English directors deserved to be arrested and tried. The solicitors deny that the directors connived at the outrages, and demand that Canon Henson shall make amends.

The clergyman has replied that his sermon was entirely justified. He states that when the directors took over the business they retained men who, as the company's own representative subsequently confessed, were murderers, pirates, and bandits.

"The directors," Canon Henson states, "ought to have hastened to Peru, and done something personally to atone for the infamies perpetrated."

TH

A

Krupp's Nachrichten holding of manœuvres. next war the united and Russia.

DE

Mr. C

Referring "Standard" miralty (M cent naval office, and manders u Mall Gazet ously again The writer mislead the Churchill by Admira Home fleet strategical

LINK

OVERS

MEM

The ove General S ing:— New Ze Robin, Chi Canada.— Inspector Australi military a the Imperi It is e shortly be officer.

SOU

Ships

General vaal Legis chairman ence, is a to discuss million a y Intervie ral Beye

Melbourne *Argus*, 26 August 1912.

traditional élites, particularly at the secondary level, and fanned and controlled the play of conflicting tribal loyalties, the Dutch generally curbed the power of traditional powerholders. Early this century they began construction of a trunk road from Kupang to the centre of the island and moved population to settlements around the road system.[40] Portuguese attitudes reflected the smallness of their numbers and limited economic resources. Pursuing the policy of divide and rule, they allowed certain kingdoms to retain private armies and proscribed movement between *concelhos*. After 1912, they forbade, too, traditional intermarriage between the *liurais*.

Clearly 'pacification' on either side of the island was the main prerequisite to border settlement, although depleted Portuguese coffers could also be a lever. In 1850 Governor Lopes de Lima caused a scandal when, empowered by Lisbon to negotiate with the Dutch, he signed a convention ceding Solor and Larantuka in exchange for Maubara and 200,000 florins. The florins were payable in three instalments and the Dutch were entitled to occupy Larantuka after payment of the first. De Lima was recalled to Portugal and arraigned. The Portuguese repudiated the convention, but Holland had by then already occupied Larantuka, and Lisbon could not find 200,000 florins with which to repay them. Thus in 1860 Portugal was forced to ratify an agreement in almost exactly the same terms as de Lima's.[41]

A number of enclaves now remained in east and west and both parties expressed a desire to tidy up the map. These included Oecusse and Noimuti in west Timor, Maucatar (part of the realm of Suai-Camenassa) in eastern Timor, and around the proposed central border, the small kingdom of Djenilu west of Batugadé, and some of the central Bunak and Kemak-speaking areas.

In 1893 a convention was signed in Lisbon providing for a mixed commission to draw up the final lines. The convention included a 'most favoured nation' clause by which if either party wished to relinquish their colonial claim the other should have first preference to it. The commission sat between 1908–9 but disagreements led to a conference at The Hague in 1902. The final outcome was agreement that Portugal should have Oecusse and in return would cede Noimuti, Maucatar and disputed border areas to the Dutch. A convention was signed in 1904, although minor disputes stretched on until 1914, largely due to inaccuracies in the 1902 map. The final agreement divided a number of traditional kingdoms, the most important of which was Suai–Camenassa, formerly of the Waiwiku–Wehale kingdom.[42]

In 1926 the violence-wracked democratic republic which was established in Portugal in 1910 gave way to what was to become Europe's most enduring fascist government, António de Oliveira Salazar's corporate state, or *Estado Novo*.

In 1930 the 'Colonial Act' reduced the already slender civil rights held by inhabitants of the colonies. Under the pre-1910 constitutional monarchy the colonies had the status of 'provinces' and their inhabitants held, in theory, the same rights as Portuguese citizens. Salazar's new Act stressed the supremacy of the metropolis through the use of the term 'colonies' and heralded legislation in which constitutional rights were made dependent upon 'assimilation' to a 'Portuguese standard' of civilisation.[43]

How this worked in practice can be seen from the following 1950 table, in which 'assimilated' are listed as '*indigenous—civilizado*':

Table 1. Composition of Portuguese Timor's Population in 1950

European	**568**
***Mestiço* (mixed blood)**	**2,022**
Chinese	**3,128**
Other non-indigenous (Goan, etc.)	**212**
Indigenous – *civilizado*	**1,541**
Indigenous – *nao-civilizado*	**434,907**
Total	**442,378**

***From* Donald E. Weatherbee, 'Portuguese Timor: an Indonesian Dilemma', *Asian Survey* 6 (Dec.1966), p.684**

On this classification only 7,471 of the population, 1.8% (all those outside the last category), were regarded as eligible to vote. Before World War II *não-civilizados* had neither citizenship nor suffrage; in 1950 they had citizenship but no vote. Even those who had reached the required level of 'assimilation' to find urban employment worked for wages of around one thirteenth those of European workers.[44] The chances of a Timorese acquiring this privilege were small. Education in government schools was restricted in 1950 to families of *assimilados*, leaving the Catholic mission schools as the only option for children of others. Adult illiteracy was then estimated to be between 95–99%. By 1960 primary school enrolment accounted for 6% of the total school age population.[45] The rate of illiteracy in Portugal itself was almost as high. In the nineteen-fifties it was almost 45 per cent, although separate surveys of the rural population revealed its average as 60%.[46]

Another instrument of Portuguese dominance under Salazar was PIDE, the secret police organisation which, through the use of terror, censorship and a web of paid informers, existed as a state within a state. Timor between the wars was a closed book to the outside world and existing accounts of PIDE activities are mostly post-World War II. Enforced isolation and obscurantism were the hallmarks of Salazar's state, to which accounts of the loneliness of dissidents in those years, written since the 1974 Lisbon coup, bear eloquent testimony. Nevertheless it is clear that it was in this period that the brutal practices of twentieth century Portuguese colonialism were founded—the secret terror of PIDE, forced labour under the knout and the application of the *palmatória*. This latter disciplinary measure was used in all the colonies and Australian soldiers saw it applied during the second world war:

> This was the normal form of punishment ... The stick used was fifteen to eighteen inches long and comprised a handle and a flat disc three to four inches in diameter at the end. The wood was hard, and an inch or more in thickness. The punishment was inflicted by delivering blows as hard as possible on to the palms of the hands with the flat of the disc, which was perforated with a few holes to reduce any cushioning effect due to the air. I was told that twelve or fifteen blows on each hand was as much as a white man could possibly stand, but for severe crimes as many as fifty blows on each hand were sometimes administered to natives. In such cases the native's hands were entirely useless for two or three weeks ... [47]

The Australians also obtained a glimpse of forced labour practices:

> it is a common sight to see gangs of natives roped or chained together working on the rice fields or marching back to the calaboose at night.[48]

When war broke out in 1939, Portugal was quick to declare neutrality. In Asia, the Japanese move south went primarily through Malaya and Singapore but it was not long before they reached Timor. The Dutch, Portuguese and Australian governments became increasingly nervous about Japanese intent; the Dutch reinforced their Kupang garrison and in mid-December 1941 Australia landed pre-emptive forces in Kupang and Dili, the latter against the Governor's protests of neutrality. These men were the first graduates of the Australian army's jungle warfare training scheme.

The Japanese followed soon after. On 19 February 1942 they landed 1,000 troops at Dili and 5,000 at Kupang, reinforced with new waves in the following days. The Australians at Kupang resisted in fierce hand to hand fighting. In the space of several days they fought the Japanese for a few metres of land, until forced to surrender. Casualties on both sides were heavy. One of the keen nineteen-year-olds who participated in this resistance, and who spent the rest of the war on the notorious Burma railway, was Australian Labor politician Mr Tom Uren. The Dili force was luckier. It numbered only 327, but in deference to the pride of the Portuguese Governor had disembarked a little down the coast from Dili. A high proportion of the troops were quite soon stricken with malaria, and so a hospital camp was established at a place called Three Spurs (near Railaco) in the hills behind Dili, and the command headquarters was moved to Railaco. Thus when the Japanese landed the Australians there did not suffer the brunt of the offensive as those in Kupang had. They demolished Dili airstrip before making good an escape to the hills with the loss of only a few men.

For the next thirteen months they worked with sympathetic Timorese to conduct a remarkable guerilla campaign from behind Japanese lines. In the first months they were totally isolated from their command in Australia and became bearded guerillas, living off the land and eventually speaking Tetum as a second language. They were joined by the few Australians who escaped from Kupang, some Dutch forces and small 'international brigades' of *deportados*, Portuguese exiled before the war for anti-Salazar activities.

In Australia it was believed that the Dili force had been

eliminated. It was with some incredulity that a radio signal from Australians in Timor was received in Darwin two months later. The guerillas had built a transmitter from scavenged parts. First radio contact was made on 22 April and supplies were being airdropped within days. A month later first surface contact was established when a Catalina seaplane, guided in by signal fires lit by Timorese, landed off south-coast Beco and evacuated seriously wounded personnel. Henceforth the Australians used the radio to direct strategic bombing missions from Darwin.

Most of the Portuguese were interned by the Japanese at Liquiçá, although others were cut off in the interior. With the breakdown of the administration, tribal fighting erupted in some areas and in others Timorese took the opportunity to settle scores with the Portuguese. In Maubisse the administrator was murdered and Australian soldiers witnessed at first hand the typical Portuguese response to insurrection:

> ... the Portuguese prepared to deal with this uprising as their hundreds of years of colonization had taught them. Their army was collected; it consisted of two companies, each about one hundred strong. The troops were Timorese, and the non-commissioned officers and officers were Portuguese ... At the same time the natives in the surrounding areas were ordered to arm themselves and prepare for war ... The Portuguese prohibition of natives travelling from one area to another had prevented any concerted action, and had maintained the local jealousies and rivalries ... It was also fortunate that the natives in the two areas around Ainaro and Same were Christians and not at all friendly with the non-Christians of Maubisse ... there was a concentrated drive into the Maubisse area ... Compared with this, the Japanese efforts at subjecting areas were just child's play. Every village and crop was burnt; every woman, child and animal was driven off and fell as spoil to the victors. The tracks through that area were foul with the bodies of natives killed and just rolled out of the way.[49]

In the first months of the war the Japanese had been content to occupy the north coast without attempting to move inland. However, the Australians of Independent Company became a gadfly too troublesome to ignore and in mid-1942 the Japanese brought reinforcements, including a counter-insurgency unit under a commander known as the 'Singapore

Tiger'. Australian prestige was enhanced when the Singapore Tiger was assassinated during his first foray against them, near Remexio. Nevertheless, in the coming months the Australians were pushed south until in January 1943 a full-scale evacuation was effected from the south coast, leaving Timor under Japanese occupation until the surrender in 1945. In the course of their campaign they had lost forty men for approximately 1,500 Japanese casualties.[50]

In the following two and a half years of Japanese occupation a brutal toll was exacted from the Timorese. The post-war population was estimated to be 40,000 less than in 1942, the result of Japanese brutality, war-induced famine and ruthless food-expropriation policies in which the whole harvest of an area would be taken, leaving the Timorese to glean what they could from root-gathering and hunting.[51]

Allied military briefings spoke constantly of the Timorese terrain as a dominant factor in all military activity:

> To the infantryman Portuguese Timor is one lunatic contorted tangle of mountains. There is no main system of ranges, for the mountains run in all directions and fold upon one another in crazy fashion.
>
> The mountains determine that warfare ... must be of a guerilla nature ... one geographical feature, mountains, determines the whole nature of life and fighting on the island.

Most of the Australians who fought in East Timor during the second world war developed a lasting affection for the Timorese and many have taken an active interest in Timorese affairs since. The literature of the war in Timor is, however, tinged with the racism which has historically characterised Australian attitudes to South-East Asia and the Pacific. A 1943 report discussed the Timorese thus:

> Money, of which they have very little, is their god ... On the whole, they are very lazy and prefer to gamble rather than work. Good use, however, can be made of them by our troops as carriers and runners ...
>
> The natives are excellent porters, and for hours on end can carry 40 lb loads on their heads. They must be well fed, as food shortage can cause desertions. Pay for the native carriers would be 10 avos (2d) per day in the beginning, but towards the end they were earning 2d per hour ... The only really reliable natives now

are the creados (servants)[52]

As in most areas of South-East Asia under pre-war colonial rule the war involved local people in a choice of lesser evils in which Japanese brutality finally tipped the scales towards the Allies. In the long term the weakening (and in some cases breaking) of the grip of white colonial power by the Japanese fertilised the soil for post-war nationalisms.

In the Netherlands East Indies most of the major nationalist leaders collaborated with the Japanese in exchange for assurances of independence. With Japanese defeat, the independent Indonesian Republic was declared in August 1945. Its authority over the whole country was established only in 1949, after a war of independence against Dutch restorationist forces. West Timorese played a part in some Indonesian nationalist organisations established in the 1930s and many were active supporters of the Republic of Indonesia in the 1945–9 period. The present Governor of the Eastern Lesser Sundas, El Tari, was one of a number of west Timorese who fought against the Dutch in Java. The Dutch were able to re-establish control fairly easily in west Timor in the years after 1945, but few Timorese mourned their departure after the 1949 settlement. West Timorese, Savunese and Rotinese played important roles in the civil administration of Indonesian Timor after 1949, though some senior posts were held by people from Java and other parts of the archipelago.

By contrast, the post-war years in East Timor were a time of unprecedented harshness. The economy was in ruins and the Portuguese were preoccupied with re-asserting their authority. The first signs of insurgence were apparent in Portuguese Africa. It was in these years that FRETILIN's president Xavier do Amaral developed his nationalist ideas.

In 1947 a member of the Australian War Graves Commission visited East Timor to search for the remains of war dead. Glen Francis's glimpse of East Timorese life shocked him:

> After centuries of colonial rule the natives are as backward and helpless as ever ... Forced labour under the whip goes on from dawn to dusk, and the Portuguese colonists, including those exiled from Salazar's Portugal ... live with the same mixture of civility and brutality as they had 350 years ago.

In the course of his mission he travelled to Viqueque, where he was invited for a meal at the administrator's house. Afterwards they sat drinking liqueurs and smoking fine cigars, until the sounds of human industry aroused Francis's curiosity. He was told that a new wall was being built for the *posto* and the road repaired. On asking to watch he found a gang of Timorese working under forced labour conditions. Two teams worked on the road repair, one carrying boulders about two feet in diameter from a nearby quarry, using a canvas sling, to the other team which was breaking the boulders with sledgehammers. His account gives a fascinating picture of the Portuguese practice of rule through hierarchical division of the local population. The labourers were being whipped to action not by Portuguese, but by three Timorese overseers. Two wearing a red cloth of rank were flaying the road gangs with a short thick length of rope. The third, wearing a purple diagonal sash, beat the other two with a birch if they paused in their work:

> In a moment he darted forward and brought down his flagellum again and again on the backs of the red-clothed men who themselves had relaxed a moment too long. They arched backward with the pain, then ran amok, their ropes swishing in the air to right and left, and cracking anew upon searing flesh. As one gang moved out, another moved in ... the creatures in pain turned their eyes upon me in passing, eyes dull with stupefaction, glazed with that lustreless opaqueness to be seen in an abused animal when it collapses exhausted. The ropes swished on, cracked on, the feet pattered back and forth, the flesh came up in new weals, the foundations of the road crept forward foot by foot.[53]

In 1956 Portugal was admitted to the United Nations, finally overcoming long-standing opposition by Eastern bloc and some Western European nations. Although membership was eventually to subject Portugal to increasing pressure over its 'non-self-governing territories', culminating in economic sanctions in the early seventies, the immediate question was obviated by a constitutional sleight of hand by which the term 'colonies'—in official use since Salazar's 1930 'Colonial Act'—reverted to 'overseas provinces'.

The first eruption of anti-colonial rebellion after the war took place in 1959 in the Viqueque region. Little is known outside of East Timor about the 'movement' of 1959, although both APODETI and FRETILIN claim it as a formative influence. Existing accounts vary; what is known is that in 1959 fourteen Indonesians who claimed to be refugees from the secessionist Permesta movement in the Celebes (Sulawesi) landed in Portuguese Timor and requested political asylum, which they were duly granted. They established residence in Baucau. The administrator at Viqueque was particularly unpopular in the *concelho* (although not the same man who entertained Francis twelve years before), and the area was ripe for rebellion. The Indonesians apparently encouraged Timorese there to attack Portuguese posts at Uatolári and Uato Carabau. Telephone lines from Baucau were cut by pre-arrangement, isolating these villages, and a series of riots and sporadic attacks followed in which houses were burnt. It has also been claimed that a truck laden with armaments was almost to the gates of the central barracks in Dili before it was discovered by the Portuguese as the result of an informer in the rebel ranks. The Portuguese dealt with the revolt in customary fashion: accounts of the number killed vary between 160 and 1,000, a number of people were gaoled, and 58 Timorese exiled to Mozambique, Angola and Lisbon.

The main discrepancies in accounts are of the origin and intent of the 14 refugees. On the one hand it has been suggested that they were conscious agents of Indonesia's Sukarno government, on the other that they were genuine anti-Javanese secessionists with the half-formed idea of using East Timor as a base for eastern Indonesian secessionist movements after their forced departure from Sulawesi. Regardless of the origins of this rebellion its repression rankled in Timorese minds as a recent bitter injustice and a number of its protagonists were prime movers in the political associations formed in Timor after 1974.[54]

The new Indonesian Republic held territorial claims to all that was formerly part of the Netherlands East Indies, including West New Guinea. Between 1949 and 1962 the claim to West New Guinea, where the Dutch had succeeded in maintaining control after the 1949 settlement, was a major focus of Indonesian foreign policy concerns as well as a rallying point for domestic unity. Indonesian leaders often spoke of the need to combat colonialism throughout the world, and occasionally made references to Portuguese colonialism in Timor in this context. But they were careful not to give the impression that they aspired to incorporate Portuguese Timor (or the territories of North Borneo). There were good reasons for this: their claim to West New Guinea was advanced on the grounds that Indonesia was the successor state to the Netherlands Indies, and they would have weakened their case significantly if they had argued that East Timor was included in the campaign to eliminate anachronistic colonial boundaries. In 1961 Sukarno assured Salazar that Portuguese rights in Timor would be respected. A UN background paper saw it in this light:

> For its part the government of Indonesia has declared that it maintains friendly relations with Portugal and has no claim to Portuguese Timor, which has never been part of the Dutch East Indies and therefore is not of the same status as West Irian [West New Guinea][55]

Donald E. Weatherbee, writing in *Asian Survey*, described the policy as one of 'irresolute indirection'; meaning that any 'liberation' policy held by Jakarta was unofficial but at the same time a movement emerging in the territory itself would be sympathetically heard if it applied for support: 'With specific reference to North Borneo and Portuguese Timor, General Nasution has said: "We support their struggles, but do not claim their territories"'.[56]

Whether or not Jakarta encouraged actions such as that of 1959 is unclear, but in 1961 the semblance of a movement did appear, and was noted by the United Nations. The 'Unirepublic Timor' movement declared itself in April 1961, naming its acting president as A. Mao Klao. Its founding document, in Indonesian, declared Batugadé the capital of a united Timor, nominated the cabinet of the new republic and proclaimed 'Long Live Malay Melanesia!' An office was said to exist in Jakarta but several callers to the address between then and now have failed to find evidence of an organisation there.[57]

In 1962–3 Indonesia realised its long-standing aspiration to incorporate West New Guinea. After a long campaign of domestic agitation and international lobbying, combined with military moves in the last stages, Sukarno succeeded in forcing the Dutch out of this last vestige of their eastern empire.

Sovereignty was transferred to a UN Temporary Executive Authority in late 1962 and the UN handed it to Indonesia the following May. Indonesian sovereignty was formally confirmed in May 1969 by an 'Act of Free Choice'—neither freedom nor choice, as the journalists quipped, but certainly an act. Aware that it had failed to win voluntary support from the people of West New Guinea, the Suharto government decided not to risk a plebiscite. Instead a handful of foreign observers were invited to witness local assemblies in which selected local notables raised their hands in favour of continued Indonesian control. The architect and supervisor of the Act of Free Choice was Brigadier-General (now Lieutenant-General) Ali Murtopo. Irian Jaya, as it is now called, has been isolated from the world since 1969 and sporadic but persistent reports of armed resistance suggest that the Jakarta authorities have reason to fear international scrutiny.

Quite apart from the special case of Irian Jaya, the Indonesian Republic has had national unity problems since its foundation. The Dutch had ruled over a wide variety of ethnic communities, some of which had little contact with each other in pre-colonial times, some of which had a history of conflict with each other and others of which were united in suspicion of the Javanese. Most of the leaders of the pre-war nationalist movement had been from the Javanese ethnic community, which accounts for a little over half of the country's population, and the Javanese emerged as a strong group in the period after independence. (Sukarno was a Javanese, as is Suharto. Hatta, the former Vice-President, and Prime Minister in 1949–50, is from West Sumatra.)

Coming into existence with a weak and divided army, at a time when arms had been distributed widely among the population and when there were still many Dutch in the country willing to back anti-nationalist causes, the new state was forced to contend with a variety of rebellions, both in the heartland island of Java and in the outer islands. The secessionist 'Republic of the South Moluccas', proclaimed in a small region just north of Timor in April 1950, kept sizeable numbers of central government troops pinned down for over a decade, as did three distinct rebellions launched under the symbol of Darul Islam (House of Islam) in West Java, South Sulawesi

(South Celebes) and Aceh (an area of the northernmost tip of Sumatra). Moreover, a further series of regional rebellions broke out in February 1958 when the government's own military commanders in several areas of Sumatra and Sulawesi backed a 'Revolutionary Government of the Republic of Indonesia' (PRRI), in an action which was anti-Sukarno and anti-leftist as well as anti-Javanese.

It was only around 1962 that the central government succeeded in gaining supremacy over these various rebel movements. In the case of the South Moluccas Republic and the West Java and South Sulawesi segments of the Darul Islam movements, the government achieved its ends by predominantly military means. In the case of the PRRI (including its North Sulawesi division, Permesta) and the Aceh segment of Darul Islam, the rebels 'returned to the fold of the Republic', agreeing to lay down their arms on the basis of a negotiated settlement involving amnesties for the rebel combatants. In settling the Aceh rebellion the central government conceded that the province should become a Special Territory with greater autonomy than is accorded to other areas.

In these years the Sukarno régime was sliding into the pattern of corruption and authoritarianism which frequently afflicts newly-independent nations drained by the preceding colonial power and the fight to break free of it:

> Sukarno's Indonesia resembles the authoritarian models of Latin America: a flamboyant leader, backed by the military, popular with the masses, supposedly progressive but, in fact, conservative, in that no radical domestic reforms are introduced.[58]

The government was an uneasy coalition of army and civilian elements which was beset by tensions between right and left. The populist Sukarno was a sympathiser of the Nationalist Party and the Communists whose politics stirred powerful apprehensions in the ranks of the urban upper classes and those army leaders who were his partners in government—apprehensions which culminated in 1965 in a bloody coup. On 1 October 1965 a group of pro-Sukarno officers reached for power in the capital, killing six senior generals. By the evening of that day the generals had struck back, under the leadership of Major-General Suharto of the Strategic Reserve. Somewhere between 500,000 and one million supporters of the Indonesian Communist Party were killed in the next six months.

On 11 March 1966 Suharto forced Sukarno to cede virtually all his powers to him and the next nine months saw the consolidation of a military régime whose economic and foreign policy postures were characterised by a sharp shift to the right. Granted aid on a generous scale by the U.S., Japan and other Western-linked states including Australia, the Suharto government set out to achieve the kind of development which the World Bank and International Monetary Fund would support and fund, and to which foreign investors in minerals, fuels, timber and manufacture would be attracted. The result has been the 'showcase state', an Indonesia in which foreign-induced economic growth has created a series of boom cities and a newly prosperous civil servant class, but in which the mass of the peasantry is no better off than before, and some groups of it a good deal worse off. Military rule has given Indonesia greater political stability than it had in the Sukarno years, but at the expense of democracy—and, to a large extent, of the interests of the workers and peasants. Civilian 'technocrats' play a significant role in the government as allies of the army but political parties are either banned or circumscribed. Amnesty International estimates between 55,000 and 100,000 persons are being held as political prisoners, many of whom have been imprisoned since 1965.

By the mid-twentieth century the colonies were a disastrous drain on Portugal's economy. From the early 1960s the cost of counter-insurgency wars in the African colonies increased the burden. In 1964 Salazar was forced to take the unprecedented step of inviting foreign investment. The first decade of guerilla war in Portuguese Africa saw a spectacular expansion of exports and budgetary revenue in Angola and Mozambique. The opening of the metropolis to foreign capital, and thus industrialisation, sowed the seeds of social change which reached fruition in 1974.[59] Although these changes did not better the lot of the Angolan or Mozambican peasant (if anything they were used to subsidise the war against them) they contrasted with Timor's tiny budget, which was annually subsidised from Lisbon. In 1964 budgetary expenditure was less than $A3m., of which $A2m. was a direct subsidy.[60] In 1973 it was $A5.5m., of which more than half was raised locally, the balance subsidised. Local revenue came from exports (mainly coffee, but also copra, beeswax, sisal and timber) and the imposition of a wide range of taxes, including $A1m. from the poll tax levied on each adult male. This tax was a long-standing hardship for the Timorese (the 1912 rebellion was attributed in part to it) and the *corvée* labour gangs usually comprised people unable to pay. By the seventies East Timor was heavily dependent on imports, of which Australia supplied some 15%, although there was no return trade. Average annual income was estimated at around $A30.[61] Details of the last wage increase before April 1974 give an indication of standard daily wage rates. These were tabled in three forms—'total' wages, subdivided into 'cash' and 'food provisions':

Table 1. Rural workers and workers utilised for the construction and repair of roads

Designation	Total	Cash	Food Provisions
1 Workers over 18 years of age	12$00	7$00	5$00 [escudos]
2 Workers more than 14 but under 18 years of age	10$00	5$00	5$00

Table 2. Other workers on a level with rural workers

Designation	Total	Cash	Food Provisions
1 Workers over 18 years of age:			
In Dili	17$00	11$00	6$00
In other localities	15$00	10$00	5$00
2 Workers more than 14 but under 18 years of age:			
In Dili	12$00	6$00	6$00
In other localities	10$00	5$00	5$00

From *Diplomas Legislativo 11/73 and 12/73:*
Increase in the Salaries of Public Servants and the Minimum Wages of Workers–*A Voz de Timor,*15 June 1973 (reprinted from *Boletim Oficial*)

The escudo (0$00) was worth approximately 33 to the $A at this time. The highest rate on this table—17$00 per day for a Dili worker over 18—was therefore equivalent to about $3 per week.

In 1963 Osmar White, a Melbourne journalist, visited East Timor. 'I have travelled a great deal in parts of Asia where white men are disliked and distrusted', he wrote,

> but I have never been so sensible of fear-paralysed hostility as I was in Timor ... One of the most extraordinary things about life in Portuguese Timor is that ranking Portuguese officers seem genuinely unaware of the social and spiritual squalor of their environment.

He predicted that the Indonesian Republic would soon 'swallow' East Timor:

> ... for much the same reason as the Union of India swallowed Portuguese Goa ... many Australians are going to feel a shock of alarm as unpleasant as that they experienced when the Dutch yielded to world pressure and surrendered West New Guinea ... We would be electing to confront Indonesia on very shaky moral grounds indeed if we expressed any strong disapproval or resisted any move to liquidate this last and most lamentable example of European colonialism in South-East Asia.

White further estimated that the colony would explode from within, as Portuguese Africa was then doing. He suggested several ways this might happen, all assuming degrees of Indonesian complicity or interest, stemming from Sukarno's anti-colonialist rhetoric. Firstly, native Timorese could revolt, Timorese troops defect to the insurgents, killing white officers, and independence be declared in the belief that Indonesia would prevent Portuguese intervention; more probably, an army revolt headed by dissident Portuguese officers and supported by Timorese could spark the explosion:

> However the success of an officer led army revolt could be jeopardised if the Indonesians next door regarded it with less enthusiasm than a spontaneous uprising of their Timorese brothers and so witheld support at the crucial time.

The last possibility he noted was an uprising which was the outcome of Indonesian infiltration of skilled agitators into the colony. The actual course of events in East Timor in 1974 and 1975 combined elements of these several prognoses although with an outcome bloodier than even White could predict.[62]

In the late 60s and early 70s *Seara*, a Catholic newspaper, became a focus for growing unrest in East Timor. Church publications stood outside the normal censorship laws and *Seara*'s columns soon filled with contributions about issues of Timorese life: traditional marriage law, traditional housing customs and attendant problems, scientific humanism *v.* Christianity, the morality of violence, the principles of education. The paper gave regular space to the teaching of Tetum (in the state education system pupils were obliged to use only Portuguese). Many of *Seara*'s contributors emerged to prominence after 1974: Nicolau Lobato, José Ramos Horta, Xavier do Amaral (writing as 'Ramos Paz'), Domingos de Oliveira, Manuel Carrascalão, Francisco Borja da Costa, Inácio de Moura, Mari Alkatiri.

Between December 1972 and January 1973 the increasingly political nature of the paper was made apparent in a polemic between Ramos Horta and Mari Alkatiri. Alkatiri, a practising Moslem, could hardly have been involved with Church affairs. Ramos Horta argued that East Timor was a beautiful country but the Timorese did not appreciate it. If they did, he said, they would work harder and make something of it. Alkatiri replied that the problem was not that the Timorese had no will to work; the malaise of Timor was more complex—it was structural; agricultural production was retarded by the colonial system. Ramos Horta hotly retorted: 'Our problems will not be solved with Utopias or sophisms!'.

On 24 March 1973, despite its apparent immunity, *Seara* was closed down, on the intervention of PIDE.[63] But a kernel of active resistance had aready formed. Some of the *Seara* contributors were already meeting regularly in Dili, in conditions of utter clandestinity. Nicolau Lobato, Mari Alkatiri, Alarico Fernandes, José Ramos Horta, Justino Mota and others now met and talked each Sunday in Henry the Navigator Square, outside the *palaçio*. Some had been to Africa, in exile, or in the course of their studies, and silently observed the nationalist movements. In a period of exile in Mozambique Ramos Horta narrowly avoided aggravating his problems with the Portuguese. He worked there as a journalist and was called to account for a review he had written of the Australian film 'Ned Kelly', starring Mick Jagger, in which he characterised Kelly as a democrat fighting colonial oppression. But more important than the ensuing brush with the authorities was the fact that he saw FRELIMO in action, although he had no opportunity for direct contact. Mari Alkatiri had studied in Angola, where he met secretly with an MPLA representative. However, both were so consumed with suspicion that the other may be a PIDE agent that no useful bond could be forged.

In December 1972 after 23 years of conservative Liberal Party government a Labor government under Mr Gough Whitlam came to power in Australia. It was noted by the young radicals in Dili. In October 1973 Ramos Horta devoted an article in Dili's only newspaper, the weekly *A Voz de Timor*, to a discussion of the new government, in particular, its attitude to the Aboriginal people and its foreign policies.[64]

The foreign policy style of the new government contrasted with that of the Liberals. Australian involvement in Vietnam immediately ceased, as did the system of military conscription in Australia, friendly relations were established with the People's Republic of China and Australian UN representatives were instructed to support certain anti-colonial resolutions.

In early 1973 Timor provided a test case for the consistent application of these principles. On 14 November and 14 December 1972 Australia supported two resolutions condemning Portuguese colonialism, the first under the Liberal McMahon government, the second under the Whitlam administration. The first affirmed the right to self-determination and independence of Angola, Mozambique and 'other Territories under Portuguese domination'. It called on member nations to cease all activities and to discourage individuals or companies from making any agreements, which 'contribute to Portugal's domination over those Territories'. The 14 December resolution went further, calling for cessation of all forms of assistance used to 'repress the peoples of the colonial territories and their national liberation movements'.

The consistency of Labor support for these resolutions was called into question when it was revealed in the *Australian Financial Review* that the government-owned Trans Australian Airlines, which provided the only regular air service into the territory, had been transporting Portuguese troops between Darwin and Dili and that most foreign investment in the territory was Australian.[65]

Until 1971 there was only one mining concern in East Timor,

the Australian-owned Timor Oil, which had been there since 1956. In January 1972 the Australian BHP company obtained a concession to prospect for minerals for an initial period of four years. BHP was particularly interested in iron, manganese and chromium. The agreement with the Portuguese administration was renewable for a further three years with an option at the end of that time of an extra twenty years. In June 1972 Timor Oil farmed out concessions to twin affiliates, International Oil Exploration N.L. and Amalgamated Petroleum N.L.

Australia was also involved with Portugal in negotiations over seabed rights. Since 1953 Australia had laid claim to the potentially oil rich continental shelf to sixty miles from the coast of Timor. Australia's north coast is characterised by an extensive shallow seabed which drops at this point, known as the Timor Trough, to a depth of over 10,000 feet. Portugal claimed that this trough was merely a depression in a contiguous continental shelf and that under the Geneva Law of the Sea Convention of 1958 the boundaries between the two countries should be set at a median point. Australia pressed a similar claim against Indonesia in the Arafura Sea between Irian Jaya and Australia, and in the Timor Sea west of Portuguese Timor. In October 1972 Indonesia conceded the 'Timor Trough' principle to Australia and a boundary was drawn up which gave Australia a little less than originally claimed. Portugal, however, remained obdurate.[66]

To the accusation that its involvement with Portuguese Timor violated the UN resolutions Senator Willesee for the Labor government replied that they applied only to Africa:

> operative paragraphs of the resolution are ... specifically directed to the situation in Portuguese African territories. Portuguese Timor is not named in the resolution.[67]

Although the Labor government's vigorous policies of support for Third World countries elsewhere raised unfulfilled hopes for Timorese nationalists, the government itself thus served early notice that the decolonisation issue in Timor might be a little too close to home.

In Portugal, the death of Salazar in 1970 gave impetus to the decay already eating at the *Estado Novo*. He was replaced by Marcelo Caetano, a long-standing colleague, who was forced

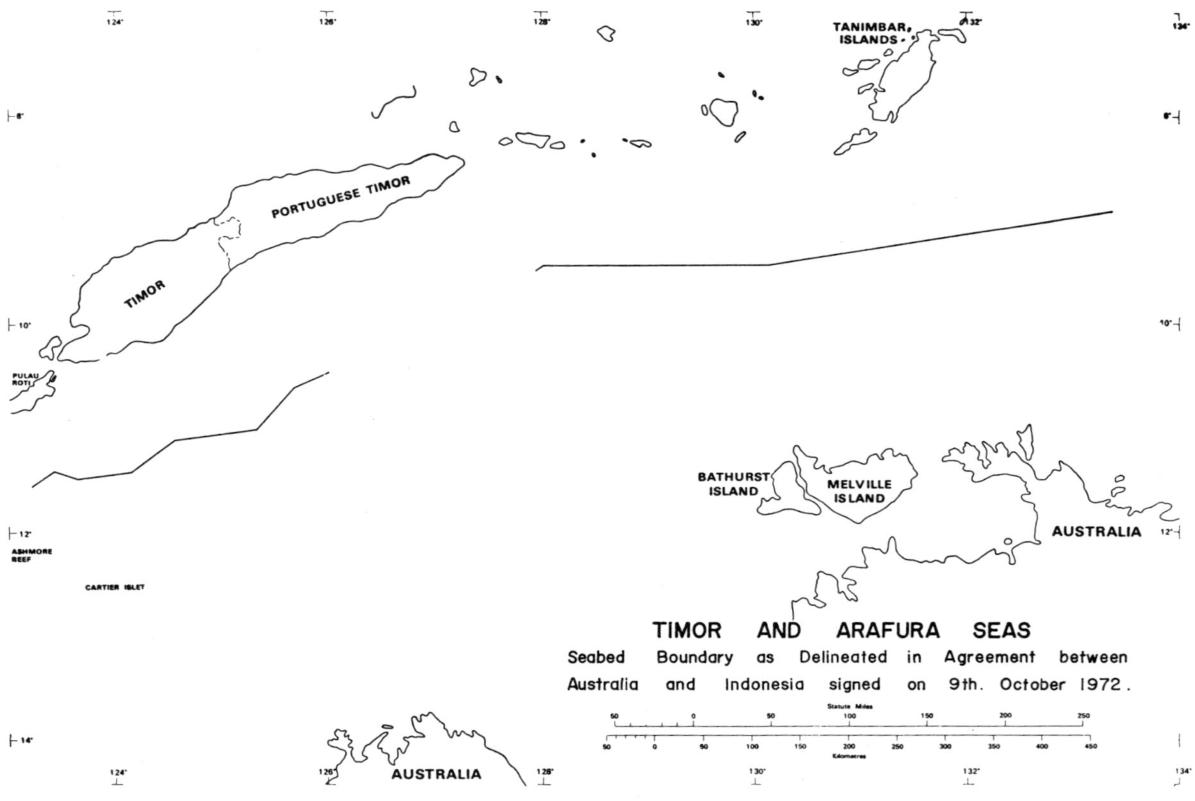

TANIMBAR ISLANDS
PORTUGUESE TIMOR
TIMOR
PULAU ROTI
ASHMORE REEF
CARTIER ISLET
BATHURST ISLAND
MELVILLE ISLAND
AUSTRALIA
AUSTRALIA
124°
126°
128°
130°
132°
134°
8°
10°
12°
14°
TIMOR AND ARAFURA SEAS
Seabed Boundary as Delineated in Agreement between Australia and Indonesia signed on 9th. October 1972.
Statute Miles
50 0 50 100 150 200 250
50 0 50 100 150 200 250 300 350 400 450
Kilometres

14869/74

to some mild liberal reforms, but they were insufficient to save the old order. The Portuguese people were war-weary. More and more Portuguese sons were dying in Africa since the launching of FRELIMO, PAIGC and MPLA guerilla campaigns, the national debt was soaring astronomically, but the average Portuguese grew no richer. Caetano changed the name of PIDE to DGS but the organisation remained the same.

In late 1973 and early 1974 there were rumours in Lisbon of a 'Captains' Movement'. In recent years there had been an influx of educated young officers into the army, forming a new layer whose interests conflicted with those of career officers. The movement, soon to be called the Armed Forces Movement (MFA), centred around two main demands—peaceful decolonisation as a solution to the African wars and the restoration of democracy in Portugal. On the morning of 25 April 1974 word spread through Lisbon that army units had taken over broadcasting stations and key government installations. Caetano and his Prime Minister were reported under arrest.

> In less than twenty hours a régime that had lasted nearly half a century had collapsed... The 'April Revolution' found its symbol in the seasonal red carnation and was singularly deprived of feelings of revenge ... The mass demonstrations on 1 May 1974 were one of the happiest explosions of liberal acclaim any country could ever see. It recalled the mood of victorious nations at the end of the war ... Freedom had been late in arriving but when it came it had generosity and style.[68]

2

APODETI, FRETILIN, and UDT

There were technically no political parties in East Timor before the UDT coup in August 1975 and the subsequent withdrawal of the Portuguese administration from Dili. Under the Caetano regime, the formation of political parties was forbidden; only the Acção Nacional Popular, the political organ of the corporate Portuguese state was allowed. By August 1975 the necessary legislation to allow political parties was yet to be enacted, although the machinery had been put in motion at the first session of talks to initiate the decolonisation process, held in Dili in May 1975. Thus when the political organisations that sprang up after the Lisbon coup were formed they were called 'unions' or 'associations'.

The news of the Lisbon coup first reached East Timor through Radio Australia. Although the political groupings were quickly formed—the three major ones within five weeks of the news—structural changes were relatively slow-moving, probably in part due to the remoteness of the colony from the metropolis. In June the Portuguese administration announced that there were three options open to the East Timorese in the decolonisation process: continued links with Portugal, integration with Indonesia, or complete independence. Although there were MFA delegates in East Timor soon after 25 April 1974, it was not until Dr António de Almeida Santos, Minister for Overseas Territories in the Lisbon junta, visited in September that things stirred. Then, the first group of international press correspondents to visit the territory under the new order (Australian journalists, at least, had been unwelcome for some time under the Caetano administration) accompanied the Minister's tour of the former colony. On 18 November a new Governor and administration officials drawn from the MFA presented themselves in Timor, some months after former Governor Alves Aldeia returned to Lisbon. Colonel Mário Lemos Pires replaced Governor Fernando Alves Aldeia bringing with him a group of officers who were to serve in the administration and form a decolonisation commission. One of their first tasks was to investigate the activities of former colonial régime officials and recommend arrest or dismissal where necessary.

On 11 May 1974 the União Democrática Timorense (Democratic Union of Timorese, UDT) was formed. In a statement of principles published on 1 August, UDT declared its aims to be:

> Accelerated promotion—proceeding in the shadow of the Portuguese flag—of the social, economic, cultural and political development of the Timorese people ... Self determination for the Timorese people oriented towards a federation with Portugal, with an intermediary stage for the attainment of independence ... Integration of the Timorese people through the use of the Portuguese language ... Acceptance and observance of the Universal Declaration of Human Rights ...[1]

The UDT leadership predominantly comprised Catholics who were smallholders or administration officials. Two, Lopes da Cruz and César Augusto da Costa Mousinho, had been representatives of the Acção Nacional Popular in Timor's Legislative Assembly. The Carrascalão brothers, João and Mário, sons of a Portuguese Communist youth leader deported to Timor in the thirties, were also prime movers.

A little over a week later the founding meeting of the Associação Social Democrática Timor (Social Democratic Association of Timor, ASDT) was formed. According to one of its founders, José Ramos Horta, the association was formed from a strike committee established almost immediately after 25 April:

> ... immediately after the coup the first thing we did was to organise a strike of the labourers who were getting only $[A]10 per month. The strike was called because some of the workers were asking for an increase of salary and were sacked. They came to see me and we organised a meeting. The company complained to the government and called me a reactionary against the coup. They were trying to discredit me in the eyes of the people and arrest me. Two officials from the junta in Lisbon came to Timor and they

> realised that I was an activist against the old order. The result was that the laborers got a 100% increase in salary to $[A]20, and they can now form a union. This is the first trade union in Timor. The governor condemned this, but I made a statement calling him a neo-fascist. The next day he retracted the statement and said that he was not very informed about what had happened in Lisbon.[2]

The ASDT's first manifesto, published on 22 May, called for the right to independence, rejection of colonialism, the immediate participation of 'worthy Timorese elements' in the administration and local government, an end to racial discrimination, a struggle against corruption and a policy of good neighbourliness and co-operation with countries of the region.[3] Included among the founders were Nicolau Lobato (later to be Prime Minister of the Democratic Republic of East Timor), Mari Alkatiri, Ramos Horta and Justino Mota, all members of the clandestine anti-colonialist group which had met in a Dili park prior to 25 April. Francisco Xavier do Amaral, later to become a leader of the movement, was not present at the founding meeting, but identified with the group a few days later.

In September the ASDT changed its name to Frente Revolucionária de Timor Leste Independente (Revolutionary Front of Independent East Timor, FRETILIN). That the leadership were impressed with and influenced by the African nationalist movements was obvious from the choice, in its similarity to FRELIMO. Ramos Horta had himself spent some time in Mozambique, Mari Alkatiri had studied for a similar period in Angola and Timorese in Portugal had made limited contact with the Africans. The main political direction of the developing Timorese movement was towards the ideas of African nationalists from the Portuguese colonies like Eduardo Mondlane, Agostinho Neto and the martyred Amílcar Cabral. They styled themselves 'the sole legitimate representatives' of the Timorese people, a slogan used by the liberation movement in Guinea Bissau. Some observers have pointed out that the adoption of a fiery name did not necessarily mean a sharp leftward political turn,[4] although there was a policy change to demand an immediate declaration of independence 'de jure'. The change reflected two things: a move away from a party type structure (although the internal organisation of the front was and is in many ways in the style of a party rather than a united front), and a desire not to restrict the movement to a particular political philosophy of labour-oriented social democracy. The creation of the front was meant to open the way for all Timorese nationalists, of whatever shade of the political spectrum, to participate around one common principle: national independence.

> [FRETILIN] is called a *front* because it calls for *unity* of all Timorese patriots. The experience of failures of our ancestors in their struggle for liberation warns us that at the moment it is necessary that all nationalists and anti-colonialists must unite without discrimination of race, religion, political ideology, sex and social background.

FRETILIN maintained the concept of the front throughout 1975. In an interview with journalists two weeks before the Indonesian assault on Dili, Nicolau Lobato was asked:

> FRETILIN *embraces people of any ideology who defend independence. Does it include Communists?*
> —I do not know of any Communists here, but I cannot read minds. We have a discipline of the Front, so everybody respects the programme of FRETILIN which was drawn up according to social realities.
> *How would you describe the programme? As populist? socialist?*
> We don't know about such names. We study our own circumstances. As you know, we have lived under a colonial government. We must transform that system to help the people to progress ... we are not a Communist party. We are a liberation front which gathers together people of any ideology, who will defend the independence of East Timor.[5]

The Associação Popular Democrática Timorense (Popular Democratic Association of Timorese, APODETI) was formed in late May around the principle of integration with Indonesia. It was originally called Associação Integração de Timor—Indonesia (Association for the Integration of Timor into Indonesia, AITI), but changed its name soon afterwards. APODETI was opposed to Indonesian annexation but expressed the wish to be an autonomous province of the Republic, for which there was no provision in the Indonesian constitution. The association invoked ancient mystical ties with the people of west Timor, 'realizing, at last, the existing culture of traditional mysticism of our Timorese ancestors which has been forgotten

. . . ' It advocated the teaching of Indonesian as a compulsory subject in all secondary schools and the opening of elementary schools teaching Indonesian as a first language (co-existing with the existing school system). Among the APODETI founders were a Dili schoolteacher called José Osório Soares, José Martins (a *liurai* from Ermera), Abel Belo from Baucau (reportedly a protagonist in the 1959 rebellion), and Arnaldo dos Reis Araújo, owner of a cattle property at southcoast Zumalai and later leader of the Indonesian-sponsored Provisional Government of East Timor.

After the administration's announcement of the three options, José Ramos Horta travelled to Jakarta. He sought assurances from the Indonesian government that they would respect the right of the Timorese to organise around the independence principle, given assurances that ASDT intended to pursue a policy of non-alignment and regional co-operation. He came away with a document of moment in East Timor's history—a letter from Indonesian Foreign Minister Adam Malik guaranteeing the integrity of a future East Timor. It stated:

> The Government of Indonesia [until] now still adheres to the following principles:
>
> I. The independence of every country is the right of every nation, with no exception for the people in Timor.
>
> II. The Government as well as the people of Indonesia have no intention to increase or to expand their territory, or to occupy other territories other [than] what is stipulated in their Constitution. This reiteration is to give you a clear idea, so that there may be no doubt in the minds of the people of Timor in [expressing] their own wishes.
>
> III. For this reason, whoever will govern in Timor in the future after independence, can be assured that the Government of Indonesia will always strive to maintain good relations, friendship and cooperation for the benefit of both countries.

In June a team from Australia's Foreign Affairs Department visited East Timor to investigate the changed situation. It included Mr. J.S. Dunn, the Australian consul in Dili from 1962 to 1964, who had retained his links with the territory. On his return he reported that the Portuguese had in mind a plebiscite to be conducted to determine which of the three options the

Adam Malik

Menteri Luar Negeri

Republik Indonesia

Jakarta, 17th June 1974.

To :
Mr, Jose Manuel Ramos Horta
D i l i
Portuguese Timor.

Dear Mr. Horta :

I was pleased to meet you during your recent visit to Jakarta, Indonesia.

We, the people of Indonesia, and the Government of Indonesia, have been heartened by the recent changes that have taken place in Lisbon, Portugal.

This change og government and of policy outlook came as something of a surprise to most people, including you and your people in Timor.

In our view, these developments offer a good opportunity to the people of Timor to accelerate the prosess toward independence, as well as to generate overall national development and to promote the progress of the people of Timor.

The Government of Indonesia untill now still adheres to the following principles :

I. The independence of every country is the right of ever nation, with no exeption for the people in Timor.

II. The Government as well as the people of Indonesia have no intention to increase or to expand their territory, or to occupy other territories other that what is stipulated in their Constitution. This reiteration is to give you a clear idea, so that there may be no doubt in the minds of the people of Timor in expresing their own wishes.

III. For this reason, whoever will govern in Timor in the future after independence, can be assured that the Government of Indonesia will always strive to maintain good relations, friendship and cooperation for the benefit of both countries.

Please convey my message to your people in Timor.

With my best wishes and warm regards to you and to all the people in Timor.

Sincerely yours,

ADAM MALIK.

Letter from Indonesian Foreign Minister Adam Malik to FRETILIN's Jose Ramos Horta, 17 June 1974 (reproduced by courtesy of Helen Hill).

East Timorese would favour. Of these choices, he commented:

> The option of integration with Indonesia, the objective of APODETI, has attracted very little support in Timor and it seems inconceivable that the Timorese would freely choose this solution to their future. Indeed, it is something of a concession to Indonesian apprehensions at the implications of a change in the status of the territory that integration with Indonesia is being offered as an option.

Speaking of possible Australian attitudes, he continued:

> It may seem tempting to pander to those influential elements within Indonesia, who may wish to incorporate Portuguese Timor, in order to avoid the risk of endangering our present good relations with Jakarta. In the long term, however, this policy seems unlikely to serve Australian interests in the region. We could well lose respect in other South East Asian capitals, particularly in Port Moresby, and, further, we might find ourselves encouraging a dangerous trend in Indonesian politics, with implications inimical to regional security.[6]

He concluded that there was a strong case for the government to resume consular representation in Dili as soon as possible, in order to be informed of developments within the territory and to consult with Indonesian consular representatives there.

Apart from the formations representing the three main options in the decolonisation process, three other grouplets were later formed, two of which were to play out their near-phantom existence in dramatic fashion almost a year later.

On 20 November, 1974, Klibur Oan Timur Aswain (literally, (in Tetum) the Sons of the Mountain Warrior-dogs,[7] KOTA) was formed by a group representing a number of principally Tetum Terik speaking *liurais* who traced their ancestry to the fabled Topasses and claimed to be the tribal aristocracy of East Timor. The grouping had existed before November as the Popular Association of Monarchists of Timor. Some of its members initially identified with APODETI. Indeed KOTA appeared to be a racially pure satellite of APODETI, based on an inner circle of tribal leaders with access to the mystical rites of the traditional culture. According to one of its leaders, José Martins, all the business of KOTA was transacted in the *uma lulik*, the animist religious centre.

The other grouplets were Partido Trabalhista (a 'labour party') and the Associação Democrática Integração Timor-Leste-Australia, ADITLA, which supported integration of Timor with Australia. Little is known of Trabalhista except that its members did not number more than ten.[8] ADITLA's future prospects were sharply dashed with the declaration in the local press that the Australian Government had outrightly rejected the possibility of any such links.

When a team of Australian Labor parliamentarians visited East Timor in March 1975, they reported that Portuguese decolonisation authorities did not consider these groupings as legitimate parties to any discussion because they lacked a political programme; presumably, also, they were all regarded as too small.[9]

The groups which merit attention are clearly ASDT/FRETILIN, UDT and APODETI. In the context of developing Timorese nationalism, the strength and depth of nationalist sentiment within the emerging formations must be the litmus test for a real understanding of their role in the period preceding the Indonesian invasion and, indeed, in East Timor's long-term future.

There were certain initial similarities in the leadership of the groups which, in the course of events following the Portuguese abdication of power in Timor, took on a growing importance. J.S. Dunn has written on this point:

> The polarization of the three parties around three distinct aims tends to exaggerate the differences at this early stage in the political development of Timor. In fact, the basic aims are rather similar. All oppose racial discrimination, support freedom of expression and religious liberty, and oppose corruption. In Australia, Horta has several times referred to UDT as "neo-fascist", but in Timor he, and other ASDT leaders, admitted that there was much common ground, at least with the leaders of UDT. The leaders themselves come from similar backgrounds most of them employed as middle-level officials in government departments. Some of the leaders of the two main parties are interrelated. For example Ramos Horta is Carrascalão's brother-in-law ... [10]

FRETILIN leaders have constantly stressed confidence in their belief that no matter to which party they claim allegiance, the followers must ultimately be 'oan Timur', true children of Timor. The concept of the people united against the *malai* is an enduring one in Timorese politics.

The *curriculum vitae* of many of the leaders of UDT and FRETILIN is strikingly similar: from the family of a *liurai*, primary school education at the Jesuit college at Soibada, higher education in the seminary at Dare, on completion of which they generally entered the Portuguese civil service (there was usually little opportunity to continue studies beyond Dare). The children of Portuguese *deportados* were a second source of leadership, Horta and the Carrascalãos being the most obvious example.

But if cross-party profiles of the leaders followed a common pattern and some similarities of political ideas existed there were also important political and social differences. Soon after 25 April 1974, a member of this urban élite produced the first theoretical work of modern Timorese nationalism. The significance of Abílio de Araújo's modest work, *Timorese Elites*, was not so much that it was the first attempt by a Timorese after 25 April to come to grips with the role of Portuguese colonialism, but that it expressed an advanced consciousness of the position of Timorese politicians as people drawn from the urban élite.[11] De Araújo saw the creation of élite groups in Timor as a function of Portuguese occupation from the earliest times. He argued that the corruption of the traditional ruling layers by the bestowal of privileges on tribal leaders willing to serve the Portuguese (especially in exchange for the right to work the island's sandalwood) functioned by setting Timorese against Timorese while facilitating Portuguese exploitation of the natural resources of Timor.

This consciousness and the attempt to redefine Timorese history were to form an important distinction between UDT and FRETILIN. For it was those young radical Timorese, especially the Lisbon-educated, alienated from their own culture, who were most eager to search for their cultural origins. Later they were to lead the FRETILIN drive into the villages, initiating consumer and agricultural co-operatives and a literacy campaign conducted in Tetum along the lines used by Paulo Freire in Brazil. De Araújo's argument, logically extended, meant that by understanding Timor's colonial history, the work of

Timorese in the decolonisation process was to end the divisive system of élites, thereby creating a Timorese national consciousness.

Both UDT and ASDT/FRETILIN leaderships were predominantly Catholic, but the Catholicism of the FRETILIN leadership was of a different quality. After training for the priesthood, Xavier do Amaral left the Church because legally and politically it was an arm of the Portuguese state in the colonies. He nevertheless retained his faith. Rogério and Nicolau Lobato also remained believers at odds with the role of the established Church. As FRETILIN grew these people responded with growing indignation to the local Church's accusations that they were 'Communists'.

Although the mainstream FRETILIN leadership was nationalist Catholic, it also included a number of practising Moslems. By contrast, UDT has always been seen as the party of Portuguese Catholicism and has retained close links with the established Church.

Of the Dili élite, FRETILIN cadres were generally drawn from the pool of young under-employed professionals who occupied middle-level positions in the Portuguese administration. The UDT leaders tended to be older men more entrenched in the administration and often involved in business ventures, especially coffee plantations.

At 38 Xavier do Amaral was the oldest of the FRETILIN founders. At its inception on 12 September 1974 he was proclaimed president of the front. Described by J.S. Dunn as a 'quietly spoken, extraordinarily humble man',[12] Xavier is the true populist leader of the East Timorese; Wherever he travels he is mobbed by people and is known at the village level through most of the territory. He maintains a constant air of bewilderment at the injustices he feels have been imposed on his people. He is the one nationalist to whom the traditionally stiff Portuguese administration officers afforded a grudging natural respect. Others, like Nicolau Lobato, earned it.

Xavier was born the son of a *liurai* at Turiscai, in the heart of East Timor's mountainous interior. His aged mother remembers the Great Rebellion of 1912. Outrage at post-war repression under the Portuguese established a basis for his nationalist ideas. After graduating from Dare he went to Macau

Xavier do Amaral

to extend his studies. There he received letters from friends telling of the imprisonment of a number of his schoolfellows from the Catholic primary college at Soibada for their part in the 1959 disturbances. Subsequently he left the Church before ordination and on his return to Timor worked as a schoolteacher for six years and then (up until 25 April 1974) as a customs official. In those pre-coup days he became known as a public critic of the Portuguese.

The founder and early leader of FRETILIN best known to Australians was José Ramos Horta. He was influential in winning Australian support for the Timorese cause in the first months after the formation of ASDT:

> The Party Secretary, far better known in Australia and Indonesia is Ramos Horta, a youthful, romantically good looking mixed Timorese–Portuguese ... Where Xavier is cautious, Horta is incautious and impulsive ... [13]

Perhaps more than any other of the FRETILIN personalities Horta expressed the cultural conflict of the Timorese élite. The son of a *deportado*, the similarities between UDT and FRETILIN were expressed in his cultural and familial closeness to the Carrascalaos, founders of UDT. As FRETILIN defined itself as a black nationalist movement sharply divided on most points from the Portuguese Catholic UDT, Horta's influence within the leadership was to change.

Horta was identified with Alarico Fernandes, a meteorologist who was then Secretary-General of the Central Committee. Fernandes worked closely with Horta in the foundation of ASDT/FRETILIN and later accompanied him to Jakarta and Australia.

Perhaps the most important person to emerge from ASDT, apart from Xavier do Amaral, was Nicolau Lobato. At the age of 29 Nicolau carries the tragic history and compounded experience of a much older person. An intense, handsome man of proud demeanour, more than anyone he is the spirit of Timorese nationalism; he emphasises self-reliance and discipline. A key influence in his life has been the drive for education, socially expressed and politically applied as a drive for dignity for his people. At the time of the Lisbon coup Nicolau was employed in the finance department of the administration and was studying economics at night in the hope that he would be able to study abroad later.

Of the three parties, ASDT quickly gained the support of the majority of the thirty-nine Timorese studying in Portugal. The Lisbon events had a deep personal effect on them, although as

Nicolau Lobato (Jill Jolliffe).

a small national and racial minority in urban Europe they no doubt had some reservations about an officers movement aimed primarily at the liberation of metropolitan Portugal. The Timorese argue that it was not in fact the Portuguese people who made the 'flower revolution', but the people of Mozambique, Guinea Bissau and Angola, who had fought these war-weary officers since 1960.

These overseas students formed a valuable support group. In May 1974 Abílio de Araújo travelled home to work with the ASDT leaders on the design of a literacy campaign and the preparation of printed material to build the movement. He and another student Francisco Borja da Costa had already composed a new song in the Tetum language, to be a component of the literacy campaign. The song, called 'Foho Ramelau' (Mt Ramelau) was based on a traditional song form and was soon to be known and sung throughout East Timor.

In September a general assembly of ASDT was held. It produced a manifesto which stated that the ASDT, which 'wants full independence for Portuguese Timor has been hardening its policy' and went on to proclaim the foundation of FRETILIN, under the leadership of Xavier do Amaral:

> The [ASDT] considers itself the interpreter of the profound ideals of the people of all East Timor and, because of this reason, declares itself the only legitimate representative of the people and will now be called "Revolutionary Front of East Timor"—FRETILIN.

The 'hardening' of policy appeared to refer to independence. FRETILIN now demanded an immediate declaration of 'independence de jure' from the Portuguese and the achievement of 'independence de facto' through a transitional programme of social development, aimed at the 'total abolition of colonialism'. The transitional development programme called for:

> a) profound and quick transformation of the old colonialist structure, implementing new forms of democracy.
> b) Cultural development [inspired by] a new process and concept of the culture which is to be from the people, with the people and for the people.
> c) Active movement against corruption and exploitation of the people.
> d) Multi-racial living without discrimination of race and religion.

In the transition from 'independence de jure' to 'independence de facto' Portugal was to be recognised as the 'only mouthpiece for discussion' of the decolonisation process.

The call for the abolition of colonialism was accompanied by a call for the rejection of 'neo-colonialism'. This referred to several possibilities: the reformation and retention of Portuguese colonial rule in the guise of a federation (initially proposed by UDT in Timor, reflecting an early current within the MFA in Portugal), the exchange of Portuguese colonialism for a new colonial ruler, Indonesia, or the exploitation of East Timorese resources by foreign capital from whatever source. In practice the attack on neo-colonialism was principally directed against UDT's advocacy of foreign investment as a solution to the ills of Timorese underdevelopment.

The front's foreign policy was relatively unformed at this time. It stressed regional co-operation but in the context of a rather unreal stress on the primacy of the Portuguese African colonies:

> FRETILIN defends the policy of closer international co-operation with Portugal, Brazil, Guinea-Bissau and the future countries of Portuguese expression, as well as the countries of the geographic area in which Timor is integrated, safeguarding the superior interests of the people of East Timor ... FRETILIN will resort to international aid and the goodwill of all nations and international organisations in order to solve the most urgent problems in the social, economic, cultural and political fields.

By December 1974 FRETILIN had articulated and developed its programme to a detailed statement embodying an extensive programme of social development. It called for economic reconstruction through the creation of co-operatives of production, distribution, and consumption as the basic unit of economic life, the elimination of 'excessive' dependency on foreign imports, the discouraging of monoculture and the implementation of agrarian reform defined as the expropriation of all large farms and the utilisation of unused fertile land to be worked within the co-operative system. Agricultural development was to take place through mechanisation and the development of pre-existing local industries—fishing, cattle and food processing.

As well, policies were expounded on education and culture, social justice, health, internal administration and national defence, all with the emphasis on economic self-reliance, the combating of former colonial structures, and rapid development of Timorese participation.

Educational and cultural policies called for an 'extensive programme' to eliminate illiteracy and ignorance, the replacement of the colonialist education system with one promoting Timorese culture and freedom of religion for all people, with the state guaranteeing protection of native religious houses, churches, mosques and temples. 'The Portuguese language will be retained as the official language of the country' it stated, while calling for:

> A program of research and study ... into the Tetum language, as well as other local languages. A further aim is the fostering of literature and art of the various ethnic groups through cultural exchanges for the enrichment not only of Timorese culture as a whole, but also as a contribution to universal culture.

The programme of reconstruction and development was seen as a practical one in which FRETILIN cadres would begin the work of implementation. It called for the co-operation of the Portuguese government in this work. In at least two key areas, literacy and agriculture, work began immediately.

Foreign policy by this time specified that the independent state should be non-aligned, while FRETILIN would work to:

> immediately develop widespread diplomatic activity with all the countries of the world and with international organisations, in order to gain moral, diplomatic, political, technical, economic, financial and military support, with a broad view to constructing and developing the country, but always safe-guarding the policy of non-alignment ... FRETILIN defends a good neighbour policy of no interference and co-operation with all countries of the world.

By contrast, UDT's first published programme of 1 August 1974 was neither extensive enough nor specific enough to give a good picture of the Union. In particular it lacked a coherent programme of social development, although it did speak rather paternalistically of its task to 'enlighten those of the interior, and ... give knowledge to the Timorese people'. Whereas the FRETILIN programme took special account of the diversity of dialects and local cultural differences (while advocating the continuation of Portuguese as the official language of the immediate future), for the UDT, Portuguese was to be the vehicle for the 'integration of the Timorese people' in the interior. According to Evans, the UDT leadership do not generally speak indigenous dialects. Certainly they have not, as FRETILIN has, used them in written form to propagate their ideas.

UDT has generally been regarded as the proponent of continued Portuguese rule. However, as Dunn has pointed out, it has never overruled the possibility of independence. Its original programme called for 'progressive autonomy' within a Portuguese federation, allowing for the possibility of eventual independence in '15 to 20 years'. By September 1974 the policy was changed to one of federation with Portugal as an intermediary stage towards total independence. On the common principle of independence UDT came together with FRETILIN in February 1975, both modifying their attitudes in the interest of rapprochement: UDT diluting the pro-Portuguese content of its programme and FRETILIN articulating acceptance of a longer period of transition.

Nevertheless, UDT's rhetoric was often deceptive. By March 1975, for example, it was outflanking FRETILIN in anti-colonialist rhetoric, claiming a commitment to

> destroy monopolies, capitalism and the class system in Timorese society ... [not as a] dogmatic principle but ... a permanent guide to action.[14]

although such ideas were clearly at odds with the social fibre and the actual anti-communism of the leadership. Even accepting the nominal commitment of UDT, as their programme evolved, to some measure of social change, there was little which could link the leadership to a popular movement of the people of the interior.

Some commentators on Timorese affairs have written of the incorporation of the Portuguese flag into Timorese culture as a *lulik* object and its display at demonstrations after 25 April 1974 as a symbol of support for continued Portuguese rule (and thus for UDT). *Lulik* flags were displayed in strength during Dr Almeida Santos's September 1974 visit. On his return to Portugal, he was reported to have said that he found in Timor 'a phenomenon of which I was unaware, a mythology of love for Portugal'. Interpretation of the display of the *lulik* flags as either a 'mythology of love for Portugal' or an indicator of support for UDT assumes a great deal about what their display expresses in the consciousness of the Timorese bearer. Both the Portuguese and UDT have chosen to see and use the *lulik* flags to their own ends, attaching a glib significance to the sanctity afforded these historical relics in Timorese folklore.[15]

The effects of centuries of Portuguese indoctrination should nevertheless not be underestimated. Old Timorese still bow when they pass Europeans in the street. In the early months of the new régime in East Timor the ability of UDT to muster support in the interior despite the chasm which separated the leadership from the mountain people reflected the strength under the old order of the social authority of *chefes de posto*, hoteliers, and plantation owners in each local area. If the repercussion of Lisbon events was slow to reach Dili, it took even longer to affect the hinterland. In the following year those areas which remained divided over support for FRETILIN or UDT in a period of general swing to the assertive nationalism of FRETILIN were areas where such authority ran deepest—the coffee-growing Ermera district (home of the Carrascalãos and Lopes da Cruz and an employment centre for wage labourers), the prosperous rice-bowl area of Maliana, and Maubisse, a military, administrative and commercial centre under the old régime.

The question central to a description of the UDT leadership is not so much whether it was a nationalist formation but whether any Timorese nationalists could be found within its ranks. 'Everbody knows' one leader of a rival Timorese faction commented scornfully, 'that UDT are really white men with black faces, that this is a party of the Portuguese!'[16] As well as being generally regarded, not entirely correctly, as the formation merely representing an extension of the old régime, UDT has been seen as the party of the economically privileged, although the leadership deny this claim. The Australian Labor parliamentarians who conducted an investigatory tour of East Timor in March 1975 asked at a formal meeting with UDT representatives:

> *Is your party ... mainly composed of people who have interests to protect even though the interests may be only minor? For example, shopkeepers, minor employers of labour, some people engaged in plantation culture?*
> Perhaps we started off that way but the majority of our members are now a broad section of the people.

A distinction has been drawn by some observers between a 'right wing' and a moderate section of UDT, the former including Lopes da Cruz and César Augusto da Costa Mousinho, the latter the Carrascalãos and Domingos de Oliveira. Those who have had personal and political contact with Domingos de

Oliveira, at least, have been impressed with him as a fervent Timorese nationalist.

Perhaps UDT can best be understood by reference to Portugal's *assimilado* policies and the creation of a caste of honorary Portuguese. Both FRETILIN and UDT can be subsumed under the category of the urban élite and sections of both were drawn from *assimilados*; but while the policy of the one has been to seek a return to and the redemption of its own people, the function of the other has been to preserve the élite status. One is a self-conscious, and to that extent self-dissolving élite, the other the product of a colonialism which functioned by isolating a section of the colonised for use as an ally. De Araújo expresses it thus:

> This type of élite is the best ally of colonialism ... However, when it observes that its interests are not satisfied because colonialism imposes certain barriers, that is, when its interests conflict with those of the colonial power, it changes into a mentor ... for the anti-colonialist struggle. Because this attitude results from the refusal of the former ally (colonialism) to share the cake that was promised and later denied, its situation in the post-colonial era is identical or even worse.[17]

Some observers have seen the pro-Indonesian APODETI as simply a 'quisling' grouping. Certainly only pro-Indonesian propagandists have ever seen it as representing more than a very small percentage of the population. It has been claimed that the founders of APODETI were paid Timorese agents of the Indonesian government recruited through the Indonesian consulate in Dili, which had been involved in political disruption and intelligence-gathering activities within Portuguese Timor for some years.[18] In March 1975, senior officers of the Portuguese administration declined to answer a question by Australian Labor parliamentarians as to whether they believed the Indonesian government was conducting intelligence operations in the territory, although the Governor added:

> There are problems here because Jakarta is not well informed by the Consul and I believe that he may be replaced soon. I have invited Antara [newsagency] to come here and see due to this lack of information.[19]

Against accusations that it was a creation of Indonesia,

APODETI claimed that its political roots were strong, having grown from the 1959 uprising. The association's social base was drawn from certain tribal groupings under the leadership of some of the more despotic traditional rulers, the small Moslem community, some conservative Timorese Catholics and those Timorese who for various reasons closely identified with Indonesian Timor (because they had families there, because they were strongly anti-Portuguese, or because they had been influenced, perhaps, by the Indonesian independence movement as it affected west Timor). Most followers of APODETI in the period before December 1975 viewed themselves as nationalists and anti-colonialists. The rhetoric of APODETI was anti-colonial and anti-white, calling for unity with their fellow people in west Timor from whom they had been dispossessed. (By an historical irony, in August 1975 APODETI followers joined with FRETILIN to fight against the imposition of UDT military rule following the coup of 11 August, and to drive UDT forces over the border into west Timor.)

From its inception in 1974 until the invasion of Dili in December 1975, APODETI followers believed that from their support for integration with the Indonesian Republic would flow the right to be an autonomous province within it. In October 1975 in a television interview conducted with the Melbourne television reporter Greg Shackleton (later killed at Balibó), José Osório Soares reiterated the group's opposition to forcible annexation by Indonesia. No Timorese politicians (with the possible exception of a minority of pro-Portuguese *assimilados* in the leadership of UDT) have ever expressed opposition to unification with Indonesian Timor per se. Even the argument of East Timor's cultural distinctness which has been put forward by FRETILIN supporters does not run very deep. The argument for independence is more advanced than this: it is an argument against neo-colonialism, a political, not a cultural or racial argument. After four centuries of colonial rule FRETILIN nationalists argue, they have no desire to subjugate themselves anew to a foreign power. The key issue for them is the right for a Timorese identity to develop freely in the post-colonial era. On this point J.S. Dunn comments:

> Economic conditions in the Indonesian sector of Timor appear to be little, if at all, better than in the Portuguese territory removing

> an important incentive to join Indonesia. Integration with Indonesia holds little attraction for most Timorese leaders, if only because it would deny them the satisfaction of developing their own identity, and of reaping the prizes of office, as well as the opportunity to accelerate social and economic development, through direct appeal to other countries, such as Australia and Portugal ... [20]

In informal conversation young FRETILIN supporters argue that if the people of Indonesian Timor desire to be free they must build their own independence movement; given the prospect of freedom, the East Timorese cannot allow their development to be retarded by responsibility for their fellow-people in the west.

On the other hand, APODETI and its Indonesian sponsors have used racial sentiments to muster support. In late May a journalist from the Indonesian newspaper *Suara Karya* interviewed José Osório Soares and Arnaldo dos Reis Araújo in Dili:

> The consideration for integration with Indonesia is Portuguese Timor's geographical location and racial sentiments of the native Timorese of the two parts of the island ... It's probably not difficult to attract the people of Portuguese Timor to join AITI [APODETI]. According to some observers, the racial sentiments can be raised in the hinterland via the priests.[21]

But the difficulty was greater than envisaged. Most of the personnel of APODETI were not held in high regard locally. The *Suara Karya* interview also featured comments by dos Reis Araújo that he had been imprisoned by the Portuguese for 29 years for collaboration with the Japanese during World War II. A concerned APODETI backer in Indonesia wrote in October 1974 to his superior officer complaining of the crassness and disreputability in East Timor of the APODETI leadership:

> When Mr. Arnaldo dos Reis Araújo visited Indonesia, practically all the Indonesian newspapers uncritically echoed his exaggerated description of the colonial misproportions and suppressions in the province ... Indonesian interest requires that we have to be very selective about subjects coming to East Timor as self-made—or drafted—information agents. They should be a high-souled people, of a fine character, sincere and [of integrity] ... Indonesia has enough to offer to make an integration appealing and

> attractive and to convince also politicians with a critical attitude. Let us keep away opportunists and profiteurs [sic] from this delicate job'.[22]

In the history of East Timor, those who have employed the backward practice of fomenting racial (anti-white, anti-Portuguese) feeling for political gain have been equally prepared to employ Portuguese-fostered tribal divisions to fan and contort such sentiments. It is interesting that those geographical areas where APODETI sought to use fundamentalist anti-colonial sentiment and tribal jealousies correspond closely to those used by the Japanese during World War II. In the Atsabe area, in the long-suffering rural poor area of Maubisse, in Viqueque and in the Arab quarter in Dili, the pattern of over three decades ago has prevailed.

APODETI and UDT represented polar opposites in Timorese politics: APODETI's social base tended to be anti-white and anti-Portuguese, drawing support from conservative full-blooded Timorese Catholics (including some priests), a section of conservative tribal leaders and the majority of the small Timorese Moslem community. Of the minority ethnic groups, Moslems generally supported APODETI, a small proportion of progressive Moslems supported FRETILIN, none supported UDT.

Events of 1974 caused East Timor's Chinese community to feel insecure for its future. Perhaps they were the group in East Timor with the deepest interest in the old order, which maintained their position as a dominant, imported trading class holding in check the political development of a national bourgeoisie. Like most overseas Chinese in South East Asia the Timorese Chinese are an urban educated people who have kept themselves separate socially, economically, and in their education system. They held a stranglehold on East Timor's economy. OECD figures for 1974 gave East Timor a GNP per capita of about $A80 (although the head of East Timor's Economic Department put it lower, at $A30, based on a report of the Banco Nacional Ultramarino),[23] yet prices of essential commodities in Dili's almost exclusively Chinese-owned shops were generally slightly higher than Australian prices. A black market in foreign currency also operated through the Chinese business community.

The Chinese thus tended to be the butt of some local resentment after 25 April 1974. Slogans which appeared around the capital proclaiming, 'death to the traitors!' and 'whoever sells our country is a traitor!' were frequently on Chinese shops. The Chinese community was equally apprehensive at the prospect of Indonesian rule, having some knowledge of the pogroms which occurred in 1965 after the overthrow of Sukarno. Generally Chinese regarded themselves as political 'neutrals'. If they expressed a preference it would be to UDT, the group most linked to the status quo, although a few young Chinese identified with FRETILIN. As an urban educated group they had some sensitivity to progressive ideas; in an interview with the Australian parliamentarians in March 1975 nominally pro-Taiwanese Chinese community representatives expressed interest in the literature of mainland China. In the same interview, they were asked: 'Do you have any feelings about the three political parties? Do you fear APODETI, or any political party?', to which they replied: 'In some ways APODETI is anti-Chinese. If we have difficulties we will have to adjust'. The politicians observed in their notes that the Chinese were reluctant to discuss the question further.

In March 1975 the *Australian*'s Bruce Stannard reported the beginnings of a Chinese exodus from East Timor, and an incident in which two Chinese were detained attempting to leave the country with suitcases stuffed with paper currency.[24]

From the outset, APODETI pursued a policy of non-co-operation with the Portuguese government. Their refusal to treat with them in any way was so complete that after their final withdrawal from the territory in December 1975 members of the Portuguese administration knew almost nothing, for example, about Arnaldo dos Reis Araújo. They commented that the personality of the leader of the Indonesian-installed government was 'a mystery' to them and that they only knew that he had travelled frequently to Kupang and Jakarta in the preceding year and a half. It was known that APODETI made no decisions without him, and he was seen as the real power behind the scenes. In *Suara Karya* dos Reis Araújo was reported to '[speak] Indonesian fluently and [have] some knowledge of the Pancasila and the 1945 Constitution obtained from his association with Indonesians'.[25] Throughout 1974 and 1975 de Araújo insisted that the Portuguese Decolonisation Commission was 'colonialist' and that he recognised only the Republic of Indonesia as his government.

From late 1974 Indonesian attitudes were more actively expressed. In a cable published in the APODETI newspaper *O Arauto de Sunda* on 18 September, a week after ASDT's transformation to FRETILIN, Adam Malik gave his blessing to APODETI.[26] As part of the development of the political movements in the decolonisation process, the Portuguese gave free time to each of the groups on the government radio station. APODETI broadcasts were backed from inception by regular transmissions beamed into East Timor from the government Radio Republic Indonesia station in Kupang. At the end of February 1975 the APODETI air time was suspended for 45 days for 'inciting violence'. Broadcasts had regularly commenced with bursts of machine-gun fire. The Kupang broadcasts henceforth played a more prominent role; they featured aggressive propaganda in local dialects which continued right through 1975. In these early broadcasts FRETILIN was denounced as 'Communist', UDT as 'neo-fascist'.

On 12 September the Jakarta daily *Sinar Harapan* reported that Governor El Tari had received APODETI leaders in Kupang, Indonesian Timor, and declared the provincial government's willingness 'to assist the struggle of APODETI'. José Osório Soares reportedly told the Governor that APODETI's programme had the support of 70% of the people. In March 1975 J.S. Dunn wrote of this claim:

> This claim was of course a gross exaggeration. In July '74 support for APODETI was estimated at less than 5% of the total following. Reports from Timor since that time indicate that it is still very much a minority force.[27]

The Jakarta press by now was giving concerted support to Radio Kupang. Sensational stories of FRETILIN 'atrocities' against APODETI supporters, of mainland Chinese officers giving military training to FRETILIN supporters, and denunciations of a group of Lisbon-educated students as 'Maoist' were rife around the end of 1974, particularly in the army newspaper *Berita Yudha*.

The quickened pace of events in September, in Timor as abroad, also manifested itself in a FRETILIN-organised demonstrated outside the Indonesian consulate in Dili.

Delegates from the demonstration handed a note to the consul, Mr Elias Tomodok, requesting Indonesian non-interference in the internal affairs of East Timor.

The month closed on two events of even deeper significance for the territory's future: the fall from power of the First Provisional Government under General António de Spínola in Lisbon as a result of which the mainstream of the Armed Forces Movement assumed control, and talks held in Yogyakarta between the Australian Labor Prime Minister Gough Whitlam and Indonesia's President Suharto.

In a bitter resignation speech Spínola spoke of movements towards 'over hasty' decolonisation, the 'lack of discipline' among Portuguese workers and the alleged collapse of constitutional authority in Portugal. Spínola had been the champion of the concept of an international Portuguese community in which the former colonies would move from the status of 'provinces' to equal states in a federation (the basic idea of the original UDT programme). One of the issues of Spínola's demise was the question of decolonisation. Under the First Provisional Government General Costa Gomes had flown to Mozambique and Angola in May and called on the liberation movements to surrender their arms in order to participate in this 'pan-Portuguese fantasy', as Robin Blackburn described it.[28]

In metropolitan Portugal supporters of the liberation movements applied mounting pressure for recognition of the emerging African states. Spínola's resignation finally ended the colonial dream. Genuine decolonisation became a meaningful prospect. An important by-product of the fall of the first MFA government was the abandonment of the idea of referenda to be conducted in the colonies to determine their future. In Guinea Bissau and Mozambique Spínola had offered the near-victorious liberation movements a ceasefire in return for the promise of a referendum, in the hope of retaining Portuguese power there. Knowledge of this could have been responsible for FRETILIN's early resistance to the idea. If Malik's letter to Ramos Horta can be accepted at face value, it can also be seen in the pre-September context of Jakarta not regarding Portuguese withdrawal claims seriously under Spínola.

In Yogyakarta Whitlam was reported to have told President

Suharto that 'an independent East Timor would be an unviable state and a potential threat to the area', although he believed that the East Timorese should make the ultimate decision about the territory's future. Peter Hastings described Whitlam's statement thus: ' ... uninvited, he practically gave East Timor to Indonesia' and added that the views expressed were very similar to those guiding Australian policy *vis-à-vis* Irian Jaya in 1962. Regardless of Whitlam's intentions Jakarta interpreted the Australian attitude as a sanction for Indonesian incorporationist policies.[29]

Australian journalists working in East Timor in early 1975 reported that Radio Kupang made generous use of the Whitlam statement, usually reiterating the first sanction without the meekly qualifying 'self-determination' clause.[30] The East Timorese were consequently quite conscious of the Whitlam stance. Given that the political leadership was aware of Labor's professed policy towards liberation movements in Africa, the Yogyakarta statement and the Whitlam government's subsequent postures were a constant bewilderment to politically conscious East Timorese—as they were to many Australians.

Just as East Timor's future could not be separated from social and political developments of the countries of the region no matter how studiously Timorese politicians pursued a policy of non-alignment, neither could it be separated from the fate of the stunted revolution which was occurring in metropolitan Portugal.

The officers of the MFA were very often themselves the educated sons of poor peasants whose emergence from the era of Portuguese fascism was tempered by the backwardness and political isolation that régime had entailed. The biography of the average Portuguese soldier was not markedly different from that of a 'subject' Timorese, Angolan or Mozambican. The poor sons of Portugal typically expended the best years of their lives—and their lives—fighting in a foreign country against people not much poorer than themselves, their families divided and reduced by colonial wars:

> The champion of civilization in Africa had an adult illiteracy rate of 40 per cent and the highest infant mortality rate in Europe. Nearly a fifth of Lisbon live in shanty town dwellings (*barracas*), while there are virtually no medical services in the countryside and

> many villages even lack electricity.[31]

The Portuguese could not free themselves overnight from their own colonial attitudes. In late 1975, by which time FRETILIN had conducted a successful de facto administration of East Timor for three months against enormous odds, senior Portuguese of the former administration, including those MFA officers regarded as most 'left', still refused to acknowledge that the Timorese could be capable of running their own affairs. Throughout 1974–75 Portuguese attitudes to the Timorese remained tainted with a deep-running paternalism exacerbated by the traditional pride of Portugal's military élite.

Progressive Timorese nationalist attitudes to the Portuguese after April 1974 were mixed. On the one hand the mutual bondage of the colonised and coloniser was recognised and the prospect for freedom opened by the MFA was greeted with enthusiasm and excitement. On the other, the legacy of bitterness from a long colonial occupation could not be simply erased. Nevertheless, FRETILIN responses to the Portuguese have been of a political, not of a racial nature. Writing of Africa, Basil Davidson has argued:

> ... the general sentiment among responsible men and women in the national movement ... is ... that the bulk of Portuguese have become the victims of a disaster from which they are able to extricate themselves far less than the Africans, who suffer from it worse.[32]

In one sense, at least in Africa, liberation lay within the reach of a gun for the nationalists. In the case of Timor, Indonesian expansionist perspectives arguably created a special case. For the deformed society that is European Portugal, long isolated from the rest of urban Europe and the course of industrial development, the problem is more complex. It is equally true that responsible Timorese nationalists are free of racial responses to the Portuguese: in intensive interviews in Darwin in early 1976, former administration officials reported that they had not encountered racist or anti-white sentiments from FRETILIN, in sharp contrast to the political attitudes of APODETI.

The seventeen months of MFA rule opened with high hopes for the Timorese. The spruce officers who presented themselves in November, who typically lined their bookshelves with volumes of Rosa Luxemburg, Marx and Lenin, seemed a far cry from the old order. As events ground on, the incapacity of the Portuguese to deal with the situation became obvious. They felt that while they were tidying up a situation in the colonies which they didn't create, events at home were slipping through their fingers. Colonial settlers from the African colonies were flocking back to Portugal altering the new balance of power which had been created by the MFA. On the individual level, Portuguese in the colonies were consumed with war-weariness and the yearning for Lisbon. The brutal colonialism of the old order in East Timor was consequently replaced by the irresponsibility and incompetence of the new.

Given that a decolonisation process could occur from above, the Portuguese's limited capacity to supervise it in East Timor was given little assistance by the Australian government. One of the first requests of the MFA was for the re-opening of the Australian consulate. According to Governor Lemos Pires he first requested this in November 1974:

> We asked for a Consul in November and have asked about 10 times since. Mr Taylor was asked last week, Mr Woolcott was asked this week. We have asked in Lisbon and I believe Dr Matias has or will be asking again in Australia. At present, Australia cannot compensate for Indonesian propaganda or understand the day to day happenings in the colony. It would seem better to us if there could be discussions between an Australian Consul, the Indonesian Consul and myself as Governor before our parent governments were informed of various events as information gathered on the spot would be more accurate. We have also asked for agricultural technicians.[33]

The 'delinquent Portuguese' were to provide a convenient excuse for Australian politicians, who later placed responsibility with Portugal for the catastrophe which befell East Timor. Their case would have carried more credibility had they responded sympathetically to these early requests from the administration in Timor for assistance in the decolonisation process.

The Portuguese critique of Timorese political developments went beyond colonial attitudes carried over from Caetano days. MFA officers who had served in Africa claimed that Timor was a separate and special case from the other colonies, a claim which has some substance. In Africa, remoteness from the metropolis was not so acute a problem, nor was there a nervous expansionist power waiting in the wings. Less than a year after the formation of ASDT, President Xavier do Amaral predicted in a sad irony that East Timor would be the only one of the former Portuguese colonies to experience a peaceful transition to independence.

But the Portuguese also claimed that Timorese nationalism did not have the developed identity which years of armed struggle had lent to the African movements and that there was no pre-existing movement of profound resistance to colonialism. As evidence, they cited the case of the 16 PIDE (DGS) agents operating in the territory. One of the MFA's first tasks was to call for complaints from the populace against these security agents, conduct hearings based on the evidence and recommend arrest and imprisonment where necessary. According to the Portuguese, no complaints were lodged in East Timor, even from FRETILIN which had been in existence for some months.[34] The conditioning of centuries could, of course, have made Timorese reluctant to trust the new situation—for a Timorese to denounce a Portuguese to other Portuguese was a major political step. Helen Hill hints at this in discussing the PIDE question, commenting that 'fear of blackmail, intimidation, etc. was still present and hampering the decolonisation process'.[35] In the absence of complaints, the MFA were powerless to act against the agents, but advised them to leave the colony, which they did.

As events were to show, regardless of its alleged lack of history Timorese nationalism was alive and flourishing by the end of 1974. All indications were that, unformed and inexperienced though its proponents were, it had touched the imagination of the East Timorese: it was to develop a dynamic of its own.

Most observers agree that in the intial months after April 1974, UDT attracted the most support of the three formations. The FRETILIN statement of September tacitly acknowledged this:

> Everything indicates that in the very near future the Revolutionary Front of Independent East Timor will win the great majority of Timor's population.

And indeed this prediction did appear to be moving towards fulfilment in the early months of 1975. The unpopularity of the integration option and the UDT's inability to articulate a

FRETILIN demonstration, Baucau, March 1975. Banner reads: 'Only one force—the people, only one guide—FRETILIN, only one aim—independence' (Jill Jolliffe).

programme of social development or build links with the common people in the hinterland could not provide serious opposition to the FRETILIN literacy and agricultural development campaign. In February 1975 journalist Robin Osborne observed that:

> [UDT] is thought to have the support of about 10 per cent of the people ... APODETI supporters are said to be few, perhaps only 5 per cent and of those I met most seemed unaware of the party's specific aims ... FRETILIN could possibly command about 60 per cent of the vote. It is said of the people that 25 per cent are thought to be too remote, illiterate or apolitical to take part in an election.[36]

Nationalism is not merely an abstract idea. The central and frequently forgotten question of Timorese politics is that of underdevelopment—chronic underemployment, systemic poverty, virtual absence of public welfare services, illiteracy, the stagnation of agriculture and the absence of industrial development. A cornerstone of ADODETI ideology (echoed by Whitlam in Yogyakarta) was the belief that East Timor could not exist economically as a small state—integration with Indonesia was viewed as a panacea, despite the comparable economic depression of Indonesian Timor and the outlying regions of the republic. UDT's strategy was to argue for the injection of foreign capital. By September FRETILIN had articulated and developed a course characteristic of ascendant nationalisms in the Third World: the development of modest self-sufficiency through a programme of public education, co-operative agricultural self-reliance schemes and the controlled inflow of foreign capital including inter-governmental aid.

In the decolonisation process the choice of a road for economic development manifests itself as political choice, the right to self-determination. A Timorese in the remote interior village of Namoleço expressed the dilemma in a more articulate and real fashion than any political theorist discussing East Timor could: 'We are not buffalos or potatos or mice to be sold to the Indonesians', he told visiting journalists. 'We are Timorese and this is our country'.[37]

3

From Coalition to Coup

At the beginning of 1975 the 650,000 people of East Timor faced the possibility of a new kind of life, a new identity.

The outside world knew little about them. They knew little about it, or indeed, about themselves, in the reflective historical sense. No coherent recorded history of Timor from the Timorese point of view existed, for their history had been written for them by Portuguese colonists, through Portuguese colonists' eyes. A few missionaries and anthropologists had recorded some of the languages of East Timor, but others had never been heard or described outside Timor. Since Lord Alfred Russel Wallace and his peers explored the East Indies in that nineteenth century spurt of natural scientific energy stimulated by Darwinism, little scholarly work had been done independently of the Portuguese. For the Timorese themselves, their history comprised the oral histories of land ownership, their archives those relics preserved in *lulik* tradition—the objects of foreign occupation, ancestral resistance and before.[1] The Timorese story had not been told abroad, nor Timorese identity freely expressed at home in the preceding centuries: reconstruction lay ahead.

Many factors lay between the wish and the realisation. For such a tiny country, international influences and pressures were wide flung. Located in South East Asia, the hope for change sprang from Africa, then Lisbon. The future was now dependent (apart from domestic developments) on a precarious balance between Australian foreign policy, Indonesian military intentions and Portuguese domestic politics. The excuse for invading East Timor in December 1975 will be that the warring giants of the world stage, the U.S., China and the U.S.S.R. might be interested in its 14,953 square kilometres.

Internally, the local Catholic Church's response to the new

situation provided one obstacle to change. On 25 January 1974, the Bishop of Dili, Bishop Dom José Joaquim Ribeiro, issued a Pastoral Letter, 'Regarding the New Situation'. The letter asserted the Church's willingness to move with the times:

> All priests and missionary personnel are glad to see new opportunities opening up. The Church is aware of the social and political conditions affecting the life of the people. Times are different for the Church as well as the people ... The Bishop and the priests are looking forward towards the future: we want a Timor that is progressive, just, peaceful and Catholic.

All Timorese, whether Catholic, Moslem or animist, had in common a belief in God, the Bishop argued, expressing an unshaken confidence in the commonality of Henry the Navigator's monotheistic deity with the *lulik* beliefs of the Timorese. At the same time he went on to warn:

> We must guard against materialistic and atheistic Communism and socialistic Marxism which is seeking to estinguish [the] positive values of the Timorese people ... People must respect the rights of property ...

and to remind his flock that the Church forbade Catholics to vote for Communists or socialists in any election.[2]

In all Portuguese colonies the Catholic Church had been the linchpin of Portugal's 'civilising mission'. The power this role gave is revealed in amendments to the Portuguese Constitution made in 1971 in response to the deteriorating situation in Africa. While recognising separation of Church and State 'so far as freedom of worship is concerned', they reaffirmed the Church's role as the 'traditional religion of the Portuguese nation', and reinforced the principle of protection and aid by the state for the teaching and welfare institutions of the Church as 'centres for spreading civilisation'.

In an interview with the Australian parliamentary delegation to Timor in March 1975, Bishop Ribeiro expressed apprehensions about the Church's future in the territory and underlined his comments of the Pastoral Letter:

> You must realise that the Church is very suspicious of Communism and one only has to see other Communist countries where religious freedom has been promised ... We believe that although the people of Timor are very anti-Communist, there are

> influences coming in from other parts of the world ... Dialogue is alright at the European level of culture but not here where the people are not as sophisticated ...

He made it clear that the 'influences' referred to were within FRETILIN.

Although unofficially identified with the established Catholic Church, UDT did not see the need to articulate a policy on religion. By contrast FRETILIN specifically proposed the complete separation of church and state. In the 'pure democracy' which was their goal, there was to be no place for a privileged church; it could not expect state patronage in an independent East Timor, but would be expected to take an equal place with the traditional religion of the majority of the people—animism—as with the Moslem community.

Despite such differences, UDT and FRETILIN formed a coalition in January 1975. The context was increasing pressure from Indonesia expressed through Radio Kupang and the Jakarta press. The immediate rationale for coalition was a united front on the common principle of independence. The coalition was also a product of Portuguese desire for a national front formula to expedite the decolonisation process, a formula which they had pursued in Angola. In early 1975 the UDT, with their inferior links with the village people, their lack of social development policies and the apparent swing towards FRETILIN, were the main short-term beneficiaries of the partnership, although a pattern of ebb and flow of common interest between sections of both UDT and FRETILIN was to recur.

The two groups reached agreement on a common programme for transition to independence. This coalition programme rejected the notion of a referendum for independence, arguing that it was a fundamental human right guaranteed by the UN Declaration of Human Rights, and proposed the formation of a transitional government. It proposed that it be led by a High Commissioner representing the Portuguese government, and that the Cabinet positions should be shared equally by FRETILIN, UDT and the Portuguese. This would function over a minimum of three years and if circumstances determined, to a maximum term of eight. During its term the projected transitional government would reform all internal political and administrative structures and implement a programme of reconstruction and development. The coalition pledged, finally, to 'promote friendship, goodwill and cooperation with all countries of the world, particularly with Australia and Indonesia, for the peace and security of the whole region' (Appendix B). By combining around the independence principle the two largest formations hoped to express the popular support which existed simply for independence and isolate APODETI which was then claiming mass support for the integration option.

In February the Portuguese administration publicly protested in the territory's newspaper about a telegram which had been sent to the UN by APODETI. Major Francisco Mota, Chief of Cabinet of Political Affairs, alleged in *A Voz de Timor* of 20 February that a 'profoundly demagogic' telegram containing 'utterly slanderous' assertions had been sent. It had claimed that the Portuguese had cancelled electoral rights, were oppressing the people, and that violence and chaos existed in the interior. Further, the UN cable accused, the Portuguese wished to retain East Timor. It was ironic, Major Mota commented, that APODETI, which had refused to collaborate in any small way in the decolonisation process, should distort the political situation in East Timor: 'The association is so preoccupied with explanation and enlightenment for the population of the interior that it holds to the tactics of corruption and intimidation'.

Nothing could be more remote from the truth than APODETI's accusation that the Portuguese wished to retain Timor. Soon after the cable incident Australian journalist Bruce Stannard interviewed a senior Portuguese officer who informed him that if the Indonesians invaded Timor, the Portuguese would simply pack their bags and leave. 'Portugal has enough problems of her own at the moment', he told Stannard, 'We have our own revolution to attend to at home. We would say to the Indonesians "Hello, come on in if you want to!"'[3]

Already 25 Portuguese schoolteachers had been dismissed by the MFA and returned to Portugal, partly, at least, as a result of agitation by progressive Timorese students against the continuation of colonialist teaching methods. A company of military police had also been sent back in 1974. They were replaced in April 1975 with a force of paratroopers.

In late February, the Australian press reported that an Indonesian invasion of East Timor was imminent. The reports of a planned amphibious landing in Dili and a parachute drop at Baucau airport emanated from an Australian Defence Department 'leak'. In response the coalition cabled Andrew Peacock, Foreign Affairs spokesperson for the Liberal opposition, stating that they represented the overwhelming will of the East Timorese for independence and were prepared to hold talks with the Indonesian and Australian governments towards 'peace, political stability in South East Asia'. A parliamentary debate ensued in which the acting Minister for Foreign Affairs, Mr Morrison, outlined the Labor government's policy as one of 'Support [for] a measured and deliberate process of decolonisation in Portuguese Timor through arrangements leading to an internationally acceptable act of self-determination'.[4]

If invasion reports proved to have no immediate substance, there were more substantial reports of APODETI subversion and intimidation. These ranged from stories of the political activities of the Indonesian consul in Dili, the entry of Indonesian agents into the territory as 'tourists' in order to make contact with APODETI delegates in the villages, the distribution of Indonesian-supplied bribes (such as T-shirts and transistors) to local people to join APODETI, to the activities of a pro-APODETI traditional chief, the *liurai* of Atsabe, in recruiting East Timorese to go over the border into Indonesia for guerilla training. In March Governor Lemos Pires complained to the Australian parliamentary delegation of distorted information emanating from the Indonesian consulate. He had recently returned from Jakarta where he had informed the Indonesian government that he regarded the Radio Kupang broadcasts as provocative. He expressed the view that his discussions there had resulted in a more reasonable attitude: it had been conceded that the broadcasts were inflammatory.

The 'Atsabe incident' was to prove an event of long-term significance. The Melbourne *Age*'s South East Asian correspondent Michael Richardson reported from Dili in March that a small East Timorese guerilla army was being trained in Indonesian Timor by Indonesian army commandos:

> The training site is said to be near Atambua, the main town on the Indonesian side of the frontier.
>
> Portuguese intelligence officers claim about 100 citizens of Portuguese Timor have been trained in commando techniques at the camp ... recruits were selected from a group of several hundred Timorese "enticed and pressured" to cross the border ... in the past few months.
>
> They claim recruits have become disillusioned by promises of girls, money, good food and rapid promotion which did not materialise.[5]

At the centre of the incident was Guilherme Maria Gonçalves, the *liurai* of Atsabe. In a story with an appropriate blend of Dili intrigue, parochialism and melodrama, it has been alleged that the *liurai*'s embitterment with the Portuguese stemmed from an unsuccessful attempt by them to win his support at the end of the second world war. He was initally arrested after the Japanese occupation, so the story goes, but the Portuguese then sought to pacify him by the offer of a trip to Portugal. On arrival the *liurai* 'remained sad, for the authorities had posted him in a third class hotel when it was the custom for other Timorese representatives to stay at the international hotel. On his return, he told his subjects of his bad reception in Portugal'.[6] Whether substantial or not, the story does demonstrate that the strength and exercise of the Atsabe *liurai*'s traditional power (representing the remnants of a formerly important Timorese kingdom) has been a necessary consideration of Timorese politicians for some time.

The outcome of the incident was that the Portuguese arrested a lesser chief who had been used as a recruiting agent by Gonçalves. This *liurai*, Feliciano Gomes, told Richardson that he had been instructed by Gonçalves at a meeting in Atsabe on 1 November 1974 to:

> urge strong people from his tribe to go to Indonesia for army training. They would then come back to Portuguese Timor to fight against parties opposing merger with Indonesia.
>
> Mr Gomes claimed that four Indonesians in civilian clothing had been present at the meeting.[7]

The detention of Gomes became the object of a new wave of propaganda in the Indonesian press which claimed he had been tortured, a claim he denied to Richardson. 'Hate Indonesia Campaign Intensified in Portuguese Timor' the *Indonesian Times* of 27 February announced, and went on to claim that APODETI supporters were 'bearing the brunt of terror inflicted by the Leftists in efforts to create a "psychosis of fear"'

Despite APODETI provocations, decolonisation appeared to be progressing well in these early months of 1975. The coalition gathered support, the transitional programme for independence looked functional, and there were no fundamental contradictions between it and the programme put forward by the administration's Decolonisation Commission at this time. If anything, the Portuguese would have preferred an earlier outside limit than the maximum eight years for transition proposed by UDT and FRETILIN, but were adamant that they would accept this if it was the wish of the parties. One point on which the Portuguese were consistent was that they would not be happy about UN involvement in the transfer of power although FRETILIN at least had spoken in varying terms of the desirability of UN supervision. Conscious of their limited capabilities and, possibly, of the future inability to supervise decolonisation, they were not eager to expose themselves to international scrutiny.

In this period, two important development projects based upon foreign investment were under discussion. One involved Australian capital, in a cattle project in Lospalos, the second was a joint Australian-Japanese tourist development venture.

Although the initial project for the Lospalos development was agreed to in May 1974 (which was the period before significant MFA involvement in the administration), the project was in abeyance one year later. The Portuguese had initially insisted as a term of the contract—undertaken by a Darwin businessman to the value of 18,000 contos ($A545,454)—that work on it must begin within a year. Just before the expiry date the Darwin party contacted the administration and asked if the formation of a company to manage the venture would be acceptable. The Portuguese replied that as the political situation had changed in Timor, the project's future would now depend on the attitudes of the newly-formed political associations to it. In April the associations made their views known. APODETI refused to attend discussions. It sent instead a letter saying that the project was 'neo-colonialist and fascist'. César Augusto da Costa Mousinho, the UDT representative, waxed enthusiastic at the project and declared his support for it. He himself had cattle in Lospalos, he said, and the people of the area could only stand to benefit by the technical expertise such a project would introduce. FRETILIN's response was initially negative, but their representative, José Ramos Horta, changed ground and asked for more time to study the proposal.

Negotiations for the second project had been underway well before the Lisbon 'revolution'. The poverty and isolation of East Timor under Caetano had had the fortunate side-effect of saving the country from the sort of tourist development which co-exists with glaring poverty in other parts of Asia. This project, planned as a joint venture by the Japanese-based Daiko Kanko Company with the Australian Thiess Holdings, projected just such an international tourist complex near Baucau airport. It would comprise a four-wing hotel, villas, a marina, golf course, shopping centre and a 175 sq km zoo. Press publication in 1973 of details of Australian involvement in the project caused some controversy. Earlier, in November and December 1972, Australian UN representatives had voted for resolutions in the General Assembly opposing foreign investment in any of the Portuguese colonies.

The new administration also subjected this proposal to the examination of the parties. Again UDT was enthusiastic while FRETILIN expressed reserve, reiterating the principle that they would accept foreign investment so long as it was controlled. 'FRETILIN accepts foreign investment for production but never for consumption, which will produce new habits', Nicolau Lobato commented of the project.

Generally, FRETILIN's attitude to foreign capital, in contrast to UDT's, was close to the MFA position (at home and in Timor)—investment was necessary for the future, but foreign capital should not be allowed to dominate the economy. However, the administration's public postures were not always consistent with its private attitudes. On 11 December an agreement was quietly signed between the Portuguese government and Oceanic Exploration Company of Denver for oil exploration rights in the territory. This project was not discussed with the associations and caused anger in Australian government circles because it involved rights over the large slab of disputed continental shelf between Timor and the north west coast of Australia. It also cut across a number of concessions, granted or renewed, to oil companies by the Australian and Western Australian governments since 1963.

The question of oil in East Timor was of some potential significance. In March 1975 Bruce Stannard reported in *The Australian* that the Woodside Burmah company had completed a series of seismic soundings off Suai. 'If there is oil in commercial quantities', he wrote, 'the discovery could be the single most important factor influencing the course of the colony's future as an independent state or as yet another part of the sprawling Indonesian Republic.' For an independent state it could mean the economic viability so constantly disputed as a consideration for its political future, especially if a nationalist régime demanded equity. 'Oil may not be a watertight guarantee of perfect political harmony, but the political theorists who abound in Timor say that at least it would ease the Indonesian generals' fears of communist interference ... If petro-dollars mean petro-security, the Timorese may well be on the road to real independence', he concluded.[8] (Timor Oil and BHP were also active but it seems none were prepared to commit themselves to long-term projects in view of the country's uncertain political future.)

In this period East Timor's 650,000 inhabitants witnessed a number of important changes in the patterns of village life. The FRETILIN literacy programme was formally initiated after planning of several months including the printing of a literacy booklet in Lisbon. The booklet's text and illustrations centred on an anti-colonialist view of Timor's history and future: attacking the greed of the colonists, economic exploitation under the Portuguese, the collaboration of feudal chiefs in exploiting the people and the methods of the colonial teaching system.

In March 1975 two Australian journalists and a tutor from a Melbourne university witnessed the literacy programme in action in a village school in a remote mountain area. The programme worked in a school system separate from the official Portuguese system. The school visited at Namoleço was built of mud slab and grass thatch right in the middle of the village, two kilometres away from the nearest Portuguese school.

Between 2 pm and 5 pm each day over 100 men and women attended classes in company with the village children. Although the school was in Mambai-speaking country, the lessons were conducted in Tetum, the most widely-spoken language of East Timor and the future lingua franca of a nationally independent country. Full-time FRETILIN cadres had been working in this village and others in the Aileu area since November 1974. A year after the Lisbon coup, this village had yet to see UDT or APODETI representatives.

Agricultural work was also underway at the village level. Before the close of 1974 FRETILIN had piloted agricultural co-operatives and consumer co-operatives. Neither of the other two associations had articulated or developed policies on this question. Problems of agricultural change in East Timor are daunting. In the brief time open to it, FRETILIN appears to have merely scratched the surface, although this was more than either of the other two associations had done. Natural harshness of terrain and climate compounded by various features of Portuguese colonisation have left East Timor's land ecologically depleted and the people ill-equipped for agricultural reconstruction.

The average Timorese's horizon is restricted like that of most peasant people by bondage to the soil and thus the vagaries of nature. Direct dependence on the soil narrows options for change. In Timor the dependence is deepened by the extremities of climatic conditions, which make planning—short-term or long-term—difficult. Natural disaster or social disorder, when the daily routine of subsistence agriculture is broken, can thus bring severe famine in its wake. The massive death toll from World War II (around 40,000) was largely the result of famine.

In the progression from a hunting and gathering economy to the practice of swidden agriculture today, it is difficult to isolate the influence of colonial rule on patterns of existence. (A comparative history of the Portuguese colonies would be enlightening in this regard.) Some features are clear. The introduction of cash cropping (coffee, copra, tobacco, cotton) and with it day labour, forced and voluntary, has altered population patterns and disrupted traditional life in the villages. The initial destruction of the sandalwood stands eroded

Timor's mountains, as it created new social formations. The particularly stagnant style of Portuguese colonial rule in the twentieth century meant that the changes which gained impetus in the nineteenth—coffee planting in the interior, the introduction of poll taxes bringing the penetration of a money economy to the village level, the creation of an urban labour force which drew people from the land—were not compensated by economic planning which could remedy the problems created. The drawing of population to coffee planting areas like Ermera, Hatolia and Maubisse for example, was not offset by the introduction of food storage facilities, a transportation system, or irrigation systems which could ease life on the land. It is not in the nature of colonial systems to be locally benevolent: all colonialisms are characterised by the economic drain from the colonised territory to the metropolis, but by the twentieth century the exhaustion of Portuguese colonial power rendered it less capable of local window dressing than most.

Ormeling has pointed to the enduring influence of the *liurais* in Timorese history, whose power was strong long before the Portuguese occupation:

> In the course of time central governing agencies, borne by sacred chiefs, have been superimposed upon the simple suku [suco] life.

Despite the debasement of their power effected by the Portuguese around the turn of this century, the *liurais* continued to wield great power:

> Experience has taught that social and economic modernisation only has a chance of success in this unindividualised society if introduced or imposed by its leaders ... All innovations ... [fail] or [succeed] according to their co-operation.

He compares the relationship between the *liurais* and their subjects to the feudal regimes of mediaeval Europe, based on superstition and passivity of the masses.[9] The importance of the *liurai* has been understood by coloniser and colonised alike in Timorese history. If the land is the key to deep-running social change, the *liurais* are the key to the land.

In the village, land is held collectively by the *suco*, based on descent from a common ancestor, and worked by its constituent family groups. It is regularly re-allocated by the *liurais* in consultation with the *datos*, elders of the clan. But 'it would be a grave mistake to imagine that this is some system of egalitarian democracy. The *sucos* are dominated by a few wealthy and powerful families'.[10]

Much has been written of UDT as the party of the *liurais*, and of the influence of a certain few more traditional chiefs in exploiting their power to give APODETI a public face. However, although FRETILIN's populist aspect derives from its identification with the Maubere, the common people, in those areas where it has pioneered agricultural co-operatives—Bucóli, Aileu and Bazartete—FRETILIN has had the political support of the local *liurai*. Again, the role of Timorese élites is underscored: generally, the traditional rulers have been concerned to preserve power, but they also represent an educated layer. It was inevitable that, of these, some should turn to democratic ideas. The problem created here is not whether, as the Portuguese paternalistically claim, local people only support FRETILIN (or APODETI, or UDT) at the direction of the *liurai*. There is overwhelming evidence to suggest otherwise. It is whether under a future nationalist régime a contradiction will be engendered between the thrust for change from below and the attempt to implement agricultural change by working through sympathetic *liurais* who have traditionally controlled the land.

Like their approach to most problems, FRETILIN met the challenge of agricultural change in a gradualist and pragmatic way. The first co-operative was initiated by Nicolau Lobato in 1974 in his home village of Bazartete:

> The people are still suspicious of the idea ... They have been drawn into similar collective projects by either the Portuguese or the Japanese only to find themselves dispossessed. We have started off with a small number so that we can work out the problems that arise easily, and when it has shown itself to be successful then others will follow quickly. It demands the creation of a great deal of trust among the members and that all decisions taken by the co-operative be taken democratically.[11]

This and other areas under co-operative cultivation were collectively worked at *suco* level with the use of shared implements. It was proposed that land tenure remain with the constituent families. Half the produce would go to the state, through the *suco* consumer co-operative, and half to the family. The main targets for co-operation would be the more fertile lowland (wet rice) areas until production was increased, when the problems of the poorer subsistence agriculture areas could be considered.

In traditional agriculture the digging stick is the main implement of production and although water buffalo are abundant in Timor they have not generally been utilised except to trample the soil before planting, a practice unique to Timor. Animal husbandry and agricultural production are not integrated, even though the buffalo could be used to pull a plough, and the numerous herds of goats and sheep cultivated for milking. An Australian Council for Overseas Aid team which saw the FRETILIN co-operatives at work in October 1975 commented on these problems:

> Unlike most other Asian and S.E. Asian countries, the necessity for more efficient production methods in East Timor is reflected in the amount of land in many areas which remains unutilized or under-utilized due to lack of manpower.
>
> [For example] ... a large tract of paddyfields at Seical ... is cultivated such that each field produces only one crop in three years. The reasons for this wastage are twofold ... the difficulty and inefficiency of preparing the fields for planting by the time honoured process of trampling the mud under the hooves of a herd of water buffalo, and ... the depletion of the soil's fertility due to constant planting of the same crop without addition of any type of fertilizer.
>
> In the ... less fertile highland areas, a vicious circle almost certainly exists, in that digging-stick cultivation methods demand heavy work from a population whose available energy is already depleted by inadequate nutrition. Thus one crop is often grown where there is potential for two—and so food shortages persist.[12]

The same team reported that the FRETILIN co-operatives which they inspected at Bucóli, Aileu and Malinamo (on the edge of Dili) were 'working enthusiastically but under severe handicaps through lack of resources'.

On their arrival in November 1974 the MFA administration established an agricultural extension centre at Maubisse to work with local people. Of the three Portuguese officers there, one had done similar work in Angola for five years. They aimed at 'forming production attitudes in an anti-paternal way, by resolution of indigenous problems ... all work to be with the rural family ... to always reach agreement with the population where possible'. One of the main problems they saw was to establish availability of credit in order to break the traditional cycle of annual agriculture and thus work towards the building of storage facilities and the purchase of fertilisers and new strains of seed. The area is one in which pressure on the land is high. The training of young Timorese towards self-reliance was also stressed. Local people appeared happy with the project and delegates from both UDT and FRETILIN were active in forward planning. Maubisse, a *posto* town, was initially regarded as a UDT area. The Union was formed here in August 1974, FRETILIN in October/November of that year.[13]

All the associations claimed to represent the 'common people' and all, credibly, to have the support of certain *liurais*. Of the first claim, only UDT and FRETILIN gave visible evidence. FRETILIN acknowledged UDT's early numerical superiority. 'UDT is the largest organisation', José Ramos Horta told Helen Hill in August 1974, 'however it is only a matter of time [for FRETILIN] because after 500 years the people have completely lost their nationalism'.[14] The growth of the front's popular strength in subsequent months derived in part from its identification with the 'Maubere'. Ramos Horta later attempted to elevate this concept to an ideology, 'Mauberism', but it is better described as a populist catchry expressing a general political orientation. Maubere is simply a very common Timorese name, like 'Mr Smith' or 'Mr Jones'. Its feminine equivalent is 'Bibere'. Under the old régime, Maubere was a term of contempt for the poor mountain people, the most backward, illiterate and superstitious section of Timorese society. FRETILIN turned the idea on its head to make Maubere a term of national pride. 'O Maubere, Bibere, East Timor our land', runs a popular FRETILIN song. APODETI and KOTA antagonism to FRETILIN stemmed in part from its identification with the rural poor. 'The trouble with FRETILIN is that they are of the Maubere, they are not *liurais*', a KOTA leader remarked in a comment superficially inaccurate, (given the fact that many of the front's leaders are of *liurais*' families), but expressing a fundamental truism.[15]

These three components: the literacy campaign in Tetum, the commencement of limited agricultural reform at the village level, and the political elevation of the Maubere were irreducible components of FRETILIN's theory and practice. Another was the organisation, in the urban centres, of the small force of wage-earners and students.

The strike organised by ASDT after the Lisbon coup resulted in the formation of a National Union of Workers, on a 'one big union' principle, to include professional and manual workers. (The craft divisions which bedevil union organisation in Western countries could have little basis in East Timor's tiny force of wage-earners.) A reception by the workers' union for the Australian trade union and student delegation which visited East Timor in March 1975 drew near 1,000 people.

A national students union was formed early in 1975. The National Union of Timorese Students (União Nacional de Estudantes de Timor, UNETIM) was established at the technical school in Dili. Soon afterwards it had a branch in Dili and delegates in various village schools: The founding manifesto proclaimed:

> We, the students of Timor conclude: that it is necessary to create a students' association ... which will ensure the unity of all Timorese students in their actions within the broader sphere of action involving the people of Timor in their fight for freedom and progress.

Among its aims, it stood to:

> promote the general reform and democratisation of the education system in collaboration with progressive members of the teaching staff ... combat the deification of teachers and the subsequent segregation of students from teachers which can only exist in a paternalistic education system; such a system neglects the creative capacity of students and is alienating ... to fight for the consolidation of the democratic liberties already obtained in the teaching institutions in particular and in the political life of the country in general, as well as contributing to their expansion ...

In a letter to Australia a member subsequently described the drive into the countryside in the following dry season, to consolidate and expand UNETIM:

> On Easter holidays we formed many groups to the inland, getting traditional stories and some superstition of people, in each region. I went to Baucau with our group. I stayed there for a couple days and after I went to my home country in Baguia.[16]

In the democratising spirit of the times a sergeants commission was also established to air grievances within the army. It was initiated by MFA officers and was based on the committee system fundamental to the MFA in Portugal. A principal figure in the commission was Fernando Carmo. Expressions of party politics were discouraged in army life and the commission was not established on party lines. Nevertheless the Indonesian press saw its establishment as a further step in the direction of 'absolute power take over by the communists', commenting that eleven of the twelve sergeants involved were FRETILIN men.[17]

Local elections initiated by the Decolonisation Commission gave the opportunity to gauge the success of the political work of the various associations. Michael Richardson witnessed the conduct of one such election at the *suco* of Chau Luturo in the eastern Lospalos area. The first of a number of elections of traditional chiefs began here in March after the local people complained to the administration that they were dissatisfied with some of the *liurais*. There were complaints against 33 of several hundred in the *concelho*. The elected *liurais* would form an electoral college with the unchallenged, or 'confirmed', *liurais*. The college would then choose a 35-member council to administer the *concelho*.

Portuguese officers described the local electoral process thus:

> [These are] local assemblies to confirm traditional chiefs as having influence and to convince the people that there are options. The council would not be deliberative but administrative—no economic power. The political parties are involved in the process but not to a high degree. The councils will be situated in 13 regions composed of 35 chiefs elected out of which a 5-man executive will be chosen.[18]

In the election Richardson observed, a Filipe Quintas was challenging Fernando Sanches, the Chau Luturo *liurai* since 1959. Quintas was the president of FRETILIN's regional subcommittee although the election was not contested on party lines:

> It is a unique process, designed to marry local custom with the basic principles of one man one vote and the secret ballot ...

> Instead of ballot boxes they use woven baskets made for carrying farm produce. And small stones take the place of voting papers in a region where very few people can read or write.

An MFA officer supervised the process. Two small baskets were placed inside another basket set on two chairs. One of the small baskets had a handkerchief tied to it. This was Quintas's basket. Those who wished to vote for him placed their pebble in it. For Sanches they put it in the other. All those over 18 years old were electors—489 of the *suco*'s population of 1,259. After each voter placed his or her pebble in the basket the votes were counted. Quintas was elected 259 to 92 with one informal vote (a pebble which missed both baskets) and one abstention, a man who explained that he didn't want to vote because he was related to both candidates.[19]

Of the three political associations, only APODETI supported the idea of a pre-independence referendum. The Portuguese themselves were not well-disposed to the idea, but proposed instead an initial formal process of decolonisation. In these first steps they hoped to operate through consultation and consensus with and between the associations. Subsequent steps would involve the legalisation of political parties and the establishment of a transitional government which would plan a general election. The Portuguese canvassed the idea of a pre-independence referendum with UDT and FRETILIN, both of whom rejected it by reference to the UN principles of decolonisation. The relevant General Assembly resolution they invoked, ' ... on the granting of independence to colonial countries and peoples', states:

> Immediate steps shall be taken, in Trust and Non-Self-Governing Territories or all other territories which have not yet attained independence, to transfer all powers to the peoples of those territories, without any conditions or reservations ...

and:

> Inadequacy of political, economic, social or educational preparedness should never serve as a pretext for delaying independence.[20]

FRETILIN saw the political forms of East Timor's future as rather different from the Westminster model of party pluralism identified with democracy in most western minds. In styling themselves 'sole legitimate representative of the Timorese people' and calling for the participation of all Timorese patriots irrespective of class, race or religion in a broad national front, populist in concept, they were identifying themselves as part of a tradition of Third World nationalism as old as Sun Yat Sen's Kuomintang and as recent as Samora Machel's FRELIMO. In this model, which is characteristically the foundation of the post-colonial nation state, political differentiation typically springs from within the front.

Not that they were opposed in principle to national elections, but independence before any other question could be discussed was a non-negotiable principle. The people were free to choose integration with Indonesia, FRETILIN argued, but the mechanics of declaring independence first must be a preliminary—a colonised people could not be seen as expressing a free choice.

There was another reason for this policy. Fundamental to FRETILIN thought was a deep-running almost nineteenth-century liberal (indeed a number of the leaders had read J.S. Mill) belief in the power of education, in the Brazilian Paulo Freire's *conscientização*, as a force for social change. They saw the task of preparing the people, through education and the creation of the minimal requirements for a decent standard of life (health care, agricultural development, economic self-sufficiency), as a long-term one inseparable from future expressions of choice. This process required time.

The atmosphere in the first months of 1975 was one of hope. Events of the past year had been propitious. Change in the colonial metropolis had opened up new perspectives overnight. In a neighbouring South East Asian country a movement which had begun as a tiny and disorganised nationalist force was delivering the final blows against the world's mightiest imperial power. Fighting Vietnam was an inspiration and a comfort when pondering the possibility of armed defence against Indonesia. The whole region reverberated with change. Papua New Guinea was heading for independence. Above all, at the end of 1972 a government had been elected in Australia which would support the struggle of a small nation for self-determination. It had been elected to office partly on its policy of withdrawing Australian troops from the American assault on

Vietnam. Australian Labor Government support for liberation movements in Southern Africa was internationally recognised. The new Prime Minister, had in 1963, when still a rising star on the Labor horizon, even specifically raised the question of the rights of the long-neglected Timorese, calling for UN action against Portugal in order to bring about East Timorese self-determination.

Between 25 April 1974 and mid-1975 the people of East Timor lived briefly in this atmosphere of change, hope and growth. On 20 May, one year after the formation of ASDT, FRETILIN held a celebration in Dili. Thousands of Timorese came in from the mountains. *Liurais* and common mountain people in traditional dress marched and celebrated in the streets. The evening was devoted to cultural events: poetry-reading in Tetum, traditional songs and dances and a film from across the sea—of the now-victorious liberation struggle of the people of the former Portuguese colony of Guinea Bissau.

Domestic reconstruction was proceeding apace, but no group could afford to neglect the important field of foreign relations. FRETILIN, conscious from its inception of the Indonesian danger, embarked on a course of vigorous and ambitious foreign policy activism. UDT were eager to build their own standing (even in the coalition period) through separate approaches to Canberra, Jakarta and the ASEAN nations, a programme which got off to a late start. APODETI foreign policy was inbuilt, with little need for external contacts. Apart from regular visits to Jakarta, Bali and Indonesian Timor, their only foreign politicking appears to have been a visit to Australia in mid-May.

Ramos Horta was nominated by FRETILIN for diplomatic work in the local region. In June 1974 he visited Jakarta for the first time and was well received, returning with the Malik letter described in the previous chapter. His exchange with Deputy Parliamentary Chairman John Naro (who also stressed respect for East Timorese sovereignty) was noted in the Indonesian press:

> Horta declared that the view about Indonesia [in East Timor] to date was ... apt to be aggressive. On my return from Indonesia, I will explain conditions in Indonesia in the present period, when it

> prefers quiet and cultivates peace, he said.
>
> Horta expressed the hope that Indonesia would help Timor 'because we have been dosed with the Western way of living, and now we understand what is the significance of Indonesia ...' He hoped that the demands of the party would be recognised, including that the Indonesian language would be a compulsory subject in schools in Timor next year ...[21]

In August he went to Australia. He hoped for, but did not obtain, from his meeting with Senator Willesee (then Minister for Foreign Affairs), similar guarantees to the one received from Malik. This first visit heralded a slow and limited stirring of Australian curiosity about the territory which had previously been known to hardly more than a few 'top end' holiday travellers, oil company staff and consular officials.

By December 1974 Ramos Horta was back to persist with the independence case—for the re-opening of the Australian consulate (formally requested by the Portuguese in November), aid for education, health and agricultural development, and above all recognition of the Timorese right to self-determination. Ramos Horta's personal political development in this period was apparent. A number of Australians took a personal interest in his political development including J.S. (Jim) Dunn the former consul, and Professor Fred Fisk of the ANU. Fisk organised for Ramos Horta to return to Australia in the following June for a course of private tuition at the university's Development Studies Centre.

Before the June 1975 visit, Ramos Horta and Alarico Fernandes preceded UDT leaders on a trip to Jakarta where they were wined and dined but apparently offered no prospects of serious discussions.[22]

In April 1975, Nicolau Lobato left for a grand diplomatic tour of Africa and then to Lisbon; following his departure Xavier do Amaral and Mari Alkatiri (later to emerge as the front's most competent Third World diplomat) left to attend Mozambique's independence day celebrations, at the invitation of President Samora Machel.

In mid-April UDT ventured into the diplomatic world with a trip to Jakarta, and then Australia. Like FRETILIN, the UDT delegates (Lopes da Cruz and César Augusto da Costa Mousinho) had been invited. In their case, however, Indonesian officials, including Generals Murtopo and Surono spoke with them in some detail. On the UDT leaders' own account 'Indonesian officials all stressed the dangers of Communism. It was ... suggested that Timorese leaders link up with APODETI, the party in favour of integration with Indonesia, to form a common front against Communist subversion'.[22] It was also reported that on their return through Australia, UDT leaders were reinforced in their anti-Communist apprehensions by rightwing Australians who had formerly served as commandos in Timor.[23] The path of UDT foreign policy from this time onward was inextricably bound up with the general deterioration of domestic events, as with the machinations of Portuguese foreign policy.

The MFA's eagerness to supervise a decolonisation process acceptable to the Timorese was tempered by anxiety to rid themselves of this South East Asian colonial millstone. The principled facade masked an actuality which has been described as 'a mosaic of semi-secret negotiations and undertakings'.[24] In late March 1975 Indonesia's Ali Murtopo and the Indonesian ambassadors to Britain, France and Belgium met in London with a number of senior Portuguese representatives to discuss East Timor's future.

Lieutenant-General Murtopo was and still is one of President Suharto's closest advisors and deputy chief of the state intelligence co-ordinating body (BAKIN). The previous October he had taken command of a military/political operation aimed at the incorporation of East Timor into Indonesia, 'Operasi Komodo'. In 1969 he was a central figure in the *Pepera*, the so-called act of free choice which integrated Irian Jaya into Indonesia.

The Portuguese delegation included Almeida Santos, his Secretary of State Dr Campinos and Major Vítor Alves (a member of the MFA Supreme Revolutionary Council and a presiding spirit of the subsequent decolonisation talks in Dili and Macau). Major Mota also participated.

The talks resulted in a verbal agreement in which the Portuguese accepted that the easiest outcome was incorporation into Indonesia through an internationally acceptable act of self-determination. They agreed, too, to take Indonesian interests into account in the decolonisation programme and to permit Indonesian support for APODETI, on condition that the support was not 'embarrassingly obvious'. Both sides opposed UN involvement, which they saw as 'internationalising' the issue. Indonesia, for its part, agreed to encourage APODETI co-operation with Portuguese authorities, in particular, attendance at the imminent decolonisation talks.

Portugal's private delivering up of their former colony to Indonesia in the 'London Agreement' was one of a series of Portuguese–Indonesian–Australian connivances from April 1974 to August 1975 to determine East Timor's future above the heads of its people.

Political circumstances degenerated in the territory itself from around April–May 1975. Ramos Horta wrote on 24 May:

> We are having now a lot of troubles. The reactionaries are trying to divide us, launching rumours among the members, pamphlets attacking some of being communists, opportunists, etc ... We are getting full control of East Timor, but indeed ... UDT and APODETI are trying hard to undermine FRETILIN. We still are in coalition with UDT but it is in hot point ... I am trying hard to keep it because if it breaks, we shall have a lot of troubles here, even bloodshed. The only one that can win from such a situation will be APODETI. You don't imagine how we are worried about the future. I have been working hard to keep unity in the Party and to keep the coalition, but time will come when the tensions explode ... [25]

On 7 May the first phase of formal decolonisation talks began in Dili, presided over by Governor Lemos Pires and the Decolonisation Commission. The second phase was to be held in Macau. At the time of the Dili talks, both UDT and FRETILIN representatives had just returned from Jakarta, but the coalition was still intact. APODETI did not participate, but the Decolonisation Commission held separate talks with them after the discussions with the coalition. *A Voz de Timor* hailed the talks in a front page spread as: A LANDMARK IN THE HISTORY OF TIMOR![26] FRETILIN was represented in May by Xavier do Amaral, Alarico Fernandes, Juvenal Inácio, José Ramos Horta, Mari Alkatiri, Aleixo Corte Real, António Carvarino, Abel da Costa Ximenes, Guido Valadares, Djafar Alkatiri, Hélio Pina and Vicente Sa'he. Nicolau Lobato was abroad. UDT representatives were Francisco Lopes da Cruz,

César Augusto da Costa Mousinho, Mário Carrascalão, António Nascimento, João Carrascalão, Mariano Lopes da Cruz, Fausto do Carmo Soares, Fernando Barreto da Luz, João Saldanha de Melo, António Sarmento, Jacinto dos Reis Soares and Vasco Senanes.

This phase of the planned two-phase talks was to discuss several points: Portuguese attitudes to the FRETILIN–UDT coalition's demand for an immediate declaration of legal ('de jure') independence; the formation of a transitional government and an interim consultative assembly in October 1975, the latter to deal with legislation for the formation of political parties, electoral laws and the distribution of portfolios in the transitional government. Elections to be held one year from the formation of the transitional government and consultative assembly, and the possibility of co-ordinating them with a declaration of actual ('de facto') independence, were also points of discussion.

The formation of the transitional government in October 1975 was agreed upon, and elections for a national consultative assembly to be held in October 1976. The immediate declaration of legal independence which the coalition hoped for was not acceptable to the Portuguese, although they tentatively proposed a proclamation in three years. No decisions were made on the allocation of portfolios.

Acceptance of APODETI was a sensitive topic in the Dili talks with the coalition and was a theme relentlessly employed by the Decolonisation Commission, especially the possibility of their presence at Macau. The Commission spoke of bringing APODETI 'out of clandestinity'. It proposed that they should participate in the Macau talks, would not have a portfolio in the transitional government, but would compete in the October 1975 elections.

In the communique issued after the talks, the Commission noted comments attributed to Nicolau Lobato (then in Portugal) in the Lisbon press. He had complained that the decolonisation process was proceeding at a 'minimal' pace and that the choice of Macau for the summit 'significantly circumscribes our struggle for independence in the geographic area in which we are situated'. Of the legitimacy of APODETI, he argued that 'decolonisation to allow a new coloniser is simply a contradiction, an absurdity'.

Following the Dili talks, Ramos Horta left for Australia after discussions within the front on the formation of 'revolutionary brigades' to intensify and extend the agricultural and literacy work then in motion. The FRETILIN leadership had claimed that they were unable to provide handbooks or teachers to meet the demand for literacy schools in the interior. It was proposed that the Dili organisation become a branch not the centre of FRETILIN, and that the Dili members, principally students and teachers, should leave their positions to work full-time on this ambitious '*conscientização*' programme, living and working with the villagers. It was scheduled to begin on 10 June. This new expression of organisation, determination and strength seems to have increased the growing points of abrasion between UDT and FRETILIN.

In mid-May, an anonymous inflammatory leaflet appeared in Dili. It called for the expulsion of a group from FRETILIN who were commonly regarded as the 'left wing'. 'Carapinha, Roque, Carvarino and Vicente Reis [Vicente Sa'he] are Communist-Maoist extremists!' it declared, 'Mauberism is synonymous with Maoism!' Under the heading 'dangerous work', it declared these four to be 'lackeys, ignorant defenders of the MRPP [a Portuguese Maoist party: Revolutionary Movement of the Portuguese Proletariat] in Timor ... The people demand the immediate expulsion of these real malefactors, because they are also traitors ... OUT WITH THE TRAITORS! He who hesitates doubts the Maubere people', it concluded. Three of the four named in the leaflet were Lisbon-educated Timorese who had returned from Portugal after 25 April. The fourth was a Portuguese member of FRETILIN's Central Committee who had been in East Timor for some years and now taught at the technical school. The leaflet was signed 'Das Armas' (from the armed).

Rumours and occasions for friction intensified in this period. From March, when the elections in the countryside began, there had been fights between UDT and FRETILIN supporters in the marketplaces in Dili, Maubisse and Oecusse. By the end of May, UDT had withdrawn unilaterally from the coalition. In the communique announcing their withdrawal they accused FRETILIN of distorting the principles laid down in the basic document creating the coalition and bringing about an atmosphere of 'insecurity' among the population.

It has been suggested that the UDT withdrawal was an attempt to push the FRETILIN leadership into breaking with the 'left wing' group under attack and even to collaborate in expelling them from Timor. This possibility was supported by the fact that some time before, private discussions were held between certain FRETILIN and UDT leaders with a view to having the 'left' of FRETILIN expelled from the territory after a mutual approach to the Portuguese Governor.[27] In both cases, FRETILIN's growing self-definition as a black nationalist movement and the loyalty within the front between people of quite different political complexion, were underestimated.

Despite the breakdown of the independence coalition, the Macau talks went ahead in mid-June, but without the participation of FRETILIN. FRETILIN's decision to boycott Macau appears to have been mainly due to APODETI's participation which resulted from the successful persuasions of the Decolonisation Commission. According to Dunn, 'strong opposition to participation with APODETI in the Macau talks developed in FRETILIN's central committee. It was unthinkable, they argued, to discuss decolonisation with a party committed merely to changing the form of East Timor's colonial status'. Ramos Horta and a number of other FRETILIN leaders evidently supported participation at Macau throughout, but were outvoted in the central committee. When he arrived in Australian in June, Ramos Horta gave the principal reason for the FRETILIN boycott as the changed position of the Portuguese *vis-a-vis* APODETI. He claimed that FRETILIN's position had not changed, but that of the Portuguese had, even though he personally advocated participation at any cost. It does not seem that FRETILIN had any conscious knowledge of the London Agreement at this stage. The Macau boycott later became a weapon in the hands of the other associations and Indonesian propagandists.

The result of Macau was the announcement of a constitutional law for the ultimate decolonisation of Timor, around the terms discussed in Dili. Governor Lemos Pires was expected to continue to head the Portuguese sector, becoming High Commissioner in the transitional government. Portuguese sovereignty would continue until October 1978.

From this time, events in Timor moved quickly. UDT followers arrived armed at a demonstration to farewell their delegation to Macau. In response, FRETILIN supporters stoned the trucks carrying them as they drove through Dili streets. The Timorese also felt insecure becasue they believed a political split to be apparent in the Portuguese administration, between Majors Jonatas and Mota on the one hand and Governor Lemos Pires, Major Barrento and Major Coelho on the other, although the Portuguese have since vigorously denied this. Rumours of an impending coup were rife. MFA officers reported that in this period they were approached by both UDT and FRETILIN leaders claiming that the other side was planning a coup. According to Major Barrento, UDT claimed FRETILIN had two secret military training camps, one near Baucau, at Bucóli, the other near Aileu. The Decolonisation Commission raised this question with FRETILIN, who invited a representative to inspect the camps. Major Mota travelled to both the centres and confirmed that they were agricultural and literacy camps, with no evidence of military training. He reported, instead, that he felt they were 'doing a very good job' there:

> working beside the peasants and at night they would have political discussions ... They were using the method of that Brazilian Paulo Freire. One does not have to be a Communist to say that if we are to educate these people and increase their literacy, the most capable people must work near the people. UDT does not do this. I have talked to many UDT people and have said this to them. They agreed, but they are *funcionalismos*, [public servants], they are officials, and if they go and live in the mountains to work, they will lose their jobs.[28]

It has also been claimed that FRETILIN approached the police unit in Dili at this time with the idea of a coup, but administration officers once again said they found no evidence of any such plans. The only irregularities they reported were that FRETILIN was 'exerting its influence' in some areas—at Aileu they were reportedly stopping and checking vehicles passing through, asking to see FRETILIN membership cards.

Something, on the other hand, was afoot with UDT. In late July two UDT leaders travelled to Jakarta; several days after their departure, João Carrascalão was summoned to join them. Barrento spoke to Carrascalão on his return:

> I gained the impression that he had been deeply influenced by

> what he had been told in Indonesia ... He mentioned Ali Murtopo in conversation ... He told me they [UDT] were convinced there would be no independence for East Timor under FRETILIN and they were doubtful there would be independence even under UDT. Perhaps this was important for the action they took. They were very conscious of ... the need not to offend Indonesia. Carrascalão was also convinced that a Communist-influenced East Timor could not survive next to Indonesia.

He did not have the same success in talking with Lopes da Cruz:

> With me he kept his mouth shut and maintained the face of an angel. João Carrascalão was open, but with Lopes da Cruz I never knew what was in his mind.[29]

UDT were not the only party involved in the conspiracies and frictions of July. The splinter group KOTA was also planning to take power. While the other parties 'made noises with microphones, flags and demonstrations', KOTA worked in its own style of intrigue and superstition. With the aid of six machineguns stolen from the army by a supporter, they hoped to lure the leaders of UDT and FRETILIN to a common meeting in order to arrest them. The ruse failed but the planners instead took an oath in the *uma lulik* on the outskirts of Dili that if certain nominated people ever came to power in East Timor, they would assassinate them: 'at the same time, the same hour, the same second, in different places, we will make justice, from our ancestors'.[30]

In late July Bishop Ribeiro allegedly summoned UDT and KOTA leaders and informed them that the Portuguese had 'allowed 26 or 28 North Vietnamese through Macau and Darwin as merchants ... but they are terrorists. These Communists from Vietnam are already in our land', supposedly to give military training to FRETILIN. According to this account the Bishop urged the leaders, as Catholics, to accept his word for this and to 'take action'.[31] The 'Vietnam terrorist' story was circulating in the Indonesian press and appears to have emanated from Jakarta.

On 6 August the UDT leaders returned from Jakarta. In the preceding weeks, FRETILIN leaders had been attempting to contact Ramos Horta, who was still in Australia, urging his immediate return. Xavier had just returned from Mozambique.

He did not report to the Governor on his return, as was the custom, but according to the MFA, the speech he made on arrival was 'very moderate'.

On the weekend of 9 and 10 August UDT staged a series of anti-Communist demonstrations of mounting intensity. They demanded the arrest and expulsion of five Portuguese, including Cristóvão Santos and Majors Jonatas and Mota as 'Communists'. They did not attack the Timorese students who had previously been the focus, perhaps in the hope that by directing the charge against Portuguese, they would win the support of APODETI. Already in the interior FRETILIN delegates were being arrested, and in some cases, killed.

On Monday 11 August the people of Dili awoke to find the streets lined with armed UDT members forbidding them to leave their homes. On that morning Australians switched on their radios to the headlines: 'There has been a coup in Portuguese Timor'. Ramos Horta, in Darwin, was booked on the next TAA flight to Baucau.

4

"Empty Colonial Songs..."[1]

Soon after 11pm on 10 August, Isabel Lobato and her sister Olímpia hastily gathered together a few belongings and with other members of their family including Isabel's baby son José began to climb the mountains behind Dili. They were part of a general exodus of FRETILIN leaders and their families from the capital.

At 9pm FRETILIN had received word of the UDT coup plans, which Rogério Lobato then conveyed to the Portuguese authorities. The Portuguese attitude was one of disbelief, but at 11pm the police chief, Lieutenant-Colonel Rui Alberto Maggiolo Gouveia, passed the same news to the Governor who then informed the military command and ordered security measures to be taken in the barracks.[2]

At 1am on the 11th, UDT moved. The night before, according to João Carrascalão, they invited Maggiolo Gouveia to their headquarters. On his arrival they arrested him, holding him hostage while a delegate went to the police barracks to inform the unit that their commander would be killed if they didn't declare their support for UDT's planned coup. 'After explaining our intention, 90 per cent joined our cause', Carrascalão claimed in a letter to Darwin's *Northern Territory News* a week later. There is some doubt whether the police chief was quite as unwilling a participant as characterised. According to his peers, he feared return to Portugal because he was politically identified with the old order. Whatever the case, by this means the UDT leadership had access to arms and the support of the police unit which they then used to take control of strategic points of the capital: the water station, the airport, the two main crossroads and the Marconi communications centre in the town square. The police unit also encircled the central military barracks in Taibesse, although they allowed traffic to move in and out. Seven of the UDT leaders, including Mousinho, left for Baucau, one left for Suai and Mário Carrascalão went to the Same district.

After they controlled the Marconi centre, UDT cabled Australia, to the 'base comander', Darwin. (Whether 'base commander' referred to the Australian military or the responsible telecommunications official is unclear.) 'Situation very bad for us in Timor. Emergency exists. Communist Portuguese Army officers attempting to massacre the population to make them surrender. Request immediate help. We need help in Dili. Request base commander also contact Guam.' This was the first of a series of messages. It was signed by Lopes da Cruz. An addendum informed Darwin that the person doing the communicating was Australian pilot Roger Ruddock, 'because of his English language'. Ruddock was a pilot with Transportes Aéreos Timor (TAT), the domestic East Timor airline.

One FRETILIN leader didn't go to the mountains. Despite the obvious danger to his life, Rogério Lobato stayed in Dili that night, but did not sleep in his own bed.

When the coup began the military chief of staff, Major Barrento, informed the Governor who immediately convened the Decolonisation Commission. The Commission consisted of Governor Lemos Pires, military commander Lieutenant-Colonel Magalhães, Majors Barrento, Coelho, Mota and Jonatas and three MFA officers elected by the military. They agreed on three principles in their approach to the situation: to avoid bloodshed at any cost, to try to get UDT and FRETILIN to talk, and that they 'couldn't support the position of UDT in trying to eliminate FRETILIN leaders'. Entailed in the first principle was the intention to avoid 'putting Europeans against Timorese, or putting Timorese against Timorese on party lines'.

This consensus was conveyed to João Carrascalão and at 4.30 am the Commission made its first contact with FRETILIN, asking Fernando Carmo to attempt to reach the leadership to organise talks. Carmo was not on the Central Committee of FRETILIN and although he was regarded by both the Portuguese and UDT as a FRETILIN man, the leadership were a little unsure of his loyalty at this time. He had been editor of *A Voz de Timor* before the coup and in his coverage of the Macau talks had been publicly critical of FRETILIN for their absence. The Portuguese were aware of his political influence in the army and that the position he took as a moderate nationalist would be a guide to the rank and file Timorese soldiers. According to the Portuguese, they contacted Rogério Lobato later in the morning and also requested him to make contact with the leadership, in particular with Nicolau. Rogério, however, replied that he had been tricked by Governor Lemos Pires, who was having secret dealings with João Carrascalão.

At 8am Carmo returned to the Portuguese with a list of FRETILIN people contacted. They were all secondary figures, so the Portuguese again went to Lobato. Next morning, the twelfth, he returned with a reply—fifteen conditions FRETILIN demanded as preliminaries for negotiation. The most important of these were that UDT be disarmed, retire from its positions and cease 'provocative demonstrations, disorders and murders'; that Timorese soldiers from the Dili garrison resume control of the city; that communications with the outside world be re-opened, with access for all parties; that the Portuguese paratroopers be used only for the Governor's personal protection and that of the Portuguese authorities in Dili; that prisoners taken by UDT be released; that safe conduct be guaranteed for all FRETILIN negotiators, including a Timorese military escort; and that negotiations be conducted only through the Governor, as the representative of Portugal. A further condition was that FRETILIN must be able to check that all demands had been carried out before their representatives sit with the Portuguese.

Meanwhile, the situation in Dili remained outwardly quiescent. Only a little shooting had taken place on the night of the tenth, with two or three deaths. UDT troops, sometimes hardly more than children, patrolled the streets forbidding people to leave their homes. In Australia, the nearest communications link, there was almost no information on the situation although Lopes da Cruz's cables were being monitored in Darwin and passed on to government officials in Canberra. On the twelfth the *Macdili*, a small merchant ship then in Dili harbour, left with families of the Portuguese garrison, some Chinese and the few tourists who were in the territory. They had been rounded up by Portuguese paratroopers and advised to leave for their own safety. The first public information on the situation in Dili apart from news that the coup had occurred came with *Macdili*'s arrival in Darwin. Some of the tourist witnesses told of being woken by gunfire at about 4.30am on the 11th:

> In the morning there was a complete curfew ... We were not allowed out on the street. The only people who could move around were Timorese with special UDT badges. There were men with rifles all around the administration buildings. All day long trucks with boys of only 12 or 13 carrying rifles were driving through the streets. They were UDT people ...[3]

Unknown to those on board the *Macdili*, UDT had threatened to mortar the embarkation area. On 11 August they re-presented the demand for the expulsion of Majors Jonatas and Mota. The Governor refused, saying he would not bow to pressure, to which UDT replied that if he didn't agree they would bomb the wharf area where the families of the Portuguese administration were boarding the *Macdili*.

The accusations against, and the demand to expel, the two officers were repeated insistently in Lopes da Cruz's communications to Australia. One of the several 11 August messages read: 'Today the Communists commanded by Majors Mota and Jonatas and by all the Communist officers are trying to make a counter-revolution to deliver Timor to the Marxist FRETILIN'.

On 13 August the messages reflected a slightly changed situation. The first reverberations of the UDT coup were being felt. Word had arrived in the capital that the Lospalos military company under a Portuguese officer, Captain Lino, had declared for UDT and was marching on Dili. In Dili Maggiolo Gouveia also declared himself openly UDT. UDT forces from Baucau were reported to have marched on the FRETILIN camp at Bucóli and arrested FRETILIN cadres including Vicente Sa'he, regarded by them as one of the more notorious FRETILIN 'leftists'. They were now said to be marching on to Vemasse and Laleia. It was also the day marked for Indonesian independence day celebrations in Dili and on the Portuguese account an APODETI demonstration outside the consulate drew 6–700 people. A press statement cabled to Darwin publicised UDT demands presented to the Portuguese government at 7.30

that morning:

> To get rid of the Communists in Timor, including the immediate departure of some members of the Government Cabinet insistently requested by UDT.
> The immediate departure from Timor of the Communist members of the FRETILIN party ...
> A meeting with the moderate members of FRETILIN to work together to constitute a movement for independence.

Tension mounted throughout the week. The Portuguese, between two sets of demands, appeared increasingly helpless. The systematic arrest by UDT of leading FRETILIN members and supporters was underway: by 15 August around eighty had been detained in Dili. On the 15th an Australian Foreign Affairs official, Dennis Fisher, flew into Dili and reported that the situation was 'uncertain but calm'. Reports of fighting in the interior and firing of village settlements by UDT were trickling in.

In the mountains the Central Committee of FRETILIN proclaimed a state of 'general armed insurrection against the traitors of the homeland and for the genuine liberation of the Maubere people'. The text read:

> Considering that:
> 1. There is a necessity to impede the advance of the reactionary forces, which with the system of terror, are prolonging the system of domination and exploitation of the Maubere people;
> 2. The local Government, with the mounting arrests, is in the position of having looked on at the pillaging, assassinations, rape of women, etc ... and is responsible for the arming (supply of arms, training of forces) of the UDT and permitting also, the reaction and terror which spreads to all corners of our country of East Timor ...
>
> The Central Committee ... proclaims ... at ... 15 hours and 45 minutes on 15 August 1975 a general armed insurrection against all traitors and enemies of the people ...[4]

One reason the Portuguese offered for their inaction was that they awaited the arrival of officials from the Lisbon government, which had been notified of the coup immediately it happened. A peace-keeping mission left Lisbon soon afterwards bound for Timor. Its failure to arrive in this important period was almost entirely due to Indonesian obstruction.

The principal mediator, Major António Soares, arrived in Jakarta on 14 August, without a visa. The Indonesians granted him a special three-day permit and he then set out for Dili via Kupang. On reaching Denpasar, Bali, on the 15th, his way was blocked by immigration officials who held him until his scheduled flight had left. The incident was reported in full because three Australian journalists were on board the same flight, having received permission from Soares to accompany him on the Portuguese government plane into Dili.[5] When they arrived in Kupang on 15 August they waited for the envoy to appear on the following flights. Two flights with empty places arrived, but without Soares. On Sunday 17 August the Portuguese government plane flew into Kupang from Dili. Its pilot carried a letter from Portuguese authorities for the Governor of Indonesian Timor requesting his assistance to expedite the mediator's journey to East Timor. After waiting a day, the pilot returned to Dili with an empty plane. The three journalists' requests to travel back on the flight were agreed to by the pilot but refused by Indonesian authorities. Soares waited in Bali until the seventeenth when he was flatly informed by an Indonesian colonel that he could not travel on. He returned to Jakarta and took a plane back to Europe the next day. Portuguese authorities later called in the Indonesian ambassador to Lisbon and registered a formal protest. The first Lisbon peace-maker to arrive in the area was Dr Almeida Santos who arrived in Darwin on the twentieth, after full-scale fighting had already begun in Dili.

But the most important reason for Portuguese inaction was *apartidarismo*. This policy was a fundamental tenet of the MFA both in Portugal and in the colonies. It asserted that the armed forces must stand above the political process. Their role was conceived as politically neutral, their task in Portugal to prepare the populace for the exercise of democracy after fifty years of fascism and, in the colonies, to prepare the people for genuine decolonisation. Two members of the Decolonisation Commission explained the application of this policy. In an interview in Darwin shortly after the UDT coup, Major Mota said:

> Well, Portugal is decolonising—that means, is tranferring power to the people of Timor. We have no forces in Timor because the process of decolonisation is pacific and we were hopeful that the

> problem of Timor could be solved by pacific means ... In this context ... we have one company only of Portuguese troops ... UDT tried to put the Portuguese government on the side of UDT to fight FRETILIN. The government would never do that, because the new Portugal respects all opinions ...
>
> Of course what's going on in Timor reflects what's going on in Lisbon, but we can say that the Administration in Timor has only one point of view: to respect the population, with no interference. Perhaps certain officers would like to interfere, like Mr Maggiolo and Captain Lino, but we think, and Lisbon thinks, that Portugal has no right to interfere—it's a question for the Timorese people.[6]

Also speaking after the coup, Major Barrento reinforced the neutrality principle:

> I am certain that the Governor had no sympathy with UDT. The Decolonisation Commission was on the side of a new country in Timor. If the people would like to be Indonesian, OK. We told El Tari [The Governor of Indonesian Timor] this very clearly, [but said], that we didn't see much sympathy for APODETI in East Timor ... Portuguese decolonisation stands for new countries in all of our territories, not another colonialist power.

The administration was at pains to deny claims that Jonatas and Mota had actively supported FRETILIN. This impression was perhaps gained, they said, by the fact that Mota was the public face of the Decolonisation Commission and Jonatas deputised in this role when Mota was away. Both Jonatas and Mota had more physical contact with the associations than other members of the Commission and also announced all of the Commission's decisions. They were thus regarded as more political:

> In Timor we all worked as a team, very closely ... and the final decision was with the Governor ... so when UDT said this, it was an accusation against the Governor and against Mota, because Mota was very loyal to the Governor at all times. He would speak out in discussion, but if he had differences, he would always abide by the Governor's decision.

However, there was some displeasure expressed by other members of the Commission over interviews Jonatas and Mota gave in the Lisbon press in early 1975. 'UDT never forgave them for saying that UDT was not a progressive party' Major Barrento continued, 'Jonatas called them bourgeois, but they didn't have the right to say this ... This was very important for the way UDT thought. They were private views they were expressing, which were taken as the views of the administration.'

Although the possibility of private agreements with the UDT or the Indonesians cannot be overruled, especially against the backdrop of the London Agreement, non-intervention rather than direct complicity was nevertheless the administration's greatest crime in FRETILIN and also UDT eyes. Certainly some Portuguese lower in the hierarchy sided with the respective parties, as occurred in Africa, but they did not express the administration's view.

According to Barrento the policy of *apartidarismo* had already been questioned by the Timorese associations which urged instead a policy of 'active neutrality' as practised by the Portuguese in Mozambique. Indeed by the end of 1975, too late for the Timorese, Portuguese MFA people themselves questioned the policy. Expressing the growing sense of failure abroad among MFA officers, they debated whether the MFA had ever existed as a separate force or whether it had merely been the sum total of the party political loyalties of its followers.

FRETILIN anger towards the Portuguese was primarily directed towards their attempts to impose *apartidarismo* on the Timorese soldiers:

> The chief commander proves his part ... by his apparent passivity, when he should vigorously and severely discipline the criminal action of UDT against the population, which is contrary to the position taken by the Lisbon government, which does not recognise the legitimacy of the movement taken by UDT ... [He] has proved his propositions unworkable and has shackled each and every initiative of the armed forces to re-establish peace in our Homeland, gravely altered by UDT.[7]

In the week after 11 August the Portuguese attempted to confine the Timorese soldiers, whom they knew to be overwhelmingly pro-FRETILIN, to barracks and to convince them that they should be 'above' politics. By 18 August, after contacting all the units to determine rank and file attitudes to the coup, the Portuguese were hopeful of achieving a negotiated settlement.

But it was then too late, for the political situation had degenerated considerably. Imprisonment of FRETILIN people continued unabated. On the night of 18 August the FRETILIN headquarters in the suburb of Santa Cruz was sacked by UDT forces led by João Carrascalão and Maggiolo Gouveia. A large armed demonstration marched on the house and arrested the 80–100 FRETILIN people inside. On the eighteenth they also went to the home of Inácio de Moura, a Portuguese named by the 8 August demonstration, and arrested him. Several prisoners were shot in the UDT gaol in this period, including José Sequeira, a popular founding member of FRETILIN. In these days the formation of the Revolutionary Anti-Communist Movement (MACR) was announced, drawn from members of all anti-FRETILIN parties.

FRETILIN bitterness to Portuguese inaction at this time was later expressed by Timorese poet, Francisco Borja da Costa, in a prose poem describing events of the coup:

> Crimes litter the land,
> the people flee
> or are drawn into fractricidal carnage.
> Corpses mount,
> soaking in bloody rivers.
> In the confusion of black smoke
> Timor's skies darken,
> the stench of burning bodies drifts
> from the flaming *palhotas*,
> fired by order of the UDT gangsters.

STILL THE GOVERNOR FOLDS HIS ARMS

On the seventeenth, the Portuguese sent Majors Jonatas and Mota out of Timor. They insisted that the decision did not represent a concession to UDT pressure, but was based on two considerations: firstly, the administration needed to liaise more effectively with Lisbon, in view of the failure of the peace delegation to arrive; and secondly, as their own position was becoming more insecure, they claimed that the safety of Jonatas and Mota could be threatened. As they had to send somebody, they reasoned, it may as well be Jonatas and Mota especially if it would also cool the political situation. Mota was deeply disburbed by the political attacks on him and, according to his peers, wept when he heard of the demand for his expulsion. On his arrival in Darwin he spoke in disillusioned tones of the accusations against him:

> I know Domingos Oliveira a little; he is a strong nationalist, and they are introducing anti-communism as part of a political strategy. Some Portuguese officials like myself and my friend Major Jonatas have been attacked as Communists, but we have good relations with these men and they know we are not involved in Communist activities, but are working for Timor.[8]

His bitterness was not confined to UDT; he claimed that FRETILIN had been consistently unco-operative in the decolonisation process.

If the Portuguese did not regard their departure as a concession, UDT did. 'Yesterday we had a great victory', João Carrascalão wrote in a dispatch sent out the next day to the *Northern Territory News*, 'the two Majors, Mota and Jonatas, were expelled and flown out of Timor.'

Major Mota's helpless tears symbolised the Portuguese position. But was there an alternative? Mota claimed in Darwin that the use of Timorese troops against UDT would have initiated generalised fighting. Although to disarm UDT was clearly a sensitive military operation (in which the Indonesians would probably have claimed that the Timorese were being oppressed anew by white colonialism), the actual military weakness of UDT, revealed in the following week, demonstrated that a wisely-planned police action could have restored order easily. Nor was there anything to suggest that in such an action Timorese troops would have broken discipline, at least in the early days before UDT killings accelerated. Perhaps the most important aspect of *apartidarismo* was the Portuguese resolve not to participate in any armed activity whatsoever in the territories after 25 April 1974. They believed that the firing of one shot in the decolonisation process would signify a new Portuguese involvement in foreign wars.

Because he politically distrusted the Portuguese as well as their capabilities, Rogério Lobato spent his time in the week following the coup not in attempting to persuade FRETILIN to negotiate as requested but in lobbying the army units for their support, in liaison with FRETILIN's Central Committee in the mountains. The FRETILIN position had been put to the Portuguese in the fifteen conditions for negotiation served on them on the morning of the twelfth.

The twenty six year old Rogerio Lobato underwent an experience of intense responsibility and testing in this and following weeks. One of eight Timorese above the rank of sergeant in the Portuguese Army, he was described by Portuguese officers as having 'good discipline, a great leader of men ... he has a good intuition for guerilla war'. He was one of four people chosen for officer training from a list of sixty applicants. As recently as March 1975 he had been an activist in the student movement. Rogério Lobato emerged from the civil war period with a position of respect from his fellow Timorese, military and non-military.

The Portuguese believed he was trying to bring about negotiations. On the fourteenth he returned to Dili after travelling to Aileu at their behest to contact Nicolau, without results. On the seventeenth, one hour after the two Majors departed for Darwin from the UDT-held Dili airport, the Portuguese took Rogério by helicopter to Maubisse with the request to bring Xavier do Amaral back to Dili, a request which they were later to regret. 'This is the last chance to bring Xavier and some of the members of the Committee to the conference table', Major Mota said in Darwin that afternoon. 'Now the soldiers are quiet, yet it is very difficult to get them into the barracks ... But we only need Mr Xavier ... because he is a charismatic figure, symbolic, and we think that if he agrees to sit at the conference table that will be the beginning of peace'.[9]

The next forty eight hours were decisive. The Portuguese left Rogério in Maubisse, where he learnt that Xavier had left shortly before for Aileu. For twenty hours he followed Xavier and his accompanying band through the mountains on foot until he arrived in Aileu in the early hours of the next day.

On 17 August the Central Committee in the mountains announced that it no longer hoped for satisfaction of the fifteen conditions put to the Portuguese. The administration, FRETILIN claimed, had ignored its request that their willingness to negotiate, and the terms, be publicised. And the Portuguese had not contradicted UDT radio claims that FRETILIN had refused to negotiate. Now the Central Committee called on supporters throughout the territory to 'actively collaborate with all elements of the Armed Forces of Timor to safeguard order and peace in our territory'.

The administration's helicopter and its pilot did not return to Dili from Maubisse. By 18 August they were prisoners of FRETILIN. Rogério Lobato had gained the support of the Aileu garrison. The Central Committee announced:

> On the night of 17/18 August 1975, within 24 hours of the return of the people of Aileu, conducted by ... FRETILIN, FRETILIN took charge of the Central Company of Instruction at Aileu, detaining all the forces which did not support the movement, including all the European officers and sergeants ... This position has been taken due to the incapacity of the commander of the company, that is to say, due to the game of UDT and the Governor Lemos Pires in permitting our people to perish, murdered by the troops of UDT ... Certain elements of the government ... trained UDT, at their Centre of Instruction in Dili, with the approval of Governor Lemos Pires ... the situation in Portugal is not favourable for those individuals and they consider our country of East Timor to be their final fortress, because they are all Spinolists, Marcellists, Salazarists and colonialists.

The announcement went on to attack the Portuguese government for 'divisionism':

> The Portuguese government in Timor pursued concrete divisionism in the contact with members who did not belong to the Central Committee, for the formation of a new FRETILIN, in the likeness of the colonialists.[10]

The Portuguese had made a serious mistake in FRETILIN eyes by attempting to deal first through people they regarded as more moderate than others, through Xavier before the Central Committee, and in attempting to treat with Nicolau individually. Once again, the unity of the leadership had been underestimated.

On the nineteenth a long political statement was broadcast through the territory from Aileu. It came from the armed forces—the command at Aileu and the Light Infantry Company No. 10 at Maubisse. This was the first statement from the army as distinct from FRETILIN. The statement began:

> Attention:
> 1. The forces of UDT are armed and covertly have the complicity in this initiative of responsible figures in the Government of Timor.
> 2. The same forces of UDT have practised a criminal action of murder, massacre, burning and robbing the undefended people.

> 3. The armed forces are the strong arm of the undefended people and have to guarantee the order and security of the population and ought never to turn their arms against their own society, that is, the people.

and went on:

> 7. It is urgent to emerge from the situation of doubt, confusion of spirit and unclear politics in which our people and our land find themselves.
> 8. The FRETILIN wanted to arrive at an agreement when it presented 15 conditions for possible discussions with the government ...
> 9. The FRETILIN propositions have never merited any formal reply on the part of the government of Timor, which yet denounces the conclusion that it is with UDT.

On the basis of these considerations, it declared:

> The Armed Forces of the Centre of Instruction at Aileu and the Light Infantry Company No. 10 at Maubisse, in defence of order and security of the lives and well being of the population and the superior interests of our people, breaks with its *apartidarismo*, defining clearly and unequivocally that its position is with FRETILIN for the defence of our people ...[11]

It asserted anew the desirability of negotiations between FRETILIN and UDT but demanded four preconditions, including the disarming of UDT, control of the territory by Timorese military forces, and the transfer of military command from Portuguese to elected Timorese officers and sergeants.

The winning of the Armed Forces in Aileu and the use of the Aileu radio was the key means to the general support of the soldiers. In Dili, Carmo and an NCO called Domingos Ribeiro declared themselves for FRETILIN, with certain provisos, and the support of the Dili garrison seemed close.

Having won Aileu, by the evening of 18/19 August the elusive Rogério was back in Dili, hidden by the soldiers in the central barracks at Taibesse. By the nineteenth he was in full command of the Dili garrison and the struggle began in the streets to wrest control of the city from UDT. On the twentieth he radioed Nicolau and the Central Committee in Aileu:

> The Timorese Armed Forces, united from the DSM, CPM, QG and the ENG., [military] units set out on the streets last night. They were

> directed by Aspirante Lobato and Alves, of the first line, against the UDT. Positive results. Arrested ex-lieut.-Col. [Maggiolo] Gouveia and some other UDT elements surrendered. All the Dili units supported FRETILIN. Unified command was assumed by Timorese personnel. A large number of people went to General Headquarters at Taibesse. This morning the flag of FRETILIN was raised at General Headquarters in Taibesse and 'Foho Ramelau' sung ... Await my orders return to Dili. Palapaço surrendered. Political prisoners freed.[12]

In Third World narratives, events of the capital are often mistakenly regarded as tracing the country's history and, conversely, the influence of rural events on the capital ignored. The outline of the UDT coup in East Timor's countryside is difficult to trace. Generally, it occurred slightly earlier than in Dili and its forms were sometimes complicated.

A good proportion of the FRETILIN leadership, including Xavier (who was in Turiscai) were in the countryside in August carrying out the 'revolutionary brigades' policy. The coup took many of these cadres by surprise, in some cases at the cost of their lives. Where possible the news was telephoned or carried to them by other FRETILIN members but because it happened in certain parts before the action in Dili, there was sometimes no chance for warning.

Rui Fernandes was a Dili schoolteacher in August 1975 and a FRETILIN Central Committee member. He went to Hatolia on 7 August to visit relatives. When he arrived local UDT officials came to the house where he was staying, arrested him at gunpoint and gaoled him:

> Almost all of the Hatolia activists of FRETILIN, maybe 10 or 12 people, were arrested and they forced the others, the Maubere, to take guns and fight FRETILIN in Aileu and Ermera. One of our delegates, Gaspar, was killed. We were both in the same room. In the night they took him out and I didn't know where they took him. Only a week afterwards, they told me he was killed, shot ... I was not treated well by them there ... I only ate every two days, sometimes only coffee or tea and bread, without anything with it. I was there for 21 days, from August 9 ... if FALINTIL hadn't come near to us, I think they would kill me too'.

'Did they beat you?' 'They didn't, because the UDT delegate there was a *mestiço* and his children were my pupils ... When I went there [Hatolia] they said "Oh, he is our teacher"'. There was no fighting in Hatolia itself. When FALINTIL came to the area on August 30, the UDT ran before them, but in the early days of the coup they had burnt houses, and there was some fighting in the surrounding bush. 'I came from Dili with a boy and afterwards, when UDT ran away, [the villagers] told me that the boy was killed by them and his body eaten by the cows'.[13]

Rui's story was characteristic of accounts of the coup in the countryside. The usual pattern was that houses were burnt by local UDT people and FRETILIN supporters gaoled. Most village centres suffered one or two dead, sometimes up to a dozen, either in the initial UDT attacks or in the fighting that followed FRETILIN retaliation. There were some instances of atrocities including the murder of eleven FRETILIN militants engaged in literacy work near Alas. A message warning of the coup failed to reach them. They were arrested and taken to the gaol at Same, which was crammed with FRETILIN supporters. Over a week later, as FALINTIL advanced they were taken from the prison and in early September their trussed bodies were found on a south coast beach near the hamlet of Bi Susu. They had been bound in pairs, shot and then run through with traditional catana knives. Four of the victims were leaders of UNETIM, the national student organisation and included the president, Domingos Lobato, younger brother of Nicolau and Rogério.[14]

The Same prison was allegedly also the scene of a mass execution. In early September an Australian press party travelling to Maubisse in company with Xavier do Amaral gave transport to a group of people stranded by a road accident. One was a woman who had come from Same. Through an interpreter she said that her husband was one of thirty nine people in the gaol bound together and executed in like fashion.

In the Maubisse area, the fighting following UDT attacks degenerated into the tribal conflict which has constantly blighted Timorese hopes of national unity since Portuguese occupation. The Portuguese knew by 16 August that at least 200 were dead between Maubisse and Turiscai. By the end of August, that figure was multiplied several times. The death toll was originally thought by FRETILIN to be in the several thousands, but by the end of November when electoral rolls had been revised and the situation calmed, the local FRETILIN military commander estimated the final death toll in the whole of this *concelho*, of Ainaro, to be around 1,000. In its wake the fighting in this traditionally rebellious zone left acrimony, misery and hundreds of displaced or orphaned children.

In World War II local wars erupted in this area when the Portuguese administration broke down. At least some aspects of the fighting then were simply anti-Portuguese, but fratricidal fighting was also observed. There is too little information to offer reasons for the ferocity of conflict here during times of social disruption. However it is one of the few areas where local *liurais* still retain private armies. It is also a densely populated area of rural poverty.[15]

Soon after the fierce conflict subsided here, the FRETILIN leadership moved to discipline their own forces. A Central Committee edict stated that:

> various FRETILIN delegates in the Maubisse area have taken advantage of the present situation to exact personal vengeance, in the name of FRETILIN, and have been tempted to exploit the people ... They do not contribute to the re-establishment of the unity of our people or assist in the conquest of national liberty for our complete independence.

The crimes listed included the taking of personal vengeance and the use of military weapons to assault, loot and burn houses. Any FRETILIN soldier found guilty of such acts would be immediately disarmed and put to productive labour in the fields and in repairing roads, the statement said.

Caught at Turiscai near the intense Maubisse conflict, FRETILIN president Xavier do Amaral narrowly escaped the UDT net. Taking to mountain tracks, he walked for days through the bush towards Aileu with a band of FRETILIN people. Exchanging his usual Western dress for a traditional *lipa*, he was protected by local people who called him only by his traditional Timorese name. With him on this trek was a twenty one year old Central Committee member Goinxet Bonaparte, who later acted as an interpreter for press parties and was affectionately dubbed 'Gunshot' in deference to lazy Western tongues. The Macau-educated Bonaparte was identified with the student left wing of the front. The bond between the thirty eight year old populist leader and the youthful revolutionary intellectual, expressed in this journey, spanned the political poles of East Timorese nationalism. They arrived in Aileu as FRETILIN prepared to strike back at UDT.

In the following days Dili exploded. From 20–27 August, after Rogério had won over the Dili garrison, a fierce and bloody battle was waged for control of the capital.

Having won Taibesse, FRETILIN controlled the capital's food, petrol and other supplies. It was the logistic nerve centre. Lobato then captured the Portuguese Army's materiels detachment, the main source of arms and ammunition. Pro-FRETILIN NCOs took over from the Portuguese at gunpoint. On Lobato's account, however, the counterattack did not properly begin until 2 pm on the twentieth, due to the unreadiness of some of the military units.

Between them, FRETILIN and UDT now had the entire Portuguese arsenal and the Timorese personnel of the former colonial army under their control. The active troop strength of the Portuguese Army at this time consisted of 2,500 first line (regular) soldiers and 7,000 second line, mainly conscripts. Beyond this, most Timorese adult males had done thirty months national service training.

UDT forces were drawn from Captain Lino's Lospalos company, the second line troops from Baucau and the Dili police unit, comprising a task force of between 1,500 and 2,000 in all. In Dili they possessed the police unit's arsenal of light arms. From 11 August the heavier armaments from the Lospalos and Baucau companies were ferried to Dili by the Australian pilot Roger Ruddock with the assistance of another Australian, Randall Riseley. Riseley was an adventurer who had come to Timor some months before the coup to work as an engineer for the state-owned Portuguese company SAPT. He was a friend of the Carrascalaõs and may have been involved in the hasty preplanning of the coup.

As a NATO partner, the Portuguese Army was a relatively well equipped light infantry force with a generous supply of the standard G3 automatic rifle, ageing but efficient second world war Mauser rifles, grenades, bazookas, mortars and light infantry pieces. Mercedes-manufactured UNIMOG vehicles provided excellent troop transportation, even over East

Timor's terrain. In the course of the fighting a fleet of new road construction vehicles imported by the Portuguese for work on the Dili-Baucau road was also commandeered for troop transport. Although FRETILIN had a helicopter in their possession at Aileu, they had no-one trained to fly it. The other Portuguese helicopter was under guard by the Governor's paratrooper unit on Dili wharf. UDT however had air power in the form of the TAT de Havilland Dove which was soon to be put to use by Ruddock and Riseley. Neither side had any form of 'naval' transport at this time although FRETILIN later rigged up a former Portuguese fishing boat with a 75mm artillery piece and used it to chase UDT forces down the north coast.

Following the early arrest of Maggiolo Gouveia and the taking of Taibesse, FRETILIN's main task was now to dislodge UDT from their camp at the airport end of town, in the suburb of Palapaço. A number of neutral zones, including the hospital were agreed to, but these agreements were reportedly never very enduring.

The Portuguese sought refuge in two areas proclaimed as neutral zones—the harbour buildings and the Governor's new residence in the Farol suburb. With the force of paratroopers they blocked access to the roads surrounding the residence. They were under the direct authority of the Governor, carried a superior variety of automatic weapons, were apolitical (their brief time in the territory meant they had built no ties with it), and were combat ready. In the early days a few patrols forayed around the capital with messages from the Portuguese, but the practice ceased as fighting intensified.

Although the battle's vortex was located more definitely towards the airport and the harbour in the closing days of the week of 20–27 August, fighting was generalised through Dili from the beginning. Power supply was soon disconnected and in the black tropical night only the flashes of grenades and mortars lit the sky. When fighting began, one FRETILIN Central Committee member, Aleixo Corte Real, sought asylum in the Indonesian embassy, until he was talked into joining the FRETILIN counterattack by his brother-in-law Fernando Carmo. A conservative black nationalist, Corte Real was reported to have capitulated to the Indonesians after the 7 December invasion of Dili.

In the Hotel Dili on the waterfront six Australians sheltered from the battle, although they consistently refused offers of evacuation. This was the hotel of Frank Favaro, a Northern Territorian whose favourite boast was that he introduced fast food and milkshakes to East Timor.

A couple of days after the fighting began, an elderly figure emerged from the Hotel Dili and began to walk unarmed down the main esplanade towards the quarter where the Portuguese took sanctuary. Of unmistakeable military gait, he wore a floppy-brimmed cotton hat with a boomerang insignia on the front, a pair of baggy grey army shorts and a smartly-pressed shirt with a shoestring tie. Behind almost every tree on the esplanade was a sniper. As he approached each tree he stopped and waved his hand in a regal gesture. Proceeding thus and dodging and diving through the crossfire he reached the Portuguese. In many cases the soldiers held their fire while he passed. This was Mr Samuel Kruger, an Australian pensioner who had become well-known to Portuguese and Timorese in Dili during his eighteen months' residence. During the Pacific war he saw active service at Guadalcanal and had since spent his life exploring the islands to Australia's north. Although around the time he made his harbour trek the Australian press was surmising (from the list of Australians still in East Timor) that he was a 'paraplegic', the sixty five year old 'Major' Kruger as he was known to the Portuguese, had recently been in a fistfight in a Portuguese officers' club over an alleged insult to a woman.

From the people in the Hotel Dili, Kruger was nominated to take a message to the Portuguese asking them for their estimation of the situation and what course they proposed. They advised the Australian contingent to get on the nearest boat and leave, advice they were preparing to follow themselves.

As the week progressed the fighting became heavier. Ruddock and Riseley used the de Havilland Dove to fly over Dili dropping mortar shells over FRETILIN positions.

A couple of days after the first excursion, Sam Kruger made a second trip to the harbour. The fire was now predominantly mortar and artillery bombardment. Despite the intensity of conflict there appeared to be no dead or wounded around—he saw no bodies in the streets, although the muzzles of G3s and Mausers protruded from most windows. On his return he hitched a ride in the back of a makeshift ambulance where he crouched with his feet in a wash of blood.

'Major' Kruger was surprised to find that the Portuguese were still at the harbour. They were soon to leave. Since the fighting started they had maintained radio contact with the nearest Portuguese territory, Macau. Describing the situation by this means, the Governor had two vessels diverted to Dili harbour to evacuate the crowds gathered there. On 25 August the *Macdili* and the 9,000 ton freighter *Lloyd Bakke* were in the harbour. They could not berth because the bombardment of the harbour area was too heavy. Instead, refugees from the fighting were ferried onto the vessels by landing barges. By this time fires burned all around Dili.

The loading of the *Lloyd Bakke* began in the afternoon and continued until the early hours of the next day, upon which it sailed for Darwin. The *Macdili* stood off until early on the morning of the twenty seventh.

On 26 August Governor Lemos Pires cabled Macau to say that the administration's position was such that it could remain no longer. By now an Indonesian warship, the *Monginsidi*, was in the harbour, ostensibly to evacuate consular staff. The attack on the harbour during the transfer of refugees was so heavy that the Governor had difficulty restraining the paratroopers, who were threatening to retaliate. They subsequently sent out two patrols—one to the FRETILIN headquarters, the other to the UDT, to threaten intervention if the bombardment of civilians in the harbour area did not cease.

Both leaderships denied culpability and the question of who bombarded the harbour remains a mystery to this day. The fire did not come from the direction of either the FRETILIN or UDT strongholds. Perhaps this was the first manifestation of a third force in Dili politics. From its direction it was surmised that the bombardment could have come from the military police headquarters, situated between the FRETILIN and UDT positions, although when the Dili garrison sided with FRETILIN on the nineteenth this included the MPS.[16]

Another non-combatant ventured into the streets during this period of heavy fighting. Bishop Ribeiro braved the fire to escort nuns to the harbour area for evacuation.

On 26 August the *Lloyd Bakke* arrived in Darwin to expectant crowds of reporters, Red Cross and government officials. This evacuation brought 1,115 refugees of whom 400 were Timorese, the remainder Portuguese and Chinese. The first *Macdili* voyage had brought almost no Timorese and the higher proportion on this voyage was testimony to the heavier fighting. The refugees who came ashore in Darwin brought with them the stock tales of refugees everywhere: of race war, the razing of Dili, the deliberate mutilation of children. The *Sydney Morning Herald* rose to the occasion with a story headed 'Fleeing white children blown up'.

At 3.30am on the twenty seventh the *Macdili* towed landing barges with members of the Portuguese administration aboard to the island of Ataúro, north of Dili. The *Macdili*'s Captain Dagger had earlier acted as an intermediary between the captain of the *Monginsidi* and Governor Lemos Pires. On the twenty fifth the Indonesian captain radioed him and asked him to arrange an interview with the Governor. He claimed that he had come to evacuate the Portuguese administration at their request. He also asked the *Macdili* captain how many Indonesian consular officials and citizens were ashore in Dili and if he knew the location of the consulate. Lemos Pires rejected the Indonesian offer and asked for evacuation to Ataúro by the *Macdili*. After they were safely established on Ataúro the Portuguese requested the *Monginsidi* to withdraw from Portuguese territorial waters.

Soon after the administration's departure a shore party landed from the Indonesian vessel to evacuate the consul. The first Australian press party arrived in time to obtain dramatic photographs of Indonesian paratroopers kneeling on Dili beach with weapons cocked, covering the shore party.

An Australian aid group, the Australian Society for Inter-Country Aid (Timor) ASIAT, with a team from the Channel 9 television corporation, had hired a fishing trawler and embarked from Darwin, ostensibly bound for Bali. They sailed into Dili harbour in the early hours of 29 August under the protection of a Red Cross flag. They were then unaware of who controlled Dili or what sort of reception they would meet.

On board was Dr John Whitehall, a Sydney paediatrician. Whitehall and other ASIAT delegates had been to East Timor earlier in the year and discussed the establishment of a rural

Indonesian paratroopers, Dili beach, August 1975.

health scheme with leaders of the three political associations. Further discussions were conducted with Ramos Horta during his June visit to Australia. ASIAT-supplied medical goods were in the house sacked by UDT on 18 August. Although a non-party organisation, some ASIAT members were associated with the Liberal Party. At various times during its Timor operation, Michael Darby, son of Australian Liberal politican Douglas

Darby was also involved with ASIAT. In the strange confluences of Dili politics, Darby later facilitated the return visit to Dili of two of the March Labor parliamentary delegation, Ken Fry and Arther Gietzelt.

Whitehall recorded in his diary their first view of Dili:

> After two days of chugging across the Arafura Sea we arrived outside Dili harbour at 3 a.m. on Friday the 29th August, to find Dili ringed with fire but obviously darkened itself. Only the lighthouse insisted that Dili was alive ... Blackness of mountain turned to greyness and then dark green as we slowly edged into the harbour at first light. Fire was leaping from a block of houses beyond the waterfront and the steady crackle of gunfire with the deeper explosions of mortars strained our senses as with hesitating slowness we approached the docks. Soldiers could be seen darting from house to house ...[17]

On investigation, the situation in Dili had calmed. UDT forces had fled to Liquiçá and FRETILIN was in full control of the city. Journalist Gerald Stone was accompanied by a television cameraman, Brian Peters. Stone reported:

> All previous reports of fighting in Timor had been filtered through the eyes of frightened and exhausted evacuees or worse, had come dribbling down from Portuguese, Indonesian and Australian officials—all of whom have reason to distrust FRETILIN ... Our drive through Dili quickly revealed how much distortion and exaggeration surrounds this war.
>
> The city has been taking heavy punishment, with many buildings scarred by bullet holes. But all of the main buildings are standing.
>
> A hotel that was reported to have been burned to the ground was there—with its windows shattered out but otherwise intact.
>
> Even the Portuguese flag still flew over government administration buildings. And that, in fact, could be a symbol of FRETILIN's willingness to reopen negotiations with Lisbon.[18]

In Dili hospital John Whitehall set to work operating on battle casualties who had been there for four days without treatment following the evacuation by the Portuguese of their remaining doctor, an army surgeon. Some patients awaited amputations, others suffered the agonies of peritonitis from stomach wounds. Most injuries were the result of mortar and grenade fire.

The day after the ASIAT arrival, an International Red Cross assessment team went into Dili. Chief delegate André Pasquier flew over the countryside in a low-flying aircraft with binoculars trained on the landscape. Fires were burning all around Dili and the smoke still curled from the burnt remains of some village settlements. In most villages very few people could be detected. In times of crisis, Timorese have historically 'clung to the mountains', fleeing from officialdom to live close to the land, in caves, in the mountain bush and jungle undergrowth.

Nevertheless, the general devastation had been grossly exaggerated. Speaking of their potential to work from the pre-existing medical system, the Red Cross reported:

> Considering the general situation [in Dili], and the work load at the hospital ... the local staff had coped admirably ... With reference to the hospital and Health Department buildings, it was observed that both institutions had been respected by the combatants and there was no evidence of looting. The staff had continued working during the conflict uninterrupted.[19]

5

Interregnum

In the weeks following the arrival of the ASIAT medical team and the first journalists, FRETILIN forces were engaged in 'mopping-up' operations against UDT.[1]

After FRETILIN gained power in Dili there was a period of tension in UDT–controlled Baucau. Would FRETILIN attempt to take the second town by force? On 31 August António Mota, who had commanded UDT forces there after the departure of Augusto César da Costa Mousinho at the head of the force marching on Dili, arrived in Darwin on an evacuation flight. He expressed apprehension at the possibility of an attack on Baucau. It was soon clear that Baucau would not be contested. In the first days of September a surrender was negotiated between FRETILIN and the UDT forces remaining (apart from those marching on Dili a number of UDT leaders had left for Australia on the RAAF flights which marked the final stage of the Australian-sponsored evacuations). Mousinho was captured in a goatpen on the Baucau–Dili road after he sent a surrender note carried by a priest to FRETILIN leaders. On his capture, the former mayor of Dili was transported back to the capital; he arrived severely beaten and suffering from concussion. Placed under guard in the Dili hospital, he remained there until the Indonesian attack on Dili in December 1975.

On 11 September two planeloads of press representatives flew from Darwin to Dili on a forty eight hour visit. Ramos Horta's return on the same flight ended his temporary exile. Peace was clearly re-established in the capital and the whole of the territory to the east and south-east, although a dusk-to-dawn curfew was in force in Dili and until the end of September there was sporadic street shooting during curfew hours. Between Dili and the border town of Batugadé fighting continued as FRETILIN pushed UDT forces towards the border.

On 24 September the majority of the exhausted UDT troops crossed into Indonesian Timor at Batugadé after short-lived fighting at Liquiçá, Maubara, Atabae and Balibó. The crossing signalled the effective end of the civil war in the territory. About 200 UDT supporters who chose not to cross into Indonesian Timor surrendered at Maliana.

Despite their publicised interest in incorporating East Timor, the Indonesians attempted no direct military intervention during the confusion of the civil fighting. There had been the *Monginsidi* incident in Dili harbour. Adam Malik had also pressured the Lisbon government to agree to the entry of Indonesian troops in a police capacity at the height of the fighting, after the breakdown of Portuguese authority, but the Portuguese insisted that the only acceptable peace-keeping force would comprise troops from several regional powers, including Australia.[2] Dunn concludes that Indonesian failure to intervene in this period, when external political circumstances were most favourable for intervention, was largely due to political miscalculation:

> ... it is quite possible that they were acting on a poor intelligence assessment of the abilities of the leaders of [UDT] and the extent of the support they enjoyed. While there is evidence that Indonesia knew about the coup at least 24 hours before it was launched, it seems that the subsequent shape of events took them by surprise ... It is tempting to conclude that Indonesia failed to act, simply because the quick collapse of UDT forces took Jakarta completely by surprise and by the time the Indonesians had decided to invoke the military dimension of 'Operasi Komodo' the civil war, as such, was over. Of course, it is also possible that the Indonesians deliberately waited for the contending forces to wear each other down.[3]

The 900-strong force which crossed into Indonesian Timor on 24 September were mainly UDT, accompanied by a sprinkling of people from KOTA and Trabalhista. Despite press reports to the contrary, APODETI leaders were not among their number, although of the thousands of civilians who crossed the border during the whole of the civil war period to escape the fighting, there were no doubt APODETI supporters. In the course of events from 25 April 1974 to the end of the civil fighting in East Timor in 1975, APODETI forces did not generally fight alongside

UDT. In some cases they fought against them, with FRETILIN; in others they were neutral.[4]

The only significant APODETI figure to cross into Indonesian Timor in this period was Guilherme Maria Gonçalves, the *liurai* of Atsabe. On 12 September he was plucked over the border by an Indonesian helicopter assigned to rescue him after the FRETILIN victory. An on-the-spot observer commented of the incident: 'If the raja [*liurai*] was dead, APODETI was dead'.[5]

Before 24 September FRETILIN reported some border incursions by Indonesian regular troops. On 14 September raids from Indonesian Timor were conducted in the Bobonaro, Atsabe and Suai regions. An Indonesian corporal captured during this incursion later identified himself to journalists as Corporal Welly of the 315 Battalion of KOSTRAD (the Strategic Reserve Command); his number he gave as 368113. He said that he had travelled from Jakarta to Kupang by plane, and thence by road to the border. He had been inside East Timor five days before his capture on 14 September, part of a task force of three platoons which crossed at various parts of the border. But the turning point for Indonesian intervention in East Timor was 24 September. It was then that 'Operasi Komodo' became a serious military reality, lending historical significance to the border crossing.

Batugadé is the site of an ancient fort which faces on to the Ombai-Wetar Straits. Bamboo houses shaded by coconut palms cluster around the flat expanse of the fort. Before it, traditional canoes tuck into scrub which fringes the white tropical beach. It is one kilometre from the Indonesian border, marked at this point by the Motabiacou river, known here at its estuary as Mota Ain. Between Batugadé and the border is a straight flat track leading to the bridge which crosses Mota Ain into the territory of the Republic of Indonesia. Until this time an Indonesian flag normally flew at one end of the bridge, a Portuguese at the other. Although the track to the crossing runs straight, on either side it is surrounded by the endlessly pleated razorback ridges which typify East Timor's terrain. From the top of these ridges one can look far into Indonesian Timor.

To UDT, the loss of Batugadé would mean they were a discredited force in East Timorese politics, without territorial power. They lost it to FRETILIN on 24 September when

125°

East Timor: the border area.

FRETILIN soldiers entering Batugadé, 24 September 1975 (Bob Hannan).

FRETILIN casualty, Batugadé (Bob Hannan).

FRETILIN casualty, Batugadé (Bob Hannan).

Australian press correspondents observed FRETILIN forces finally secure the town.

In the preceding weeks, as UDT came under increasingly heavy attack, negotiations had begun with Indonesian officials for conditions of entry into Indonesian Timor by the besieged forces. With their supplies running low and with responsibility for feeding a large refugee population, UDT leaders Lopes da Cruz and Captain Lino appealed to Indonesian leaders for food, ammunition and access to Indonesian Timor. In response, two Indonesian officials came to Batugadé—a Colonel Sugiyanto and a BAKIN agent called Louis Taolin. They told UDT leaders they would assist on condition that the UDT forces address a petition to President Suharto appealing for integration with Indonesia. Although most of the Timorese were reluctant to take such a course, described by one as a 'confidence trick', in the face of dwindling options they signed the petition on 7 September and thus obtained access to Indonesian Timor.

Notes from a military diary kept by KOTA leader José Martins tell the story of the final retreat in precise detail:

September 24
6.30—heavy mortar fired by FRETILIN; immediate defence and cover.
7.30—still fighting, 60 and 81mm FRETILIN guns, G3. Big fire. Isolated shots.
7.35—keep positions by all means, open vee, large, total evacuation—crossing the border. Indonesian forces have no force to support us on the other side of Mota Ain.

With the defeated UDT were twenty eight prisoners, twenty three of whom were Portuguese from the Bobonaro garrison arrested by UDT as FRETILIN sympathisers. They had been arrested as they made their way by foot from Bobonaro to the north coast in the hope of being picked up by a Portuguese government barge and re-united with Portuguese authorities on Ataúro. In the whole course of the civil war these were, ironically, the only Portuguese who took action against the coup, attempting to wrest control of the barracks from UDT. Now they crossed the border as prisoners of the Union:

7.35—Portuguese army men cross the border.
8.15—we have wounded; everyone must evacuate. More mortars coming; hold the positions.
9.00—I went to the other side, Indonesia, with Palma Carlos, under fire. The Portuguese are safe. I give cigarette to the captain. I told him to go to Atapupu with the civil columns ...
9.15—we prepare to shoot strongly—mortars, G3 and Mausers. Crazy noise.
9.30—destroyed mortar position at 500 metres from the sea.
10.00—many mortars and bullets inside Indonesia ... Many people run from death. The 23 are o.k. plus five FRETILIN. We release them. Major Viçoso was paralysed under fire, the captain was shouting obscenities. Killed some FRETILIN ... Our camp completely destroyed. I picked up at this hour in our destroyed camp some new cats and some little dogs, just born.

At 3 o'clock in the afternoon, the first signs of Indonesian military involvement appeared:

15.00—Colonel Dading arrived by helicopter. We had an immediate meeting.
18.00—there are already 40 or 50 special commandos from the

Indonesian Army at Mota Ain.
21.30—João Carrascalão, Mau Sako and Indonesian commandos prepare to take action against Batugadé. We progress to Batugadé about 400 metres from the fort.

They joined several thousand refugees who had crossed the border from as early as March 1975 when the *liurai* of Atsabe began his recruiting campaign. These refugees became a political bargaining point for the Indonesian government.

The relatively quick victory of FRETILIN after the retaliation of 20 August gave impetus to the political spirit of nationalism among the general population, but also accentuated certain trends within the leadership of the front.

For all public purposes the leadership of FRETILIN presents a disciplined unity to the world. At the time of their victory in late August, attempts to break its unity had met with assertive statements of common purpose in response to the UDT's anti-Communist demands of 13 August and the Portuguese attempts to deal with sections of, and not the whole, leadership. There was, nevertheless, a discernable shift in power distribution when FRETILIN emerged victorious. At the beginning of 1975 the pro-Western José Ramos Horta and Alarico Fernandes were publicly seen as the key figures in FRETILIN, along with Xavier, and then perhaps Nicolau Lobato. Rogério Lobato was an organiser of UNETIM, the students union, and did not appear a significant figure. After 28 August a group around Nicolau Lobato, including Rogério, came to represent the dominant political trend.

For some months the FRETILIN President Xavier do Amaral had wielded little effective political power. Portuguese administrators noted this decline around May 1975. After the civil war period it was clear that Nicolau was the real spokesperson for the front. Most of the details of the military retaliation appear to have been planned by Rogério and Nicolau. Xavier was sometimes out of touch with the everyday working of FRETILIN decision-making, although his potential political power and the esteem he enjoyed was expressed by the unwieldy corps of enthusiastic young bodyguards who were assigned after the coup to watch his safety at every move.

The ascendancy of the Lobatos, with their limited overseas

experience, stress on self-reliance and the prestige of military victory they carried, rendered the leadership in some ways less accessible to negotiation, a characteristic of mixed value in the coming period. Although the extent of their real political experience was compressed into the months of August and September, with Nicolau shortly before having visited Mozambique as a guest of honour of President Samora Machel, the new leaders perhaps more truly expressed the core of Timorese nationalism, in their blend of the ideas of revolutionary African nationalism, pragmatism and conservative self-reliance.

It did not follow from the dominance of the inward-turning Lobato stream in the front that the left wing of FRETILIN were removed from influence. On the contrary, although the left's past activities had aroused extreme hostility from the conservative urban élite, their popularity in other quarters, stemming from their work in the literacy campaign, was too great to ignore. The common ground of the African influence allowed an accommodation between the two trends. Mari Alkatiri was the spokesperson for the left wing of the front, which was generally younger and emphasised ideological development. Their theoretical sources were primarily the African nationalists —Amílcar Cabral, Samora Machel, Frantz Fanon—but secondarily Marxist works and the Chinese and Indo-Chinese experience.

Despite their reading of Marx, the left did not regard themselves as Marxists but as nationalists who believed they could draw on Marxism and adapt it to nationalist ends.[6] Nicolau Lobato, on the other hand, operated from a solely nationalist framework with the stress on meeting local needs by whatever means necessary, whether socialisation or foreign investment. The platform of the front always included a clause on the necessity of foreign investment after independence, with the proviso that it should serve local interests.

The consequence of the marriage of these two streams was a Timor-isation of the leadership following the coup period, accompanied by an emphasis towards black nationalism rather than social democracy.

Certain concessions had also to be made to Army personnel who had been instrumental in FRETILIN victory, but were not members of the Central Committee. Of these, Hermenegildo Alves, Guido Soares and Fernando Carmo were the most important. Alves had a reputation as a clever strategist, perhaps the real brain behind the FRETILIN success. Although Rogério Lobato was also regarded highly as a military leader, his importance as head of the newly-designated FALINTIL (the armed forces of FRETILIN) was perhaps more political than military. Generally, the drawing of the military men under the FRETILIN umbrella introduced a conservative influence in its political development.

When the fighting stopped in Dili FRETILIN addressed itself to the problem of defining policy to meet the situation. On 16 September the Central Committee met. There was no question at this point of declaring independence. After the meeting the Committee announced that while 'the affairs of East Timor must be decided by the Timorese people within national territory without external pressures', Portugal remained sovereign in its eyes. It called for the Portuguese to return and supervise the decolonisation process. Talks to this end with Portuguese government representatives were requested and Baucau was nominated as the venue, 20 September as the date. This first post-coup statement also called for a joint peacekeeping force of Indonesian and East Timorese troops to patrol the border, 'to avoid any misunderstandings and unnecessary conflicts'.

On their attitude to other powers in the region, FRETILIN underlined anew its non-alignment policy: 'now and in the future, we will strive to promote friendship and co-operation between ourselves and the countries of the region'. Further, they expressed interest in joining ASEAN after independence:

> The Central Committee of FRETILIN considers that ASEAN is a factor of stability and a driving force of regional co-operation. East Timor would greatly benefit from integration into ASEAN after independence.

The eighth point of the statement re-asserted that the front was not opposed to foreign capital. On the contrary:

> The Central Committee of FRETILIN believes that the development of East Timor will depend greatly on foreign capital. We therefore welcome foreign investments provided that the superior interests

of the people of East Timor are safeguarded.[7]

In continuing recognition of Portuguese sovereignty FRETILIN avoided violation of key state institutions. They placed armed guards on the Portuguese bank, the Banco Nacional Ultramarino, and forbade use of the Governor's residence, his official black Mercedes Benz, and the administration building in the city square. They also ordered the Portuguese flag to be flown throughout the territory. Speaking of the FRETILIN policy, Alarico Fernandes told an AAP reporter:

> ... FRETILIN controls East Timor and intends to provide stable civil administration until the Portuguese colonial administration resumes its responsibilities in this territory. FRETILIN has never taken up arms against the legitimate colonial government.[8]

The UDT which crossed the border on 24 September was politically a different party from the UDT which staged the coup in Dili. It has never been a pro-Indonesian party. Now, it ostensibly supported integration. At the time of the coup UDT had declared that it still wanted independence. João Carrascalão claimed:

> We want to be independent, but only when we can see that we can support ourselves ... we definitely want linkage with Portugal, because we need their help.[9]

In other words, he was re-stating the post-September 1974 policy of a tutelage relationship with Portugal over a long transition to independence. In August, after the coup, Lopes da Cruz had been placed under house arrest by the other UDT leaders on the grounds that he was too pro-Indonesian. In Dili itself, of the UDT supporters remaining, some gaoled, others free, there was no expressed support for the integration petition extracted from those who crossed the border, even among the most conservative of UDT supporters. Mousinho in Dili hospital specifically repudiated the policy to the few people he agreed to see.

In Indonesian Timor an Australian journalist managed to speak to the UDT leaders in their newly-occupied headquarters in Atambua. Domingos de Oliveira told him that the Union's position was 'hopeless' and that they had lost the civil war. The interview was given before the integration petition. He complained that the Indonesians were pressing them to sign and he said he was personally opposed to signing.[10]

After the coup the leadership was in any case scattered in three directions. Apart from those who had crossed the border, around one third had gone to Australia as refugees and the remainder were prisoners of FRETILIN in East Timor.

During the fighting of 20–28 August in Dili many APODETI supporters clustered around the compound of the Indonesian consulate and in the grounds of the SOTA Timor emporium which backed on to the compound. In early October FRETILIN arrested and detained all APODETI Praesidium members, and most supporters. Their grounds were twofold: they claimed that APODETI people were using the empty Indonesian consulate to create provocations in the streets at night (indeed, shooting in the streets did generally cease after their detention) and that they were held for their own protection from the local population. It was also apparent that their detention made them potential hostages in the event of Indonesian escalation.

A few leaders, such as Arnaldo dos Reis Araújo, were imprisoned in the Portuguese military prison. The majority, numbering around 150 and including José Osório Soares, were detained under armed guard in the empty Museum building, but under more casual conditions than those under which UDT prisoners were held at the FRETILIN military headquarters at Taibesse and at Aileu and Baucau.

This was the most significant remaining section of APODETI. It was in no position to play a future role in East Timorese politics. The only other APODETI figures, apart from village supporters, were the *liurai* of Atsabe who had been rescued by the Indonesians on 12 September and his son Tomás who had been in Kupang since March training the East Timorese sent over the border by the *liurai*. Tomás was regarded as culturally Indonesian by other leaders of anti-FRETILIN formations.

In the first weeks of October APODETI re-entered the political scene when Tomás brought his force, which had not participated in the civil war, back to the border area, to accompany Indonesian regulars in a planned large-scale attack on East Timor.

Journalists who arrived in Dili in the weeks after the UDT coup regarded the de facto FRETILIN administration with a mixture of bemusement, admiration, cynicism and humour. At the Hotel Turismo where they stayed a Portuguese poet shouted his poems to the night air till the early hours of the mornings and Rita the monkey chattered in the splaying branches of the mango tree. FALINTIL soldiers who looked like black Abbie Hoffmans drank the copious quantities of Mozambican 'Laurentina' beer bequeathed by the Portuguese and juggled grenades across white linen tablecloths. The hotel owner had left, owing several million escudos to the Portuguese administration. Nobody knew who now owned the hotel, but real accounts were paid to a phantom owner. 'Foho Ramelau' and other songs of Timorese nationalism blared into the bar from Radio Maubere, the newly-established radio station. The large, pious Portuguese woman who managed the hotel abused the bar workers about the radio. They grimaced and giggled behind her back but stubbornly persisted.

For one hour each night they tuned to Radio Kupang. In between the Beatles or Tom Jones the voice of Lopes da Cruz or José Martins assured listeners that anti-Communist forces would soon liberate Dili. Frequently they claimed to be in Maubara or Liquiçá. Lights from Indonesian warships sometimes winked in Dili harbour at night. After the anxiety engendered by their first appearances they became part of the unreal scenery.

In the tropical evenings the reporters sat under the mango tree with Rita and spoke of writing Graham Greene novels. After his nightly fill of 'Laurentina' at the Turismo 'Major' Kruger broke the curfew by regular arrangement and weaved home to the Hotel Dili. 'The soldiers ... [look] like a "Dad's Army" of Timorese hippies,' Michael Richardson wrote. 'In the shade of silver-trunked gum trees this incredible collection of long-haired slovenly soldiers [form] into ranks of parade. [I've] never seen an army like this one, not in Vietnam, nor Cambodia, nor Laos nor anywhere else in South-East Asia'.[11]

The *National Times*'s John Edwards also noted the unreal casualness of post-coup Dili:

> 'Even in the midst of war and revolution, it is impossible to resist the indolent charm of Timor ... Dili is such a pleasant place that it

> is difficult to regard the Timorese revolution with proper gravity. Nothing ever happens on time; some incongruously absurd event (like a herd of goats wandering among the guard of honour during the raising of the FRETILIN flag) always spoils the solemnity of great occasions; the army is the least Prussian of military forces and its troops the most amiable; and the central committee of FRETILIN is in age and style not very different from the students' representative council of a major university.

'None the less' he added 'there are plenty of reminders of the awful seriousness of the fighting during August, and of the perilousness of the situation in which this newly independent nation is being born'.[12]

One reminder was the mound in the cemetery at Santa Cruz in which 158 victims of the fighting in Dili lay. A few bodies were buried in a smaller cemetery at the eastern end of town, fifteen were buried in the Chinese cemetery and a number had been burnt in the streets under Red Cross supervision. In all, the death toll in Dili was probably around 300; other estimates have placed it around 500.

The city showed little evidence of war damage. In typical Dili style a number of unexploded mortar shells poked out of the asphalt around the airport and at various points of the city; one had to remember not to trip over them. Many buildings were pockmarked by bullet and mortar fire and there was a good deal of broken glass, but little structural damage to the city proper. On the outskirts, as in most of the villages, some traditional houses had been burnt to the ground.

By the time the journalists arrived the de facto administration had restored essential services to the capital and shops were re-opening; control of prices and currency exchange rates was strictly enforced. Food was rationed and distributed under FRETILIN administration. Stocks of flour in private warehouses were confiscated for a central pool to deal with the food shortage. East Timor normally depended on importation of essential goods from Australia, but since the coup supply had ceased, a situation which was to continue for the three months of FRETILIN administration.

In these first weeks the Central Committee, now an embryo civil administration, was located at Taibesse with the central military command. Early morning crowds queued outside for food rations and for transportation to country centres: the resettlement of village people who had fled before the fighting was a central preoccupation. Civilians came here not only for food supply and transport but also to inquire about imprisoned relatives, for requisition forms and, principally in the case of the Chinese, exit visas. At the same centre, volunteer soldiers drilled daily on the parade ground and departed for the border. Radio communications between the central command and the border zone were maintained from here.

Prisoners were also kept in a gaol compound at Taibesse. They were predominantly UDT, although some were FALINTIL soldiers charged with crimes against the civilian population—looting, murder or rape. In some cases UDT prisoners were direct family members of FRETILIN leaders—the deeply political nature of the differences within the urban élite in the post-colonial era was expressed in family divisions.

All prisoners were divided into two categories: leaders of the coup and 'Maubere followers'. Those in the first category, who were often Portuguese, were kept in cells and in some cases had been beaten, although prisoners were generally well-treated. In this group, Lieutenant-Colonel Maggiolo Gouveia, the former police chief, was now a wretched unshaven figure clutching at his beltless trousers. The 'Maubere followers' were frequently old mountain people. They were kept in a compound and taken out daily on work detail, digging fields or restoring war damaged buildings.

When the press party visited the gaol in early September the 'followers' were delivered a political lecture in rapid Tetum by Xavier do Amaral and Alarico Fernandes. In the pause following the harangue a bent, toothless old man clutching a rosary stepped forward and replied, gesticulating, to the President of FRETILIN. A fast exchange followed. With an ingenuous giggle Xavier turned to the journalists and translated: 'He said that he fought against us because he was fighting the Communists, so I said to him "Where are the Communists? Can you give me a list so that we can find them? What are their names?"'

The hospital presented another reminder of the grim seriousness of the August war. People lay encased in plaster or peppered with gunshot wounds; other faced the future lacking one limb.

In the centre of town, at what used to be a casualty clinic

known as the Banco Urgencia, or just the 'Banco', Swiss delegates from the International Committee of the Red Cross (ICRC) directed the Red Cross relief operation, working with doctors recruited through Australian Red Cross. Under the direction of chief delegate André Pasquier, they administered Dili hospital, ran a daily outpatients clinic at the 'Banco', inspected the condition of prisoners in the FRETILIN gaols and operated a tracing service to link people separated by the civil war, whose relatives might now be in Australia or Indonesian Timor. The ICRC was at Baucau during the surrender and at Maubara. Liquiçá and the villages on the route to the border when FRETILIN forces advanced against UDT. During this last military action they treated war casualties, provided relief for the civilian population, and enforced Geneva Convention conditions for the treatment of prisoners of war.

With the siege of the Hotel Dili ended, Frank Favaro was back in business, although prospects for a boom tourist season were dashed. He had made the decision to sit out the UDT coup in order to protect his property—the Hotel Dili, a coffee and pineapple plantation in the mountains and a light aircraft. He was in Maubisse when the coup broke but had spent most of the time besieged in his waterfront Dili hotel. Now he emerged to greet incoming Australians at the airport, in a Landrover with a large Australian flag aloft, the same flag which had been hoisted and floodlit over the hotel during the time of heaviest fighting. Outside the Hotel Dili a notice posted during the coup, like a Timorese *pomali*, warned: 'This is the property of Frank Antonio Favaro, Australian citizen and representative of the Australian government in Timor'. In the coming months Favaro's brash manner and outspoken conservative opinions, his flights to various parts of the territory and his reluctance to accept the authority of the FRETILIN administration embroiled him in a series of sometimes comical situations which eroded his dogged determination to stay.

That the country was securely under FRETILIN control was demonstrated by the ability to travel throughout the territory without fear of ambush. Only the border area was an exception. The recentness of the civil war was brought home everywhere in these first weeks of September, however, by the road blocks which checked travellers every few kilometres.

Unsleeping peasants with traditional weapons staffed these points, usually marked by bamboo poles pivoted from kerosene drums. With razor sharp reflexes mountain soldiers would leap into the headlights' glare to train bows and arrows or spears through the open window of the vehicle until papers were checked, an unnerving experience heightened by some FRETILIN drivers' habit of braking at the very last minute, when the nose of the jeep nudged the bamboo pole.

Remarking on the extent of popular support, Dunn wrote:

> Whatever the shortcomings of the FRETILIN administration, it clearly enjoyed widespread support from the population, including many hitherto UDT supporters. In October, Australian relief workers visited many parts of Timor, and, without exception, they reported that there was no evidence of hostility towards FRETILIN. Indeed, FRETILIN leaders were welcomed warmly and spontaneously in all main centres by crowds of Timorese. In my long association with Portuguese Timor ... I had never before witnessed such demonstrations of spontaneous warmth and support from the indigenous population. The FRETILIN administration was not without its critics and opponents, but opposition appeared to be confined to expressions of dissatisfaction rather than hostility ... FRETILIN authorities had requisitioned certain goods from Chinese shops, but there was little evidence of looting. The Authorities dealt swiftly and harshly with thieves, hoarders, and occasional offences against the civilian population by FRETILIN soldiers.[13]

Three Australian parliamentarians, two Labor and one Liberal, visited East Timor in early September and echoed Dunn's sentiments. Two of them, Senator Arthur Gietzelt and Ken Fry, were members of the March 1975 delegation. The third was Aboriginal Liberal Senator Neville Bonner, who quickly developed a rapport with the Timorese. At the conclusion of their brief visit the trio issued a mutual statement to the effect that the FRETILIN administration appeared to be a 'responsible and moderate government' with widespread popular support.

Dunn added that for one sector, the Chinese, the war had been a 'profoundly disrupting experience'. Although the loss of life was small, Chinese shops were looted extensively by UDT during the coup. In the villages traditional hostility from the local population surfaced, forcing many to flee to Dili. Although they generally came to terms with the three-month administration, and were assured by FRETILIN that they had a place in Timor, it was clear that their status as a privileged merchant caste had ended. As well, they perhaps had a greater dread and better understanding of the possibility of an Indonesian invasion than most sections of the community.

The revival of economic life was a major problem. With the Portuguese departure had gone the little technical expertise which existed in Timor. With them had also gone the key to the Banco Nacional Ultramarino. As a consequence there was little currency circulating in the territory and the foreign currency which visiting journalists and aid workers used to pay for food and accommodation was welcomed. In mid-October FRETILIN formally opened the offices of an economic commission.

On 28 August, the day of FRETILIN victory in Dili, the Central Committee had met to plan the urgent work of restoring the country to normality. The Popular Organisation of Timorese Women (Organização Popular da Mulher, Timor, OPMT) was formed on that day and allocated the task, to be shared with the Popular Organisation of Timorese Youth (Organização Popular da Juventude Timor, OPJT), of establishing crèches to care for war orphans and feed the displaced. In the process they were to keep the literacy campaign in motion. These crèches, at Turiscai, Maubisse, Baucau and in Dili, were already functioning by the first weeks of September.

As well, three economic commissioners were nominated to plan a structure for economic administration. The three commissioners were José Gonçalves (a son of the *liurai* of Atsabe), Juvenal Inácio and Domingos Ribeiro. The troika principle which applied in their selection was one generally applied to FRETILIN administration in the post-coup period. Gonçalves was not a member of the Central Committee but was nominated to organise the Commission by virtue of his technical skills. Juvenal Inácio represented the Central Committee and Domingos Ribeiro was drawn from the military leadership.

The 11 October opening of the economic commission offices was presided over by Xavier do Amaral and Nicolau Lobato and attended by journalists then in Dili. The Commission for the Control and Supervision of the Economy was to administer nine departments related to the central economy: the Depart-

Nicolau Lobato (armed), Xavier do Amaral (centre) and José Gonçalves (right) arrive for the opening of FRETILIN's Commission for the Control and Supervision of the Economy, Dili, 11 October 1975. (Jill Jolliffe).

ment of the Secretary-General; Department for the Inspection of Banking; Department of Commerce (Internal); Department of Commerce (External); Department of Customs and Port Authority; Department of Military Maintenance—Supply; the Border Authority; Department of Fuel Supply; and finally, perhaps the department which would most express the shape of the new Timor, Department of Information for Agricultural and Consumer Co-operatives.

When the commission opened, some of the offices were no more than empty rooms with a desk, a typewriter, a chair and the designation of the department on a sign outside. By the end of the next week some fifty people were in full-time employment there and the daily queues outside Taibesse for food, fuel and transport allocations had switched to this downtown office. The de facto public service's workforce expanded steadily in the period thereafter although the workers had to content themselves with employment without wages. The only rewards they received for their service were priority in food rationing, the right to requisition essential goods and authorisation of credit for other goods. The commission occupied offices formerly used by the Commercial, Agricultural and Industrial Association of Timor. Next door stood the deserted offices of the former administration. The Portuguese flag still hung at the mast.

On 8 October Batugadé fell. Several hundred Indonesian troops supported by artillery, naval and air bombardment retook the town, forcing a FRETILIN retreat. Initial reports of the attack by FRETILIN claimed that jet aircraft were used, but later reports revealed that this first aerial attack on East Timor since the second world war was inflicted by one of the vintage B26 bombers in the Indonesian arsenal.[14] The artillery-mounted boat which had provided offshore support for FRETILIN during the UDT retreat was present during the attack on Batugadé. Now renamed the *Mau Bulac*, meaning 'crazy man' in Tetum, the seven-metre timber boat and its crew survived the attack. The captain and his crew hid under the boat's tarpaulins as the Indonesian aircraft zoomed in over Batugadé to drop its payload.

Two days after the town fell, a light aircraft wheeled over the glistening Fatocama beach and levelled itself to land at Dili airport, at the other end of town. After nearly an hour's flight along the mountainous spine of the island, the capital appeared as an abrupt break in the mountain chain. Greg Shackleton, Gary Cunningham and Tony Stewart saw below them a flat sunny settlement of whitewashed buildings fringed by suburbs of traditional bamboo houses. Pigs, goats and small ponies could be seen moving around the ground and as the plane bumped down on the dirt runway some people on tracks adjoining the airport stopped and waved.

When they landed, the journalist, cameraman and sound technician from Melbourne's Channel 7 television network presented their credentials to the FRETILIN administration, shot some film around town for dispatch on the plane's return flight and booked in to the Hotel Turismo. There they ate a hurried meal, and without waiting to unpack their bags, left within five hours of their arrival for the border.

Forty eight hours later two members of a rival television corporation arrived. Journalist Macolm Rennie came with Brian Peters (the first cameraman into Dili after the coup). Although they were also in a hurry to leave Dili, Brian Peters first went to Alarico Fernandes's home to renew their acquaintance. It was Sunday, when Timorese swim and fish in Dili harbour, and before leaving for the war zone they strolled along the foreshore watching the nets being hauled in.

In the early hours of the next morning four Portuguese television reporters followed the Australian crews to the border. This was their second excursion. On the road they passed an Australian Broadcasting Commission television crew and an Australian Associated Press journalist on their way back to Dili.

By the time the Portuguese and Australian television crews were established on the border there was another influx from Australia. Four people comprising a task force from the Australian Council for Overseas Aid (ACFOA), including Jim Dunn, the former consul, flew into Dili on 16 October.

Late that night Nicolau Lobato asked them, and all journalists still in Dili, to come to the Marconi communications centre. There, he announced the grim news of a massive attack on the territory. Seven soldiers had escaped from Balibó on foot and run to Atabae with the story. From there, they had driven to Dili. They told of an attack on Maliana and Balibó in which Balibó was razed by shelling from Indonesian warships and heavy artillery bombardment from Indonesian Timor. The soldiers had last seen all the television crews in Balibó. Their fate was not known.

6

Balibó and Beyond

Until the fall of Balibó the FRETILIN border defence was characterised by the same casualness which affected life in Dili. In the newly-created FALINTIL there were no ranks, only soldiers and commanders. The latter were drawn from the small pool of Timorese who had undergone officer training with the Portuguese, particularly those who had trained overseas. In those early September days commanders argued with soldiers over their casual approach to border defence.

FALINTIL was by any standards a democratically disciplined army, although its appearance belied its actual efficiency. One reporter described it thus:

> [It had] a core of hard professional soldiers, an outer layer of sinewy Timorese jungle fighters, most of whom prefer working with bolt action Mauser rifles, and a mass of keen volunteers who had been in uniform for six weeks at the most. The professionals identify themselves by the way they move in the field. So do the newcomers, who survive in action more through the lack of an effective opposition than their own efforts at self preservation. Yet the army wins actions ... [1]

Weapons were frequently handled in cavalier fashion. If the tension press parties experienced in journeying to the war zone was great, it did not stem only from an anticipated Indonesian presence. The FALINTIL men were known to slumber over cocked rifles, muzzles swaying at dangerous angles; hand grenades rolling around dashboards mesmerised civilian passengers. One party reported driving over a live grenade.

The seriousness of the border situation was nevertheless soon understood. From a traditional and then a legal division which had altered in detail but not in essence over the past century, it overnight became a sensitive international concern. In the past, families had crossed with comparative ease, legally or illegally, to visit relatives or trade at neighbouring markets. At most a 'border incident' might arise from a foray into the adjoining territory to settle a local dispute.

Ramos Horta with his developed sense of international relations moved quickly to warn soldiers at the border of the new situation. 'Indonesia is trying to get an excuse to move into our territory', he claimed in early October, 'We have instructed our troops not to fire on Indonesian territory and not to cross the border under any circumstances'.[2]

The Indonesian government had already complained of trespass during the final routing of UDT on 24 September:

> Reports reaching here from Jakarta say FRETILIN killed people on the Indonesian side of the border, while FRETILIN says two of its troops were killed when heavy weapon fire was directed at FRETILIN positions in East Timor from the Indonesian side of the border.

'Our military action was directed solely against ... UDT which on August 11 attempted to usurp the legitimate authority of the Portuguese colonial administration in East Timor', Rogério Lobato replied, 'FRETILIN forces at Batugadé behaved in a restrained manner and did not violate Indonesian sovereign territory'.[3] It was urgent that those fighting at the border see themselves in a national setting; a village view of the border was now dangerous.

The news from Balibó had a dramatically sobering effect. On the morning of 17 October Taibesse was astir with tense activity. New detachments of volunteers assembled on the parade ground to be briefed and quickly packed into convoys for the border.

The press corps at the Turismo did not know who exactly comprised the crews caught at the border. It was 'normal' for at least one group to be down there at a time. An extract from the hotel register revealed that the missing nine were Brian Peters, Malcolm Rennie, Gary Cunningham, Tony Stewart, Greg Shackleton, Adelino Gomes, Jorge Teofilo, Herlander José Mendes and Manuel Patrício. The first two were from Sydney, three were from Melbourne and the latter four were from the Portuguese government television network.

The four Portuguese had worked in Angola and Mozam-

New Zealand television crew reporting border war, Batugadé, 27 September 1975 (Jill Jolliffe).

bique during the anti-colonial wars and Adelino Gomes became well-known in Lisbon through his reporting of the 'flower revolution'. A tall beanpole of a man with a bald pate fringed with shoulder-length hair, Gomes was the opposite in appearance to the lightman, who was short and rotund. This team had a natural advantage over the Australians: apart from their war experience, they shared a common language with the local population. Of the two Australian teams only Gary Cunningham who had been briefly in Vietnam, and Brian Peters who knew some tense moments in East Timor's interior during his early trip, had any military experience.

That afternoon the first slender news of their fate reached

Dili. A FRETILIN Central Committee member who had accompanied the Portuguese to the border arrived in the capital. Mau Kruma reported that they were in Maliana, not Balibó, when the attack occurred the previous day, Thursday. They had gone there after calling in to Balibó on the Wednesday afternoon, when they spoke to the Channel 7 and Channel 9 reporters. Kruma said they saw the Australian crews at about 2 pm on the Wednesday and left them at about 3.30 pm. They were in good spirits, he said, and asked the Portuguese if they had any beer or wine. They said they intended to stay in Balibó 'a few more days to film some action', including the anticipated recapture of Batugadé by FRETILIN forces. The Portuguese decided to go to Maliana because they thought they would get better footage there.

When the attack began in Maliana, Mau Kruma and the Portuguese attempted to reach Atabae by car, but found themselves encircled and forced to return. From Maliana, they then set out on foot for Cailaco, fifteen kilometres away. But the reporters decided to turn back to Maliana, where they sheltered in a mission building with a priest. Mau Kruma said he urged them to continue to Cailaco with him but they were reluctant to abandon their equipment. The area came under heavy fire soon after.

With hope of finding any of the reporters alive rapidly receding, the Portuguese crew arrived unexpectedly in Dili on the eighteenth. When the bombardment became intense they had asked the priest to direct them to an escape route. He showed them to a track which led over the razorback Cailaco, the mountain theatre of ancient anti-Portuguese wars. Word was passed by FRETILIN that the Portuguese were friends and in every hamlet they passed through, mountain people stood waiting with food and water. By some misunderstanding they believed the reporters to be 'Portuguese tourists' at large on the mountain. Timorese assisted with their equipment, although they had been forced to abandon some of it back at the mission. For forty hours they trekked over the mountain, away from the Indonesian attack. On the slopes of Cailaco they counted the headlights of an Indonesian convoy passing between Maliana and Balibó. They counted between thirty and forty headlights. FRETILIN commanders claimed that at least 100 vehicles had crossed the border. The Portuguese observation was consistent with this: 'When we saw the lights of streams of cars passing between Balibó and Maliana on Thursday night we believed that Indonesia must be invading East Timor', Adelino Gomes commented later. They finally arrived exhausted, sunburnt and blistered, at Atsabe. Adelino Gomes and the rotund lightman collapsed before reaching the village and had to proceed on the last leg laid over Timorese *kudas*.

They came back to Dili with film showing an Indonesian helicopter landing in the centre of Maliana, and their last sight of the Australian crews at Balibó. The film showed the five drinking beer in the Balibó town square, sitting shirtless in locally-made chairs outside the Chinese shop which was one of two houses used to accommodate press crews en route to the front.

Adelino Gomes reported:

> They asked me if I thought there would be any fighting there which they could film. I said I thought so because UDT and Indonesian forces might move in there in the next few days because the rain was setting in. They were happy at the prospect of getting some film and would not leave because this was what they had come for.[4]

That night an armed guard was placed around the Hotel Turismo lest the precious evidence in the film should become a focus for attack. The next day the Portuguese flew out, carrying it by hand to Lisbon.

There was also an armed guard ringing the neighbouring Hotel Dili that night. It was an expression of FRETILIN displeasure with Frank Favaro. For the second time unscheduled guests had arrived in Dili without notice to FRETILIN authorities. Three people flew in that day in a light aircraft. They declared ignorance of the war and remained at Favaro's Hotel Dili for a few days before continuing on their travels. They and a red-haired Canadian hippy who arrived for a holiday constituted the backbone of FRETILIN's tourist industry in their three months of administration.

Nothing more was heard of the Australian crews until 20 October. Then, Radio Australia reported that the Jakarta daily *Kompas* had published an interview with Lopes da Cruz, taken

Television reporter Greg Shackleton painting 'Australia' sign on house in Balibó, Tuesday 14 October 1975—two days before his death. (From television film). *Courtesy of HSV7, Melbourne.*

in Batugadé on 17 October. In it he said that the bodies of four Europeans had been found with eleven others in a shop in Balibó. Near the bodies was a sign saying 'Australia' and a drawing of the Australian flag. Da Cruz later denied to Australian officials that he had given the interview.

On hearing the news in Dili, the Portuguese reporters recalled the 'Australia' sign. They said the letters on the sign were at least a foot high. The Australians had joked, they said, about Balibó's 'Australian embassy'. As some of the crew members were of English and New Zealand origin they discussed writing the words 'Commonwealth Secretariat' under the sign (Gary

Cunningham was a New Zealander, Brian Peters and Malcolm Rennie travelled on British passports.)

Balibó in more peaceful times was a pretty little hamlet set on a rocky crag. From its highest points it overlooks the coast. Vermilion flame trees offset stucco Portuguese villas. Really the town is little more than a junction—houses do not extend far beyond the edges of the town square where three roads intersect, one to Nunura and Maliana (and thence Dili), another to Batugadé, the third to Cová. Above the town an old fort provides a coastal watchtower. In the past Balibó's main significance was strategic and administrative. Its junctional location made it a *posto* town and the site of a regional market, its geography a strategic defence point. Now, in October 1975 war had faded its past charm. The civilian population had fled as FRETILIN chased UDT towards the border and the town had a derelict appearance. One of the journalists wrote in his notebook: 'The buildings are deserted, dirty, strewn with rubbish, and rent with holes or smashed windows'. Piles of excrement fringed the town square where the soldiers had relieved themselves at will.

The house with the 'Australia' sign was the last on the fork of the road to Batugadé, that is, the first from Batugadé as one walked into Balibó. There, a fire burnt constantly in the courtyard, which was strewn with forty-four gallon drums. In the early hours of the morning Timorese crouched over the fire discussing the war and preparing breakfast for the troops. These were the only civilians remaining in the town. Further back in the town square was the other house used as a base by passing press crews. Like the corner house it was in actuality a Chinese shop. It faced on to the town square: it was here that the Australians sat and drank on the Wednesday afternoon when filmed by the Portuguese.

On 20 October Timorese in Dili reported hearing a broadcast from Radio Kupang quoting Lopes da Cruz as saying the Australians were Communists who were 'integrated' with FRETILIN forces and deserved to be killed. As a result, on the night of 21 October Radio Kupang was monitored and a similar statement recorded. In the garbled rhetoric of the Revolutionary Anti-Communist Movement it read:

> The forces who are fighting against the Communists are from UDT,

PAUL GAMA

Dili

Indon prisoner

UDT prisoners

Teacher - Francisco Xavier Amaral, Pres

Atauro garrison — Gov. Lemos Pires

Fretilin political

Fretilin left - Caravena, Pena

Darwin

Rebuilding

- Mayor DR Ella Stack

Thurs Left Melb 7 am - arrived Darwin 2pm - refused permission to leave -

Fri Left Darwin 8.30am - arrived Dili 11am - pics at airport, in town, at barracks, at Marconi office, i'view 1 with Horta, i'view 2 Horta - pics at museum, i'view Apodeti - prisoners at museum - plane gone, [illegible] - left Dili 4pm

Sat Stayed at Maliana 6 am, flood - slept & Radio story

Left Maliana 6am - [illegible] b'fast Atabai - met ABC [illegible] before Nunura sent film 12pm (inc standup) - drove past Balibo, 3 pm - any near Balibo shower wash man ? food hand grenade at night

Sun Fretilin abandons Balibo - paint 'Australia' on walls - standup on street - saw chopper - we withdraw to Maliana lunchtime - standup FILM GOES - any near missions night at Maliana TALK -

Mon Standup on talk at village - try to return to Balibo turn back before Nunura after meeting retreating soldiers - prisoner at Maliana - lunch - go Balibo with reinforcements - 2 ships - meet CTV - beer - Horta too - sleep Balibo

Tues - 6 ships - patrol - FILM GOES - with Horta - Comm Secretariat - Shower / wash - chopper lands on ship?

Sleep [illegible] Balibo

Wed Paul & Masters take car - shower

close, [illegible] with

Cartridge sticks - [illegible]

Extract from Greg Shackleton's notebooks, handed to Australian officials in Jakarta in November 1975 by BAKIN Chief General Yoga Sugama. This diary of events records the television crew's movements until October 15, the day before their death. *Courtesy of Shirley Shackleton.*

Timorese villagers prepare food for FRETILIN soldiers, Balibó, September 1975. (Bob Hannan).

> APODETI, KOTA and Trabalhista ... We will do our best to reach Dili and then go to Tutuala to liberate this land from the hands of the Communists. We only want to remove their livers ... We attacked with mortars, machine-guns and various kinds of guns and aircraft all the peaks of Balibó. The Australian Communists were supporting and aside FRETILIN to fight against our forces showing their heroism to our traitors during the fights at which they camped. How could they fight us, if as soon as our guns began crying, they all disappeared? Three Australians could run away so they want to tell the others we were anti-Communist forces. We are not afraid of FRETILIN, nor the Australian Communists. You can send them to the border to play with us. We have also many friends in Asia.[5]

The statement was made in the name of Lopes da Cruz, who continued to deny any knowledge of the deaths until 22 October, when he was a signatory to a statement forwarded to Mr Richard Johnson, a representative from Australia's Jakarta embassy who had travelled to Kupang. The finding of the bodies was then officially acknowledged for the first time.

Stories were meanwhile seeping into Dili of FRETILIN eyewitnesses to the entry of Indonesian troops into Balibó. Journalists working from the capital requested that any such witnesses be brought in as early as possible. As a result, on 27 October Guido dos Santos, a medical orderly, was interviewed. He claimed to have seen Indonesian troops fire on the five. He said that he left Balibó around 7am, retreating from an attack which began at 4am. When the attack began with distant mortar and bazooka fire from the hill above the town, FRETILIN soldiers moved their positions forward a little, so that the fire was falling behind them. They retreated through Balibó as 'many soldiers' came into the village with machine guns, bazookas, grenades and automatic weapons.

According to his account, when the initial shooting began the television crews took their equipment and went out to film around the village. They never left the village area. The last time dos Santos saw them they were standing in front of an 'Australia' sign pointing to it. In the orderly's words, as the invading troops entered:

> They fired on the building where the Australians were and I saw one fall. The others pointed their hands at the sign on the wall and were shouting 'Australians! Australians!'.

Dos Santos said he was about fifty metres away when he saw this, and that FRETILIN soldiers fired on the group attacking the reporters. This was his last glimpse of them. As he left the village he could still hear them shouting 'Australians! Australians!' for some time, heard continued shooting, and eventually the voices ceased.

In response to questioning dos Santos said he never saw the Australians handle weapons in the whole time they were in Balibó, and they were in civilian dress throughout. He described the uniforms of the attacking troops thus: some wore red helmets, some wore white, some of the uniforms were khaki, others of a fawn colour, and they wore, in his words, 'long white socks', presumably gaiters. He estimated that about 300 soldiers entered the town, based on the fact that he personally saw 'many' and that he could hear many others shouting and singing behind them. He said that the soldiers entered the town from the Maliana-Nunura road and the Cová road, as well as over the hill between them. However, all roads from Balibó appear to have been blocked by troops—retreating FRETILIN soldiers went over the mountains, to Sanírin and Leolima.

On 10 November Australian newspapers published an interview by Australian freelance journalist Roger East with three soldiers who also claimed to be eyewitnesses. The interview was taken quite separately from that of dos Santos but tallied in most essential respects. These soldiers said that when the dawn attack began, Indonesian troops entered Balibó. As they advanced into the town the FRETILIN men crawled into the undergrowth and urged the Australian teams to do the same but the reporters continued to film the battle. When the Indonesians appeared, 'some walked, some trotted', one of the soldiers, Lucas Jeronimo, said:

> . . . The Australians ran toward their house about 200 metres away. One kept stopping, looking back and pointing his camera. He was a big man, but I didn't know his name. We ran into the vegetation and called out 'come on, come on' but they didn't listen. The Indonesians kept firing. The man with the bald head [Peters] was still filming, then he cried out and fell down. The other Australians were screaming 'Australians, Australians' with their hands up. The soldiers circled them and made them turn their

backs and face the wall of the house. The firing died down and we crawled away through the undergrowth. We heard the Australians screaming and then there was a burst of automatic fire.[6]

After Balibó, the population of Dili held its breath: would the Indonesian advance continue? Would the death of the journalists cause the Australian government to take a stand against Indonesia at last? Despite editorialising on the part of several leading dailies, it was soon obvious that the latter would not be the case. On the contrary, although transcripts of all available evidence were forwarded to Canberra by Australians in Dili and it now seemed extremely difficult to deny Indonesian involvement in East Timor, the Labor government gave early notice of its willingness to accept Indonesian accounts of the deaths at face value.[7]

Pitched fighting continued in the Balibó/Maliana region in the weeks after the original attack, but the Indonesians launched no new offensives. Perhaps they, too, were waiting to gauge Australian responses. Tension in Dili nevertheless ran high. Dili's defences had been re-organised and reinforced since 28 August and the FRETILIN command was confident of the city's security. Troops occupied strategic posts behind the capital and along the beachfront. The few available artillery pieces were also located in the surrounding hills. Indonesian warships continued to sail through the harbour area with alarming regularity but until this time no incidents had arisen from their excursions.

On the night of 27 October the capital was for the first time placed on full alert as a consequence of one such visit. The memory of Balibó was still fresh in people's minds and perhaps there was a greater anxiety abroad than before. This was the evening of the wedding of José Gonçalves and Olímpia, sister-in-law of Nicolau Lobato. For some hours the guests had been feasting at the Lobato house near the centre of town. Nicolau looked relaxed and easy for the first time in weeks. Alarico Fernandes was present with a number of other FRETILIN Central Committee members. Most of the guests, however, were women and children. At about 10pm some gathered to leave, only to find their way blocked at the gate by FALINTIL soldiers. An Indonesian ship had sailed close inshore and an emergency had been declared. No-one was permitted to travel through the city and street lights were blacked out. Soon afterwards the sound of mortar shells and artillery thundered through the night. A terrible fear passed across the faces of the children: they began crying almost with one voice. It was only a little over two months ago that every night had been filled with the sounds of war. Some of the women clutched at the nearest arm: everyone strained to detect the direction of the fire. The shells came from FRETILIN guns on the eastern and western fringes of Dili. The fear was that the intruding vessel would respond. It did not: the incident was perhaps an attempt to flush out FRETILIN artillery emplacements around the capital. It was the only occasion on which FRETILIN fired on any of the Indonesian vessels who entered the Dili harbour area. The commanders claimed that on this occasion the ship had sailed closer than usual to the shoreline.

Two nights later there was a complete blackout in Dili for about two hours from 9pm. It was preceded by several bursts of gunfire in the streets, although FRETILIN claimed that its cause was entirely due to a technical breakdown.

The events of these nights wore on the nerves of a section of the foreign aid workers. On 29 and 30 October most members of the ASIAT team, believing an Indonesian landing to be imminent in Dili, returned to Darwin until the situation cleared. On the night of the twenty seventh the scene in the 'Toko Lay' apartments where they lived had been one of panic. When the shooting began the many Chinese who lived here had all huddled on the same level of the building as the ASIAT staff, heightening the general sense of insecurity which most residents of the capital were then experiencing. The ASIAT departure coincided with the scheduled departure of a number of International Red Cross doctors and the last members of the ACFOA task force. In the days after this apparent exodus of foreign nationals from Dili there was an air of demoralisation among the locals who stopped to question the few Australians remaining about the apparent flight of the aid workers.

Soon after, his dreams of fast-food fortunes in ruins, Frank Favaro followed their example. Events had overcome him. The final erosion of his determination to stay came from his belief that an Indonesian invasion would occur in early November, his generally strained relationship with FRETILIN, and a cable from the Australian government informing him that Jakarta had accused him of spying for the Australian government in Timor. On arrival in Darwin Frank Favaro voiced his belief that an Indonesian invasion was imminent. Ramos Horta, then in Darwin, heard of Favaro's claims and relayed them to FRETILIN. Partly on the basis of this they believed Favaro to have access to Indonesian intelligence sources and accused him of being an Indonesian spy. The accusation was also made on the basis of air trips made within Timor. FRETILIN claimed that on a trip made ostensibly to Oecusse some time after the coup Favaro had actually landed in Atambua. A sequel to this confused course of events was the dismissal in October of the head of the Australian Security Intelligence Service, Mr Robertson, reportedly because he had commissioned the hotelier for intelligence activities in Dili without the knowledge of the Whitlam government. Favaro's spying activities were alleged in this accusation to be 'pro-FRETILIN'. Favaro denied the story, although the Foreign Affairs sources from which it came held to it.

On 1–2 November the Portuguese Foreign Minister Melo Antunes met in Rome with the Indonesian Foreign Minister Adam Malik to discuss the future of East Timor. Ironically, this was the only occasion in the whole period between the UDT coup and the Indonesian invasion of 7 December on which any of the parties principal met to negotiate, yet no East Timorese representatives were present.

Although FRETILIN viewed the talks with suspicion, on their commencement they sent a telegram to the Portuguese government in Lisbon reiterating their willingness to negotiate with Portugal as the 'only legitimate mouthpiece' of the decolonisation process:

> FRETILIN controls all of the territory except Maliana, Batugadé and Balibó in the border region which are occupied by the military forces of Indonesia .. FRETILIN does not consider itself to be a force for instability in the area, but the act of aggression by Indonesian troops which constitute a force for instability in the area. Peace at the border can only be re-established ... when the invading troops of Indonesia retire from our territory'.[8]

The edge of bitterness which attended the FRETILIN view of

the talks was sharpened by the fact that on 25 October they had put a proposal to the Portuguese for negotiations, to which they received no reply. Xavier commented:

> The talks suggest to me that Portugal has made some compromise with Indonesia beforehand. If the Portuguese government did not wish to invite representatives from FRETILIN it should at least have invited ASEAN nations, the UN Committee of 24, Australia or other south Pacific nations to participate.

He detailed the 25 October proposal: the talks were proposed for the first fortnight of November and confirmation by the Portuguese government was requested by the end of October. The proposal was accompanied by an invitation to representatives of the former administration now on Ataúro to send a delegation back to the mainland to witness the present political situation.

Why did talks between the various protagonists never occur? Was the failure to negotiate the result of incompetence and a series of misunderstandings, or of a conscious design? On the eve of the Rome talks Foreign Affairs Minister Willesee claimed in the Australian parliament that the earlier meeting proposed by FRETILIN for 20 September did not take place

> at least in part because of the intransigence of FRETILIN, which has continued to claim to the United Nations and the world in general that it is the only authentic and legitimate voice of Portuguese Timor.[9]

Dunn, on the other hand, claims that FRETILIN leaders 'were effectively isolated by a combination of skilful Indonesian propaganda and diplomacy, and by Portugal's inaction', and that the failure to establish contact with the Portuguese had led to a general hardening of attitudes in the leadership. Thus the call for the return of the Portuguese was accompanied by a set of 'stiff demands'.

While it is correct that FRETILIN terms were stringent (for example, after Macau a basic principle had been that all discussions about the territory should take place in East Timor itself and certain Portuguese negotiators were also considered unacceptable) the actuality was, as Dunn goes on to say, that FRETILIN existed in a framework in which no meaningful opportunity for negotiation was ever presented:

> ... failure to interest countries such as Australia in the fact that Indonesian military intervention had already begun caused a general hardening throughout the Central Committee ...
>
> FRETILIN leaders saw themselves as victims of an act of aggression, a cruel injustice which outside powers were choosing to ignore.[10]

Certainly the Portuguese did not regard FRETILIN as the obstructing party to negotiations.[11] They were prepared to accept that the leaders would not negotiate at the same table as UDT and APODETI and had already accepted this principle and practice in the Dili talks of May 1975.

Perhaps what was of more concern than an outward hardening of attitudes was the atmosphere of unreality in which FRETILIN functioned. Dunn pointed to the warping effect of isolation on political perspectives. The new leadership, he observed, appeared to place most emphasis on their capability to resist an invasion.

> Their success so far may have blinded them to the serious problems ahead on the diplomatic plane ... Underlying these attitudes is a lack of understanding of the situation in this region and of how to go about coming to terms with Portugal and Indonesia.

With their limited view of the outside world, a fundamental and persistent tenet of FRETILIN thought was the belief that boundless enthusiasm and goodwill were sufficient conditions for success and that it inevitably followed that the world must see the justice of their cause. The corollary of this approach was the bitter, tough self-reliance to which it periodically gave way with the realisation that this was not the case.

This unreality was expressed in the failure of Portuguese–FRETILIN negotiations. While high-sounding cables passed between Lisbon and Dili, the former Portuguese administration sat watching Dili from only thirty kilometres away at a time when the mere establishment of any kind of intercourse had the potential to prevent a tragedy of massive proportions. When Dunn arrived with the ACFOA team in mid-October he made talks between FRETILIN and the Portuguese on Ataúro an important priority. He travelled to the island and reported:

> We were particularly disturbed to find that there is not merely no contact between the parties to this conflict (FRETILIN, UDT and the Portuguese), no effort is being made to establish such contacts. The Governor, Col. Lemos Pires, with his staff, is on Atauro, and appeared to be opposed to seeking contact with UDT or FRETILIN. His attitude seems dominated by his hurt pride. For example, he was opposed to sending food ... he said: 'I want to help the people of Timor but I will not help FRETILIN. If I send food to Dili it will go to the war'. I have nevertheless suggested that he establish some contact with FRETILIN and if possible with UDT at an informal level, if only to keep some kind of communication link open ...[12]

FRETILIN had requested negotiations initially on 20 September and then again on 25 October. On both occasions it appears that mutually acceptable conditions were never arrived at and the dates slid by. Ramos Horta liaised with the Portuguese delegation based in Darwin on the details and at times negotiations appeared close, but they soon took on a mirage-like quality.

The inaccessibility of the APODETI and UDT leaderships in Indonesian Timor was a major obstruction, especially to the scheduled September talks. The Indonesians continually blocked access to them, as they had obstructed passage of the António Soares delegation. In September the Portuguese sent a plane from Ataúro to Atambua in an attempt to persuade UDT and APODETI to join in talks. A Timorese then in Atambua described its arrival:

> In September, 1975, a TAT plane arrived in Atambua. Its objective was to deliver a message to the MAC leaders. In this message the delegation from the Portuguese Government in Ataúro asked for a meeting with the parties in order to discuss the situation. To begin with the plane was grounded, and its crew put in Wisma Sabtha [a hotel] under armed Indonesian guard. Only some days later did BAKIN inform MAC of the aforesaid message. By this stage, Taolin had been able to relay Jakarta's orders regarding the sort of reply that should be given. The reply was made precisely as Jakarta ordered. As Jakarta was concerned to prevent any contact whatsoever with the Portuguese government, it was decided to mark time so that the Portuguese government would give up waiting. For this purpose, when the TAT plane returned to Ataúro it was excessively late arriving; for, according to Taolin, 'We want no more talks with them'.

The same account also claims that all messages to the Portuguese government from the Timorese parties in Indonesian Timor were drafted in Jakarta.[13]

Despite its not very flattering references to FRETILIN, the front regarded the Willesee statement of 30 October as the first sign of a thaw in Australian attitudes. While he spoke in general terms of the desirability of inter-party talks and of the positive outcome of the Rome talks, Senator Willesee also referred for the first time, albeit euphemistically, to Indonesian military involvement in East Timor. He went on to offer Australia as a venue for talks. Although they generally held to the view that all negotiations should take place in Timor, FRETILIN were sympathetic to this offer. Until this time the Whitlam government had publicly claimed no central regional interest in the decolonisation of East Timor. Long after this statement, by which time the Fraser government had taken power in Australia, FRETILIN leaders harked back to it as a sign that the Labor government may eventually have changed its political position, even though subsequent statements by Mr Whitlam and newspaper disclosures of certain private dealings between the Whitlam government and Jakarta suggested that this was not really the case.

The outcome of the Rome talks was a twelve point accord signed between the Portuguese and Indonesian Foreign Ministers. Although most reporting of the agreement in Australia characterised it as a step towards peace, more informed commentators saw it differently. Michael Richardson wrote of it as a 'bitter setback' for the Timorese independence movement.

The Rome negotiators agreed that Portugal was the legitimate sovereign power with responsibility for the decolonisation process. 'To this end' the communique issued at the end of talks stated,

> the two Ministers concurred on the necessity to convene at the earliest possible time, a meeting between Portugal and all political parties in Portuguese Timor simultaneously and aimed at ending armed strife and bringing about a peaceful and orderly process of decolonisation in Portuguese Timor.

In this context, the twenty three Portuguese POWs and the refugees from East Timor now in Indonesian Timor were also discussed as 'two questions of urgent importance to their respective governments'. Further, 'in the implementation of decolonisation of Portuguese Timor it would be essential also to safeguard the legitimate interests of the countries of the region, particularly the interests of Indonesia as the closest neighbouring country'.[14] The 'simultaneous discussions between all parties' clause was certainly a term favourable to Jakarta and a setback for FRETILIN desire to deal with the Portuguese on a one-to-one basis.

In Australian eyes FRETILIN non-participation in such a settlement would appear unreasonable, but in reality the Rome Agreement made the possibility of independence through political settlement remote. Participation in talks on these terms would almost certainly lead to a settlement conducive to merger with Indonesia regardless of political feeling in East Timor. On the other hand a FRETILIN boycott would leave only one course: to fight on in isolation in the bitter knowledge that the question was no longer one for UDT or APODETI, it was one for the Indonesian military. Richardson saw it as an agreement carved out on the battlefield by Indonesia:

> Canberra strongly suspects that the successful military comeback staged by UDT, APODETI and two allied pro-Indonesia parties in the past few weeks has been buttressed by military assistance from Indonesia.
>
> Canberra also knows that Indonesia was able to undercut FRETILIN's hopes of a favourable political outcome to the struggle in Timor and negotiate the new agreement with Portugal on the basis of the battlefield advances by anti-FRETILIN forces.[15]

Xavier do Amaral, FRETILIN's president, commented of the outcome:

> It is unreal to suggest talking with representatives of UDT and APODETI. In Rome they talk of self-determination, but self-determination has been decided already, the people have chosen their course. We have made an appeal to the nations of the world and the UN. If they do not accept this definition of self-determination it will mean continued fighting for us ... The defeat of UDT was not a defeat by the FRETILIN army, but the people who supported it. The revolution was not only made by soldiers but by women, children and even old people as well.[16]

7

The Fragile Peace

At the conclusion of the Rome talks the internal security of Dili came under threat for the first time. Since UDT's border crossing, the use of material from Dili sources in Radio Kupang broadcasts had added credence to speculation that fifth columnists operated a secret transmitter out of the capital.

On 4 November it was rumoured that a section of the military police had placed a cordon around Dili to prohibit movement to and from the city and that a delegation to the FRETILIN leadership had demanded the recall and arrest of a list of FRETILIN militants, including some OPJT and OPMT delegates working in Maubisse. The alleged 'Communists' included Francisco Borja da Costa, Secretary for Information on the Central Committee, and Rosa Muki Bonaparte, Secretary of the OPMT. The MPS were rumoured to be under the influence of the Bishop of Dili.

As an élite military group the military police were known to be reluctant to accept political leadership from non-military figures. This latter problem had already occurred in a wider framework. In early October Mau Lear, one of the FRETILIN theoreticians, wrote in the new national newspaper of the need to break traditional prejudices and enter into new forms of relationships. 'Divisionism' was a traditional enemy of the Timorese people, he wrote, which had led to the defeat of their ancestors in the anti-colonial wars. It was a problem which persisted even after FRETILIN victory:

> There are comrades of ours among the military who say to civilians "If it weren't for us you would have all been killed by UDT" or "We have left our own region to defend you". Such statements are mistaken and indicate a regional outlook. The Armed Forces, in defending the people, perform a revolutionary duty—the freeing of our country from foreign colonial oppres-

> sion and the freeing of the entire population from exploitation between one man and another ... The problems that exist between the military leadership and the members of the Central and Regional Committees, deserve special consideration here ... Having broken down the *apartidarismo* desired by the colonialists by means of the unconditional unity of the FRETILIN Armed Forces, the definition of new functions begins to take place ... The basic difficulty stems from a failure ... to utilize the problem-solving methods outlined by FRETILIN. Thus, mutual debate and self-analysis are replaced by suspicion. While such a spirit of mistrust and lack of openness prevails, the internal problems which exist ... will not easily be solved.[1]

It was by just such means of 'mutual debate and self-analysis' that the impasse with the military police was resolved: in four hours of discussion with the soldiers on 4 November they were persuaded that their accusations were falsely based. In a later statement confirming the rumour Nicolau Lobato described the aborted revolt as:

> a manoeuvre of the reactionaries to divide our people ... designed to coincide with the talks in Rome between the Indonesian and Portuguese Foreign Ministers. The defeat of the reactionaries is regarded as a great victory.[2]

Despite the tension in Dili, of which the MPs revolt was an expression, life was generally calm and orderly, with the work of reconstruction a central preoccupation. On a clear day with the wind blowing in the right direction, the sound of Indonesian naval bombardment down the north coast could be heard, but otherwise the war at the border seemed distant. A newcomer would take some convincing that a bloody war had raged in the capital only a little over two months before. There was now a general air of business about life. Glaziers, carpenters, painters, street cleaners and gardeners worked on repairing battered buildings and tidying city streets. Sometimes at a closer glance it became apparent by the presence of an armed guard that the 'gardeners' or 'street cleaners' were prisoners. An occasional European face appeared among these groups, usually a Portuguese accused of involvement with UDT.

Most of the Chinese-owned shops were now open daily, although there were shortages of certain goods. The school of the Chinese community re-opened in October and the babble of the children in their neat blue and white uniforms at the building near the 'Banco' was a reassuring sound. Outside its fence, vendors sold Timorese street food—a sort of short soup soused with *ai manus*, extra hot Timorese chili sauce, and served on communal enamel plates. The Timorese school system had not yet resumed. The structure of the state school system had almost totally collapsed with the exodus of the Portuguese from the territory and any Timorese teachers remaining were involved in vital economic reconstruction work. As well, if at least some teaching was to resume in Tetum, the whole curriculum required overhaul. It was hoped that schools would re-open in December.

The 7pm to dawn curfew remained but the presence of the military in Dili was markedly less evident than it had been. Around the middle of October the Central Committee moved house from Taibesse to a former student residence building opposite the territory's only technical school. The military headquarters now functioned more effectively as a training centre where volunteers who were formerly wildly undisciplined were drilled daily by the best of the experienced regulars. Even away from the Taibesse command the soldiers of FALINTIL drilled to the sound of their own war whoops, but they drilled earnestly under the command of former Portuguese Army men.

The Central Committee's move marked a clear separation of the political from the military functions of the front. The new centre now being repainted was airy and light. Each department of the Central Committee had its own suite of offices. The FRETILIN President and Vice-president also worked from this location. The economic commission remained physically separate, partly to accommodate the workforce it employed. The Central Committee headquarters became the real heart of business. It was the place where all policy was determined, usually after long meetings. Policy statements were also issued from here.

Although the economic commission was physically separate, the Central Committee had sovereign authority over it. One of the main problems the commission experienced was the overburdening of Dili resources after the civil war. José Gonçalves commented:

> It is a centuries-old problem for Timor. Dili is the home of a privileged class. At the moment Dili has an artificial population of people who consume but do not produce. It is the base for the soldiers for the frontier and thus for their families, which involves feeding many more mouths.

The chief economic commissioner also argued that a main priority must be to reverse the flow of population to Dili: 'Chinese and Timorese are concentrating here for security, but this is not security for the stomach. The families of prisoners in Dili also constitute an extra unproductive group'.[3] The food situation in Dili by this time was poor. Flour had run out altogether and on 13 November only 100 tonnes of rice remained.

A major obstacle to East Timor's economic recovery was dependence on the restoration of banking facilities which, as long as Portuguese sovereignty was recognised, depended on negotiations with Portugal. Neither foreign trade nor the internal economy could function while the bank remained locked with no prospect of re-opening. Here was the quintessence of a dilemma which was to grow sharper. If negotiations were not soon forthcoming FRETILIN would be forced to think about nationalising the bank and thus abandoning the call for a return of Portuguese authority.

Gonçalves hinted at this option in the same interview: 'We cannot wait eternally on [it] to function' he said of the state-owned bank, '[It] is already nationalised, but we may think of perfecting the process'. The economic commission controlled the Timorese escudo at the rate of exchange set by Lisbon and a major economic transaction conducted by FRETILIN in November demonstrated that ingenuity could meet many economic problems, but time and again the administration was forced back to the fundemental problems of finance facilities and circulation of currency.

Another function which FRETILIN at least initially regarded as dependent on Portuguese return was the processing of prisoners. They wished the leaders of the coup to be tried in a Portuguese court of law on the return of the colonial power. The remainder, the 'followers', were systematically processed from the end of September when FRETILIN established a military/political commission of inquiry to hear prima facie evidence against those held. Members of the public were asked to come forward to present evidence. By 14 November some 250 prisoners had been freed by this process. At the end of that month, when Portuguese return seemed more remote than ever, the original policy was under review and the possibility of FRETILIN-conducted trials of coup leaders was being considered.

On 13 November the first food aid to reach East Timor since the coup arrived on the barge *Alanna Fay*. The barge was chartered from Darwin by the Australian Council for Overseas Aid (ACFOA), although the relief was provided by both ACFOA and ASIAT. The barge carried one tonne of milk powder, thirty tonnes of rice, twenty five tonnes of corn, 4,000 metres of cloth, five tonnes of flour, and penicillin and other drugs to the value of $A10,000. Diesel fuel and petrol came too, for the distribution of the relief. This item had caused difficulties with Australian authorities for an unofficial blockade of fuel for East Timor had been in force for some time. Although the civil functions of East Timor's economy normally depended on the importation of fuel from Darwin, the Australian government claimed that the sale of fuel could be construed as military support for FRETILIN. It was finally allowed on the barge on condition that the quantity was proportionate to the amount of aid to be distributed. The *Alanna Fay* also carried twelve tonnes of assorted seed, expressing the ACFOA task force's recommendation to the Australian organisation that the self-reliance principle on which the FRETILIN administration operated should be interfered with as little as possible. It was hoped that the seed would be in time for planting before the wet season set in.

On their previous visit ACFOA representatives had established an independent local commission to facilitate fair distribution of relief. It consisted of three representatives of the FRETILIN economic commission, a representative of the Catholic Church nominated by the Bishop of Dili and an ACFOA representative, Dr Bob Richards.

Two days later the barge sailed out of Dili harbour laden with coffee. It represented the first successful export sale of the FRETILIN administration. From the time they took power on 28 August FRETILIN had set people to work processing the coffee crop. The sale had been transacted with the assistance of aid

Processing the coffee crop, Dili, October 1975 (Jill Jolliffe).

Unloading the *Alanna Fay*, Dili harbour, November 1975.

groups and in particular with Jim Zantis, an independent aid worker close to ASIAT. The $A40,000 proceeds of the sale were deposited in a bank account in Darwin—it was hoped that the opening of this account would temporarily resolve some of the economic problems engendered by the uncertain legal status of the de facto government.

The crew of the barge returned to Australia impressed by their experience of the FRETILIN administration. They were surprised to find the political situation quite different from the impression given in Australia ('There is no troube here. It is calm and peaceful' the captain remarked). All their stevedoring labour had been provided by Timorese.

The distribution of the aid consignment in the countryside was a test of the effectiveness of the FRETILIN government. In the early hours of 10 November two ageing Bedford trucks lumbered out of Dili bound for Maubisse. They were laden with rice to be distributed in this interior centre which was suffering deprivation as a result of the August war. On top of the sacks of rice sat Chinese and Timorese going home for the first time since the coup. The journey was punctuated by the regular boiling of the engines of both vehicles, long and lively discussions on how to heal the wounded monsters and the final demise of the second truck on the Dili side of Aileu.

The remaining Bedford finally lurched into Maubisse town square. The ACFOA delegate accompanying the consignment had been told in Dili that the distribution of the rice would be supervised by local FRETILIN delegates, but the details had not been specified. Hearts sank as the truck turned in: about a thousand whooping, cheering Timorese milled around, making progress impossible. But after initial disorder a smooth distribution was soon under way, with Regional Sub-committee members, mainly young schoolteachers, overseeing the process. They worked from census lists revised under the direction of the local police commander in October. When the crowd quietened the delegates set up school desks at six points of the square, then proceeded to call out family names from the roll. Scales set up at each point weighed the villagers' allocations, collected in a colourful range of containers, from plastic bags, tins, blankets to battered hats.

The Maubisse administration area covers some 300 sq kms divided into nine *sucos*. The revised census lists gave a population of 22,000 persons in the area. It was calculated that some people had walked at least fifteen kilometres to collect their ration, distributed on the principle of one kilo per family for the first distribution, with the exception that extra rations were earmarked for the crèche and hospital. There was also a special list for distribution to people held in FRETILIN custody in a house in the town centre. These were relatives of UDT people, allegedly held under protection for their own safety—as distinct from prisoners, who were held at the Maubisse military post.

The consignment was transported from Dili using the

The ACFOA food consignment bound for Maubisse—despite mechanical setbacks—November 1975.

Villagers in Maubisse town square for distribution of ACFOA food consignment, November 1975.

resources of the SAPT company, a former Portuguese co-operative which was largely state-owned. Both the invalid trucks and the drivers had worked for the SAPT before the coup. The employment of this structure meant that the relief was handled by civilians at every point. The day's distribution done, villagers danced and sang in celebration. The war had been cruel to the people of Maubisse. It was normally a poor place in which many people wore little more than rags. Most of the population are subsistence farmers, the success of whose harvest depends on the daily tending of crops. In times of social disruption like the coup they faced famine.

Nevertheless the marks of the town's recovery in the months since August were apparent. When the ACFOA consignment ar-

Crèche *Mau Koli*, Maubisse, November 1975.

rived the ground had already been dug to receive the seed allotment. The distribution of the rice by the Regional Subcommittee was orderly and their authority seemed to be generally accepted. The OPMT/OPJT crèche in the former hotel above the town was functioning and there was even a Maubisse 'medical school' established by the local infirmarian. The infirmarian was a skilful, dedicated nurse, a pious man, who had been in charge of the hospital since the Portuguese left. Now he spent his evenings imparting his skills to a class of local people in the village schoolhouse.

The number of displaced or orphaned children cared for at the crèche had been reduced from the several hundred of early September to ninety-four, the balance having been placed with local families. The women's movement and youth movement delegates from Dili worked here alongside local people, and International Red Cross, (which had already provided some support), kept a check on the food level. The staff of the crèche had also initiated a *loja de povo* in the town, a 'people's shop' which sold essential goods like kerosene, cooking oil and sugar, at low fixed prices.

Maubisse is set on a mountain plateau surrounded by the higher peaks of neighbouring mountains, including Ramelau. The slopes of the village are lightly wooded with eucalypts; one could be in the Australian bush. In the early morning a mist swirls down around the town. Walking through the town the day after the distribution, the misery of the war still showed in many faces, of wounds not yet healed, of divisions still rankling. In the main street the crowd engaged in a favourite diversion: baiting a mad old beggarwoman. Through the eucalypts a doleful procession wound up a mountain track. At its head moved a large red, yellow and black FRETILIN flag. Behind walked several Timorese *kudas* led by people bearing a coffin and beating a dirge on a drum. This was the funeral procession of the *liurai* of the nearby village of Fatubesse, a FRETILIN *liurai*.

That afternoon people streamed from far around to join the funeral feast and pay their last respects. The village settlement stood just outside Maubisse on a green knoll which afforded a grand view of the area's sweeping valleys and peaks. Half a dozen grass huts surrounded by a common fence housed the *liurai's* extended family. Pigs, goats and children played within the enclosure, smoke from household fires curled into the mountain air.

Januário Soares, the FRETILIN military commander of Maubisse, was a special guest at the wake. Januário was a dashing figure who sported a beautiful oiled mop of black locks, stovepipe trousers pressed into razor-sharp creases and, always, a starched white handkerchief in his hip pocket. Since the coup he had occupied the finest Portuguese villa in town, the former administrator's house.

In the distance people trekked in from surrounding districts; closer in they climbed the last stretch of track to the settlement. Immediately below white and pinto *kudas* grazed, Gauguin-like, on the green.

In the main house the old fellow lay at peace, his chin strapped up under his best embroidered felt hat, his body draped in a traditional rug. Relatives conversed in hushed tones around the candlelit bier. Outside, people sat under the verandah thatch chatting quietly over the funeral feast. Watching this tranquil rural scene it seemed inconceivable that in a little over two weeks bombs would be dropping on these village houses.

In October and November the Indonesians intensified the campaign of distortion of information which was now an integral part of 'Operasi Komodo'. One observer set the beginning of the propaganda campaign as June 1975:

> After the Macau Conference, as a result of secret talks in London, the Indonesian government decided to initiate a news battle over Timor. Accordingly, the Antara Agency received daily instructions to fabricate articles about phony happenings in Timor ... The Indonesian government ... sent various delegations to its partner countries of ASEAN attempting to communicate the reasons which later would lead to military intervention into Timor. The activities ... regarding ASEAN were always based in news allegedly originating in Timor and published in the Indonesian press. The purpose was to completely falsify the Timorese political picture.[4]

The two essential components of this campaign were Antara newsagency for international purposes, and Radio Kupang for domestic consumption. The local operation took on various names: originally identified just as Radio Kupang, after the UDT coup it became 'Radio Ramelau' and later still its programs were designated 'Radio Loro Sae'. It was a secret operation from the outset:

> What was simply called Radio Ramelau was in fact quite a complex organisation. In a modern building situated on the heights of Kupang, there is a firm known as P.T. Arjuna which carries out various activities. Inside the building a powerful transceiver is installed, and there is a recording studio. There, the government agents from Jakarta operate a direct contact with the Atambua centre. Radio Ramelau transmits on various wave-lengths, and is able to muffle the broadcasts from Radio Dili. Some young Timorese work at Arjuna. They were taken to Indonesia by Tomás Gonçalves.[5]

The Timorese were necessary for the broadcasting of programmes in local dialects, a practice which commenced in early 1975.

From August the main concern of this campaign was to give the impression to the outside world that several rival parties still existed in East Timor (the elevation of KOTA and Trabalhista to parties of equal status with UDT and APODETI after the border crossing was part of this distortion), that the anti-FRETILIN parties were making substantial military advances against FRETILIN, and that the territory was in a state of generalised turmoil.

The incidence of false reports, many of which were carried uncritically in the Australian and international press, increased after the fall of Balibó. On 22 October Antara claimed that 'anti-FRETILIN forces' had taken Bobonaro and then on the twenty third that they were in Maubara. On-the-spot investigation by journalists who travelled from Dili to Maubara proved this report quite false. On 3 November Antara issued a report, widely used in Australia, that there had been a landing in Baucau. On 5 November it was claimed that there was fighting in Dili itself and also that Lebos had been taken; on 14 November Dili was reported under attack again. The reality was that the military situation was unchanged. The border fighting continued to and fro while life in Dili was orderly and peaceful. Red Cross doctors reported no substantial increase in war casualties treated at Dili hospital during this period. After 16 October the regular toll from border fighting registered at the hospital was around three to five wounded daily, with one or two deaths from injuries every several days.[6]

FRETILIN thinking in the November period was deeply influenced by the MPLA's declaration of independence in Angola. The Angolan war-time declaration was a politically strategic decision designed to contribute to final military victory. On 8 November *Timor Leste* carried a stop press announcing that the MPLA intended to declare independence around 11 November. In the 15 November issue, the first three pages of the six-page edition were devoted to articles explaining and discussing the MPLA's unilateral declaration and comparing the strategies of Portuguese colonialism in Angola and Timor. They included the text of Xavier's speech to a demonstration held in Dili on 11 November to mark the day and the news that thirty countries had already recognised the new Angolan government, including fifteen African countries, the Soviet Union and most eastern bloc countries, Brazil, Syria and North and South Vietnam (then separate states).

The 11 November demonstration was perhaps a turning point on the road to independence. It was remarkable as a FRETILIN demonstration in that the ninety minutes of speeches were delivered entirely in Tetum (in most previous demonstrations at least some Portuguese was used). More important was the tone of deep and irrevocable bitterness against the Portuguese, a bitterness previously felt privately by the FRETILIN leadership but not spread abroad. The speeches ran on two themes: undying opposition to Portuguese colonialism and the need for international solidarity or 'militant internationalism' as it was often called, expressed by this demonstration of identity with Angola. From that day it seemed that the option of Portuguese return was narrowing rapidly, that even if the FRETILIN leadership were to negotiate a new decolonisation relationship it would have great difficulty finding popular acceptance.

Another public meeting followed quickly on the heels of the MPLA demonstration. The next Saturday a 'conscientisation' rally held in Dili stadium was addressed by Rogério Lobato in an unbroken hour-long speech, followed by a twenty minute speech from Nicolau devoted mainly to the situation in Angola.

Although these signs seemed to point in only one direction,

there was nevertheless an expressed awareness of the danger of a glib analogy with Angola. On his return from Africa, Alkatiri was asked for his impressions of the Angolan situation and whether he felt FRETILIN would be forced to declare independence:

> Our political situation is not the same as Angola, our economic/political situation is different and our military/political situation. We want to solve our problems in our own way, considering what is relevant. Our situation is different because we are faced with resisting an invasion by more powerful forces. We know that if we declare UDI Portugal will not send warships and we cannot take responsibility for an Indonesian invasion. This is a problem which we would prefer to solve diplomatically.[7]

If in its early days FALINTIL was a slipshod fighting force, by the early weeks of November there was a stubborn prowess about its military capacity. The experience of two months fighting Indonesian regulars proved invaluable, and the army had considerable success in its ground encounters with Indonesian troops. FALINTIL soldiers had the advantage of knowing the local languages, knowing the terrain and having a high degree of political motivation. All Indonesian victories to date had been won with naval and air support, principally along the sparsely-populated north coast. The more mountainous and densely-populated southern border zone had remained in FRETILIN hands despite concerted and regular attacks on Suai, Lebos and the other villages dotting the frontier.

Even Maliana, scene of the massive 16 October attack, was not secure for the Indonesians. In Dili in mid-November three FALINTIL soldiers described an offensive in which they claimed they had forced Indonesian troops out of Maliana by an ingenious guerilla action. Using only light weapons, a small force of soldiers fought for the whole day of 13 November after attacking the town from three sides in the early hours of the morning. On their account the enemy troops were forced to retreat into Indonesian Timor in some of the vehicles they had used to cross the border on 16 October. This exercise bore the imprimatur of Manuel Soares, the diminutive military commander of Bobonaro, a clever tactician whose skills were noted by the Portuguese. His brother Lemos Soares was the Tapó military commander. The fierce defence of Tapó and Maliana was later confirmed by sources on the other side of the border.

In the last week of November it became public in Dili that Atabae had been under attack from Indonesian naval bombardment since 14 November. When Balibó and Maliana fell on 16 October, Atabae and Bobonaro had become the FRETILIN front line. On 23 November two journalists travelled to Atabae in an attempt to observe the bombardment. FRETILIN claimed that since the bombardment began, Atabae had been subjected to an attack which sometimes involved as many as eleven vessels at the one time.

Freelancer Roger East was already observing regular aerial attacks on Bobonaro, thirty kilometres inland from Atabae, where he watched FALINTIL troops in action over a period of ten days:

> The two Second World War bombers which stooge around each morning are largely toothless at this hour. From the safety of about 3,000 metres they machine-gun at random. To date, no bombs have been dropped and their daily targets are mainly the former Portuguese cavalry outpost at [Bobonaro] or Atabae to the north. One is silvery white, while the other is brown, and both are unmarked.[8]

At nearby Tapó he saw in action a brigade of women recruited in Bobonaro to fight with FALINTIL.

The Loes river is an important East Timorese waterway, geographically and in folklore. From the river flats at its estuary one has a prime view of Atabae which, like Maubisse, is a plateau town. At this point it is about ten kilometres inland on the other side of the Loes. Further along towards the border the hump that is Balibó can just be made out; Batugadé is tucked behind the sweeping curve of the coastline.

From a base camp just north east of the Loes crossing to Atabae, FALINTIL commanders kept radio contact with Aquiles Soares, the Atabae commander. The site of the camp was a concrete house set a little to one side of some traditional Timorese houses, on a flat wooded expanse providing good air cover. It was the logistics centre for the defence of Atabae—as well as maintaining radio contact, men were dispatched from here to staff the various beach sentry posts or on hunting parties to supplement the camp rations with deer or pigeon. Here, too, local villagers brought in chickens, eggs or vegetables to help feed the soldiers. Relieving troops were also sent regularly into Atabae from here, although the Loes was becoming more difficult to cross with the onset of the wet.

From this camp a jeep traversed the undergrowth to a beach patrol post. Nothing along the white sandy strip indicated that the undergrowth was studded with similar posts. The soldiers here told the reporters that the naval shelling of Atabae was a daily event, as was aerial bombardment. They assured them that if they waited long enough they would observe an attack. As they spoke a plane flew high overhead and shortly afterwards the distant 'phut phut phut' of artillery fire could be heard. By breaking the beach cover the plane could be seen diving over Atabae in a series of runs. Far offshore the pale forms of warships could also be seen.

The soldiers explained that the bombardment occurred mostly at night—if the journalists wanted to observe it, then was the best time. Later that night on a hillpost a few hundred metres from the beach position FALINTIL soldiers shared their dinner with the reporters and talked about the offensive. Only that day, they said, a plane had ploughed up the ground metres from where they stood. The day before, the power station at Atabae had been demolished in the bombardment. The ships shelled every night and sometimes for stretches of six hours at a time.

The FALINTIL men ate well. That evening they had locally-supplied eggs as omelettes, rice, tapioca, roast pigeon and sweet potatoes washed down with Aguardente, a particularly evil brand of Portuguese spirits. Their shelter was a three-roomed bamboo house set on a hillside. Their assigned watch was further up the hill from where there was a good view of Atabae, the Loes, and the coastline less than a kilometre away. A mountain gun camouflaged by a palm frond stood aside a small grass shelter.

What sort of men were these front-line soldiers of FRETILIN? One said he was a dentist from Maubara: the saturnine 'Nixon' took great pleasure in describing the weaknesses of President Xavier when faced with an extraction. His cousin César, also from Maubara, drove trucks in Dili before the coup. Nixon, who hadn't much schooling despite his dentistry, felt that some

FRETILIN sentry post, Atabae, dawn, 27 September 1975. (Jill Jolliffe).

of the Central Committee people might be too 'timid' to stay long at the front, expressing a soldier's distrust of politicians. Both César and Nixon were typical of the city workers who before the coup formed the ranks of FRETILIN's Workers Union. Others of the soldiers were from Liquiçá or Dili but many were local people. Some dressed in a combination of the simple *lipa* with a Portuguese Army cap or shirt, a Mauser slung over one shoulder, a bag of betel nut on the other. Perhaps they had only occasionally seen cars, let alone the mechanised arsenal of a modern army.

FRETILIN border patrol, Batugadé, 27 September 1975. (Jill Jolliffe).

The dinner broke up around 10pm, lights were extinguished and the Aguardente quickly soothed the hut's inhabitants to sleep. The arrangement was that when the bombardment began the soldiers would take the reporters to the hill lookout. At several hours after midnight a sound like soft but regular thunder broke the silence. After shaking the sleeping guide awake, the journalists trooped noiselessly up the hill. There, from several kilometres off the Loes a destroyer class vessel was shelling Atabae. The flashes from each round of shelling lit the night sky, followed by a series of 'booms' in Atabae after each burst. For half an hour from around 3am the shelling continued, at one point using a starshell flare to light the target. The ship remained in position until dawn when at least two vessels were revealed, one of which moved closer inshore soon after first light.

At 6.15am the bomber seen the day before appeared from the west. This time its closeness rendered recognition possible as a B26 'Invader' bomber with camouflage markings. The plane dived over Atabae with the same 'phut phut phut' sound heard from the beach hideout and then disappeared towards Maliana. Ten minutes later it re-appeared flying off-shore from the west, wheeled and dived, raking the area between the beach and the reporters' position with a deafening burst of artillery fire. The observers on the hillpost dived for cover on the impact. As the bomber dived there was a 'woosh' signifying the release of rockets which detonated on the west bank of the Loes.

Watching the bombardment of Atabae, the naval shelling in particular, it was difficult to believe that the soldiers remained in the town centre. Yet the very attack the journalists witnessed claimed at least one victim, Eduardo Moreira, who was interviewed in Dili hospital some days later. Moreira had just finished his regular morning task of distributing ammunition around the various points when the plane came. He took shelter behind a coconut tree but in the strafing an artillery bullet snapped the tree trunk and entered the soldier's leg. How did he feel during the bombardment of Atabae? he was asked. At first the soldiers were very frightened, he said, because they had never seen bombing, rocket or artillery fire before. Now, however, they were used to it: 'Only the ones who

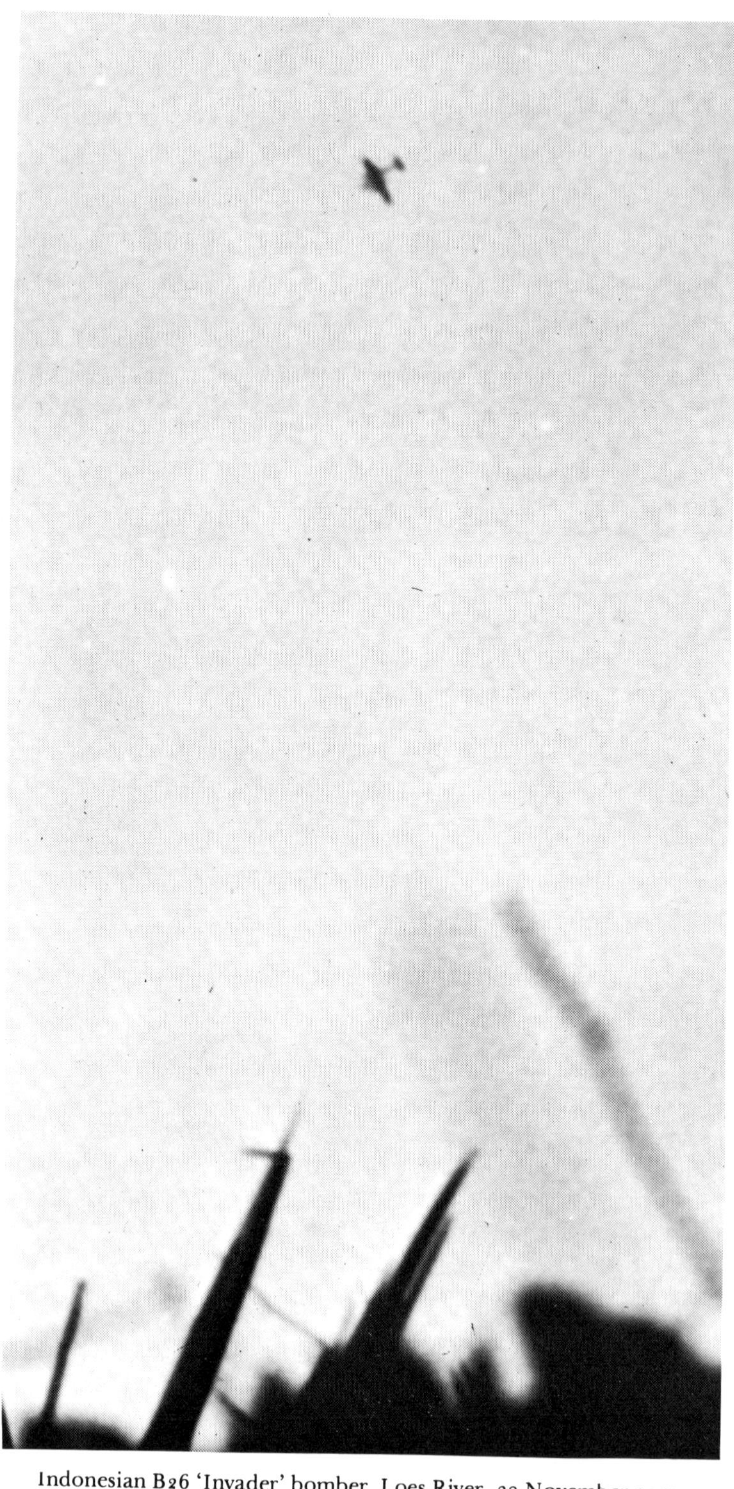

Indonesian B26 'Invader' bomber, Loes River, 23 November 1975. (Michael Richardson, courtesy of the *Age*).

Indonesian naval presence off Atapupu, Indonesian Timor, September 1975. On the left is the destroyer *Monginsidi*, centre the patrol boat BC704 and on the right the destroyer *Nuku*, an old Soviet ship. (Michael Richardson, courtesy of the *Age*).

aren't afraid are there'. As soon as he recovered he too would return, he vowed: 'My fellows are there and I must be with them'.

On 24 November Rogério Lobato announced that the situation in Atabae had reached crisis point. An appeal was addressed to the UN Security Council and to world leaders including the Foreign Ministers of Papua New Guinea and Australia:

> We inform you that Indonesian forces with the support of eleven warships and approximately ten aircraft and infantry forces have attacked the border zone at Atabae for the past five days. The area is still under FRETILIN control but the situation has reached crisis point today.[9]

Ground troops had attempted to enter the town but been successfully repelled. The following day they succeeded in occupying Hatás, a few kilometres south of Atabae.

On 27 November an Indonesian helicopter dropped propaganda leaflets bearing the signature of Lopes da Cruz over Atabae and Beacou, on the west bank of the Loes. 'Combined anti-Communist forces of UDT and APODETI are on the road to Dili', it proclaimed, 'it is useless to resist us. On arrival present yourself without arms and show the sign of peace—a white flag'. It was addressed to 'Believers and pious people of Timor and soldiers of FALINTIL who are not Communists' and concluded 'God exists! God is great! We will win!'.[10]

After fourteen days of intense aerial and sea bombardment Atabae fell to Indonesian occupation at 7am on 28 November.

8

Independence

At the rear of the SOTA Timor, one of Dili's largest shops, were several spacious apartments which had been occupied by Portuguese army officers before the UDT coup. Since their flight, the Portuguese poet had staked a claim on one of the apartments. His next door neighbour was 'Major' Kruger, who also had a good eye for a bargain. The poet rose late on the morning of Friday 28 November. Next to Sam Kruger's door he drew a sketch, an outline of a flag which looked like this:

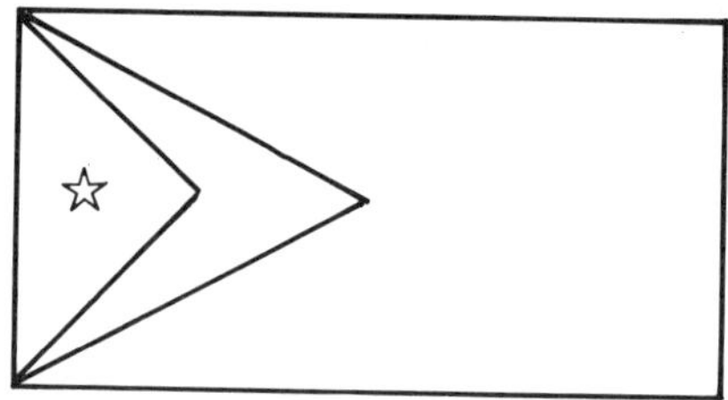

He suggested to his war veteran friend that he wear a clean, pressed shirt and his military medals that day. Some hours later a resident of the Hotel Turismo returned to the hotel for the midday meal and reported that Henry the Navigator Square in the centre of town was filling with armed soldiers and that travel was being controlled at most points of the city.

Michael Richardson, one of three remaining foreign journalists, had an after-lunch interview scheduled with the Bishop of Dili. The Bishop's residence was on the way to the city square. Notebook in hand, he hastened down and conducted a foreshortened interview with Bishop Ribeiro through his aide Father Martinho da Costa Lopes. Pale-faced nuns in the grounds of the presbytery spoke together agitatedly. They beckoned urgently to an Australian walking past to take sanctuary in the church grounds. The interview concluded, Richardson turned quickly into the main street and strode towards the city square. Armed soldiers at each junction checked passing cars, in some cases turning them back. Chinese were gathering anxiously in shop doorways. No doubt a few knew of the narrowly-averted trouble with the military police.

The square was full of soldiers. They wore the brown and green mottle of Portuguese camouflage dress, offset by sartorial white gloves and brilliantly-coloured bandanas, red, blue or orange, according to the group in which they were roughly assembled. They carried G3 rifles. On questioning, none would volunteer a reason for the gathering. There was no leading FRETILIN figure in evidence.

After what seemed an interminable time, a few Central Committee people appeared—José Gonçalves, Juvenal Inácio, Aleixo Corte Real. Still there were no leaders present. Then, a while later, Rogério Lobato appeared. He was unshaven although he wore, for the first time, a Portuguese Army dress uniform which reporters had seen lying on his desk some days before. It was a light shade of olive with a red fleck through it. Even the normally outward-going Rogério would say nothing at this stage. A few civilians gathered in the square, all looking rather uncertain of what was in store.

The hot Dili sun beat down and an hour later the observers knew no more. Other Central Committee members, however, had appeared. They wore khaki uniforms with red bandanas and assembled in front of the arch entrance of the former Portuguese administration offices. The soldiers were assembled facing them, on the road in front of the offices. It was a reflex action to peer beyond them to scan the horizon for Indonesian ships. Beyond lay Ataúro, where the Portuguese Governor Lemos Pires and his commandos sat uselessly. On clear days one could almost see every goatpath and crevice on the island: on other days it shimmered or disappeared altogether in tropical haze. Along the Dili esplanade heavy Portuguese cannons, probably embedded in the facing cement when Dili was little more than a malarial swamp, pointed out to sea.

A van drove around the perimeter of the square, with a loudhailer blaring a message in Portuguese or Tetum. Some of the young 'leftists' appeared to be on it. After touring the square it disappeared into the Dili streets. Women in freshly pressed dresses were also gathering now, heralding the presence of a growing crowd of civilians. From the left came the sound of voices singing. A demonstration was moving towards the square. As the sound grew nearer a group of youth and women's movement leaders turned the corner at the head of a procession of children singing FRETILIN songs. A small cheer went up as they entered.

Over an hour after the assembly commenced, Rogério Lobato came up, a characteristic shy grin on his face. 'Do you know what we are doing?' he asked. The observers murmured ignorance. 'We are going to declare our independence!'

The crowd grew quickly, although tension still hung over it. Some of the Red Cross doctors had driven down from the hospital and occupied key positions on the top balcony of the administration building. Roger East was there, looking florid in the Dili heat. Even 'Nixon' was present with some of the soldiers from the front, all displaying a generous application of spit and polish. Next came 'Major' Kruger, resplendent in a crisp fawn military shirt and his service medals. Then, an unexpected turn: round the corner glided the Governor's black Mercedes-Benz, the iron cross of the state of Portugal still on the bonnet. A soldier snapped to attention and swept the door open to present Xavier in a fancy red fleck uniform twin to Rogério's.

Everyone was here, after what seemed an anxious eternity. The Central Committee were ranged a little to the left of the portico, at the head of the assembly. In the centre Muki, secretary of the OPMT, carried a flat package.

In front of the Central Committee was a table with a white lace tablecloth on which was the text of the declaration of independence. Xavier stood squarely behind. On his right was Nicolau Lobato, then Mari Alkatiri, on his left Rogério Lobato, then Guido Soares, chief of staff of FALINTIL. A little further to the right stood 'Major' Kruger, proudly to attention. In a kindly touch of Timorese generosity the Central Committee had invited the Australian pensioner to take a prime position at the ceremony, near the President.

At 5.55pm Muki moved to the flagpole base with her

package. A fanfare sounded. The Portuguese flag had flown inviolate through the three-month absence of the Portuguese, as it had for four centuries before. That afternoon it was lowered in East Timor for the last time. To the mast fluttered the new flag of the Democratic Republic of East Timor, the outline of which Sam Kruger had seen that morning. Central Committee members had worked all night on the design and final sewing; it was a variation of the red, black, yellow and white FRETILIN banner.

Independence day, Dili, 28 November 1975. The crowd assembles. Freelance journalist Roger East is at far left. (Michael Richardson, courtesy of the *Age*).

With the flag in place, a minute's silence was observed for those who had died in the preceding months and in all East Timor's anti-colonial wars. A twenty one gun salute boomed

Xavier do Amaral signs FRETILIN's declaration of independence. (Michael Richardson, courtesy of the *Age*).

across the harbour to mark the hour; perhaps it was heard on Ataúro by representatives of the displaced colonial power.

Xavier read the declaration:

> Expressing the highest aspirations of the people of East Timor and to safeguard the most legitimate interests of national sovereignty, the Central Committee of FRETILIN decrees by proclamation, unilaterally, the independence of East Timor, from 00.00 hours today, declaring the state of the Democratic Republic of East Timor, anti-colonialist and anti-imperialist.
> Long live the Democratic Republic of East Timor!
> Long live the people of East Timor, free and independent!
> Long live FRETILIN!

The new national anthem rang out, in the unfamiliar cadences of the pentatonic scale of traditional Timorese music:

FRETILIN leaders (from left) Mari Alkatiri, Nicolau Lobato, Xavier do Amaral, Rogério Lobato, Guido Soares and Octavio de Araújo hail East Timor's independence. (Michael Richardson, courtesy of the *Age*).

'Major' Kruger—Mr Samuel Kruger, guest of honour at FRETILIN's independence declaration. (Michael Richardson, courtesy of the *Age*).

FRETILIN leaders (from left Xavier do Amaral, Rogério Lobato and Guido Soares, independence day, Dili, 28 November 1975. (Michael Richardson, courtesy of the *Age*).

'Homeland! homeland! East Timor our nation! Glory to the people and the heroes of our liberation!'

Xavier then reviewed the elegantly garbed FALINTIL troops who drummed, trumpeted and strutted past in the goose step of the Portuguese Army. As the President took the salute 'Major' Kruger also drew himself up to his full height, medals gleaming.

The formalities over, the crowd of 2,000 erupted into cheers, embraces, singing and weeping. The journalists sprinted to the Marconi centre next door before the radio telephone line to Australia closed. Normally it closed at 5.45 but the operators had been feeding material through specially to keep it open.

Despite their efforts atmospheric conditions were so bad that it was almost unusable but Richardson valiantly screamed his piece down the line to Melbourne almost letter for letter.

By the time the story was out, night had fallen and the crowd below dispersed. The strains of 'Foho Ramelau' and a general hubbub had filled the square for an hour or so, but now the curfew was exercised. The situation in Dili was politically delicate. There had already been concern about agitation in the Moslem quarter and a provocation could not be risked at this dangerous hour.[1] Intervention from Jakarta would best be orchestrated with a signal from inside the capital itself.

It had been a rather grim, brave little ceremony, not attended by the joy which should properly accompany the birth of a new nation, or the expansive finery of neighbouring Papua New Guinea's independence day three months before. The Angolan declaration had also been made at a dark hour, but at least with victory in sight. In Dili on 28 November some Central Committee members donned uniforms and weapons for the first time since August. The ceremony was conducted in the knowledge that Indonesian forces were daily moving further into the territory and that the real testing time might only now be starting for East Timor.

Angola was not the only influence on the independence decision although African politics, generally, played some part. FRETILIN National Political Commissioner Mari Alkatiri had returned from an African diplomatic tour a little over a week before. Mau Laka, a Central Committee member, accompanied him. On Alkatiri's own account the independence decision was taken soon after their return.

At the end of September a conference of forty-nine Afro-Asian countries meeting in the Mozambican capital pledged 'total support for the struggle for national independence led by the vanguard FRETILIN'. The resolution was moved by Samora Machel and passed unanimously. Considerable significance was attached to this support in East Timor and *Timor Leste* of 4 October featured the news on the front page.

One aim of Alkatiri's tour was to consolidate this support and convert it to formal pledges of recognition in the event of independence being declared. On the delegation's return it was claimed that as a result of its work in Africa, twenty-five governments had pledged 'certain recognition' within ten days of the declaration. They included the People's Republic of China, the Soviet Union, Zambia, Mozambique, Tanzania, Guinea Bissau, Angola, Cape Verde, São Tomé-Príncipe, North Korea, North and South Vietnam, Cambodia, Romania, Netherlands, East Germany, Sweden, Algeria, Cuba, Norway and Brazil.

The East Timorese reasoned that while they existed only as a political party they carried no weight in the world political arena. FRETILIN were forced to watch helplessly as the Indonesians slowly but systematically ate into their territory, which they didn't formally administer and the formal administrator of which was either unconcerned or acquiescent.

The fall of Atabae was not disclosed for over twenty-four hours, when Rogério Lobato announced it to the press. He said it was a major factor in declaring independence. 'Nixon's' presence at the ceremony was not accidental. The soldiers at the front had been pressing for independence for some time. They wanted to fight as defenders of an independent country: if East Timorese were to die fighting for their homeland, they should die as free and independent people, they averred.

Above all FRETILIN felt they had no choice. Among other things UDI was a strategy. 'Apart from the military situation, basically the attitude of neighbouring governments and of Portugal forced us to declare UDI', Mari Alkatiri explained:

> We know that after independence we can get more aid and support from countries who are not our neighbours. We hope that their attitude will force neighbouring countries to take the same step. We would prefer them to be the first to recognise our independence.[2]

To the East Timorese it appeared that Portugal would not negotiate; it was useless to appeal to the Indonesians, and Australia, the nearest influential neighbour, would not listen. Mozambique, Guinea Bissau and Angola were constant allies, but distant and economically weak. As a sovereign nation East Timor could appeal to the UN for wider recognition and support.

In the days following the declaration Xavier worked tirelessly at the Marconi centre, speaking to African leaders by telephone, but days later only four of the promised twenty-five had recognised: Mozambique, Angola, Guinea Bissau and Cape Verde.

The Australian government (now the Fraser 'caretaker' government since the dismissal of the Whitlam Labor administration on 11 November) was quick to state that it would not recognise the new republic. The Timorese nevertheless entertained hopes of a change of policy. 'The new government does not accept the position of the Australian government as final', Alkatiri declared, 'The Australian government has been realistic in the past and we think that it is only realistic now to recognise the republic'.[3]

Although Mari Alkatiri traced FRETILIN's independence decision to the time of his return from Africa, it seems he referred to the framing of general policy rather than the specific date. The timing of the declaration took Ramos Horta and Alarico Fernandes, then in Darwin after a brief Australian tour, by surprise although in Canberra they had told sympathisers that they believed independence might be imminent. The unkempt appearance of some of the leaders, the frenetic all-night flag-sewing of the 27th and the close sequence of Atabae's capture to the actual independence ceremony suggest that the decision was taken hastily. Indeed Alkatiri (in seeming contradiction to his other statement) said on the day that it had been taken only hours earlier. Rogério Lobato told reporters that the declaration was originally planned for 1 December, an important anniversary in Portugal's history commemorating a revolt which wrested that country from Spanish control. The news from Atabae had caused them to bring the date forward.

The next day's ceremonies, scheduled to commence at 9am, were grander and more relaxed. Xavier was sworn in as president of the republic and the constitution proclaimed. As on the Friday evening, the civilian attendance was not large—again, there were around 2,000 present. It was in sharp contrast to the demonstrations of early 1975 when FRETILIN filled the same square with thousands upon thousands of supporters.[4]

In his inauguration speech Xavier spoke with some bitterness of his country's plight:

> The right of a people to independence is inalienable. Talks between FRETILIN and Portugal have never taken place because from the time of the Rome talks Portugal has stood by while Indonesia intervened ... We had to fight alone against UDT in Dili and against Indonesia at the border. We must build on the grave of fascism and colonialism a new country free and democratic where there is no discrimination ... We direct our appeal for peace to Indonesia, but we will live by the slogan 'independence or death'.[5]

Rogério then read the newly drafted constitution:

> The Democratic Republic of East Timor is a sovereign nation, united and indivisible ... anti-colonialist and anti-imperialist, born from the people's resistance struggle, guided by the legitimate vanguard of the Maubere people—FRETILIN ... The Democratic Republic of East Timor runs under the political orientation of FRETILIN in order to end colonial structures and build a new society free from domination and exploitation.[6]

The supremacy of the president over the army was stressed. He was ex officio to be commander of the armed forces, with power to expel any member of FALINTIL. The constitution also guaranteed freedom of religion and declared the principle of the separation of church and state under a policy of mutual non-interference. It defended, too, the right to sexual and racial equality, freedom of expression and political association. Universal suffrage from the age of fifteen was declared and a 'people's assembly' nominated as the supreme organ or power. Terms were laid down for the first general elections of the republic:

> Conditions, method and date of general elections will be established by electoral law. The first general elections will take place one year after the first congress of FRETILIN.

FRETILIN's first annual congress was due on 11 September 1975, anniversary of the assembly at which ASDT became FRETILIN. The UDT coup and its aftermath overruled the possibility of it occurring then. With the onset of Indonesian attacks it was shelved indefinitely and at the time of independence the future remained too uncertain to set a date. With independence the FRETILIN Regional Sub-committee structure which had functioned in the countryside as the effective unit of administrative control for the past three months automatically became a government structure. As, however, those who occupied the positions had been elected by the FRETILIN membership and not the population at large it was projected that all these positions would be declared vacant at the first election and nominations called for from the general population.

On 1 December, three days after the independence declaration, the Cabinet of the Democratic Republic of East Timor was sworn it, after days of long and apparently intense deliberation by the Central Committee. Much of their time was no doubt spent on the serious work now confronting the independence movement but the composition of the Cabinet was a difficult and, to a degree, contentious question.

The ceremony took place in the former Governor's residence, perched high on the edge of Dili, on the road to Aileu. The day was sunny and the FRETILIN men looked handsome in suits. Dili residents crowded on the terraced gardens of the ornate colonial villa which bore the inscription 'Portuguese Province of Timor'. Once again Xavier took his place behind a table with a lace tablecloth. This time an oath of office lay on it.

The Cabinet consisted of eleven Ministers with seven Viceministers to assist them. The first to be sworn in was Nicolau Lobato, as Prime Minister. Then Mari Alkatiri stepped forward, as Minsiter of State for Political Affairs. Abílio de Araújo, Minister for Economic and Social Affairs, was still in Portugal; it was planned that he should return in the next few days with the one other expatriate minister. José Gonçalves, Minister for Economic Co-ordination and Statistics, was next to take the oath, then followed Rogério Lobato, Defence Minister. Next in line were Alarico Fernandes as Minister for Home Affairs and Security and José Ramos Horta, Foreign Affairs and External Information, both just returned from Australia. Hamis Bassarewan (Hata) took the oath as Minister for Education and Culture. He was a Timorese of Arab descent who had been an initiator of UNETIM and the literacy programme. Finance Minister Juvenal Inácio was at the front—now at the Loes river—with some other Central Committee members. The mop-haired radical Mau Lear was declared Minister for Justice: he received a particularly rousing cheer from the crowd, to which he responded with the clenched fist salute of the front. The two remaining ministers were Vicente Sa'he, Labor and Welfare, and Eduardo Carlos dos Anjos, Communications and Transport. Sa'he was also at the front.

Five of the seven Vice-ministers then took their vow before Xavier—Economic Co-ordination and Statistics: Hélio Pina (Mau Kruma); National Defence (one of two Vice-secretaries): Guido Soares; Labor and Welfare: Guido Valadares; Communications and Transport: Domingos Ribeiro, and Internal Administration and Security: Fernando Carmo. Of the other two, Guilhermina dos Santos de Araújo, Vice-Minister for Foreign Affairs and External Information, was in Portugal and Hermenegildo Alves, the second Vice-secretary for Defence, was at the Loes River.

All vowed to:

> dedicate all my strength and knowledge to combat colonialism, imperialism and all forms of domination and exploitation of men by men, to defend and promote the superior interests of the people of East Timor, to work to intransigently defend the integrity of the country and the unity of the nation of East Timor.

The average age of the Ministry appeared to be less than thirty. Most were around twenty-six to thirty, some younger; Xavier at thirty-seven and Carmo, of a comparable age, were the 'old men' of FRETILIN. The two principal figures were practising Catholics, the third a practising Moslem. Three members of the Cabinet, José Gonçalves, Fernando Carmo and Domingos Ribeiro, were not drawn from the Central Committee. They were selected for their technical skills. On this principle, FRETILIN stated that they would be prepared to bring even UDT members into the government.

Following the ceremony children sang and danced in the cool green of the gardens.

Mari Alkatiri, Ramos Horta's rival, was now the third man of the front, behind Xavier and Nicolau. He had emerged as a competent and reasonable politician with an intelligent grasp of foreign affairs. He carried the prestige of his African diplomacy, while Ramos Horta had been saddled with the unrewarding work of Australian diplomacy, doomed to failure from the start for reasons quite outside his control. Ramos Horta had also lost influence through his absence from Timor during militarily crucial periods.

For some time a tension had existed within the leadership over foreign policy attitudes. There was a growing feeling, reinforced by events, of the futility of Western-style diplomacy. Some argued that because East Timor was small and isolated, ultimately the independence movement could only depend on its own strength, on the armed struggle in Timor itself. While appeals for external support should be directed as a matter of course to the provenly reliable governments of the former Portuguese African colonies and Third World governments generally, in the region the appeal to the Australian and even New Guinean government was seen as vain. The only hope, they argued, might be to form a front with popular liberation movements in the region, including secessionist movements within the Republic of Indonesia. Those who adopted this position held that neither white governments in the region nor conservative South-East Asian governments would support them. The argument was frequently coupled with disappointment at Australian Labor government attitudes.

FRETILIN had already addressed radio broadcasts to the 'brother people of Indonesia', with some apparent success. In October Timorese in Dili reported that following one such broadcast they had monitored a news report from Radio Kupang of a demonstration of students in Kupang. The demonstrators had demanded a peaceful solution to the 'border problem' represented by the thousands of East Timorese refugees then in Indonesian Timor. They petitioned Governor El Tari to return the refugees to East Timor and offered their personal services towards peace.

Although the idea of forming a front with other liberation movements had gained strength in the months between the UDT coup and the independence declaration it was far from FRETILIN policy. Officially the policy remained one of non-alignment and support for the Association of South-East Asian Nations, as it had been soon after FRETILIN's formation, when the front rejected overtures from liberation movements in Irian Jaya and the South Moluccas. From September to December 1975 repeated assurances of non-alignment and appeals for peaceful co-operation were cabled to Jakarta. But this stance was accompanied by a growing private doubt about the efficacy of diplomatic work through conventional channels.

Alkatiri's new strength in the front expressed the growing influence of the belief that armed struggle and self-reliance, in concert with the fighting tradition of the Third World, must form the irreducible core of FRETILIN thinking. In this formula East Timor lay between the expedient interests of neighbouring governments on the one hand and the major international power blocs on the other.

Portuguese influence had created a movement quite different from any other in the region. But if it had brought Amílcar Cabral to South-East Asia it had also left a barren landscape. When FRETILIN became the government of East Timor their economic inheritance was an empty shell:

> Practically all FRETILIN leaders are young and inexperienced, and therefore administrative and technical skills are spread very thinly. Professional qualifications are almost non-existent. The results of these weaknesses are weak infrastructures in virtually every aspect of FRETILIN's activities. Perhaps the army is best off, with its number of 2 to 3,000 trained soldiers, but only one of them held non-commissioned rank prior to 10th August. Thus, though the troops fight well, communications are poor, intelligence is weak, and most supporting services virtually non-existent.[7]

Assessing the FRETILIN leadership from personal observation, Dunn commented that the front lacked experience and was not fully formed politically. Military conflict was imposing strains and tensions on the leaders, he added, nor should the effect of East Timor's isolation on their perceptions be underestimated. Finally, there was 'the inevitable possibility of a power struggle, the seeds of which are already apparent'.

Their comparative inexperience was indisputable. Nevertheless the September–December experience as an administrative power had been a compressed learning process. In particular, their military capability, although lacking in many respects, had developed quickly. These months had given FALINTIL commanders the opportunity to shape their 'Dad's Army of Timorese hippies' into a fighting force. Manuel Soares's Maliana exercise had shown what could be done with a relatively well-equipped, highly-motivated peasant army. And while there was no finality about the political course they had chosen, certainly FRETILIN had by this time set its direction.

The period had been one of self-definition in which power struggles were not permitted to erupt, but considered shifts of influence had occurred in the leadership. And unformed, raw and unorthodox in its methods though the movement appeared, that was part of its character too.

The unique style of decision-making used by FRETILIN had become part of this picture. Dunn's observations of this process are worth quoting at length for the picture they give of the leadership as it was in October 1975:

> It is clear that FRETILIN is not a Communist Party, though it does have a left wing. The failure of Communist states to show any real interest in the problems of Timor has not served Communist interests. The Party structure tends to give the impression that it is Marxist, but in fact the organisation appears to have been inspired by the structures of FRETILIN and PAIGC, rather than ideological motives. I am still inclined to the view that it is more populist than Marxist. The leadership structure is, however, rather ponderous and clumsy for a country the size of Timor. There is a Central Committee of more than 30, an Executive Committee, a Political-Military Committee with what seems to be overlapping functions. The lack of experience and infrastructural weaknesses suggest that decision-making will often be a slow and painful process.

The Central Committee in fact had fifty-two members and consensus was arrived at through hours of debate and discussion. It was standard for leaders to be inaccessible because they were closeted in gruelling debating sessions within the Central Committee. The military police crisis of 4 November was resolved in this way.

Dunn added:

> On the credit side, FRETILIN has been surprisingly effective in its skeleton administration of the Province. The distribution of food appears to have been on the whole fairly equitable, the basic services to Dili are functioning more or less normally and the population appears to be quiet and orderly. There are very few reports of looting and other forms of crime.
>
> An attempt has been made to set up a transitional administration using FRETILIN members who previously worked as functionaries. The direction of "departments" is inclined to be clumsy, with a troika principle,—functionary, military and Central Committee. The FRETILIN leadership is on the whole very co-operative and informal in its dealings.[8]

After the 1 December ceremony, the sequence of events accelerated. That night Radio Kupang beamed into Dili a 'special broadcast in English to Australian listeners, from the mountains of East Timor' which sent a chill down the spines of those Australian listeners in Dili.

On 10 November FRETILIN soldiers had attacked and almost succeeded in recapturing Balibó. They reported that the Indonesians had moved a quantity of electronic and military equipment into the town and were using Balibó as an administrative base. The anti-FRETILIN parties had nominated it as their administrative centre to lend credibility to claims to represent a territorial power. The leaflet dropped over Atabae was marked 'Balibó 26 November'. Now the 'special broadcast' purported to come from here.

It was a declaration of the integration of East Timor into Indonesia and a warning to foreign nationals in the territory that 'anti-FRETILIN forces would not take responsibility for their safety in the future. Referring to the Macau conference and Rome talks, it declaimed:

> As FRETILIN ignored the above initiatives and criminally refused to allow the people of East Timor to express their legitimate interests, we declare that:
>
> FRETILIN's unilateral declaration of independence has drained out completely all possibilities of a peaceful solution to the problem in line with the wishes of the East Timorese people ...
>
> This moment is opportune to re-establish the strong traditional links with the Indonesian nation. We therefore proclaim the integration of the whole territory of the ex-Portuguese territory of Timor with the Indonesian nation.
>
> The government and people of Indonesia are requested to take the necessary steps in order to protect people's lives who now consider themselves part of the Indonesian people even though living under the terror and practices of FRETILIN allowed by the government of Portugal.

The statement was endorsed by the *liurai* of Atsabe and A. Borromeu for APODETI, Lopes da Cruz and Domingos de Oliveira for UDT, KOTA's José Martins and Domingos Pereira for Trabalhista.

According to the broadcast, the integration declaration was signed in Balibó the previous day and presented to 'a represen-

Indonesian officials with East Timorese from UDT, APODETI, KOTA and Trabalhista, declaration of integration, Atambua, 30 November 1975. Left: BAKIN agent Louis Taolin, Guilherme Maria Gonçalves, Lopes da Cruz, (next but one) António Santos of Trabalhista and UDT military commander João Tavares. Centre right is Indonesian Foreign Minister Adam Malik with, directly behind, Colonel Sugiyanto of the 'Operasi Komodo' command and, on Malik's left, José Martins of KOTA.

tative of President Suharto' that day, at a meeting 'close to our border'. The meeting was in fact held in Atambua in Indonesian Timor. The Indonesian press covered the occasion in some detail; the representative was Adam Malik and he was photographed accepting the petition from the Timorese leaders. One of those leaders later alleged that the document was drafted in Jakarta.[9]

In Atambua Malik told the Timorese:

> You are racing against time and you have a tough struggle ahead. However, you need not worry. We will give you our full support, quietly or openly.

> Now we meet in Atambua, and soon we shall meet again in Dili. I expect you to invite me to come to Dili soon.[10]

He concluded with the words: 'Diplomacy is finished. The solution to the East Timor problem is now the front line of battle'.

On the day following the broadcast, 2 December, Red Cross delegates in Dili received a cable from the Australian government warning that all Australian nationals in the territory should evacuate for reasons of their own safety. It was clear that an attack on Dili was imminent and that the Australian government had advance knowledge from Indonesian intelligence sources.

Since FRETILIN's independence declaration the International Red Cross (ICRC) had attempted to negotiate a guarantee of respect for their neutrality in the event of an Indonesian entry into Dili. This difficult task was made more so by the fact that no state of war had been declared and that Indonesia officially denied involvement. When ICRC entered East Timor in August UDT forces were still active and had agreed with FRETILIN to respect the neutrality of the ICRC. The new situation called for a new agreement. The international body now considered guarantees to be necessary from four parties to the fighting: FRETILIN, UDT, APODETI and Indonesia. Only the FRETILIN August agreement still held. Like the Portuguese negotiators, the ICRC were unable to make contact with the representatives of UDT and APODETI at the crucial time. By 2 December they still had no guarantees. They hoped to work from Dili hospital as a neutral zone in the event of an invasion but without guarantees they too would have to evacuate.

There were then thirteen Australians in East Timor on the accounting of the Foreign Affairs Department. Those in Dili were approached by ICRC delegates to determine whether they wished to evacuate in air transport provided by the Australian government. They were asked to sign a document testifying that they had been warned.

Two Australian aid workers had already been told through the Australian embassy in Jakarta that Indonesian authorities would not guarantee their safety in East Timor. In mid-November Father Mark Raper, a Jesuit priest from the Asian Bureau of Australia and Dr Bob Richards of Community Aid

Abroad—both attached to the ACFOA task force—were delivered the warning by the Australian Foreign Affairs Department. The cable outlining the warning (classified 'confidential'), was later leaked to the press and proved a source of embarrassment for the Australian government:

> On 19th of this month we have informed the Indonesian authorities of the visit to Dili by Raper and Richards.
>
> When told that Richards intended to stay in Timor for about one month the authorities commented that this was risky.[11]

On 2 December threats, ostensibly from APODETI and UDT, were again levelled at specific Australian aid workers. A message from Canberra radioed to ICRC in Dili warned that Indonesian forces had threatened to kill Australians in Dili, particularly those working for ASIAT and ACFOA. The threats were evidence of a final effort by Indonesia to clear the territory of foreign observers before the invasion began.

The decision to leave was difficult for those working there. If they evacuated, no independent witnesses would remain, no doctors would remain and, in particular, the absence of International Red Cross would mean that the important work of enforcing the Geneva Conventions could not be done. With no neutral zone, the presence of private aid agencies or of journalist observers seemed impossible, unless those concerned were prepared to retreat to the mountains with FRETILIN and remain isolated from outside contact for probably a period of years. Some had also seen the demoralisation which followed the earlier ASIAT evacuation. It was depressing to leave the capital feeling the Timorese were left to their fate. But for most of the Australians Balibó had set a precedent which they could not afford to ignore.

On hearing of the evacuation FRETILIN leaders articulated what they already knew from a number of sources: the Indonesians were coming, frontally, in a full-scale attack. Rogério Lobato issued a statement:

> Acting on information from FRETILIN intelligence sources we expect a full-scale attack against East Timor and particularly the capital Dili ... We appeal to the world to stop this criminal aggression which will cause an endless bloodbath. The people of East Timor will resist.

Most of the Australians in Dili were given the news by ICRC around midday. The evacuation flights were scheduled for 2 pm. By that time all but one had agreed to leave the mainland. 'Major' Kruger wished to stay but concerned friends insisted that he go, at least to Ataúro from where ICRC intended to commute with Dili to continue daily clinics. The ASIAT team, conscious of their miscalculation when they evacuated in October in the aftermath of Balibó, now hoped to remain on Ataúro and commute together with the Red Cross. However, when they arrived, neither the Portuguese administration nor the Red Cross were agreeable to the arrangement and they were forced to return to Darwin. Roger East was adamant that he would stay. He would go to the mountains with FRETILIN he said, and attempt to report from there even if it required being isolated for years. He had come to East Timor prepared for such an eventuality: his Bobonaro experience was a rehearsal.

SAATAS air charter, a Northern Territory-based firm which had operated between Darwin and Dili for some weeks, was to shuttle the evacuees to Ataúro. There a RAAF Caribou aircraft waited to take them on the next leg to Darwin.

As the Australians left after painful farewells to schocked Timorese friends, the Cabinet of the Democratic Republic of East Timor was in conference in the administration building. APODETI prisoners were being shifted from their foreshore detention centre to the military headquarters, with Security Minister Alarico Fernandes assuring inquirers that they would be protected in the event of an invasion. At the airport the departing foreigners said goodbye to Roger East and wished him luck. His cheerful air masked apprehension. Two of the list of thirteen Australians, Mr and Ms Rex Syddell, were in Tutuala at the eastern tip of the territory, and unreachable. The owner of one name on the list—Mr Davies of Ainaro—apparently slipped out of Dili on the SAATAS flight the day before. His presence was a mystery to Red Cross officials and others who had travelled through Ainaro, who had never encountered this Australian. In the following days a Foreign Affairs department press release announced that the list should have read as twelve Australians: the thirteenth had left East Timor the previous day. Perhaps Foreign Affairs had inadvertently exposed their man in Timor.

On Atauro the evacuees were received by the courtly gentlemen of Governor Lemos Pires's entourage. The Governor was in Lisbon but senior officers of the administration remained, with the crew of two corvettes and the Governor's commando force.

The 'goat island' bore the signs of its isolation from the mainland and its traditional social function as a place of exile. The fishing folk of Ataúro squatted under the coconut groves, chatting quietly or following the movements of the Portuguese military presence in sullen silence. Their bodies were malnourished, their garments poor. On the beachfront fleet figures moved silently around the grass houses edging the foreshore, calling children to them when Europeans passed. In this tropical pastorale there was little to divert the commandos. They wandered the island flexing their muscles, toying with weapons, eyeing the local women. The sailors kept slightly apart. Their hair was a shade longer, their gait more relaxed. They sunned themselves and swam. On a coconut tree near the village schoolhouse an MFA propaganda poster advertised the virtues of the movement to the Ataúro population: 'The MFA is the people, the people are the MFA'. The reality mocked the claim.

The corvettes patrolled the mainland from a safe distance, 'showing the flag'. Regular radio contact was kept with Lisbon and a link maintained with the Timorese administration left in charge of Oecusse, the enclave surrounded by Indonesian Timor. (The garrison on Oecusse was also withdrawn during the civil war period, although there was no fighting reported there.) The ship's radio was used for the Lisbon contact: a radio room near the officers' mess was the centre for other communications.

In the preceding three months this radio centre had provided the Portuguese with a dress circle view of activity on the mainland, through their monitoring of military communications. In August they observed the advance of UDT forces from Dili to the border. From September they recorded the onward thrust of Indonesia. Throughout, they had a rare record of the course of events from radio surveillance of all involved parties. On 16 October government personnel in Australia had been silent witnesses to the circumstances of

Balibó. From 620kms away they listened to the orders passing on either side of the border before and after the two Australian news teams died. The Portuguese on Ataúro had probably joined this secret audience.

The evacuees slept on the island that night. They lay restlessly alert, listening for sounds of military activity in the strait which separated them from Dili. Their apprehensions were sharpened by that evening's Radio Kupang broadcast. It began by repeating the integration declaration and proceeded to detail 'thirty-one conditions for the integration of East Timor with Indonesia'. 'The *sine qua non* of integration is that people should take Indonesian citizenship' it announced. Supporters of FRETILIN would be banished from East Timor for fifteen years; East Timor would become the twenty-seventh province, although its prospective governors promised to 'take into account the unique nature of East Timor'. In return, the citizens of East Timor would be obliged to 'respect Panca Sila' ... 'reject Communism' ... 'swear loyalty to Indonesia' and 'automatically' cease to recognise Portuguese authority.

The next day the journalists and aid workers flew on to Darwin. Australia was preparing for an election—in ten days people would go to the ballot box. Foreign policy was not an election issue: there was a tacit consensus between the major parties that Timor would not be debated.

President Ford of the United States and Dr Henry Kissinger, his Secretary of State, were then in Jakarta on a brief visit, for discussions with President Suharto. Their visit followed Indonesian arms negotiations with the US in October and November. It is not known whether East Timor was discussed.

On 4 December three members of the newly-formed FRETILIN Cabinet arrived in Darwin. Mari Alkatiri, José Ramos Horta and Rogério Lobato had left East Timor as the result of a Cabinet decision to send a section out to further the work of gaining diplomatic support. Rogério Lobato had married only days before: all left their families behind. Ramos Horta was to travel on to New York to put East Timor's case before the UN. Alkatiri and Lobato were to proceed to Mozambique as part of the ongoing campaign to mobilise black African support. The three had allegedly experienced difficulty leaving Dili. It was reported that dissidents (perhaps fifth columnists) had rolled barrels across the tarmac in an attempt to prevent them leaving.

In the lull following the Australian departure, Jakarta continued to disseminate false reports. On 3 December Antara reported that Indonesian forces had taken several positions close to Dili and surrounded Aileu, twenty kilometres south. A later story claimed that in a two-pronged attack on the capital on 5 December 650 FRETILIN soldiers had surrendered. In Dili Roger East reported that there was no change in the military situation apart from continuing bombardment of FRETILIN positions on the Loes river and the border fighting which had become a fact of daily life. Rogério Lobato's defence deputy Guido Soares denounced the reports as 'for world consumption'. 'Their [Indonesia's] soldiers are aware of the true situation' he added.

After months of moving tortuously between persuasion, bribery, information distortion, and military might, 'Operasi Komodo' had wound to its pitch. The dragon was poised to strike.

In Australia former Labor Prime Minister Whitlam stated on the national television network that his government would do 'nothing' in the event of an Indonesian invasion:

> Nobody would go to war over it ... We would do absolutely nothing ... Now that's a blunt, truthful answer and no political leader would give you another answer. It's the same answer Menzies gave when some newspapers said we ought to go to war over West Irian.[12]

On the evening of 6 December the Red Cross workers left Dili for the last time. Shortly before they left, they spoke to Roger East. He appeared cheerful and told them he had been invited to stay at Xavier's house but had declined. As the Red Cross plane nosed towards Ataúro at dusk, its passengers saw three warships moving down the coast towards Dili. They were the first of an armada.

In the early hours of 7 December fifteen Indonesian aircraft left their Central Java base. Nine were bound for Dili, six for Baucau. All were full of commandos.

At the border area, two forces were preparing to thrust overland in co-ordination with forces landing in Dili and

Baucau. One was to push on from Atabae, where support troops could be provided from naval transport, the other was to attempt to move overland across the border near Bobonaro and on to Atsabe, Aileu and then Dili.[13]

The main substance of Roger East's Reuters dispatch that evening was the evacuation which was underway from Dili:

> The residents of Dili have been making a quiet exodus to the hills as the security situation deteriorates. Tonight Dili is silent and almost deserted. For the fourth night a blackout is in force and the beaches and side streets are guarded by heavily-armed troops.

He also reported that FRETILIN border forces had observed the establishment of an operational command at Atabae the day before, where Indonesian troops had already been landed. Unmarked aircraft had also been active, dropping propaganda leaflets over the territory, predicting that FRETILIN would fall within five days, East said.[14]

Next morning in Darwin a radio transceiver tuned to the Red Cross radio in Dili hospital brought news of the attack. The newly-evacuated journalists sat helplessly listening to the voice of Alarico Fernandes:

> Indonesian forces have been landed in Dili by sea, by sea ... They are flying over Dili dropping out paratroopers ... Aircraft are dropping out more and more paratroopers ... A lot of people have been killed indiscriminately ... Women and children are going to be killed by Indonesian forces ... we are going to be killed! SOS, we call for your help, this is an urgent call ...

9

Australia's Role

From at least August 1975 Australian foreign policy towards East Timor was based on a full knowledge of events in the territory. This policy received its highest expression in Mr Whitlam's public 'we would do nothing' statement on the eve of the 7 December assault. When the Labor government lost office on 11 November the policy was continued and extended by the Liberal government of Malcolm Fraser.

Australian governmental attitudes to the death of the five journalists at Balibó were an important indicator that the Labor government was obdurately committed to the course it had chosen. Timorese and Indonesian assessments of their respective positions were to an extent determined by Australian responses at this sensitive stage.

The Australian government had foreknowledge of the attack on Balibó. On the Thursday on which the journalists perished, the head of AAP's Darwin bureau telephoned the Dili correspondent with the information that Foreign Affairs had warned that 'something big' was to happen in East Timor that day and that the Dili correspondent should be alerted. The 'something big' had already happened early that morning and the television crews were probably dead by the time the phone call was taken in Dili during the midday hour in which the radio telephone link to Australia was open. In this form, news of the attack reached Dili from Australia before foot soldiers brought it in from the border about 9pm that evening.

Probably by the same means that it obtained this knowledge, the Australian government also knew by the night of 17 October that the men were dead, although the first announcement from Jakarta did not come until the twentieth. From a sophisticated military intelligence base in the Northern Territory, Australian defence officials using Indonesian– and

Tetum–language speakers, monitored Indonesian and FRETILIN field radio communications on either side of East Timor's border throughout the war. By this means they first knew of the journalists' presence in Balibó during the attack. As well, throughout the months of September–December 1975 Australian embassy officials in Jakarta were briefed by Indonesian officials on their intentions in Timor. Late on 17 October an Australian intelligence operative in Darwin telephoned an executive of the Channel 9 network and informed him that the five were dead and it was useless to continue hoping that they might be found alive. (Officially, the Australian government continued to regard them as 'missing' until 24 October). An Indonesian government statement was expected to be made in Jakarta the following Monday, 20 October, he said.[1]

A statement was made in Jakarta on the Monday, but it had no official imprimatur. Then, the daily *Kompas* published the 17 October Batugadé interview with Lopes da Cruz, saying that four male European bodies had been found in a house in Balibó, after 'a mortar barrage laid down by UDT'.

In Australia Senator Don Willesee, the Foreign Affairs Minister, acted on 17 October to set in motion an investigation into the fate of the journalists, then officially 'missing' in Balibó. The Jakarta embassy was contacted and on 18 October Ambassador Richard Woolcott called on Indonesian Foreign Minister Adam Malik. The Indonesian Minister pledged to facilitate Australian inquiries and on the twentieth, following the *Kompas* interview, the embassy decided to send an officer to the border area for an on-the-spot investigation. Richard Johnson, Indonesian-speaking Third Secretary of the Jakarta embassy, was dispatched to Kupang, where he spoke to Governor El Tari who then sent a letter to UDT leader Lopes da Cruz in Atambua asking for information. Johnson's request to travel personally to the border was refused.[2]

On 24 October a letter of reply dated 22 October reached Kupang. It was signed by UDT's Lopes da Cruz, APODETI's Guilherme Gonçalves and KOTA's José Martins. They stated that they had inspected 'the troops over the areas already taken out of FRETILIN's control by the combined forces of APODETI and UDT' and been informed that when the 'combined APODETI–UDT forces' entered Balibó:

> suddenly, there was a counter-attack launched from a house against our forces. Therefore, it became necessary to blow out with heavy fire that house-position which became into flames afterwards. As soon as our front forces arrived to the house it was found that fifteen people were killed, being among them *some white people whom were previously controlling and guiding the fire of* FRETILIN *position against our troops* ... Among the 15 dead people there were several white men that might be Australian journalists ... [my emphasis][3]

The previous evening the propaganda broadcast in the name of Lopes da Cruz had been monitored in Dili, in which it was claimed the five journalists were 'Australian Communists ... supporting and aside FRETILIN'.

The inference that the Australians were combatants was continued in correspondence with da Cruz. On 23 October Johnson had sent another letter to Atambua, giving identification details of the reporters. He also mentioned the *Kompas* interview in which da Cruz had spoken of the discovery of the bodies and of the sign 'Australia' and the Australian flag drawn near them. The UDT leader replied on 27 October. He hotly denied having given the *Kompas* interview and asserted anew that the journalists were militarily involved with FRETILIN.

> 1. On the wall of one house in Balibó has been painting by hand the following inscription:
>   First, the word AUSTRALIA
>   Below, a rough drawing of the Australian flag
>   Very close to these, was written in portuguese:
>   "Falentil está sempre ao lado do povo maubere"
>   [FALINTIL is always at the side of the Maubere people]
> 2. I do question myself whether the people of that house were journalists or not. This is a point to clarify having the inscriptions in mind.
> 3. According to the words written in portuguese ... Fretilin must be responsible for any australian citizen present at Balibó at the time.
> 4. Also it must be questioned the real meaning of these inscriptions as they may seem a form of publicity to be demanded to Fretilin ...
> 6. For all the regretable situation that our territory is facing this moment we are now expecting that the Australian Government take the necessary steps to stop australian citizens to come and

> fight side by side with Fretilin and fight and [oppress] the timorese people.[4]

Although one enterprising journalist managed at the time to obtain the text of some of the first letter,[5] the full text of both documents was suppressed by the Australian government until 2 June, 1976.

After further unsuccessful attempts to reach the border area Johnson returned to Jakarta. On 12 November General Yoga Sugama, head of the Indonesian state intelligence organisation BAKIN, contacted the Australian embassy to hand over the remains of the journalists, some documents of identification and a letter from Guilherme Gonçalves. The remains consisted of generally powdered bone fragments. The documents were in somewhat better condition. Although the bodies had allegedly been burnt beyond recognition, three of the five passports, plus a health certificate, airline ticket, visiting cards, letter, notebook and various pieces of equipment were returned intact, with no evidence of charring.

Thus it was not until this date that the death of the reporters was finally confirmed by Indonesian authorities and the existence of a fifth body acknowledged. In his letter the *liurai* of Atsabe repeated the basic claims of the earlier joint statement and that by da Cruz. There were fifteen bodies found in the house in Balibó, he said—'among the victims found there were four white men burned together with the house used by FRETILIN as their strongest resistance post'. After the Australian request for identification, troops had been sent back to the scene and extracted the documents which were now returned with the remains. According to the letter the fifth body had been found with the body of a Timorese on the outskirts of Balibó 'on one of the escape routes used by FRETILIN'.[6]

In the meantime different accounts of the journalists' death had come to light in Dili. The first of these was Lopes da Cruz's propaganda broadcast of 21 October, which contradicted the story he gave to Australian authorities. Secondly, there were the separately conducted interviews with FRETILIN soldiers who claimed to be eyewitnesses to the execution of some of the journalists by Indonesian troops.[7]

In Australia the press called for stronger government action and a number of writers had already pointed to the glaring discrepancies in the stories. 'Call this Murder!—Why Guilt Lies with Canberra' Melbourne's *Sunday Press* trumpeted.

In response to the outcry, on 31 October the Department of Foreign Affairs issued a report on government action to that time. It was prefaced by the remarks:

> Statements have been made to the effect that the Australian Government and the Department of Foreign Affairs have been unconcerned or inactive regarding the case of the five Australian journalists, missing believed killed in Balibó, East Timor.

and went on to deny that this was the case.[8]

It contained an eighteen-point summary of inquiries to date and their outcome, statements from leaders of the integrationist parties and sworn statements from David Colin Rutter, Consul at the Jakarta embassy. The latter testified that the eighteen points represented 'to the best of my knowledge ... an accurate statement of the circumstances which led to the presumption of death' of the five journalists. These points made no reference to any account taken east of the border, although journalists working in Dili had carefully forwarded to Canberra recordings of the Lopes da Cruz broadcast and interviews with alleged eyewitnesses. On 17 October John Starey, a Foreign Affairs official, travelled to East Timor. According to the report he 'inquired about reports of five Australians missing in the Balibó area but was unable to obtain any additional information'. On his brief excursion into the capital, during the hour or so his plane was on the ground, Starey had made no attempt to contact Timorese who had come from the Balibó scene and were then in Dili, or reporters (including an ABC reporter) who were working full-time at marshalling information about events at Balibó.

The circumstantial evidence strongly suggested that some of the five journalists, after attempting to surrender, were executed by Indonesian troops and the bodies burnt and that another had been treated as a combatant and shot down while attempting to flee the area. Initial investigations by the Foreign Affairs department were not only 'inadequate, incomplete and incompetent', as the journalists' association described Australian government efforts: they generously accommodated the internally inconsistent accounts of pro-Indonesian Timorese, most of whom had been direct participants in the attack on Balibó, while glossing over their claims that the journalists were militarily supporting FRETILIN. No reference in published accounts of the inquiry was ever made, for example to the Lopes da Cruz propaganda broadcast, and although officials interviewed da Cruz on a further investigation which finally took them to Balibó in April 1976, the matter does not seem to have been raised with him.

Moreover, official statements encouraged the belief firstly that the journalists were killed accidently in a battle between UDT/APODETI and FRETILIN forces and secondly that they had been negligent and in some way contributed to their own deaths.

Film taken by the journalists in Balibó the day before their death and sent down the track to Dili recorded Greg Shackleton painting the word 'Australia' in large lettering on three walls of the house in which they were camped, including the wall which faced on to one of the roads from which the attacking troops are thought to have entered. The house was one in which a number of journalists before them had slept en route to various border points to report the war. A New Zealand and a Portuguese television crew, two AAP reporters and a freelance photographer had stayed in the house. Although the film of the 15th emits great tension and speaks of an impending attack, there is nothing to suggest an attack of an extraordinary nature, such as that which subsequently occurred. The blitzkreig-style attack on Balibó and Maliana was the first major Indonesian sweep into the territory. On the preceding Tuesday Greg Shackleton wrote in his notebook 'Today's patrol struck no trouble, and we have yet to see a hostile shot', and of the Tuesday night, 'Sleep beautifully Balibó'. Discussing the primitive nature of communications he added 'Rumours abound and are believed. Retreat seems to be based on rumours of attack and are believed. Retreat seems to be based on rumours of attack and little else. In this highly charged atmosphere, some grasp at straws'. The Portuguese crew's comment when they saw the headlights of troop convoys crossing the border bore out the shock nature of the incursion—'We believed that Indonesia must be invading East Timor', they said.

Despite all the contrary information to which the Australian government had access, including its own military intelligence sources, it publicly persisted with the view that it had no knowledge of Indonesian military involvement in East Timor, and in particular in Balibó. Less than a week after the journalists were reported missing, Prime Minister Whitlam reported in the House of Representatives:

> ... the television newsmen ... were filming in the border area near the town of Balibo, which was the scene of heavy fighting *between rival factions* [my emphasis] on Thursday and Friday of last week. The House will be aware of the report cited in Jakarta newspaper *Kompas* of 20 October that advancing Democratic Union of Timorese—UDT—and APODETI forces had come across the remains of 4 male Europeans in the Balibo area. The UDT leader Lopez [sic] da Cruz, was reported as saying that he could not confirm whether the four were Australian journalists but that written markings on the ruins of the house in which the four bodies had been found indicated that they might be Australians. While the Press report was sketchy, it indicated that the house could have been hit by a mortar or artillery shell, presumably during last week's heavy fighting.[9]

The Balibó five may have been guilty of not retreating from a situation which involved greater risks than they could expect to take as war correspondents, although there was little warning that it was to be more dangerous than when a dozen or so journalists had previously visited the area. (The more experienced Portuguese crew's assessment of the risks on the Wednesday afternoon did not differ fundamentally from that of the Australians, with the result that the Portuguese found themselves trapped in Maliana in an almost identical situation, but largely through luck, managed to escape.)

Nevertheless, the men were clearly unarmed and non-combatants. Regardless of whether or not Indonesian troops would understand their prominent evidence of being Australian citizens, they were clearly not Timorese, not combatants, and were unarmed persons in a battle zone. If things came to the worst they could expect to be taken as prisoners. On the FRETILIN soldiers' accounts the journalists were attempting to surrender. Even accepting the claim that four of the five were found dead in the house and were killed by fire directed at it, but not specifically at them, the case of the fifth body, found in the open in civilian clothing, can hardly be accounted for as an accidental victim of the attack. The statement that his body was found 'on one of the escape routes used by FRETILIN', lends weight to the supposition that he was treated as a combatant.

The film which reached Dili and then Australia, showed that the reporters were in a position to compromise Indonesian involvement in the Balibó operation. Although a camera and some notebooks were returned to the Jakarta embassy by Indonesian officials, there was no trace of the last film taken by either crew.

The 31 October report was forwarded to various concerned parties with a covering letter from Senator Willesee which stated that the crews had been warned on leaving Australia that they were entering a battle zone and could not expect Australian government 'assistance or protection'. The journalists were fully conscious that they were entering a battle zone in the course of their work. While they could not expect either protection or assistance beyond that to which they were entitled as citizens, they did not relinquish their citizenship on entering Timor and had the right to expect the normal protection which flowed from that, just as their relatives had the right to expect a proper inquiry into the circumstances of their deaths.

In April 1976, after Balibó had been occupied for some months, the Indonesian government finally agreed to allow a Foreign Affairs team to visit the town and interview various people who might give information about the deaths. Predictably, the team found no witnesses with evidence contrary to that originally given by the UDT and APODETI leaders and the house in which the journalists were last seen had been repainted.

In 1976 several other accounts of the deaths emerged in the course of events following the Indonesian invasion of Dili.[10] The Australian Journalists Association consequently called anew for a top-level public inquiry, but this has not been forthcoming.

A year after the deaths of the Balibó five, the Australian embassy in Jakarta erected a headstone to mark the lonely grave in which the remains of the journalists were collectively buried.

The monument bears the inscription 'No words can explain this pointless death in Balibó'.

Australian thinking towards East Timor in the twentieth century has generally regarded the territory as important to Australian defence. (Prime Minister Andrew Fisher varied the theme in 1915 when he dabbled with the idea of purchasing East Timor as a summer resort for jaded public servants stationed in northern Australia.) The 'most favoured nation' clause of the final Dutch-Portuguese border agreement in 1914, plus the chronic impecuniosity of the Portuguese led to periodic Australian fears that some power (other than themselves) might be interested in annexing Timor through purchase. From the time of the border agreement to the 1950s, Canberra chambers intermittently echoed with rumours that the Germans, the Japanese or the Dutch might be interested in lifting the white man's burden from Portuguese shoulders. Most of these rumours were without foundation, but their currency illustrates Australian concern that East Timor should not be ruled by an inimical foreign power and the belief that its occupation by a friendly power was basic to Australian security.[11]

Callinan's account of the Australian campaign in Timor during the second world war ends with the words:

> Was Timor worth holding? Was the campaign worth anything? If the answer be yes, the same reasons will apply again, because Timor has today the same strategical importance to Australia, and it is vital that the island should not be occupied by an enemy power.[12]

This view, that East Timor's political life is of interest to Australians for defence reasons, lingered on even through events of 1974 and 1975.

By the late 1930s fears of the territory falling into the hands of a hostile power found some basis. Japanese commercial penetration of South-East Asia, a prelude to military penetration, began in the 1920s and by the thirties had extended to East Timor, where in 1938 a Japanese company obtained controlling shares in SAPT, the government-sponsored agricultural company. By 1940 the Nanyo Kohatso K.K. (South Seas Development Company) had invested a total of £A1,000,000 in East Timor and was purchasing whatever export surpluses were available.[13]

At that time Australian diplomatic ties were through the British Consul-General in Batavia (present-day Jakarta). In 1937 a senior vice-consul was sent from Batavia to Timor to assess the degree of Japanese penetration. Australian defence officials were particularly concerned at the possibility of a Japanese occupation severing communications and supply between Australia and Singapore. The vice-consul found the Portuguese Governor anxious to counter Japanese influence by promoting Australian trade and shipping links and recommended that the Australian government take such a course. As a result, the first Darwin-Dili air service was established by Qantas, the government-owned international airline. At the end of 1940 Sir Frederick Stewart, the Australian Minister for External Affairs, informed the Dominions Secretary that his government would welcome the appointment of a British Consular representative in Dili. The Japanese were pressing to open a consulate and were already conducting secret reconnaissance flights in the guise of commercial test flights. Portugal at this stage did not wish a British consulate to be established openly, because it would set a precedent for the Japanese. Consequently it was decided to unofficially appoint David Ross, a senior Department of Civil Aviation (DCA) official, as Australian representative while formally designating him DCA representative in Timor. Soon after his arrival in Timor, Ross was given secret instructions from his DCA superior to apply for a clerk to assist him, and informed that a Mr F.J. Whittaker would be sent who would, on arrival, give details of his role. Whittaker was in fact 'Paymaster-Lieutenant F.J. Whittaker, RANVR, about to be posted to Dili as a Secret Naval Intelligence Officer with the cover job of a DCA clerk':

> Thus Australia's representation in Portuguese Timor—among the first of our foreign missions—initially comprised a political officer acting as a Civil Aviation Department technical representative assisted in turn by a clerk who was, in fact, a spy, a non-uniformed naval intelligence officer working on behalf of a belligerent in a neutral country.[14]

This was on the eve of the second world war. During the Japanese occupation Ross escaped from Dili after being sent by the Japanese to urge the Australian guerillas to surrender. He defected from his mission in order to join the Australians and was shortly afterwards evacuated from the south coast.

After the war Australia showed a new interest in Timor. The Liberal government's Mr Percy Spender revived the idea of annexation. However, the British government had been forced by its need to secure the Portuguese Azores as a strategic Atlantic base during the war to give Lisbon guarantees that Portuguese sovereignty in Timor would be respected. As a general principle the Australian government accepted in 1943 that responsibility for the administration of colonies should continue in the hands of the pre-war administrators, although the UK urged, also, the formation of 'regional commissions' to supervise peace treaties, establish new fields of economic co-operation, and provide a foothold for Australian security interests. The Chifley Labor government was anxious to pursue this principle and External Affairs Minister Evatt himself even spoke of the inefficiency and oppression of Portuguese administration in Timor. Typical of Australian responses, however, his motives were not entirely concern for the welfare of the Timorese:

> Australia must show a particular interest in the welfare and system of control of those islands and territories which lie close to our shores. From the point of view of defence, of trade and of transport, most of them can fairly be described as coming within an extended Australian zone ... Timor, part of which is Portuguese and part Dutch, ... in enemy hands is a constant threat to Australia. If properly placed within the zone of Australian security it would become a bastion of our defence.

The security zone was never realised, although Evatt continued to work for it; neither was a system of regional co-operation established in this area, although the South Pacific Commission provided that function in the zone east of New Guinea.[15]

Concern for East Timor's security aroused by the war led to regular Australian diplomatic representation thereafter. The turbulent circumstances of the foundation of the Republic of Indonesia also made Australia eager to establish an intelligence ear in the eastern South-East Asian region and the Dili consulate was regarded by foreign affairs commentators as a listening post until its closure in 1971, when the Liberal government decided that its maintenance was not justified by the amount of consular business it dealt with.

Despite Australian representation in Dili the territory continued to exist in isolation from Australia. The air link provided a small trickle of tourists and even a few settlers in post-war years, but it was only when inquisitive journalists like Osmar White reminded the outside world of the backwardness of this Portuguese Asian colony that it came to public attention.

In 1963 the deputy leader of the Labor party temporarily brought it into the public eye. Delivering the Roy Milne Memorial lecture in Adelaide, Gough Whitlam declared:

> Eastern Timor must appear as an anachronism to every country in the world except Portugal ... we would not have a supporter in the world if we backed the Portuguese ... they must be told in no uncertain terms that the standard of living must be rapidly raised, and the rights of self-determination fully granted ... through the UN we must act quickly to meet this problem.[16]

The same year the Federal Conference of the ALP, meeting in Adelaide, committed itself to the 'liberation of Eastern Timor', but the policy was dropped by the Federal Conference in 1966, with the result that when the Labor party came to power in 1972 it had no policy on East Timor.

In the UN, Timor was included in 1960 in the UN General Assembly's list of non-self-governing Portuguese territories and in 1962 the assembly discussed for the first time the situation of the territories as a whole. It initiated what was to become a series of annual resolutions, calling for self-determination and independence for these territories.

It was only in 1972 that Australia supported any of the resolutions. Then, in the last days of the Liberal McMahon government, Sir Laurence McIntyre, Australia's representative to the UN, was instructed to vote in favour of resolution 1918, which called on:

> all states to take forthwith all possible measures to put an end to any activities that help to exploit the territories under Portuguese domination and the peoples therein and to discourage their nationals and bodies corporate under their jurisdiction from entering into any transactions or arrangements that contribute to

> Portugal's domination over those territories and impede the implementation (on the granting of Independence to colonial Countries and Peoples) with respect to them.[17]

This break with Liberal precedent became the established pattern after Labor came to power. However, although Labor publicly pursued a vigorous anti-colonial policy in the UN, Timor soon emerged as an exception to the rule.

In 1973 the Australian press had criticised the Whitlam government over economic links with East Timor which appeared to contravene its UN stand. Senator Willesee, Minister for Foreign Affairs, was quick to claim that the resolutions referred only to Portuguese Africa, which they patently did not.

Here was the nub of Labor's dual policy towards the Portuguese colonies: the co-existence of principled attitudes abroad and expediency closer to home. Helen Hill has outlined and elucidated this policy. It contained, she wrote, two potentially contradictory elements:

> on the one hand Australia moved to support anti-racist and anti-colonialist actions and movements, particularly in the United Nations and on the other hand the Labor government moved towards close relations with the ASEAN countries. As an expression of the first Mr Whitlam banned all racially selected sporting teams from Southern Africa from entering Australia and as an expression of the second made his first overseas visit as Prime Minister to Indonesia, and initiated a series of informal talks with President Suharto.[18]

She describes these contradictory elements as the policies of 'principle' and 'pragmatism', pointing out that they did not, in these early days, come into conflict, because they were applied in geographically separate parts of the world—anti-colonialist 'principle' in Africa, and 'pragmatism' in nearby Asia.

Yet Labor policy towards Indonesia and the ASEAN countries was publicly seen in Australia as heralding a new, progressive era in foreign relations—Whitlam's informal-style 'batik' diplomacy was given free play in the press during his talks with Suharto in Yogyakarta in September 1974 and in Townsville in April 1975. It had an exciting aura of egalitarianism about it and was in marked contrast to the style of preceding Liberal governments, whose attitude to Asia was identified with the White Australia policy, the 'domino' theory, and Australian military involvement in Vietnam.

After its disengagement from Vietnam the new government was firmly opposed to the stationing of Australian troops abroad. Direct military or non-military involvement in the affairs of South-East Asia was seen as equivalent to the Liberals' military involvement in Vietnam. Although the government was at pains to deny that this trend was isolationist, Whitlam's 'new nationalism' was inward-turning. It echoed the populist 'no more foreign wars' cry recurrent to Australian nationalism. A central theme of Timor policy was that Australia was not a party principal in the future of EastTimor. The reality was that, apart from the fact that Australia obviously stood to be affected by the outcome of events, Australia was always a de facto party principal, if only by virtue of the power it held to influence events in a different direction, but chose not to exercise.

Two central tenets of the new approach were that trade was a more constructive tool in South-East Asia than defence pacts:

> We no longer look on the countries of South-East Asia as buffer states or as some northern military line where a possible future enemy should be held. Rather, we look upon them as countries having a common interest with Australia and New Zealand in consolidating the security and stability of the region as a whole.[19]

and that Indonesia and other of the ASEAN countries presented ripe fields for Australian investment, which should be exploited.

Whitlam's Yogyakarta visit highlighted an underlying conflict in government circles over the new foreign policy trend. According to contemporary press reports there was a backstage dispute between Foreign Affairs and some Defence department officials over the brief Whitlam took to Indonesia.

The Foreign Affairs department was regarded by those at close quarters to it as being prejudiced from the outset towards Indonesian incorporation of East Timor. The 'Indonesia lobby' within the department was seen as an ascendant force which wielded considerable influence in the formulation of Labor foreign policy. Its views were regarded as close to those of Jakarta embassy staff. Defence leaned towards the traditional view of Timor in Australia's defence strategy. The department's thinking reflected a current of thought in Australia which believed that Whitlam's dismantling of the system of military conscription within Australia and the pursuit of 'trade not guns' policies in Asia left Australia strategically disarmed. Whitlam's concept was that the establishment of a genuine rapport with neighbouring Asian countries was the best guarantee of regional security. The concrete application of this policy, however, meant the building of strong uncritical links with countries which, in the post-Vietnam era, were fighting a rearguard action against social change in South-East Asia—Indonesia and the ASEAN bloc. Defence's view was summarised in a press report at the time of the Yogyakarta visit, which alleged that some sections of the department were anxious to highlight:

> ... Portuguese Timor's closeness to Australia and the fact that it was used by Japan for reconnaissance flights over Australia and could again be of strategic importance. They also believed that Indonesia is not as stable as other people (particularly Foreign Affairs) think and that there is a possibility of a Government hostile to Australia emerging in Jakarta, which would make Portuguese Timor of vital importance. So they favoured the colony being independent or in some way linked with Australia.[20]

Defence officials were credited with a more discriminating view of Indonesia. They believed the régime's future to be precarious, that while secessionism may have been stamped out militarily in the early sixties its social base remained, aggravated rather than relieved by Jakarta's Java-centric economy. A forward-looking foreign policy, they believed, would not patronise an order which was doomed by historical circumstances to fall sooner or later. There would, inevitably, be a new order in Indonesia and the quality of it depended on contemporary events; the strengthening of the Suharto régime could be seen as tightening the screws of repression of political liberties in Indonesia and it was not in Australia's future interests to be identified with this. Further, the longer the régime lasted, the closer came the prospect of a communist Indonesia, in their eyes.

Thus, by a strange inversion, the Defence establishment was more inclined, for its own reasons, to support an independent East Timor and found itself at loggerheads with the incorporationist policies of Prime Minister Whitlam and the Foreign

Affairs department. Both viewpoints were predicated to an extent on the traditional Australian belief in the need to assuage a potentially hostile Asia in the interests of Australian sovereignty.

In Yogyakarta Whitlam acted on the Foreign Affairs briefing which Defence department officials believed to be based on crude political intelligence. He told President Suharto, firstly, that he felt East Timor should become part of Indonesia, but only in accordance with the properly expressed will of its people. He said he felt the territory was too small to be independent and was not economically viable, although his government upheld the right of self-determination for all remaining colonies, even the smallest. He told Suharto that Indonesia should be aware of the effects on public opinion in Australia if East Timor was forcibly annexed and reminded him that there was still disquiet in both Papua New Guinea and Australia over the conduct of the 'Act of Free Choice' in Irian Jaya in 1969. He stressed that Indonesia should bear in mind the need for Australian public support in the incorporation of East Timor into Indonesia, and for evidence that the wishes of the people had been respected.

Although the Prime Minister on the one hand stressed the need for democratic procedures, on the other he gave approval to Indonesian annexation designs perhaps even before these had solidified in Jakarta itself. If Adam Malik's June 1974 letter to José Ramos Horta, in which he guaranteed Indonesia's respect for independence if the East Timorese chose it, can be regarded as credible, it should be seen in the light of a division within Indonesian ruling circles, in which certain sections were pushing for military action while others, including President Suharto, were far from decided. And while the Whitlam statement claimed that the Australian government could only support a proper act of self-determination, it prejudged the outcome of the act, by recommending integration as the most desirable of the three options.[21] It was only in October 1974, after the September visit, that the blueprint for 'Operasi Komodo' was drawn up in Jakarta.[22]

After Ramos Horta's June visit to Indonesia he travelled on to Australia, where he was given the first indications that the government would not support independence. Senator

Willesee refused a request for an interview although Andrew Peacock and other Opposition members gave the Timorese politician a sympathetic hearing.

In September Whitlam's Yogyakarta statement became known in Timor, through Radio Australia and the Indonesian-sponsored Radio Kupang broadcasts. It was received with dismay. In December 1974 Ramos Horta ventured on a new crusade to Australia, this time with the more modest aim of gaining recognition for the right to self-determination. On this occasion the Foreign Affairs Minister saw him, but he was still unable to obtain the guarantees for which he hoped. Ramos Horta also made contact with trade unionists and members of the Australian left, as a result of which the Campaign for Independent East Timor (CIET) was formed in Sydney. Among other sympathetic contacts were members of the Australian Society for Inter-Country Aid, an aid group interested in health work in Timor, which later became the Australian Society for Inter-Country Aid (Timor), ASIAT.

In response to Labor's position in late 1974 and early 1975 FRETILIN was inclined to place more hope in the Liberal Opposition than in the Labor government. In October 1974 Andrew Peacock raised in parliament the question of Mr Whitlam's stand, accusing the government of 'pre-judging the free expression of the Timorese'. Referring to the Prime Minister's comments on the economic unviability of an independent East Timor, Peacock continued:

> The Labor Government says that the people of Portuguese Timor cannot be self-sufficient. It ought to tell that to the Nauruans, the Tongans, the Samoans or the Papua New Guineans. Evidently Labor does not realise the ramifications of its inconsistencies. So far as Portuguese Timor is concerned we would prefer to see Portugal remain in control and assist with a program for self-determination. It would then be up to the Timorese to determine their own future in a program that they can work out.[23]

In the same debate, Mr Chris Hurford, a Labor backbencher who had met and talked with Ramos Horta in July, expressed dissent from his government's policy. He referred to the Labor government's early recognition of the independence of the former Portuguese African colony of Guinea Bissau (the government was one of the first Western countries to recognise its independence). The backbencher carefully phrased his references to Mr Whitlam's Yogyakarta statement, but there was no doubt that he placed himself in dissent:

> The future of Portuguese Timor was apparently discussed at the recent meeting between the Australian Prime Minister and President Soharto [*sic*]. Although no communique was issued after this meeting ... reports suggest that the Indonesians indicated that the best solution for Timor would be for the territory to integrate with Indonesia. The Indonesians reportedly are concerned that an independent state of Timor would in some way threaten the soft underbelly of the archipelago nation ... we are traditional supporters of the principle of self-determination ... and the right of nations, even small nations, to independence. Australia cannot therefore connive at the denial of these rights to the Timorese people. This Portuguese territory may be small and basically economically unviable. But there are many other smaller and economically weaker countries in the world, among them Guinea Bissau.

He concluded by calling on the government to urge Indonesia to work with Australia on mutual support for effective decolonisation, and to re-open the Dili consulate—'I hope that this course which I advocate will be adopted by the Australian Government. I believe that it will be of benefit not only to the Timorese people but also to Indonesian-Australian relations'.[24]

On 22 February 1975 press reports that Indonesia was planning to invade Timor broke. Andrew Peacock called for an urgency debate in the parliament and swung into vigorous attack. He made six central points: that Mr Whitlam had given Australian approval for Indonesian annexation in September 1974; that when Ramos Horta visited Australia the previous July, Foreign Affairs Minister Willesee refused to see him; that the government was only then, in February 1975, sending its first fact-finding mission to Dili; that Indonesian relations were important; that the future of East Timor should be determined between the Portuguese and the Timorese alone, without interference; and, finally, that Australia should seek to bring the parties together for discussion.[25]

In reply, Mr Bill Morrison, the Acting Foreign Minister, claimed that the government supported:

> a measured and deliberate process of decolonisation in Portuguese Timor through arrangements leading to an internationally acceptable act of self-determination. We do not believe that political development in the Territory has yet reached a stage where such an act could take place ...

'We believe', he added, 'that there is time and opportunity for a political solution ... which will meet the proper aspirations of the people of the Territory and also the natural interests of Indonesia'.[26]

In March 1975 dissent within Labor ranks was reinforced by the visit to East Timor of members of the party's caucus Foreign Affairs and Defence Committee. On their return they argued strongly for more positive government action and for the re-opening of the Dili consulate. John Kerin, leader of the delegation, briefed Foreign Affairs officials. In reply to the delegation's proposals, which were put in letter form to Mr Whitlam, the Prime Minister wrote that:

> to re-open [the consulate] now could be misinterpreted, political interests in Portuguese Timor could seek to use our presence to involve us to an extent which I do not feel would be appropriate for Australia.[27]

There were also indications of dissent from Foreign Affairs Minister Willesee who in most cases bore the brunt of delivering the Timor policy to the Australian public. In a press interview in Singapore in December 1974 he openly stated his disagreement with a report that Adam Malik had, a day or two earlier, said that East Timorese independence was not a viable proposition. Asked to comment on the report Senator Willesee blunty replied 'Well, I don't agree with the Indonesians', with the implication that he didn't agree, either, with Mr Whitlam.[28]

Indeed, the Timor policy was generally identified as a peculiarly Whitlam policy. According to Gregory Clark, a former Australian diplomat and consultant to the Prime Minister's Department under the Labor government, 'A major reason was Mr Whitlam's inflexibility on the issue. He seemed to have made up his mind that the idea of an independent East Timor was an anomaly—and that was that'. Clark also alleged that Mr Whitlam had access to the details of 'Operasi

Komodo', which were studied and basically approved by his government.[29] Nancy Viviani, also a foreign affairs advisor to the Whitlam government during the formulation of Timor policy, has expanded on the contradictions of the Labor Prime Minister's role and provided insights into the Whitlam style:

> Mr Whitlam was, in comparison with almost all his predecessors, an unusual decision maker in Australian foreign policy. He had an undoubted capacity for the broad vision, well matched by rhetoric, and a confident grasp of the problems of power relations among the great powers. He conceived a new role for Australia in international relations, and he wanted Australians to emerge from the shackles of past fears and parochialism, and share his vision. He delighted in the untrammelled nature of the power involved in foreign policy making—he would not consult his Cabinet on foreign policy issues generally, and did not on Timor, and he was loath to have such issues raised in Caucus. He was confident and strong willed (some said wilful) in foreign policy ...

Commenting on Mr Whitlam's reluctance to subject the Timor policy to public scrutiny, she continues:

> It is not without significance that Mr Whitlam failed to articulate his Timor policy clearly, or argue publicly its merits and potential conflicts, as, say, Sir Garfield Barwick did when proposing the Australian policy on confrontation ... The conclusion might be drawn that he expected domestic opposition and would not encourage it.[30]

At talks held in Townsville in April 1975 Prime Minister Whitlam re-affirmed his Jogjakarta stance, although at all points the 'self-determination' proviso was added.

Although the Australian government's knowledge of events in East Timor from intelligence sources was generally complete, it did not have advance knowledge of the UDT coup of 11 August 1975. In the period after the coup, in which the Portuguese administration abdicated responsibility for the situation, the Australian government came under increasing pressure to play a positive role in negotiations between interested parties. The first and most crucial call on Australian good offices met with a negative response.

Immediately after the coup the Portuguese government in Lisbon dispatched a negotiating team for Dili under the leadership of António Soares. This was after UDT had seized power, but before the FRETILIN counter-attack began on 20 August. There was a good possibility at this point that the intervention of a Lisbon delegate may have prevented bloodshed. However, Soares was obstructed by the Indonesian government from proceeding past Denpasar, Bali, to fly into Timor. After waiting several days, he was forced to abandon hope of reaching Dili via Indonesian Timor. On 20 August he finally reached Darwin after fullscale fighting had already broken out in Timor. As Soares had other government commitments, he had to return to Lisbon the following day.

Consequently, the Portuguese government sent a second mission. On 22 August Dr António de Almeida Santos, former Minister for Interterritorial Co-ordination, left Lisbon for Timor, Indonesia and Australia, stopping on his way in New York for talks with the UN Secretary-General. In the course of Almeida Santos's talks in Jakarta the Acting Indonesian Foreign Minister proposed a plan under which Indonesia would send troops to East Timor as the first step towards a multinational peace-keeping force. The Portuguese negotiator rejected this plan, but proposed instead a multinational force of troops drawn from Portugal, Indonesia, Malaysia and Australia. This second peace proposal broke down largely because of its rejection by the Whitlam government. In a television interview the Prime Minister instead criticised Portugal's handling of theTimor crisis, saying that East Timor was a Portuguese colony and that Portugal ought to accept responsibility instead of 'clearing out and dropping its bundle'.

The government came under heavy criticism for this position, and in response to the mounting attack Mr Whitlam made a policy statement in the House of Representatives on 26 August:

> We have been ... and remain opposed to Australian military involvement. One of the first policy decisions of the Government, on assuming office in December 1972, was to determine that Australia would not intervene again in land wars in South East Asia. This applies as much to the civil war in Portuguese Timor as to the earlier civil war in Vietnam ... The Australian Government ... does not regard itself as a party principal in Portuguese Timor ... the future of the territory is a matter for resolution by Portugal

> and the Timorese people themselves with Indonesia also occupying an important place because of its predominant interest ... The Government recognises that there are some who believe that Australia should ... step in and attempt to arbitrate between the competing political factions ... acceptance of these views could lead to a situation where Australia was exercising a quasi-colonial role in Portuguese Timor.

The Prime Minister concluded with the observation that:

> the first priority is to ... restore order. This objective requires the active intervention of Portugal itself. It is a responsibility that cannot be shrugged off on to others such as Australia ... We have no ethnic or cultural ties with the Timorese which would suggest a role for Australia in substitution for Portugal ... [31]

The national capital's *Canberra Times* followed with a strongly-worded editorial the next day, 27 August:

> The Prime Minister appears to have bemused himself with some of the rhetoric of the past decade when he suggested that Australian mediation of the Timorese dispute "could lead to a situation where Australia was exercising a quasi-colonial role in Portuguese Timor" ... The fact is that ... this country is the only party—with the possible exception of Portugal ... sufficiently disinterested yet concerned enough to play such a role.
>
> The Prime Minister, after remarking that Portugal "cannot simply wash its hands of Portuguese Timor", went on himself, in Pontius Pilate style, to assert that "we have no ethnic or cultural links with the Timorese which would suggest a role for Australia ... ". But no one has proposed anything more than a temporary role, as a mediator, for Australia.

Against Mr Whitlam's 'neutrality' stand the leader of the National Country Party, Mr Anthony, claimed that the government was standing by while East Timor fell under 'Communist control', sentiments echoed by Liberal leader Malcolm Fraser, then leader of the Opposition. Prime Minister Whitlam at the time expressed strong objection to this terminology and later claimed that the labelling of FRETILIN as 'Communist' had reinforced Indonesian fears and contributed to the decision to invade.[32]

After the failure of their first peace proposal the Portuguese subsequently made a more modest proposal, through the UN, for a meeting between Portuguese, Indonesian and Australian government representatives. This was also rejected, although members of the caucus Foreign Affairs and Defence Committee urged its adoption in a letter to Mr Whitlam, with the suggestion that Timorese politicians should also be present.[33]

In the period after the end of August, 1975, when FRETILIN became the de facto administration of East Timor, the Australian government, against its claims not to be an involved party, hindered FRETILIN attempts to establish a workable situation, domestically and externally. A petrol blockade was imposed on the territory, which normally depends on Australia for fuel imports. Even private aid organisations which had organised food and medical relief for East Timor's civilian population, were initially forbidden to export petrol from Darwin. Finally, under pressure, the ACFOA relief shipment which reached Dili in early November was permitted to include sufficient petrol to distribute the aid on board. Here again, Gregory Clark reported developments within government circles:

> The strangest and least-reported of Canberra's pro-Indonesian moves was the banning of aid shipments of petrol to East Timor in October, and right through the period of the caretaker government.
>
> The aid, which also included food and medical supplies, had been donated privately. It was desperately needed in East Timor. FRETILIN said the petrol was needed for the trucks to carry the aid to inland villages. Canberra claimed the petrol could be used for military purposes.
>
> A special task group in Canberra, chaired by Foreign Affairs, monitored the movement of this aid. Officials were sent to Darwin to make sure it was not allowed to leave Australia.
>
> Meanwhile, Australia was continuing full-scale aid to Indonesia, including military aid.

Externally, the Australian government ensured that FRETILIN appeals to the UN were shelved or buried at a time when it had the power to work towards a UN-negotiated settlement. In the three months of FRETILIN administration the de facto government addressed constant appeals to the UN, initially inviting a UN inspection team and, after independence, asking for recognition of the new republic. Australia wields considerable influence in the UN's Decolonization Committee, which it could have used towards the airing of these appeals. Instead, Australian representatives worked with Indonesian delegates at the UN against the hearing of these appeals during these months which were precarious for East Timor.[34]

After the Balibó deaths, public pressure on the Whitlam government increased. In the government's last days there was evidence that it was responding to this pressure. On 30 October Senator Willesee made a major policy statement to the Senate, which began:

> The Government has viewed with concern widespread reports that Indonesia is involved in military intervention in Portuguese Timor. The position of the Australian Government is clear. We deplore the fighting in the border areas. We continue to believe that a solution to the problems in Portuguese Timor should be sought through peaceful means and free of external intervention. Indonesia has been told of our views in this regard and urged to pursue her interests through diplomatic means.

He then went on to offer Australia as a venue for possible peace talks, a measure which the government had carefully steered away from until this time, although it was known that Portugal and FRETILIN, at least, saw Australia as a mutually acceptable venue. The statement attributed the situation in Timor largely to the 'immaturity' of the various political associations. It continued:

> It is in this situation of drift ... that we view the various policy pronouncements, newspaper reports and the like from Jakarta and Timor itself. Were there substance in these reports, the Australian Government would be extremely disappointed and we have so informed the Indonesian authorities. The Australian Government has urged that Indonesia pursue her interests through diplomatic means. We have told the Indonesians that we remain opposed to the use of armed force.[35]

Having for the previous three months adopted a supine posture towards the Indonesian government, especially vis-à vis Balibó, in the stated interests of preserving the supremacy of the Indonesian relationship, the Australian government had finally adopted a mildly critical tone, and taken a first constructive step towards a solution, in the invitation to use Australia as a venue.

Unfortunately, not even this action was untarnished. The following May, 1976, a Canberra journalist revealed that this Ministerial statement had been altered to conceal the fact that Australia knew Indonesian troops to be active in East Timor. Bruce Juddery uncovered a cable to the Foreign Affairs department from Indonesian Ambassador Richard Woolcott in Jakarta in which the ambassador urged that the government alter the wording of the first paragraph to remove reference to reliable reports of Indonesian military presence in East Timor. Ambassador Woolcott had already altered the copy which had been forwarded to him to convey to the Indonesian government. In his cable Mr Woolcott said that he had conveyed the Ministerial statement minus the first paragraph, which he felt might cause problems with Indonesia. The paragraph posed a problem, he said, in that:

> If the Minister says publicly that he regrets the degree of intervention in the affairs of Portuguese Timor, will he not stir up a hornet's nest in Australia itself as well as producing a cold reaction here? Would not the first paragraph of the statement in its present form invite headlines of the type 'Willesee accuses Indonesia of Intervention' and would not this lead in turn to increased pressures on the Government to act against Indonesia by stopping the defence assistance program and, possibly by cutting aid? Such a statement at ministerial level would also stimulate hostility to Indonesia within the Australian community, which it has been our policy to minimise.
>
> Although we know it is not true, the formal position of the Indonesian government is still that there is no Indonesian military intervention in East Timor. If the Minister said or implied in public the Indonesian Government was lying we would invite a hurt and angry reaction.[36]

Senator Willesee's 30 October statement was the last substantial statement of the Labor government on East Timor before the crisis which resulted in the appointment of a Liberal caretaker government on 11 November.

Gough Whitlam, the champion of 'open' government, had emerged as the exponent of the worst kind of secret diplomacy in which the ends justified the means. At the time of the 7 December invasion, the former Prime Minister was quick to blame the caretaker government:

> We all know Indonesias's preoccupation, almost obsession, with any movements or organisations which are described as communist. And Mr Anthony's use of the term and Mr Fraser's use of the term have undoubtedly confirmed and probably exacerbated Indonesia's attitudes towards FRETILIN ... the fact that Indonesia has held her hand for so long has been due, I think it can be fairly said, to the arguments that I put to President Soeharto in Indonesia about 14 months ago and in Townsville about eight months ago.[37]

The record, however, speaks differently. In the early days of the Portuguese decolonisation programme, minimal diplomatic measures requested of Mr Whitlam's government—the reopening of the Dili consulate, assistance with aid projects, would have gone far to change the course of events and been of inestimable value to the Portuguese administration, itself preoccupied with recurrent political crises in Lisbon. The Labor government's later resting of responsibility with the 'delinquent Portuguese' may have carried more weight had the government responded to early requests for this type of assistance. More importantly, a display of Australian interest would have quietly served notice on Indonesia of Australian concern for a genuine act of self-determination in East Timor.

The path of appeasement it chose eventually produced just the effects it aimed to avoid: Indonesian hostility and the very regional instability for which it believed Indonesian annexation of East Timor was the best antidote. The duplicity and secretiveness of the Labor government, as illustrated by the Woolcott cables, earned it both the ire of its own constituents and, ultimately, loss of respect from the Indonesian government, which it tended to privately approve but publicly pillory.

Apart from questions of principle, a great flaw ran through the government's thinking—an ignorance of Timorese colonial history. Timor could be considered an exception to UN resolutions against Portuguese colonialism because it was believed its history was fundamentally different, that the colonial hand had been lighter here, resentments milder (if existing at all) and that no real movement existed or had existed against Portuguese rule. In the above-quoted letter to Senator Arthur Gietzelt, Mr Whitlam alleged that the three political associations should be regarded as immature formations, in that there had been no movement against colonial rule before 1974, and in the press release of 30 October 1975 Senator Willesee echoed the sentiment:

> That the situation in Portuguese Timor has come to its present pass is, of course, cause for deep regret. It reflects, above all, the immaturity of Timor's own aspiring political leaders.

The final expression of this flaw was in an underestimation of the ability of the Timorese to run their own affairs, and of their political will and military capacity to resist a new foreign occupation. It was instanced firstly in the unpreparedness of both Jakarta and Canberra for FRETILIN's quick military victory in August 1975 followed by the establishment of an administration, and secondly by their strong resistance to Indonesian occupation through all of 1976.

Mr Whitlam was generally regarded as the personal architect of the Timor policy, in conjunction with a section of the Foreign Affairs department. This consideration later tied the hands of members of his own party who were aware and critical of the full role of their government, and provided a perfect weapon in the hands of the Liberal party when, through 1976, it became the target of public and parliamentary criticism. Labor MPS attempted to circumvent the problem by laying responsibility at the feet of the Foreign Affairs department, but in the long run it could only be avoided by a sensitive skirting of the whole Timor question in parliament.

In Opposition in 1976 Mr Whitlam met criticisms of his Timor policy with the same duplicity which characterised his policy in office. In August, in answer to information 'leaked' from Indonesian sources that his government had approved Indonesian military action in East Timor, the former Prime Minister denied that Indonesian troops were involved in East Timor during his term of office and that he had knowledge of it:

> Any suggestion that my Government approved Indonesian military action in Timor is untrue ... We opposed any military action in Timor and insisted on the right to self-determination for the Timorese people. While Labor was in power, President Suharto's undertakings to me on these points were honoured by Indonesia.[38]

On 11 November the Labor government was dismissed and a caretaker government installed under Malcolm Fraser. Elections were scheduled for 13 December. If the Australian government refused to acknowledge its de facto political power in East Timor, the Indonesian government was well aware of it, and in the months spanning Labor's dismissal and the 13 December election the most important Indonesian manoeuvres towards full-scale military intervention occurred. In mid-November the intense bombardment of Atabae began, on 28 November Atabae fell and FRETILIN declared independence, on 30 November APODETI, Trabalhista and KOTA declared the integration of East Timor with Indonesia and on 7 December the full-scale invasion of East Timor began.

The Liberal caretaker government was obliged, under its guidelines from the Governor-General, to administer the policies of the previous government. However, it had considerable leeway: Andrew Peacock, the new Foreign Affairs Minister, was quick to acknowledge he had some freedom and did not consider himself hamstrung by Labor policies:

> I'm not restricted because we were given at the last minute a hook to hang some policy on by the Labor Party, at least talking about the need for talks regarding Timor, so that gives me sufficient leeway to be conducting Australian foreign policy effectively.

Yet the Liberals gave no sign they would act in a more principled way than their Labor predecessor, or take up the small initiative opened by Senator Willesee on 30 October. Soon after they came to power, a Foreign Affairs spokesperson was asked whether the government intended to take up the question of the presence of Indonesian troops in East Timor, referred to in the statement altered by Senator Willesee. He replied that on 26 November the Minister had acknowledged the presence of Indonesian troops, but that Indonesia had already exercised 'considerable patience' on the matter of East Timor. The *Canberra Times* commented:

> From this it was deduced that despite Senator Willesee's October 30 statement, and notwithstanding the Governor-General's guidelines, the Government does not intend to make any protest, or offer any warning to Indonesia about the danger to Australian–Indonesian relations created by its intervention in East Timor.[39]

On 28 November Andrew Peacock was again credited with a strongly critical position on Labor's Timor record. Labor's approach had been a blight on Australia's foreign policy, he said. The former government had washed its hands of Timor despite requests from the parties involved to mediate and its obvious capacity to do so. He pledged that if re-elected, the Liberals would act to reverse some of the Labor government's foreign affairs policy, including the decision to afford de jure recognition to the Baltic states.[40]

Despite the strong tone of this statement and the surgical measures pledged to the Baltic question and although they knew in advance of the Indonesian invasion of Dili, (as Labor knew of Balibó) the Liberals took no drastic initiatives for an eleventh hour action. Speaking of the place of Timor in electioneering, the *Age* canvassed the possibility of such action:

> Foreign affairs have barely rated a mention in the election campaign. But there is an important issue that does require the immediate attention of the Australian Government, and it should not be a matter of election controversy ... the fast-moving and disturbing events in East Timor call for a firm stand on East Timor *now*.
>
> ... While the Left wing of the Australian Labor Party strongly favours FRETILIN and elements of the Liberal–NCP coalition would happily have East Timor handed over to the Indonesians, there are welcome signs of a bi-partisan policy.[41]

The Labor party did put out feelers towards projecting the Timor question into its campaign, which were rapidly withdrawn with the realisation that, given its own record, there was no political gain to be made. Neither party had an interest in making Timor an election issue. Even the traditional organisations of the extra-parliamentary left generally subscribed to the consensus. The circumstances of the Labor dismissal rendered the left equivocal in their support for East Timorese independence. A few lonely campaigners from CIET in several capitals and Melbourne's Australia-East Timor Association (formed on the day of the Indonesian invasion) operated outside the consensus and distributed leaflets at Labor and Liberal meetings, where they experienced equal degrees of hostility.

On 2 December the Australian government, acting on intelligence from Jakarta, instructed International Red Cross that it wished to advise Australian nationals to leave East Timor immediately, as their safety could no longer be assured.

On December 5 Indonesia's Foreign Minister called in the ambassadors of the United States, the Soviet Union, New Zealand, Singapore, Malaysia, Thailand, the Philippines and Australia to a conference. There, Mr Malik announced that a 'grave situation' had arisen in Timor and warned that other countries should not be surprised by Indonesia's next move. Two days later, Indonesian troops landed in Dili. While both the previous Labor government and the caretaker Liberal government were prepared to warn Australian nationals of impending military action, firstly at Balibó and secondly on 7 December, neither were prepared to take political action to prevent the invasion of East Timor and the bloodshed which accompanied it.

10

Aftermath

The Dili landing of Sunday 7 December was accompanied by a Baucau landing and an overland drive from the border. Soon after the Dili assault it was known that the FRETILIN leadership had escaped to the mountains with few losses. The first news came through the Dili radio station which by the night of the eighth was in Indonesian hands. The traditional Timorese songs which had broadcast from Radio Maubere were now replaced by a combination of Western pop and of Christmas carols, interspersed with propaganda which on the one hand spoke of the benefits of surrender to the Tentara Nasional Indonesia (Indonesian National Army), and gave assurances that there would be no reprisals, and, on the other, threatened FRETILIN leaders and followers of the consequences if they did not give themselves up.

The broadcast on the night of the eighth referred to Nicolau Lobato, Guido Soares, Xavier, Hermenegildo Alves and other less senior FRETILIN figures as 'hiding in the caves, rocks and the bushes ... ',—'now you are like a deer, a wild pig, a boa constrictor, hiding in the bush':

> All FRETILIN ran away ... some to Australia and said that they were Ministers, but they ran away. Some are only walking, as Nicolau Lobato, Guido Soares ...
>
> ... the red and white flag has come to help us. Don't follow Xavier and Hermenegildo Alves that want to take you the Communist way. At this moment they must be hiding in the rocks up in the hills. They are ashamed to be in front of the people, so now you are united with us to destroy the forces of Communism. Surrender, because we are for you. With you are the Indonesian national forces ... to destroy all Communist liars.

It concluded:

> FRETILIN is no more. Radio Maubere is dead. Brothers of East

> Timor, the republic that FRETILIN declared is dead. It was alive only for nine days ... Long live the people of East Timor with the Republic of Indonesia![1]

The broadcast also included a message from Arnaldo dos Reis Araújo, president of APODETI. Dos Reis Araújo had been imprisoned by FRETILIN since the beginning of October, and although it was soon learnt that they had taken the majority of APODETI prisoners to the mountains with them, they had not taken dos Reis Araújo. Most of the APODETI prisoners were held in the Museum building under relatively casual conditions but dos Reis Araújo had been in a military prison in a suburb to the west of town, from which he was apparently freed by Indonesian forces.

In Canberra on the night of 8 December, the caretaker Australian Foreign Affairs Minister Andrew Peacock condemned the invasion and called for an immediate ceasefire in the territory. The UN General Assembly's Fourth Committee (the Special Committee on Decolonization) was then engaged in a debate on Timor which had begun on 2 December. Only a few days before, while Indonesian troops were massing for the assault on Timor, Indonesia's UN delegate told the Fourth Committee that his country respected the East Timorese people's 'inalienable right to self-determination'. Peacock now promised that the Australian government would repeat its ceasefire call when the debate resumed and also call for self-determination. He announced that he would fly to Jakarta for talks with Indonesian officials in the near future.

In Jakarta Adam Malik denied that the Indonesian government was involved in the invasion and claimed that the only Indonesian troops involved were 'volunteers', fighting at the request of UDT, APODETI, KOTA and Trabalhista. They were in Timor, he said, to enable a peaceful and orderly decolonisation process to be carried out and to maintain the security of Dili and would be withdrawn as soon as these goals were met.

In Lisbon on the night of the seventh the Portuguese government broke off diplomatic relations with Indonesia and appealed to the UN Security Council to bring about an immediate end to the invasion. An emergency meeting of the Portuguese Cabinet was held and a statement issued condemning Indonesian military aggression.[2]

At the UN a draft resolution on Timor had been circulated on 3 December in the course of the Fourth Committee debate. Sponsored by Indonesia, Australia, Fiji, Japan, Malaysia, New Zealand, Papua New Guinea, the Philippines, and Thailand it referred to 'the positive attitude of the administering power [Portugal] in making every effort to find a solution by peaceful means' through talks with the political parties in Timor. On 8 December the sponsors circulated a revised draft, which deleted this reference and substituted a preamble affirming that 'any attempt aimed at the partial or total disruption of the national unity and the territorial integrity of a country is incompatible with the purposes and principles of the Charter of the United Nations'.

Following news of the invasion this resolution was withdrawn and two others introduced, the first sponsored by Algeria, Cuba, Guyana, Senegal, Sierra Leone, Trinidad, and Tobago, the second by India, Iran, Japan, Malaysia, Philippines, Saudi Arabia, and Thailand.

The Algerian draft referred first to the UN Charter on the use of force in the settlement of international disputes and expressed 'deep concern at the critical situation resulting from the military intervention of the armed forces of Indonesia in Portuguese Timor', calling upon all member states to recognise the inalienable right of the people of Portuguese Timor to self-determination, freedom and independence'. It continued:

2. [The General Assembly] *Calls upon* the administering Power to continue to make every effort to find a solution by peaceful means through talks between the Government of Portugal and the political parties representing the people of Portuguese Timor;
3. *Appeals* to all the parties in Portuguese Timor to respond positively to efforts to find a peaceful solution through talks between them and the Government of Portugal in the hope that such talks will bring an end to the strife in that Territory and lead towards the orderly exercise of the right of self-determination by the people of Portuguese Timor;
4. *Strongly deplores* the military intervention of the armed forces of Indonesia in Portuguese Timor;
5. *Calls upon* the Government of Indonesia to desist from further violation of the territorial integrity of Portuguese Timor and to withdraw without delay its armed forces from the Territory in

order to enable the people of the Territory freely to exercise their right to self-determination and independence;

6. *Draws the attention* of the Security Council, in conformity with Article 11, paragraph 3, of the Charter, to the critical situation in the Territory of Timor and recommends that it take urgent action to protect the territorial integrity of Portuguese Timor and the inalienable right of its people to self-determination;
7. *Calls upon* all States to respect the unity and territorial integrity of Portuguese Timor;
8. *Requests* the Government of Portugal to continue its co-operation with the Special Committee on the Situation with regard to the Implementation of the Declaration on the Granting of Independence to Colonial Countries and Peoples and requests the Committee to send a fact-finding mission to the Territory as soon as possible, in consultation with the political parties in Portuguese Timor and the Government of Portugal.

On 11 December the Indian resolution, which 'did not in any way seek to blame any party or any particular country for the unfortunate situation prevailing in the Territory' and avoided reference to Indonesia, was withdrawn by its sponsors and the Algerian draft adopted by a vote of sixty nine to eleven with thirty eight abstentions. The Australian government supported the resolution, as did China, the Soviet Union, Eastern bloc countries with the exception of Yugoslavia (which abstained), Portugal, and most African states. In the vote against, Indonesia was joined by Japan, Iran, and the ASEAN countries with the exception of Singapore, which abstained.[3]

On 15 December the Security Council debated the question. José Ramos Horta was now in New York and was permitted to address the Council on behalf of the Democratic Republic. The Indonesian case was put by José Martins of KOTA, the *liurai* of Atsabe (APODETI) and Mário Carrascalão (UDT). The outcome was a resolution similar in spirit to that of the Fourth Committee, calling inter alia for the withdrawal of Indonesian troops, recognition of the right to self-determination and the sending of a special representative of the Secretary-General on a fact-finding mission to Timor. It was adopted unanimously.

Despite reservations, Australia voted for the General Assembly Fourth Committee resolution. The vote was taken two days before the general election in Australia—aware of the strength of public feeling for the Timorese cause, the Liberal caretaker government decided to take a tougher line with Indonesia. The Australian delegation recorded its reservations about those clauses which referred directly to Indonesia and Mr Peacock was quoted as saying that he 'partly shared Indonesia's misgivings' about the resolution.[4]

On 28 December it was announced that the Director-General of the UN's European office in Geneva, Mr Vittorio Winspeare Guicciardi, had been selected as the Secretary-General's emissary to East Timor and that the 63-year-old Italian diplomat was expected to visit East Timor early in the new year.

After the Red-Cross-supervised evacuation only three Australians remained in Timor. Freelance journalist Roger East declined to be evacuated and a Mr and Mrs Rex Syddell who were in Tutuala at the eastern tip of the territory could not be contacted.

None of the aid workers, journalists or various officials in East Timor since the UDT coup of August 1975 had made direct contact with the Syddells, although a number of telegraphic communications (transmitted by the FRETILIN administration) had passed between them and various people in Dili, dealing with several matters—the handling of banking from Australia, the supply of medical goods and food for the local population and a request for an Australian government representative to visit Tutuala. It was not expected that there would be much military activity in the sparsely-populated eastern extreme of the territory, although their isolation should have aroused greater concern, as they had not been offered the option of evacuation.

Roger East's plight was more worrying, given the precedent of Balibó and continuing threats broadcast over Radio Kupang against Australian journalists in East Timor. He was last seen in Dili on the afternoon before the invasion, by International Red Cross officials, and did not appear to have taken steps to leave Dili for the mountains. He was then still staying at the Hotel Turismo on the foreshore and had declined an offer from President Xavier to move to his house at the back of town. On the morning of the seventh, when Alarico Fernandes's distress messages first reached Australia, listening journalists were able to question him about Roger East. Fernandes was broadcasting from Dili hospital at the rear of the capital. Roger East had not left Dili. He was, Fernandes said, in Dili but FRETILIN were unable to find him, although they were searching for him.

In the days before the invasion FRETILIN had prepared a mobile radio unit to take to the mountains. They had at their disposal a number of radios capable of reaching Australia. At the time of the Portuguese departure each company of the Portuguese Army had a U.S.-manufactured World War II ANGRC9 transceiver. These units were portable, had the power to reach Australia and could range all frequencies. Usually powered by a car battery, the ANGRC9 also had a manual generator for use in the field. There were, too, a number of later model TR28 pack radios also capable of reaching Australia.[5]

On 7 and 8 December Alarico Fernandes's broadcasts were made on the Red Cross radio using the frequency allocated to International Red Cross for its Darwin-Dili link, but by the ninth FRETILIN were using the frequencies of the Northern Territory's Outpost Radio system. This system is designed to pick up distress messages from isolated station properties in remote areas of the Territory. Users transmit voice messages on the radios which are handled as normal telegram communications. According to Telecom officials in Darwin on 8 December they intercepted a radio call from East Timor on one of the Outpost frequencies, accepted it as a distress call and passed it on to Australian addressees as a telegram, prefaced by the phrase 'This is an unauthenticated message'. From 8 December 1975 and for most of 1976 FRETILIN used this system to pass information to the outside world, until in November 1976 the Fraser government ordered Telecom officials to cease passing on the messages.

In the days immediately following the invasion, Fernandes's communications had a life-and-death desperation about them, calling for the urgent evacuation of Timorese civilians to Australia, the return of International Red Cross and food and medical relief. They constantly reported wholesale slaughter of civilians.

On Christmas Day 1975, in the face of continuing fierce resistance in Dili and Baucau the Indonesians landed re-

Rosa Muki Bonaparte (second from left), secretary of the Popular Organisation of Timorese Women, executed by Indonesian troops during the invasion of Dili. The others, from left, are Mari Alkatiri, Nicolau Lobato and Mau Laka. (Jill Jolliffe).

inforcements—according to information later gleaned from Australian intelligence sources, a further 15,000–20,000 troops —at all key points on the north coast and at Suai on the south coast. FRETILIN were now forced to withdraw from Dili and Baucau and on 29 December Aileu fell, although it was later temporarily recaptured by FRETILIN. By the beginning of January it was clear that they had nevertheless survived the initial holocaust and were now assessing their losses. In radio messages to Australia they reported that several Central Committee members—Francisco Borja da Costa, Rosa Muki Bonaparte, Goinxet Bernadino Bonaparte—had been shot in Dili, as had Fernando Carmo, vice-Minister for Home Affairs and former border zone commander. The Portuguese poet Inácio de Moura was initially reported by FRETILIN to have been killed although it was later learned that he was taken prisoner. In the same report Economics Minister José Gonçalves was alleged to be a captive of the Indonesians, working for them under duress, Central Committee member Jorge Tomás Carapinha to have been captured, and one other Central Committee member, Mau Laka (César Correia) listed as missing believed dead.

Information from other sources in the following period established that Isabel Lobato, the wife of Nicolau, was also executed in Dili on 7 December after being denounced to Indonesian troops. Four other Central Committee members were taken prisoner: Justino Mota, Djafar Alkatiri, Octavio de Araújo and Mariano Bonaparte Soares. Another of the Central Committee, Aleixo Corte Real, had reportedly defected. Corte Real was a conservative nationalist within the FRETILIN spectrum who had revealed pro-Indonesian sympathies during the UDT coup when he joined APODETI supporters hiding in the grounds of the Indonesian consulate. Of fifty-two Central Committee members, three were reported dead, one missing believed dead, five held in Dili gaol and one working with the Indonesians. There were some not accounted for. Of the Cabinet of the new government, one was dead and another working—allegedly under duress—for the Indonesians. Neither of these Cabinet members were on the Central Committee.

In the January assessment, FRETILIN listed Roger East among those who had perished in Dili. The first reference to him was on 4 January:

> A FRETILIN soldier said he saw Roger East killed in Dili within 24 hours of the invasion, together with Fernando Carmo and Inácio de Moura. FRETILIN pays tribute to Roger East and the Timorese are mourning all the journalists, particularly Mr East, who had decided to stay on to give an independent account and put his life at risk.

The following day more detailed information was transmitted:

> Roger East was killed at 8am on December 7 by paratroopers. Soldier Fernando brought the message. Alarico Fernandes begged

> East to go with him to the hills but he said he wanted to stay in Dili to report what was happening. Fernandes then went to Carmo and instructed him to pick up East. Carmo was killed in his car by six paratroopers in Santa Cruz. FRETILIN killed three paratroopers and three got away. He didn't get to East, who was already dead.[6]

This is the only existing account of the fate of Roger East. Inquiries from the Australian Government to the Indonesian Government have produced only a fragment of further information. In early March Roger East's sister, Ms Glenice Bowie wrote to Labor parliamentarian Dr Jim Cairns seeking his assistance in determining what happened to her brother. Consequently a letter from Foreign Affairs Minister Andrew Peacock to Cairns was passed on to her. It was the first official indication that the Indonesian government held information about East. The relevant section read:

> The Indonesian Red Cross, following inquiries in Dili, has now advised us that it has received information that Mr East was armed by FRETILIN, and that a close friend of his, a Timorese journalist, was stated to be dead. The Indonesian Red Cross could offer no further information.

Referring to Roger East's refusal of the offer of evacuation, Mr Peacock continued:

> Mr East declined to leave, indicating that he preferred to remain with the FRETILIN forces.

He made no reference to his status as a journalist.

The Indonesian Red Cross statement had a familiar ring to it. Of Balibó, the pro-Indonesian leaders had claimed that the journalists were 'integrated with FRETILIN forces' and 'directing the fire' of FRETILIN soldiers. Now it was said of Roger East that he was 'armed by FRETILIN' and, by the Australian Foreign Affairs Minister, that he 'preferred to remain with the FRETILIN forces', as though in a military capacity.

The original FRETILIN report of East's death has since proved false in one detail—that Inácio de Moura did not die on 7 December. But there has been nothing to indicate that the rest of the information was incorrect, while there has been some evidence to strengthen it: in addition to the Indonesian Red Cross statement, the post-invasion seepage of information from non-FRETILIN sources in Dili has provided similar hearsay evidence of East's death. Furthermore, those who knew East are confident that had he survived the attack on Dili and escaped to the mountains, he would almost certainly have reached and used the FRETILIN radio, even if not in his own name. None of the messages monitored since 7 December bear the mark of his style.

Almost two weeks after the invasion Adam Malik announced in Jakarta that a Provisional Government had been established in Dili on 18 December. FRETILIN was then reporting continued fighting in Dili, despite Indonesian claims that 'peace and security' has been 'restored'. In a radio message of 22 December Nicolau Lobato claimed that the Provisional Government had been sworn in, not in Dili, but on an Indonesian warship in Dili harbour.

UDT leaders were not given prime positions in the installed government. After their occupation of Dili and indeed, before, the Indonesians encountered non-co-operation from Timorese leaders of the integrationist parties, particularly UDT. There had been intermittent reports of unrest in Atambua, the UDT headquarters after 24 September, throughout the last months of 1975 and the conspicuous omission of most UDT leaders from key positions in the Provisional Government gave fuel to these rumours. Lopes da Cruz, who had been placed under house arrest in Dili by other UDT leaders in August for his virulently pro-Indonesian views, was the only UDT leader regarded as reliable by the Indonesians. Arnaldo dos Reis Araújo was named Governor of the Provisional Government and Lopes da Cruz Deputy Governor. The Indonesian-sponsored APODETI had proved by its consistent unpopularity in East Timor to be an unsatisfactory medium for the Indonesian government to pursue its aims. The more popular UDT thus became the mechanism for Indonesian entry into the territory in an operation which commenced with the splitting of the FRETILIN–UDT coalition and ended with the invasion of Dili. After the invasion UDT had not only outlived its usefulness, but had become a liability through the increasing dissatisfaction of its leaders with Indonesian methods and broken promises.

The Indonesians did not claim that the installation of the Provisional Government represented an act of free choice. A ceremony held soon after in Oecusse was of a different nature. On 13 December Radio Dili reported a ceremony held in Kupang to mark the 'integration' of Oecusse, the former Portuguese enclave in Indonesian Timor, into Indonesia. It was presided over by El Tari, Governor of Indonesian Timor. The declaration of loyalty was made by the civil administrator of Oecusse, Jaime Redentor de Oliveira and the military commander José Valente. It was followed on 19 December by a further ceremony in Oecusse itself, in which the Portuguese flag was lowered and the Indonesian flag raised.

The question of who held authority in Oecusse had been the subject of some confusion after the UDT coup. FRETILIN claimed that they held political power in the enclave (administrator de Oliveira was a FRETILIN supporter) while Portuguese authorities claimed that Oecusse was loyal to the Portuguese flag throughout. No journalist went there during the months of FRETILIN administration, although ASIAT's Dr John Whitehall visited and reported the administration functioning as previously, loyal to Portugal but minus Portuguese personnel and managed under a joint agreement between UDT and FRETILIN.

After their departure from Dili, the Portuguese withdrew from Oecusse on 30 August, handing over authority to the military commander in a formal ceremony. They maintained radio contact with Oecusse from Ataúro throughout September to December.

Political turmoil between the parties had in fact erupted in Oecusse before the UDT coup in Dili. In mid-June 1975 FRETILIN forces under Hermenegildo Alves seized power in the enclave but the Portuguese regained control after sending a negotiating force from Dili as a result of which Alves was gaoled for twenty days and UDT and FRETILIN agreed to rule jointly.

Oecusse had suffered for its physical isolation from the rest of East Timor during the months after the coup. The Australian blockade of food and fuel supply created a minor crisis and at the end of November Commander Valente radioed the Portuguese administration on Ataúro asking for medical supplies, fuel, and money for the payment of government officials. The Portuguese agreed and requested the commander to provide a list of medical supplies needed.

The last direct contact the Portuguese had with Oecusse was on 30 November after FRETILIN's declaration of independence. Commander Valente then contacted the Portuguese and appealed to them to request Indonesia to relieve the pressure of the pro-Indonesian parties on them to declare for integration. He stated that because Oecusse had avoided bloodshed to this stage the population was ready to accept whatever the people of East Timor decided.

There was one more, indirect, contact with Oecusse before the 19 December ceremony. On 23 December the Portuguese corvette *João Roby* returned to Darwin after a patrol of East Timorese waters, 'showing the flag'. A brief landing had been made on Ataúro. As in Oecusse the Portuguese had delegated authority to a Timorese commander when they left. He told the landing party that soon after the invasion of Dili he overheard a radio communication in which the Oecusse commander reported that he had 'raised the white flag' in the enclave.[7]

In this early pre-empting of UN calls for a proper act of self-determination, the Oecusse integration served notice that Indonesia did not intend to comply with even formal motions of an 'act of free choice' in deference to international opinion. The Oecusse takeover was followed on 29 December by a landing on Ataúro and a declaration of its integration.

Adam Malik had told UDT and APODETI leaders in Atambua in November that he would meet them again in Dili by Christmas, but it was not until New Year's Eve that he made his first visit, escorted by Indonesian reporters. Aco Manafe, a journalist for the Jakarta daily *Sinar Harapan*, interviewed Arnaldo dos Reis Araújo in the former Portuguese government offices in the centre of town, now adorned with the Indonesian flag and photos of President Suharto. He told Manafe 'Dili is now safe, but there are still a few terrorists holed up in places outside the town, including the Comoro area. In the last few days the shots have been getting further away.' Dos Reis Araújo also complained that his government was having difficulty functioning because there was only a handful of APODETI people left to run it—the rest had been taken to the mountains by FRETILIN. He said that the most urgent assistance needed was in the form of 'typewriters, chairs and officials'.

Sinar Harapan claimed that the extent of damage to the

capital had been exaggerated in press reports, that Dili was now quiet and the curfew lifted. Although the town was mainly intact 'the general hospital had been vacated and the patients evacuated to the central clinic in Dili'. A photograph showed patients lying on stretchers in the Banco Urgencia, the first-aid clinic in downtown Dili. FRETILIN had claimed in the early days of the invasion that Indonesian warships had shelled the hospital.

In the racy style of the best social columns Manafe said that he attended a New Year's Eve function at the Hotel Resende, 'well known for its night life'. 'Several military personalities of APODETI and UDT were present', he said, 'including Comandante Tomás Gonçalves, famous for his attacks on Balibó and Maliana'. The article concluded with the observation that most of the families of Dili attended Mass on New Year's Eve. 'The churches were full of people sobbing and praying' it said.[8]

The first non-Indonesian journalists into Dili accompanied Adam Malik on his second trip on 9 January. The party was met in Kupang by Arnaldo dos Reis Araújo and taken on to Ataúro where they were met by a group of schoolchildren with Indonesian flags. The Australian Broadcasting Commission's Tony Joyce accompanied the party. He described the scene in Dili thus:

> Banners read 'UN hands off—we are already Indonesian!' and 'We want freedom now!' but it would be hard to call the Dili welcome a spontaneous demonstration of the feelings of the Timorese people. From the start Mr Malik's flying visit was carefully stage-managed. In Dili about 1,000 people were assembled outside Government House. On cue about every five minutes the crowd raised their red and white Indonesian flags and shouted pro-Indonesian slogans. I saw at least 200 Indonesian soldiers armed with automatic weapons in the capital. They wore no helmets, no badges or insignia other than an armband with the Indonesian flag and the word 'Indonesia'. This was the first visual confirmation of Indonesian troops in East Timor, though of course the Indonesian government is still maintaining the elaborate fiction that its troops are really volunteers ...

Joyce concluded that if the UN Special Envoy's visit followed this pattern he would have little chance of determining the true situation in the territory.[9]

Travelling from Jakarta, Winspeare Guicciardi visited a number of Provisional Government-held areas of East Timor in the following week, from 19–23 January, 1976. His visit was initially opposed by the Provisional Government, which later relented (according to Jakarta as a result of the good offices of the Indonesian government). Although the envoy's brief was to make contact with all parties in the territory, he was unable to visit FRETILIN-held areas 'on technical and/or security grounds'. He interviewed representatives of the Provisional Government, including José Gonçalves, formerly a member of the FRETILIN government, to whom he spoke privately at length. He visited Oecusse, Ataúro, Dili, Manatuto and Baucau. It was clear that these were the only areas secured by Indonesia. In view of his inability to reach FRETILIN, on his return to Jakarta Winspeare Guicciardi contacted their representatives in Australia to arrange radio contact with FRETILIN forces in Timor, in the hope of travelling to south coast areas from Australia. Soon after his first contact with António Belo, FRETILIN representative in Darwin, Belo was arrested by Australian Commonwealth police for possessing an illegal radio transmitter. The transmitter, which was seized and confiscated, had been the only channel of contact between FRETILIN in East Timor and their Australian representatives. It was revealed at the time that Telecom Australia officials in Darwin had known of the transmitter's existence since December and allowed it to broadcast unimpeded until then.

Winspeare Guicciardi subsequently flew to Darwin from Jakarta and despite this initial frustration of his mission by the Australian government, new contact was made by FRETILIN representatives using the radio of the Portuguese corvette *João Roby* in Darwin harbour. Nicolau Lobato then named four possible landing places for the UN envoy—Same, Viqueque, Com and Suai—but before the envoy could make the necessary arrangements to get there, Indonesian forces bombed the areas nominated and mounted a large-scale new offensive at Same. Consequently, on 5 February the UN representative abandoned attempts to visit FRETILIN-held territory and returned to Geneva. Winspeare Guicciardi's subsequent bland report to the Secretary-General spoke of a 'slender common assumption' by all parties to the Timor dispute that the people of East

Timor should be consulted on their future, although views of the means by which this should be done varied enormously. Representatives of the Democratic Republic of East Timor outside the territory proposed a referendum on a one person one vote basis, to be held after the withdrawal of Indonesian troops, the vote to be conducted on a choice between integration with Indonesia and independence with FRETILIN. Portugal also favoured a referendum after the withdrawal of Indonesian troops, he reported. The terms they envisaged were integration with Indonesia or independence in consultation with the various political associations. The Provisional Government of East Timor held that the East Timorese had already exercised their right to self-determination. Indonesian representatives, the report concluded, stated that while the future of the territory was for the East Timorese to decide, they welcomed East Timor's 'request' for integration, but believed it should be formally ratified.[10]

Although Winspeare Guicciardi's visit failed to yield much fresh information, news was now seeping out of East Timor from several sources. The 5–10 January edition of the Australian weekly *National Times* ran a detailed account of what was known of Indonesian actions from both Jakarta and Canberra security sources. It revealed that both the Whitlam and Fraser governments had access to detailed information about Indonesian military activities, including the following:

> *On Christmas Day Indonesia had launched a large-scale invasion involving between 15,000 and 20,000 wholly Javanese marines;
> *The 7 December invasion involved between 4,000 and 6,000 troops, not 1,000 as initially reported;
> *Indonesian troops had committed atrocities against the civilian population in Dili and senior officers had experienced difficulty maintaining discipline among their troops;
> *Indonesian troops had not managed to secure the territory and FRETILIN forces were waging a sustained resistance, at some cost to Indonesia;
> *Indonesian troops had first become involved in East Timor in September 1975.

The report from Jakarta filled out the picture:

> The attack by Indonesian forces on FRETILIN-held Dili early on

> December 7 was marked by a breakdown in discipline and tactical command ... Indiscriminate shooting by Indonesian soldiers is reported to have caused significant casualties among non-combatant residents of Dili. Severe maltreatment of suspected FRETILIN supporters is also reported during the occupation of the town ... Members of the attacking forces also ransacked and looted ... Paratroopers who were landed inland and marines moving into the town from the shoreline are reported to have engaged each other in firefights as their paths of attack met.
>
> Amid the attack the remaining FRETILIN forces carried out their planned withdrawal in an orderly manner, taking the radio set from the hospital as they left town.

Troops used included an infantry battalion from the Brawijaya (East Java) division, troops from the RPKAD special paratroop regiment which had been fighting at the border for some time and marine (KKO) forces.[11]

In February it was reported that certain units, mainly from the Brawijaya division, had been withdrawn from Timor as a result of their excesses against the civilian population. In Jakarta on 13 February Lopes da Cruz made a press statement which shocked observers of the war in East Timor. 60,000 people had been killed 'in the six months of civil war in East Timor' he said. It was known that the death toll in fighting in East Timor before the invasion of 7 December was around 3,000. Da Cruz said that most of the dead were women and children, and admitted that there had been some 'excesses' against FRETILIN suspects:

> Excesses often occur now as revenge for FRETILIN's cruelty when it was in power.[12]

The Australian Foreign Affairs Department subsequently went to some lengths to characterise da Cruz's statement as a description of 'victims' of the war in East Timor including the 40,000 alleged refugees in Indonesian Timor. But the East Timorese later repeated his statement. The reasons for a pro-Indonesian leader to make such a self-incriminating statement appear rather puzzling. They can perhaps be explained in terms of divisions between the Jakarta military élite over the conduct of the war in Timor, in which da Cruz became a mouthpiece for one sector: some months later it was reported that the source of the statement was a report from the Indonesian Red Cross to the Indonesian government, and that da Cruz had made the statement at the instigation of Ali Murtopo in a manoeuvre against General Surono.[13]

The emerging horror of East Timor after 7 December was also manifest in several letters smuggled to Darwin. There was already a Chinese-Timorese community in Darwin before the invasion, consisting largely of Chinese who had emigrated to Australia on their savings. In August their number was increased by Chinese fleeing the civil war. In late January 1976 letters smuggled via Kupang reached relatives in Darwin, listing whole families killed during the invasion. One letter (reprinted in the *Northern Territory News* of 29 January) claimed that the killing during the first weeks of Indonesian occupation was worse than during the Japanese occupation and that the Indonesians had looted extensively, loading their pillage, including cars, on to ships in Dili harbour. Another said that many of the inhabitants of Dili had fled to the mountains before the invasion but that of those remaining 80% of the men were killed by Indonesian troops. Later reports from Chinese sources, including the few Chinese who travelled to Taiwan after 7 December, told of groups of Chinese going into the streets with gifts to greet the invaders, only to be machine-gunned by Indonesian troops.

In early March, first news broke of the Syddells in Tutuala. On 6 March the *Sydney Morning Herald* reported that Rex and Jane Syddell were being evacuated from Tutuala to Jakarta by the Indonesian Government. The Syddells made a number of sensational allegations about recent events in East Timor. In Jakarta Mr Syddell spoke bitterly of his experiences. He claimed that he and his wife had been held under house arrest and terrorised by FRETILIN from September to December, forced to live from roots, leaves and coconut milk, and as a result were ill from deprivation when the Indonesians rescued them. He was bitter at the failure of both ICRC and the Australian government to contact him before the 2 December evacuation and accused Radio Australia of being an 'advertising agency' for FRETILIN. He also claimed that Australians had smuggled arms to FRETILIN in crates marked as Red Cross medical goods. The most important of his allegations, however, was that FRETILIN troops had killed the five journalists at Balibó, an allegation for which he claimed to hold documentary evidence. He said that FRETILIN troops at Balibó had dressed in Indonesian uniforms 'to embarrass Indonesia':

> Fifteen white people, including Portuguese soldiers, Portuguese officers and a personal friend of mine, plus the five journalists were murdered by Fretilin ... I have documentary proof, I have sworn affidavits and testaments which I am prepared to present to the Indonesian Government and to our own Government and to the United Nations. I have irrefutable documentary proof and we have the witnesses all lined up. They've been taken into protective custody because of revenge.[14]

In response to the Syddells' allegations that they had been in a state of distress throughout the period of FRETILIN rule and that the ICRC had been derelict in their treatment of them, an ICRC press release was issued on 17 March denying the claim, while conceding that the Syddells had not been contacted during the evacuation. 'However, the ICRC was asked earlier by the Syddells to arrange transfer of money in their personal account in Dili to Tutuala', the statement said, 'At no time did they express a desire to leave'.

Most of the Syddell testimony was devoid of dates and times, and although Rex Syddell claimed that he would soon produce the documentary evidence which he said he had buried in a grave in Lospalos, the evidence was not forthcoming. In April Syddell flew to the UN to support the Indonesian case at a Security Council debate and in August 1976 he travelled to Australia for a brief period where he described himself to an interviewer as a 'diplomatic observer of Indonesian and Portuguese affairs for more than thirty years who is not unknown to certain international intelligence agencies'. He held to his story that FRETILIN soldiers had killed the journalists, despite his failure since March to produce documentary evidence.

In April the Security Council discussed the question of East Timor once more, considering the Secretary-General's report since the visit of his envoy to the territory. The outcome was a resolution re-affirming the right of the East Timorese to self-determination and independence; calling upon member states to respect the territorial integrity of East Timor as well as the inalienable right of its people to self-determination; calling on Indonesia to withdraw all its forces without delay; and requesting the Secretary-General to have his special representative continue with the assignment entrusted him by the December 1975 resolution and report back as soon as possible. It was carried twelve votes to none with two abstentions, Japan and the United States.

This UN session resulted in some interesting developments. In New York to appear for the Indonesian-installed Provisional Government were Guilherme Gonçalves, Mário Carrascalão, and Rex Syddell. José Ramos Horta put the case for FRETILIN and Ken Fry, the Australian Labor MHR who had been a member of the March 1975 delegation to East Timor under the Portuguese administration and returned in September under the FRETILIN administration, spoke in support of Ramos Horta's case for independence. KOTA's José Martins, who appeared in December for the Provisional Government, was also in New York.

The debate was opened by Ramos Horta who referred to the Lopes da Cruz claim of 60,000 dead, accusing the Indonesians of systematic atrocities, the use of napalm and continued defiance of UN resolutions. Guilherme Gonçalves, for the Provisional Government, countered FRETILIN accusations with claims of FRETILIN atrocities. The Australian Ambassador, Mr Ralph Harry, also addressed the Council. He spoke of the need for a proper act of self-determination but neither specified the means nor referred to the withdrawal of Indonesian troops.

In his address, Ken Fry described the relative popularity of the three parties as he had observed them before the coup, gave evidence of the widespread popularity of FRETILIN, and affirmed the lack of support for integration into Indonesia. He did not believe that the Provisional Government represented the will of the people and that if Indonesian forces were withdrawn it would be quickly overthrown. He added that he believed the civil war between FRETILIN and UDT was fostered by Jakarta.

Rex Syddell spoke at length of the 'common characteristics of the Timorese', which he said had been reinforced by Portuguese neglect, and in support of his allegations of atrocities committed by FRETILIN. The traditional tribal system was the dominant influence on East Timorese life, he argued, and the Timorese:

> are very much dependent upon authority figures, particularly the

> tribal chiefs or sub-chiefs, to make basic decisions for them. Even these men find it difficult to make decisions in unusual or important matters.
>
> This dependence on others was illustrated by the attitudes displayed by our workers, who would frequently ask for our advice and consequently required repeated directions, even in dealing with very ordinary matters. They were incapable of following anything but elementary instructions.

Mr Syddell claimed that during the period of his alleged house arrest under FRETILIN:

> FRETILIN officials who visited us daily often boasted of the atrocities they had committed. This was done at least partly to intimidate us and in an attempt to elicit our co-operation. I should add that even during my volunteer service in the Spanish Civil War or my mission to Kenya at the time of the Mau Mau uprising, I never witnessed such atrocities, brutalities or inhumanity committed by one group of people against another.[15]

Indonesian delegates were reportedly embarrassed by the blunt paternalism and racism of Syddell's testimony, delivered in the presence of Third World UN members.

Soon after the Security Council resolution was passed, José Martins of KOTA delivered a letter to the Secretary-General announcing his party's withdrawal from the Provisional Government. A week earlier he had called an informal press conference in which he announced his defection. In the letter he declared:

> On 16th of December 1975, I addressed the Security Council of the United Nations as president of the KOTA party ...
>
> I came in December not as a free man. I was forced, like the others then, [Guilherme Gonçalves and Mário Carrascalão] as a prisoner, to read what the Indonesians had written ... I have been entrusted by my people in East Timor to tell the truth of our situation.
>
> ... After the fall of Dili a puppet 'Provisional Government' was set up. The minority APODETI Party was in prominence. The other parties were banned. Many thousands of people, including supporters of KOTA, U.D.T. and APODETI, were machine-gunned. Houses were sacked. The Indonesian soldiers took away everything they could find ... leaders of the pro-Indonesian parties were deeply shocked ... Even the long-term supporters of the 'integration' were disillusioned and many are now openly oppos-

ing Indonesian presence in the territory. The so-called Provisional Government is a one-man band. Arnaldo Araújo is the only one who is still loyal to the Indonesians.

Martins also alleged that the Indonesians had inflated the number of refugees who had fled to Indonesian Timor and that, against their claim of 40,000 refugees, the real figure was no more than 20,000 and that, of those, many wished to return to East Timor after September but were prevented from doing so by Indonesian authorities: 'Obviously the Indonesian government was using the "40,000 refugees" as a political weapon against FRETILIN'.[16]

The only Australian newspaper to run the story of Martins's defection was the *Australian* of Friday 23 April. However, the full importance of his announcement was not yet understood. It was then known in some circles in Australia that Martins had contacted two Australian diplomatic missions (in Geneva and Lisbon) and an ABC reporter in January after his first UN appearance with the intelligence that he had been privy to events at Balibó from the Indonesian side and wished to 'spill his guts' about the fate of the journalists. For reasons unknown the ABC let the story from their grasp and attempts by other reporters to re-establish contact with Martins in the months from January to April led only to dead-ends. The *Australian*'s 'Timorese Snub to Indonesia: Group to Quit Pact' story unexpectedly announced his re-appearance to public view.

The *Age*'s Michael Richardson, who was personally acquainted with the KOTA leader, worked by phone throughout the weekend from his Singapore base to elicit the story from Martins in New York. There was little doubt that Martins had been on the Indonesian Timor side of the border at the crucial time. Richardson had interviewed him there in September, and throughout the period up until the invasion Martins's voice could be monitored in Dili on Radio Kupang, disseminating propaganda for the Indonesians. A photo published in the Australian press soon after Balibó was attacked showed Martins entering the town with Indonesian troops. In the background the half-burnt house with the word 'Australia' painted on it is apparent. The following Monday, 26 April, the *Age*'s headlines read: 'Newsmen "Executed": New Claim on Deaths of Five T.V. Men'.

Martins had a reputation as a professional adventurer and had been heavily involved in the Indonesian intervention. He had not lived in East Timor since early childhood, having been reared in Portugal. His father, José Martins snr., was a *liurai* in the Ermera district and two of his uncles, the *liurai* of Atsabe and his secretary Hermenegildo Martins, were prominent in APODETI. His family claimed direct lineage from Jan de Hornay, the Topass leader. José Martins had served with the Portuguese army in Africa. He cultivated a warrior image, preaching racial superiority, tribal mysticism, machismo: in an interview with a Melbourne daily he was quoted as saying he never allowed his soldiers to rape married women. He returned to East Timor in June 1975 only weeks before the UDT coup, purportedly to re-organise KOTA, and after the coup worked with UDT and APODETI leaders from Indonesian Timor. He enjoyed the trust of the Indonesians, working closely with BAKIN agent Louis Ţaolin until his defection. He was delegated by the Indonesians to handle the Radio Kupang propaganda operation. Hamish McDonald, a Jakarta-based Australian journalist, reported that Martins threatened him in Timor in September 1975 for not reporting to his command post when he crossed the border. Martins was a signatory to the integrationist party leaders' account to the Australian government of the death of the journalists in which it was claimed that they were 'controlling and guiding' the fire of FRETILIN.

He now repudiated that statement as having been made under Indonesian duress and declared that he was prepared to tell the truth about Balibó to a properly-constituted public inquiry. Martins was in the habit of keeping a soldier's diary and as a result he was able to give a coherent account of the military operation of 16 October. According to his account approximately six companies of Indonesian troops (about 1,200 men) were involved in the offensive. At 3am tanks moved off from Indonesian territory to cross the border. At 4.30am the first shots were fired and at 6am infantry forces arrived in Balibó. 'At 8 o'clock there was word that there were journalists and at 10 o'clock they were burnt', he claimed. Martins never claimed that he personally witnessed the death of the newsmen. He entered the town behind Indonesian troops in time to see the bullet-ridden bodies being burnt in the house where they had been at the time of the attack. Two days later, he said, grenades were thrown into the house, which was why the remains were so fragmented. He was told the circumstances of their death by Tomás Gonçalves who had accompanied the Indonesian regulars into the town. Gonçalves told him that two of the five newsmen had been killed by mortar and machine-gun fire which penetrated the walls of the house in which they were sheltering, but that two had attempted to surrender. They emerged from the house with their hands up, shouting 'Australians! Australians!' Martins said. A fifth had tried to escape out of a back entrance but was 'used as a human target' by the Indonesian soldiers. Before the bodies were burnt, the Indonesian commander of the operation, Colonel Dading flew by helicopter from Batugadé to view the situation, Martins alleged, accompanied by Louis Taolin.[17]

Following the disclosures from New York, the Victorian branch of the Australian Journalists Association (AJA) decided to bring Martins to Australia. Martins was initially reluctant. He claimed that in his approach to the Australian embassies in Europe he requested officials to pass on his testimony to the dead men's relatives and colleagues while safeguarding the confidentiality of the source. He now said that the embassies did not relay the information, but breached his confidentiality with the Indonesians. In the Australian parliament Andrew Peacock acknowledged that Martins had made the approach but denied that there was a mandate to air his testimony, or that information had been passed to the Indonesians.

Under renewed public pressure the Foreign Affairs Department announced that it would question Martins and that an investigatory team was about to leave for Balibó, the Indonesian government having finally consented to allow it in.

The AJA announcement that the Victorian branch was to fly Martins to Australia was made on 27 April. By 3 May he had not materialised although the arrangements for his travel had been made. On being contacted by the AJA, he claimed that on 30 April in Frankfurt he had been threatened by the Indonesian government, through BAKIN operative Louis Taolin, that it would be 'dangerous' for him to take his testimony to Australia. Taolin reminded him, he said, that he still had relatives in East Timor.

Louis Taolin had played a role throughout the course of Indonesian intervention in East Timor. A west Timorese, son of the *raja* of Insana, he was well known in Dili before the UDT coup, describing himself at various times as a journalist and a businessman. He kept close connections with the Indonesian consulate in Dili and his house in Indonesian Timor provided regular hospitality to sporting and cultural delegations from East Timor on courtesy visits to the Indonesian territory. During the declaration of integration at Atambua on 30 November 1975 Taolin was pictured with Adam Malik and, according to Martins, was at the front with Indonesian forces at various times from September to December 1975.

Despite the threats, and after assurances that he would be dealing primarily with the journalists' association and not the Australian government, which he mistrusted, Martins arrived in Melbourne on 5 May. He was interviewed at a press conference at Tullamarine airport and then by AJA and Foreign Affairs officials where he repeated, and was cross-examined on, the evidence earlier published in the *Age*.

Martins had been in East Timor only briefly since the invasion, when he travelled to Dili by Indonesian helicopter before leaving for New York for his December UN appearance. However, through contact with other Provisional Government leaders who had been in Dili he had some picture of the situation. He claimed that Dili had been subject to considerable devastation during the attack of 7 December and that there had been indiscriminate slaughter. Asked of the fate of UDT leaders Maggiolo Gouveia and Mousinho who had been prisoners of FRETILIN, he said that he had hearsay reports that FRETILIN had executed them before leaving for the mountains, although there were other reports that they had been killed by the Indonesians.

He revealed that the Provisional government was not functioning: '[it] does not exist—it is just names'. He had no desire to see FRETILIN rule East Timor, 'But now, FRETILIN is fighting, we fight with FRETILIN. Later we may have to fight against FRETILIN'. He had counselled his supporters, and APODETI and UDT people to join FRETILIN he said:

> It is no longer a question of FRETILIN or UDT or APODETI. It is now a question of Timorese nationalism. We have one word in our

> language which is very important: *malai*. Now it is all Timorese against the *malai*, the man with the foreign language ... I am stupid, because I could have $100,000 in my pocket. But one day my son might say 'my father sold the land of his people'.

To illustrate the depth of UDT disaffection with the Indonesians, he claimed that as early as the Balibó operation João Carrascalão and Domingos de Oliveira had been disarmed and ordered back behind the lines to Atambua by the Indonesians because of their increasingly unco-operative and hostile attitudes. During the attack on Maliana, he said, twelve East Timorese civilians had emerged from the bush with their arms up in an attempt to surrender but had been machine-gunned by Indonesian troops. As a result, João Carrascalão refused to share his supply of G3 ammunition with the Indonesians and was ordered out of the operation. Captain Lino was also sent back to Atambua after trying to persuade Timorese troops to change their loyalty from the pro-Indonesian Lopes da Cruz to João Carrascalão.

In his account of the Balibó operation Martins named the Indonesian command of 'Operasi Komodo', as:

> General Ali Murtopo, General Yoga Sugama, Major-General Benny Murdani, Brigadier Pranoto, Colonel Sugiyanto, Colonel Agus, Colonel Sinaga, Colonel Dading, Major Andreas.

General Murtopo, he said, was in charge of the overall planning of the operation, but in particular its political aspects. Murdani was the key figure in the military operation from its commencement in the last months of 1975 leading to the assault on Dili. Dading has since been identified as Brigadier-General (not Colonel) Dading Kalbuadi, *panglima* (military commander) of the East Timor campaign under Benny Murdani.[18]

Martins expressed the view that FRETILIN were capable of conducting a successful campaign for a period of years, providing they 'clung to the mountains' in traditional Timorese fashion, building fortifications to protect crops and functioning as a guerilla army.

At this time there was no clear picture of whether FRETILIN were able to grow crops behind the lines and organise civil services. The messages transmitted to Darwin did not give a clear picture of the extent of their control and after the Christmas Day offensive it was clear that the Indonesians were travelling down the road system and occupying inland towns with armoured columns. In May, however, a broadcast from FRETILIN announced the convening of a Central Committee meeting 'in areas controlled by FRETILIN' and the celebration, on 20 May, of the anniversary of the foundation of the front. 'Several departments of FRETILIN have been reshuffled', they reported:

> as have, accordingly, those of the revolutionary government. In order to adjust to the situation of armed struggle, some basic structures have been altered. Vacancies left by members of the Central Committee murdered or in Indonesian prisons, or by the treason of others, have been filled by provisional members.

To mark the anniversary, the FRETILIN flag was 'solemnly raised', a Popular Centre for Culture inaugurated and an exhibition of Timorese medicines and locally made sugar displayed:

> At 10am the meeting began, followed at 12 noon by lunch when the people fraternised with the troops. The afternoon was dedicted to a sports carnival, and at 7.30pm a cultural evening began which ended at 2am the next day ... the Central Committee unanimously decided to free all political prisoners arrested before the Indonesian invasion and called on the people to remain vigilant.

Following the Martins visit the AJA requested the Foreign Affairs Department to demand reparations from the Indonesian government for the death of the newsmen. In a statement released on May 12 the Association claimed that they were killed 'as a result of illegal actions of Indonesian troops'. The Victorian branch president, Mr Geoff Gleghorn, said that if the Indonesian government refused to accept culpability in the case the Association would take the matter to the International Court of Justice.

The response of the Foreign Affairs Department to the Martins evidence was to point to the variety of accounts of the Balibó deaths which now existed, including the two different versions furnished by Martins (before and after his defection). The department pointed to the fact that two separate accounts were attributed to Tomás Gonçalves: the one he had signed with Martins and which he held to when questioned by the Foreign Affairs team in April 1976, and the account which Martins claimed he gave him in Balibó on the morning of 16 October but which Gonçalves denied to the investigators. This attitude ignored Martins's role as a defector, in which he freely admitted that he had originally made a false statement. His evidence in Australia did not introduce new assertions but corroborated a number of separate, but consistent, circumstantial accounts already given—those of Guido dos Santos, of Roger East's interviewees, and the Lopes da Cruz broadcast of 21 October 1975.[19]

In May journalists were permitted into Dili again, this time to witness a meeting of the 'East Timor Regional Popular Assembly' presided over by Guilherme Gonçalves. This ceremony was to be East Timor's 'Act of Free Choice'. The journalists were driven to the assembly straight from Dili airport and were confined to the Sporting Club building in which the proceedings were held. Some who attempted to 'stray' outside the building were politely but firmly ushered back. On completion of the assembly the journalists were driven briefly around the town and then back to the airport for take-off.

This was the first time that foreign diplomatic observers visited Indonesian-controlled Dili. In view of the resolutions before it, the UN declined to sanction the meeting by its presence, but seven Jakarta embassies sent representatives: Malaysia, Thailand, New Zealand, India, Iran, Saudi Arabia, and Nigeria. The Australian government refused to attend, as did Japan. Indonesia was angered by these refusals: Japan had voted with Indonesia in the UN but now refused to attend without UN representation.

The assembly consisted of the twenty eight Timorese delegates walking to a dais to deliver speeches in Portuguese. After an hour and a half of this procedure, Gonçalves declared the assembly's decision to petition Indonesia for the immediate integration of East Timor.

The assembly was followed within the week by a delegation of fifty Timorese to Jakarta, where they were greeted by President Suharto as 'brothers long separated by colonialism'. On 24 June a further ceremony took place in East Timor in which Arnaldo dos Reis Araújo presented a piece of local soil and a nugget of gold to Indonesian Home Minister Amir Machmud to symbolise 'the return of East Timor to its homeland'. On 17 July President Suharto signed a Bill formally merging the territory with Indonesia. The ceremony was originally scheduled for 17 August to co-incide with Indonesia's national day, but was brought forward without notice. The President called on FRETILIN members to surrender or be 'crushed'. He also announced that Portuguese nationals wishing to return to Portugal would be free to do so, including the twenty three Portuguese soldiers held since 24 September 1975.[20]

In Australia trade union leaders, parliamentarians, church and aid organisation figures, and student leaders called on the Australian government to reject the merger and request a new meeting of the UN Security Council. In response, Mr Peacock stated that the government did not recognise the integration—'Australia cannot recognise the broad requirements for a satisfactory process as having been met'.

President Suharto's reference to the repatriation of Portuguese nationals followed secret talks held in Bangkok and Jakarta in late June and early July between Portuguese officials and representatives from the Indonesian government and the Provisional Government of East Timor. The context was an election campaign in Portugal which culminated in early July in the election of conservative MFA General António dos Santos Ramalho Eanes as President. One issue of the campaign was the 'overseas question' which had plagued Portuguese political life throughout the twentieth century and which, expressing a mood of national resurgence, now returned to the fore. The complexion of the Portuguese electorate had visibly altered since 25 April 1974, with near one million refugees, or *retornados*, from Angola, Mozambique and Timor having streamed back to Portugal where unemployment was already high among the population of nine million.

Among the twenty three Portuguese soldiers still captive in Timor was Rui Batista da Palma Carlos, nephew of Professor Palma Carlos, Prime Minister during the Spínola government. His family was pressing for government action for the release of the twenty three, and there was a growing feeling in Lisbon, reflecting the conservative trend of the electorate, that Portuguese honour had been besmirched in Timor. Around this time a group of conservative officers laid charges of 'treasonable surrender' of former Portuguese colonies to anti-colonialist forces against MFA officers who had been involved in the decolonisation process. Included among the accused was former Governor of Timor Lemos Pires (now promoted to Brigadier) who faced 'serious charges of cowardice for having ordered Portuguese troops to desert thousands of Timor people who were subsequently massacred by guerilla groups'.[21] A commission of inquiry which was still taking evidence at the time of writing was established in Lisbon.

The man delegated by the Portuguese to negotiate with the Indonesians was General José Morais da Silva, a political associate of Eanes who had spent his early childhood in Timor. Subjects reportedly discussed with Indonesian officials were Portuguese recognition of Indonesian sovereignty, payment of pensions to former Portuguese soldiers and civil servants, payment of reparations to the Provisional Government, the repatriation of Portuguese citizens and the release of the twenty three.

On 27 July the twenty three soldiers and 113 East Timorese civilians of Portuguese nationality were flown to an airforce base in Java. Included among them was João Carrascalão (of UDT), still officially a member of the Provisional Government, and other members of his family. By 3 October 929 Portuguese nationals had been repatriated, mainly from Atambua. Although some of those evacuated were witnesses to the invasion of Dili, few have since spoken freely of their experiences, largely because of the selective approach of Indonesian authorities in authorising repatriation. In many cases one or two members of released families remained in Timor. The evacuation of these 929 also had the function of removing an important and potentially troublesome social layer—the articulate urban élite—from Indonesian-occupied town centres, as well as quieting public opinion in Lisbon.

Jakarta's hastening of the formal integration of East Timor was significant in that the annual conference of non-aligned nations was due to be held in Colombo, Sri Lanka, in mid-August. Indonesia hoped to present the Timor question as a closed book. Instead the summit was occasion for a stinging rebuff. The 86-member summit represented more than half the world's population and nearly two-thirds of the UN's membership. FRETILIN delegates were refused visas to the conference by the Sri Lankan government but Mozambican representatives led by President Samora Machel presented their case. Addressing the conference on 18 August President Machel called on it to appeal to Indonesia to withdraw its forces from East Timor and to give the East Timorese 'necessary moral and material aid'. At the conference's political committee Mozambique submitted an amendment adding East Timor to a list of more than a dozen 'colonial territories' named in the draft political declaration to be adopted by the conference as territories in need of self-determination and 'speedy independence'. The amendment was carried against Indonesia's bitter opposition with the result that the conference's final declaration affirmed the right of the East Timorese to self-determination in accordance with UN General Assembly and Security Council resolutions.[22]

The secretly-conducted Portuguese negotiations with Indonesia led to concern among Australian supporters of East Timorese self-determination that Portugual would soon formally recognise Indonesian sovereignty in Timor. If Portugal as the legally sovereign power handed authority to Indonesia, a large number of Western countries would automatically give recognition, including Australia. The Australian government was rumoured to be already considering recognition in its own right and talks between Prime Minister Fraser and President Suharto were scheduled to be held in Jakarta in October. This concern expressed itself in an appeal to the newly-elected Portuguese Socialist Party Prime Minister Mário Soares from the Australian parliamentary Labor party not to recognise the Indonesian takeover. (The Australian Labor Party is a fraternal member of the Socialist International with the Portuguese Socialist Party.)

On the eve of Mr Fraser's Jakarta visit a second FRETILIN transmitter was seized in Darwin. News reports from Jakarta indicated that Indonesia had pressured the Australian government to curb FRETILIN activists in Australia, instruct Telecom Australia to cease relaying messages from East Timor, and take steps to prevent aid being smuggled to Timor. In Parliament the Prime Minister and the acting Foreign Minister denied that the transmitter had been seized on an Indonesian request. Tom Uren, Deputy Leader of the Opposition, called for cancellation of the Fraser visit.[23]

Until this time the Australian government was committed to a four-point policy on Timor which included a call for the cessation of hostilities, withdrawal of Indonesian troops, a genuine act of self-determination, and aid channelled through the International Red Cross. Malcolm Fraser's claim that he had inherited the Labor government's mantle was correct; nevertheless the Liberals, if they chose to rigorously pursue this policy, clearly had scope to reverse the trend established by Labor. They chose not to do so. It was soon apparent that, as with the Labor government, tension existed between the Prime Minister and his Foreign Affairs Minister. In this case Andrew Peacock was identified with the four-point policy, particularly the insistence on the re-admission of International Red Cross to East Timor as a condition of Australian aid being sent to Timor via the Indonesian authorities. By the time Mr Fraser went to Jakarta on 7 October the policy had been partially eroded: Australia had agreed to send aid through Indonesian Red Cross, without insisting on any role for the international body.

At the conclusion of four days of talks with President Suharto, Malcom Fraser told a Jakarta press conference that he saw no need to continue to spell out the four-point policy, as it was 'on the record. I don't want to restate it. The important thing is to look to the future and work to the future'. The *Age* commented:

> We cannot go much further at present towards publicly accepting the incorporation, even though the Indonesians would like us to.
>
> The Foreign Minister, Mr Peacock, architect of the earlier strong stand, must already be sitting uncomfortably in Jakarta with his leader as the shift becomes more and more obvious.[24]

Only minutes after the Australian Prime Minister left Jakarta for Canberra an Indonesian official publicly announced that Australia had promised it would not stand in the way of Indonesia's actions in Timor: 'Mr Fraser's statement has very great importance for us. It implies that Australia has recognised the integration of East Timor into Indonesia'.

When his plane landed in Canberra, Mr Fraser was confronted with the statement, which he repudiated, saying that the only valid document was the communique signed by himself and President Suharto.

From the time of Mr. Fraser's Jakarta visit, foreign policy towards East Timor was seen as expressing the hawkish views of the Prime Minister, above those of Foreign Minister Andrew Peacock.

One incidental outcome of the Fraser visit was a multi million dollar trade agreement between the Indonesian government and an Australian oil company. For some months before the Fraser talks, negotiations had been underway between the Ampol company and several Indonesian companies including Pertamina, the state-owned oil company which became the subject of a major financial scandal in Indonesia at the beginning of 1975. The oil was needed to boost failing Australian reserves and to meet the country's light oil requirements. Mr Fraser was reported to have told Indonesia's Minister of Mines, Dr Mohammed Sadli, that although the negotiations were a private commercial concern, he would welcome an increased sale of oil to Australia to rectify the trade imbalance between the two countries. Ampol subsequently signed a five-year letter of intent with the Indonesian government to negotiate for the purchase of crude oil.

The Australian oil industry was not the only concern with a vested interest in the political outcome of the East Timor affair. Soon after Mr Fraser's talks in Jakarta it was revealed in the Australian press that a group of leading Australian businessmen were applying pressure to the government for full recognition of Indonesian sovereignty in East Timor. The Australia-Indonesia Business Co-operation Committee (AIBCC) represents 153 Australian companies, including the ANZ Bank, the Bank of NSW, Blue Metal Industries, the Australian Wheat and Dairy Boards, and the major sugar company CSR. The AIBCC's president, Mr Brian Kelman, told the group's annual general meeting that continued opposition to Indonesia's incorporation of Timor could damage Australian relations with Indonesia and that the AIBCC had made representations to Mr Fraser and Mr Peacock to accept Indonesian rule in the interests of regional security.[25]

In a further inducement to Australian acceptance of Indonesian rule it was announced in Jakarta that Indonesia would not only be favourably disposed to a generous settlement of the seabed dispute which had persisted between Australia and Portugal, but that Australian petroleum and mineral exploration companies could resume operations in Timor provided they re-negotiated their leases with Indonesian authorities. If the Australian government recognised Indonesian sovereignty, Jakarta was prepared to grant Australian seabed rights extending close to the Timor Trough, sixty miles south of East Timor, just as in 1972 it had conceded Australian claims east and west of the Portuguese territory. Of the oil companies, Timor Oil and Woodside Burmah (which had interests either side of the border in Timor) had achieved encouraging results from drilling off Suai in March 1975 but been forced by the political situation in East Timor to suspend operations.[26]

The United States was also reported to have an interest in the question of East Timor, in maintaining access to the deep-running Ombai–Wetar Straits between Dili and Ataúro, which are used for passage from the Pacific to the Indian Ocean by the US nuclear submarine fleet. In August 1976 Australian Prime Minister Malcolm Fraser, accompanied by Andrew Peacock, visited the US and held talks in Washington with President Ford. In the week following it was alleged by Michael Richardson in the *Age* that senior US officials had warned that the US would not tolerate a further deterioration of relations with Indonesia. The US considered Indonesian goodwill essential, the reports said, and believed control of East Timor by a 'friendly anti-communist' government was of direct strategic interest to them.

Richardson's story emanated from US officials in South-East Asia and although Australian Foreign Affairs officials quickly denied the allegations, the *Age* held to and expanded its story: first warning had come through diplomatic channels, it said, and the Washington warning was simply a repetition of this.[27]

The sensitivity of the question of transit rights through Indonesian seaways was heightened by the fact that Indonesia had for some time been seeking acceptance, with several other island nations, of an archipelago concept of territorial waters which would extend Indonesian territorial waters beyond the twelve mile limit and substantially increase the republic's geographic area. Although the concept had not yet been accepted in international forums, Australian anxiety at the prospect of increased Indonesian control of important regional sea routes was reflected in an Australian request for permanent corridor rights through the archipelago.

Throughout 1976 until the time of writing FRETILIN has consistently reported, against Indonesian disclaimers, that they still control most of the territory of East Timor although the war has continued with unabated intensity. Arms supply, they claim, has come from the capture of Indonesian weapons and is adequate.

The Indonesian blockade has closed access to the territory not only to the International Red Cross but to all foreign aid workers and journalists. There is, therefore, no means of independent assessment.

The majority of the population appears, from all accounts, to be behind FRETILIN lines. East Timor must thus be one of the few theatres of war in modern times in which a whole population has been exposed to conditions of open warfare—including air and naval bombardment—in which medical assistance is not available for the majority of the population. After the departure of ICRC personnel from Timor in December 1975 one local doctor remained but it is not known whether he went to the mountains with FRETILIN or, indeed, if he survived. Some infirmarians are known to be with FRETILIN but none are capable of conducting surgery.

The changes within FRETILIN's top echelons in the preceding period had, by a process of natural selection, produced a leadership well equipped to conduct the resistance. The task demands particular qualities of toughness, including the ability to buoy the population to continued resistance in a situation in which FRETILIN victories in the interior are met with Indonesian reprisals against the hostage civilian population in urban centres. Those qualities of Nicolau Lobato which were of mixed benefit before December 1975—his insistence on discipline, unbending self-reliance, reluctance to negotiate—became virtues under the occupation. It was he and his brother Rogério, in concert with the military men, who fashioned

FRETILIN as a fighting force in the closing months of 1975. And whatever political differences may exist within the front between them and the popular Xavier, the Prime Minister and the President of the Democratic Republic of East Timor are inseparably linked in Timorese eyes, both having retreated to the mountains and shared the fate of their followers after the UDT coup in August 1975 and the Indonesian invasion of December. Lobato's resolution could only have been reinforced by the execution of his wife on 7 December. Most senior members of the FRETILIN administration, inside and outside East Timor, share the experience of the general population in having some members of family living under Indonesian occupation, some behind FRETILIN lines. In their case, however, families are automatically hostage to Indonesian authorities.

Soon after the invasion FRETILIN transmitted the information that APODETI and UDT people were fighting with them, and Martin's instructions to his party members confirm this. The relationship between various sectors of Timorese society has thus been vitally altered by the invasion, galvanised to a unity embracing Timorese of a range of political groupings.

APODETI had always opposed forcible annexation of East Timor into Indonesia. Many APODETI supporters were attracted to the idea of a Timor which found its cultural location among the people of eastern Indonesia, but they had almost no concept of the nature of the political régime in Jakarta, a lesson which they absorbed in brutal fashion in December 1975. Invading forces did not, it seems, discriminate between APODETI, FRETILIN and UDT supporters: all were subject to attack.

UDT and FRETILIN had experienced a constant ebb and flow of common interest; since the invasion discussions have been held between FRETILIN and UDT people outside East Timor towards a new alliance, although at the time of writing they have not borne fruit.

The avowed willingness of most of the political associations formed after 25 April, 1974 to now fight alongside FRETILIN epitomises the truth that the force now seeking to assert itself is that of Timorese nationalism, violently arrested in the period of its first ripening, but a force which has expressed itself in varying degrees through all the political groupings. The differences between them were, and are, of a political nature, of the means to achieve a national state and the nature of that state once established.

Of the nationalists, those of FRETILIN are now in a position of natural leadership with their consistent adherence to the idea of a national front uniting 'all nationalists and anticolonialists ... without discrimination of race, religion, political ideology, sex and social background', their experience of government, their preparation for the invasion and their leadership of the resistance. Most observers of the FRETILIN administration in the last months of 1975 are generally agreed that there was nothing to suggest that an independent East Timor under FRETILIN would have been other than a moderate government pursuing a foreign policy of non-alignment and regional co-operation. Its programme of social reform is moderate, based principally on establishment of agrarian co-operatives (rather than land expropriation) and mass education. Its hallmarks are fervent nationalism, populism, political pragmatism, and while FRETILIN thinking has been stamped in the mould of Third World nationalism rather than western social democracy, the future of an independent East Timor would lie open to political change.

It is not the task of this book to discuss the problems of Indonesian society but it is self-evident that the invasion of Timor and the involvement of tens of thousands of Indonesian troops in a foreign war has affected many aspects of life in Indonesia.

In early 1975 Indonesia's giant state oil company Pertamina was unable to pay its debts—and before long it became clear that it had involved the government in a multi-million dollar scandal. Initial assessment of the total Pertamina debt placed it at around \$A3,000 million, but in May 1975 it was disclosed that it stood at \$A10,500 million. The effects on the good name of the Suharto government were devastating, as were the implications for various programmes involving fresh overseas borrowing.

In these circumstances one might have expected the Jakarta authorities to hesitate before launching what has turned out to be a highly costly military adventure. And they did indeed hesitate for a time. The final decision to attack appears to have been a reflection of four major factors. Having suppressed not only the Communists but all other popular movements within their own country, Indonesia's rulers were far more frightened than they needed to be of the radical-nationalist spirit of FRETILIN and to some extent the prisoners of their own propaganda denunciations of it as Communist. Secondly they were worried lest the successful operation of a mini-state in the eastern part of the archipelago should give encouragement to secessionist forces within the Republic, particularly in Irian Jaya where the OPM (Free Papua Organisation) was still offering armed resistance fifteen years after the territory had been incorporated into Indonesia. Thirdly they had closed off most other options by December 1975. Their long period of radio denunciations of FRETILIN as Communist had made it near-impossible for them to enter into negotiations with the de facto government of East Timor, and the withdrawal of the Indonesian troops involved in the largely unsuccessful border incursions of September-December would have meant a major loss of face. Finally the international omens were favourable in early December. President Ford's presence in Jakarta on 6 December would make an invasion launched after that date appear Washington-blessed, and the hiatus of government in Australia would minimise the likelihood of important repercussions from that side.

Soon after the invasion a series of three unexpectedly forthright articles about Timor in the Jakarta daily *Merdeka* provoked an angry response from Adam Malik. Their author was B.M. Diah, *Merdeka*'s editor and a former Sukarno Minister. Titled 'Why Are We Isolated in the World?' ('Indonesia was clearly sentenced by the world in this incident and the sad thing is: there was no-one to defend it'), the articles criticised Indonesia's dependence on foreign aid and the government view of FRETILIN as Communist. 'We even regard left nationalist movements as being communist too ...' they said, 'With this way of thinking, we fell headlong into the hole we dug ourselves. In consequence we regard FRETILIN as a communist movement'. Adam Malik subsequently accused Diah of being 'pro-PKI [Indonesian Communist Party] and a traitor to the nation' and in the following days the *Merdeka* editor repudiated his articles.[28]

The *Merdeka* criticisms were exceptional. Indonesian disaffection with the Timor enterprise has generally been confined to the means used and the failure of the military to quickly annex the territory. Even among intellectuals critical of the Suharto government there are many who believe that Timor is culturally part of Indonesia and therefore rightly belongs within the republic. The heavily censored Indonesian press offers no access to contrary information. News of Timor is scarce and most of it comes from government sources.

On the other hand, those sent to fight in Timor are bearers of news, directly or indirectly, and many Indonesian families have been touched by the war:

> ... there are unmistakable signs of discontent both in the field and among the elite in Jakarta. The troops have found that a secret war is a war without glory. There are no public heroes and the dead, possibly 2,000, have been buried without fanfare ...
>
> Fretilin resistance unnerved the cream of the Indonesian armed forces. One young officer described the Indonesian entry into Dili in December ... 'They charged unarmed to within 15 yards of our tanks. We shot them. We felt unhappy'.[29]

The disclosure of the scale of Pertamina's indebtedness in May 1976 was followed in September by an abortive 'spiritual coup', the discovery of documents in which the former Vice-President Hatta and the top leaders of four major religious groupings spoke of a 'moral decline reaching a critical point' and the 'strangling of the rule of law'. The next few months saw the unearthing by the Indonesian press of a scandal in the rice purchasing agency BULOG and by the *New York Times* of a huge kickback racket over contracts for a new satellite project. All of these are clearly generating pressure for some sort of change of government in Jakarta—and the Timor war may serve to accentuate that pressure.

In late 1976 a document reached Australia containing the first detailed description of the military/political situation in East Timor from non-FRETILIN sources. The report, from Indonesian Catholic relief sources in East Timor, confirmed the picture of Indonesian occupation (but not necessarily control) of most urban centres and the concentration of most of the population in FRETILIN-held zones in the mountains:

> —All villages and towns in East Timor are occupied by the Indonesian military forces. Beyond the villages and towns there is

no main land. And the safety is not guaranteed because of the Fretilin raids.

—The total population of villages and towns occupied by the Indonesian forces amounts to 150,000 people. Taking the total population of East Timor of 650,000 people into consideration it means that 500,000 people is [*sic*] not under their control ...

—About the territory: 80% of the territory is not under direct control of the Indonesian military forces.

The report went on to say, in broken English, that FRETILIN had 'changed its tactic to win the people. They treated the people well now and do not offend them in their believe. They tried to keep their discipline high. The Fretilin soldiers are cultivating land now and make gardens'. The writer noted some 'comments heard in passing':

—"In the Fretilin there are Communists, but among the Indonesian troops there are more Communists"—

—"There are good people in the Indonesian troops, but many of them are bad soldiers"—

—"If there should be a real referendum people will choose Fretilin"—

Discussing the death toll, the report stated:

According to report, 60,000 people had been killed during the war. We found this figure rather high, because it means 10% of the total population of East Timor. But when I asked two Fathers in Dilli they replied that according to their estimate the figure of people killed may reach to 100,000.[30]

FRETILIN leaders outside the country have a perspective of a long war of resistance. It may be ten or twenty years before they return to East Timor, they say, but they believe eventual victory is assured. They can draw some comfort from the difficulties the Suharto government is experiencing at home—the series of major scandals, the difficult debt situation and the resentment among nationalists that Indonesia's former high standing in the Third World community has been lost. They have reason, too, to be satisfied with the breadth of support they received when the UN General Assembly debated the Timor issue again in November–December 1976. They have cause to believe that Jakarta will sooner or later come under pressure to disengage from East Timor, under Suharto or his successor. International support has come principally from Third World countries, especially the new Indochinese and African states, most of whom played a role in the censure of Indonesia at the non-aligned conference. The major socialist powers have also given outspoken moral support, China more so than the Soviet Union. Chinese support has, however, yet to be put to the test and reports of Sino-Indonesian discussions towards a resumption of diplomatic relations (severed after 1965) suggest that the Chinese position may be tempered in the future by considerations of *realpolitik*.

Much of the discussion affecting East Timor and regional secessionist movements has focussed on the South Moluccas and Irian Jaya. The possibility of FRETILIN resistance stimulating support from Indonesian Timor and flaring into island-wide resistance has not been seriously discussed. Although colonially-imposed and traditional differences exist between east and west Timorese, the west Timorese share their eastern compatriots' history of resistance to foreign domination and, from the scant accounts available, the war has been profoundly disruptive of daily life in Indonesian Timor.

In early 1977 Mr Jim Dunn, former Australian consul in Dili, travelled to Portugal where he interviewed Timorese refugees (of Portuguese nationality) who had left the territory since the invasion, among them a person who claimed to have witnessed mass executions by Indonesian soldiers in Dili during the invasion, including the shooting of Isabel Lobato.

Most of the Timorese had come to Portugal from Atambua, where they had been since they crossed the border on 24 September, 1975, but a few had come from Dili. Those who had been in the capital said that the attitude of Indonesian occupation forces was one of open hostility to the local population, who were usually forced to stand to attention when addressing ordinary Indonesian soldiers. An exception to this occurred in March and April when several Indonesian officers attempted to improve relations with the Dili population, but because looting and rape by Indonesian troops continued, their efforts were in vain. Evidence was also given that:

> a special intelligence unit operating on the top floor of the Tropical Hotel regularly resorted to torture to obtain information about Fretilin. The officer in charge of this 'interrogation unit'

> was Major Yusman, who worked to the Senior Intelligence Officer in East Timor, Colonel Sinaga, a man who is reportedly disliked and feared. One woman informant said she knew two women who had been tortured in an effort to obtain information about Fretilin.[31]

From what these people knew of the situation in the mountains (and there were some with first-hand information) killing there had been worse than in Dili, with whole villages being executed in response to the discovery of FRETILIN flags, or information that villagers had supplied food to FRETILIN.

Those who came from Atambua said that they had been virtual prisoners of the Indonesians since 24 September and had been subject to forced labour conditions and general ill-treatment. They repeated the allegation that the refugee figure had been grossly inflated—it was probably half of the claimed 40,000 they said.

Among the refugees were Timorese who accompanied Indonesian troops into Balibó, including one who claimed to have seen two of the journalists shot. His account was similar to that of the FRETILIN medical orderly Guido dos Santos and to that of the soldiers interviewed by Roger East. When he arrived in the village, two of the journalists were outside a Chinese house with their hands raised and a third was on the ground. He saw the two with their hands raised shot by RPKAD soldiers, he said. Another account came from a man who said his brother had been in Balibó and had told him that he entered the same house and saw several bodies on the floor, but that one journalist was still alive. He was bleeding from a head wound and attempting to speak into a tape recorder. While he was in the room an Indonesian soldier shot the man. A third informant said that he had seen a photograph of the bodies of two of the journalists propped behind a machine-gun. He was told that BAKIN intended to use the photograph as evidence that the journalists were fighting with FRETILIN but subsequently decided against this course.

There was also a reference to Roger East among the refugee's stories. A Timorese alleged that he had seen East's passport and some notes about the paratroop attack on the desk of a Provisional Government official. He had been told by the official that East had been shot with some Timorese in an apartment in Dili between the Sporting Club building and the Banco Nacional Ultramarino.

Two irreducible features emerge from the East Timor story. Firstly, no matter which arguments are employed to support the independence case—cultural, economic, historical—there is one overriding argument, the right of the East Timorese to determine their own destiny. If as the evidence suggests, there exists a widespread will to independence, that is a sufficient argument, irrespective of questions of 'viability', of the preparedness of the population, of the sensitivity of the region in the eyes of neighbouring countries. Apart from the brief interregnum of September to December 1975, and to a lesser extent the months from April 1974 to August 1975, the population of East Timor has had no opportunity to express a choice free from foreign interference.

The second irreducible, and irreversible, feature is the killing. If the two figures cited, of 60,000 and, later, 100,000 dead since the Indonesian invasion are substantial by only half, the East Timorese population has been reduced in a proportion which can be described as genocidal and one can only exclaim, after Joseph Conrad, 'The horror! The horror!'[32]

Notes

PROLOGUE: 'PEACE AND STABILITY'

1. *Frente Revolucionária de Timor Leste Independente*, Revolutionary Front of Independent East Timor.
2. This account is a reconstruction of the invasion of Dili, culled from the most reliable available sources. There has been no reliable documentation of the fate of Roger East since the invasion, although available information suggests he was killed on 7 Dec.
3. 'No Action: Whitlam', *Canberra Times*, Friday 5 Dec.
4. *União Democrática Timorense*, Democratic Union of Timorese.
5. *Associação Popular Democrática Timorense*, Popular Democratic Association of Timorese.

CHAPTER 1: THE COLONIAL IMPACT

1. William Bligh, *Bligh's Voyage in the Resource* (Golden Cockerell Press, London, 1937), pp.243–44.
2. H.O. Forbes, 'On Some of the Tribes of the Island of Timor', *Journal of the Royal Anthropological Institute* 13 (1883), pp.402–30.
3. F.J. Ormeling, *The Timor Problem: A Geographical Interpretation of an Underdeveloped Island* (2nd impr., J.B. Wolters/Martinus Nijhoff, Jakarta/'s-Gravenhage, 1957), p.35.
4. Mendes Corrêa, *Um mês em Timor*, quoted in H.G. Schulte Nordholt, *The Political System of the Atoni of Timor*, Verhandelingen van het Taal–, Land– en Volkenkunde 60 (Martinus Nijhoff, The Hague, 1971), p.23.
5. For simplicity, terms in use in East Timor will be adopted throughout the book; hence Vaiqueno rather than Timorese, *liurai* rather than *raja*, &c. The term *régulo*, often used to denote *liurais*, is a Portuguese administrative designation common to all the colonies. In Timor the *régulos* were generally *liurais* from the pre-colonial system, but in some cases were appointed from outside traditional ruling circles.

6. Schulte Nordholt, *Atoni*, pp.19, 159.
7. C.R. Boxer, 'Portuguese Timor: A Rough Island Story: 1515–1960', *History Today* 10 (May 1960), pp.349–55.
8. *Documentos de Sarzedas*, in de Castro (1867), quoted in Schulte Nordholt, *Atoni*, pp.161–62.
9. Alfred Russel Wallace, *The Malay Archipelago: The Land of the Orang-utan and the Bird of Paradise* (Dover, London, 1964), pp.147, 152–53.
10. De Castro (1867), quoted in Schulte Nordholt, *Atoni*, p.161.
11. C.R. Boxer, *The Topasses of Timor* (Koninklijke Vereeniging Indisch Instituut, Amsterdam, 1947), p.12.
12. Ormeling, *Timor Problem*, p.180.
13. D.H. Kolff, *Voyages ... Through the Southern and Little-known Parts of the Moluccan Archipelago, and Along the Previously Unknown Southern Coast of New Guinea ... 1825–1826*, ed., G.W. Earl (J. Madden & Co., London, 1840), p.35.
14. Schulte Nordholt, *Atoni*, p.164.
15. Boxer, *Topasses*, p.6.
16. Schulte Nordholt, *Atoni*, p.169.
17. Boxer, 'Portuguese Timor', *History Today*, p.352.
18. William Dampier, *Dampier's Voyage Consisting of a New Voyage Around the World ...* ed. John Masefield (E. Grant Richards, London, 1906), Vol.II, p.493.
19. C.R. Boxer, *Fidalgos in the Far East, 1550–1770*, 2nd rev. edn, (Martinus Nijhoff, The Hague, 1948), pp.182–88.
20. Quoted in Boxer, *Fidalgos*, p.186.
21. Boxer, *Fidalgos*, pp.192–93.
22. Boxer, 'Portuguese Timor', *History Today*, p.354.
23. Boxer, *Fidalgos*, p.194.
24. Schulte Nordholt, *Atoni*, pp.177–79.
25. Schulte Nordholt, *Atoni*, pp.181–83.
26. Boxer, *Topasses*, p.16.
27. Kolff, *Moluccan Archipelago*, pp.29–39.
28. Willard Hannah, 'Reanimated Relics', *American University Field Service Reports* xiv, 7 (1966), Appendix, p.13.
29. Wallace, *Malay Archipelago*, pp.144–45, 151–52.
30. Forbes, 'Tribes of the Island of Timor'.
31. Basil Davidson, *In the Eye of the Storm: Angola's People* (Penguin, Ringwood, 1975), p.107.
32. Schulte Nordholt, *Atoni*, p.105.
33. Ruth First, *Portugal's Wars in Africa* (Christian Action Publications, London, 1972), p.2.
34. First, *Portugal's Wars*, p.7; Davidson, *Eye of the Storm*, pp.112–13; William Minter, *Portuguese Africa and the West* (Penguin, Ringwood, 1972), p.16.
35. Forbes, 'Tribes of the Island of Timor', p.408.
36. Schulte Nordholt, *Atoni*, p.3.
37. Jill Jolliffe, Interviews with José Martins, Melbourne, 5–10 May 1976.
38. Abílio de Araújo, *Timorese Elites* ed. J. Jolliffe and B. Reece (Canberra, 1975), p.3.

39. Jaime do Inso, *Timor—1912* (Edições Cosmos, Lisbon, 1939).
40. Ormeling, *Timor Problem*, p.118.
41. Boxer, 'Portuguese Timor', *History Today*, p.355.
42. William Burton Sowash, 'Colonial Rivalries in Timor', *The Far Eastern Quarterly* 7 (May 1948), pp.226–35.
43. Antonio de Figueiredo, *Portugal: Fifty Years of Dictatorship* (Penguin, Ringwood, 1975), pp.77, 172.
44. Eduardo Mondlane, *The Struggle for Mozambique*, p.49, quoted in First, *Portuguese Wars*, p.8.
45. Donald E. Weatherbee, 'Portuguese Timor: An Indonesian Dilemma', *Asian Survey* 6 (Dec. 1966), p.688.
46. De Figueiredo, *Portugal*, p.179.
47. Bernard J. Callinan, *Independent Company: the 2/2 and 2/4 Australian Independent Companies in Portuguese Timor, 1941–1943* (Heinemann, Melbourne, 1953), pp. 127–28.
48. Allied Geographical Section/Directorate of Intelligence A.A.F., Southwest Pacific Area, *Terrain Study No. 50: Area Study of Portuguese Timor* (Allied Geographical Section &c., 1943), p.69.
49. Callinan, *Independent Company*, pp.154–55.
50. Callinan, *Independent Company*, p.xv.
51. Peter Hastings, 'The Timor Problem—I', *Australian Outlook* 29 (April 1975), pp.18–33.
52. Allied Geographical, *Terrain Study No. 50*, pp.57, 67.
53. Glen Francis, 'Slavery in Timor', *Observer*, 29 Oct. 1960.
54. The 1959 rebellion remains largely undocumented. Bruce Juddery, 'East Timor: Which Way to Turn?', Canberra Times, 18 April, 1975, provides one account from interviews taken in Timor. Another is contained in an anonymous document 'The Indonesian Republic's Involvement in Portuguese Timor's Affairs' (1976), in possession of the author.
55. UN document A/AC.108/L.13, Dec. 3 1962, para. 35, quoted in Weatherbee, 'Portuguese Timor', p.690.
56. General Nasution, speech at rally at Purwokerto, 22 Jan., 1963, quoted in Weatherbee, 'Portuguese Timor', p.691.
57. Unirepublic Timor, five-page typescript document in possession of Helen Hill.
58. Bruce Grant, *Indonesia* (Penguin, Ringwood, 1972), p.226.
59. De Figueiredo, *Portugal*, pp.215–16.
60. Robert Raymond, 'Timor—Sleeping Island', the *Bulletin* (Sydney), 29 Feb. 1964, pp.13–19.
61. Hastings, 'The Timor Problem—I', pp.29–30.
62. Osmar White, 'Timor—Island of Fear' and 'From Fear to all Eternity', Melbourne *Herald*, 2, 3 April 1963.
63. *Seara* (fortnightly supplement of the 'Ecclesiastical Bulletin of the Diocese of Dili'), 12 Aug. 1972–24 March 1973 (broken series) in ANU Asian Studies Library, Canberra.
64. J.M. Ramos Horta, 'Australia: O Mito e a Realidade', *A Voz de Timor*, 5 Oct. 1973.
65. Brian Toohey, 'Timor Test for Government', *Australian Financial Review*,

15 May 1973.

66. J.R.V. Prescott, 'The Australian-Indonesian Continental Shelf Agreements', *Australia's Neighbours* 82 (Sept–Oct 1972), pp.1–2.
67. Australia. Senate, *Debates* 1973, vol. S.56, p.1824.
68. De Figueiredo, *Portugal*, pp.232–33.

CHAPTER 2: APODETI, FRETILIN AND UDT.

1. APODETI, FRETILIN and UDT Programmes, appendixes to Grant Evans, *Eastern (Portuguese) Timor: Independence or Oppression?* (Australian Union of Students, Melbourne, 1975), reproduced in this work as Appendix A. Quotations from party programmes throughout this chapter are taken from this source.
2. 'Interview: Ramos Horta', *Development News Digest* II (Sept. 1974), pp.4–5.
3. Helen Hill, *The Timor Story* (Timor Information Service, Melbourne, 1976), p.4.
4. Robin Osborne, 'That 500-year Siesta Breaks Up', the *Australian*, 26 Feb 1975. Osborne argued that 'FRETILIN ... proves that if a party's program is popular, its name is irrelevant. As moderate as its name is radical, FRETILIN was inspired by the African freedom fighters, thus the title.'
5. Jill Jolliffe and Michael Richardson, Interview with Nicolau Lobato, Dili, 26 Nov. 1975.
6. J.S. Dunn, *Portuguese Timor before and after the Coup: Options for the Future* (Parliamentary Library Legislative Research Service, Canberra, 1974), pp.18, 23.
7. The Belu people refer to their warriors as 'dogs'. C.R. Boxer, 'Portuguese Timor', *History Today* pp.349–55, throws light on this:

   > In 1719, a number of disgruntled chiefs held a secret assembly at which they swore to expel the white Portuguese and then to turn on the Black Portuguese, whom for the time being they would take as allies. This oath was celebrated by the traditional Timorese blood-pact of sacrificing an animal—in this instance a dog—and mixing its blood with that of the participants, drawn from an incision in the left breast, and a liberal dose of *tua-sabo* or local brandy.

   KOTA traces its origins to this pact, the Camenassa pact.
8. Jill Jolliffe, Interviews with former Portuguese Administration Officials, Majors Barrento and Coelho, Darwin, Jan. 1976.
9. Labor caucus Foreign Affairs and Defence Committee, Report on a Visit to Portuguese Timor (unpublished notes in the possession of the author). The Committee, which consisted of Senators Arthur Gietzelt, Richie Gunn and Gordon McIntosh and MHRS Ken Fry, John Kerin and Gareth Clayton, visited East Timor from 17–20 March 1975.
10. Dunn, *Portuguese Timor*, p.15.

11. De Araújo, *Timorese Elites.*
12. J.S. Dunn, *The Timor Affair—from Civil War to Invasion by Indonesia* (Parliamentary Library Legislative Research Service, Canberra, 1976), p.9.
13. Peter Hastings, 'The Timor Problem—I'.
14. Jill Jolliffe, *Report from East Timor* (ANU Students' Association, Canberra, 1975), p.13.
15. Anthropologist Margaret King, *Eden to Paradise* (Hodder & Stoughton, London, 1963), pp.156–57, was shown a *lulik* flag during a visit to East Timor in 1962:

    While working in the vicinity of Luro the chief of one area offered to show us the strongest *lulic* of his family ... From the dim recesses of his house the chief brought to us a small and carefully wrapped bundle which he reverently unwrapped before us. Enclosed within the wrapping was a stained and tattered cloth which, as it was unfolded to the light, proved to be a flag. The linen, discoloured with age, bore at its centre a large red cross of coarsely woven cloth, such as sailors might use, and it was sewn to the finer white linen with large, masculine stitches. Printed beneath the cross, in ink now faded to reddish brown were the words:

    Dada por Valentý Corrēa figa TENENTE DEHES [BELOS] a Phoupição de Luz, Jurdição de Same dada em Luro em 20 a Julio de 1693 annos.*

    ...* Given by Valentý Corrēa, Gentleman, Lieutenant [Dehes] Belos [in the *povoação* of Luz, administrative district of] Same—given at Luro 20th July 1693.

    The veneration of *lulik* flags is universal and is not confined to those who politically support Portuguese rule. In September 1975 a FRETILIN commander at Atabae proudly displayed several *lulik* flags to a press party. The design of the old flags bears little resemblance to the contemporary flag of Portugal.
16. Jolliffe, Interviews with José Martins.
17. De Araújo, *Timorese Elites*, p.6.
18. Anonymous, The Indonesian Republic's Involvement ...
19. Labor caucus Foreign Affairs and Defence Committee, Visit to Timor.
20. Dunn, *Portuguese Timor*, p.19.
21. 'Three Political Parties Head for Plebiscite on Portuguese Timor', *Suara Karya*, 11 June 1974, cited in *U.S. Embassy Translation Unit Press Review* 110/1974 12 June 1974), pp.4–5.
22. Timor, Dili and Indonesia (anonymous document in possession of the author), Denpasar, Oct. 1974.
23. Cited in Dunn, *Portuguese Timor*, p.6.
24. Bruce Stannard, 'Order: Toe the Line or Get Out' the *Australian*, 27 March 1975.
25. *Suara Karya*, 'Three Political Parties'.
26. *O Arauto de Sunda*, 18 Sept 1974, cited in Grant Evans, 'Timor: the Dynamics of Underdevelopment and Independence', *Intervention* 5 (July 1975), pp.5–22.
27. Dunn, *Portuguese Timor*, pp.17–18.

28. Robin Blackburn, 'The Test in Portugal', *New Left Review* 87–88 (Sept.–Dec. 1974), pp.5–46.
29. Hastings, 'The Timor Problem—I'.
30. Michael Richardson, 'Indonesia Beams Radio Propaganda at the Timorese', the *Sydney Morning Herald*, 10 March 1975; Bruce Stannard, 'The Frying Pan and the Fire', the *Australian*, 14 March 1975.
31. Blackburn, 'The Test in Portugal', p.7.
32. Davidson, *Eye of the Storm*, p.60.
33. Labor caucus Foreign Affairs and Defence Committee, Visit to Timor.
34. Jolliffe, Interviews with former Portuguese Administration Officials, Jan. 1976.
35. Hill, *Timor Story*, p.7.
36. Osborne, 'That 500-year Siesta'.
37. Bruce Stannard, 'Timor Has Long Knives and Will to Fight', the *Australian*, 17 March 1975.

CHAPTER 3: FROM COALITION TO COUP

1. Davidson, *Eye of the Storm*, p.51, has discussed the problem of recording history in Angolan society, like East Timor an illiterate society, and until 1974 culturally dominated and intellectually isolated from the world by the Portuguese:

   > A great lack of information about these peoples, a lack of written information, helps to deepen the strangeness. Urban man looks for words on paper. Here you can find next to none ... 'There are zones of Angola about which little is known,' writes the Portuguese ethnographer de Lima as late as 1964, 'about which one can really write nothing.'

   Recording history from the nationalist view (including oral history gathering) and the development and definition of cultural history has been a task inseparable from the armed struggle (1960–75) of the Angolan nationalists. In Timor the preservation of *lulik* objects gives an extra dimension to the oral tradition. For example, the battledress and effects of the *liurai* Boaventura have been preserved in the *uma lulik* at Same. The Indonesian military occupation of East Timor endangers the existence of these historical and, to the Timorese, sacred objects. It is not known whether the Same *uma lulik* and its contents survived the bombing of the town in January 1975.
2. Bispo de Dili e o seu Concelho Diocesano de Presbiteros, *Perante uma Nova Situação: Carta Pastoral* (Bispo de Dili e o seu Concelho Diocesano de Presbiteros, Dili, 25 Jan. 1975), pp.2, 3, 5.
3. Bruce Stannard, 'Garrison on Timor Ready for Immediate Surrender', *Australian*, 10 March 1975.
4. Australia. House of Representatives, *Debates* 1975, no. 93, p.644.

5. Michael Richardson, 'Guerilla Scare in Timor', the *Age*, 15 Mar. 1975.
6. Anonymous, The Indonesian Republic's Involvement ...
7. Michael Richardson, 'Indonesian Told Chief to Recruit Guerillas', the *Age*, 4 Mar. 1975.
8. Bruce Stannard, 'Black gold: a curse or blessing', the *Australian*, 26 Mar. 1975.
9. F.J. Ormeling, *Timor Problem*, pp.78–79.
10. Evans, 'Dynamics of Underdevelopment', *Intervention*, p.12.
11. Evans, *Eastern (Portuguese) Timor.*
12. Australian Council for Overseas Aid, *Report on Visit to East Timor for the ACFOA Timor Task Force* (ACFOA, Canberra, 1976), p.12.
13. Labor caucus Foreign Affairs and Defence Committee, Visit to Timor.
14. Hill, Interview with José Ramos Horta, Aug. 1974.
15. Jolliffe, Interviews with José Martins.
16. Letter to the author.
17. *Indonesia Times*, 25 Feb. 1975.
18. Labor caucus Foreign Affairs and Defence Committee, Visit to Timor.
19. Michael Richardson, ' ... As Grassroots Democracy Comes to Timor', the *Sydney Morning Herald*, 13 Mar. 1975.
20. UN General Assembly Resolution 1514 (XV) of 1960, Declaration on the Granting of Independence to Colonial Countries and Peoples.
21. 'Ramos Horta Meets DPR Deputy Chairman Naro ... ', in, ed., Molly Bondan, *Indonesian Current Affairs Translation Service*, June 1974, pp.414–15.
22. Dunn, *Portuguese Timor*, p.3.
23. Michael Richardson, 'Australian Arms Pledge to Timor', the *Age*, 18 Aug. 1975.
24. Michael Richardson, 'Why Timor Talks Upset Indonesia', *Age*, Sept. 1975. The material which follows is based on this article. The London Agreement was echoed in June 1976, after the December invasion and just prior to the formal process of 'intergrasi' performed by the Indonesian Republic on 18 July 1976. Then, to the backdrop of national election campaigning in Portugal, conservative MFA General José Morais da Silva travelled to Jakarta for the first discussions with the Indonesian government since the countries severed diplomatic relations over the Dili invasion. Negotiations reportedly centred on release of twenty three Portuguese prisoners-of-war held by the Indonesians. The cynical Portuguese preoccupation with these POWs above the fate of the Timorese during the course of Indonesian intervention earned them the contempt of the Indonesians.
25. José Ramos Horta, letter to the author.
26. *A Voz de Timor*, 10 May 1975. The material which follows is drawn from the 10 May and 24 May issues of the paper.
27. Dunn, *The Timor Affair*, p.1.
28. Jolliffe, Interview with Major Francisco Mota, Darwin, Aug. 1975.
29. Jolliffe, Interviews with former Portuguese Administration Officials, Darwin, Jan. 1976.
30. Jolliffe, Interviews with José Martins.
31. Jolliffe, Interviews with José Martins.

CHAPTER 4: 'EMPTY COLONIAL SONGS ... '

1. From a prose poem about the UDT coup, 'The Cry of the Maubere Soldier', written by FRETILIN poet Francisco Borja da Costa:
   ... The colonial leaders fret at 'the criminal conspiracy',
   work to trick the Maubere soldiers
   to a murderous silence
   with empty colonial songs of a-p-a-r-t-i-d-a-r-i-s-m-o ...

   Francisco Borja da Costa, *Revolutionary Poems in the Struggle Against Colonialism* (Wild & Woolley, Sydney, 1976), p.35.
2. Jolliffe, Interviews with former Portuguese Administration Officials, and Michael Richardson and Jill Jolliffe, Interview with Rogério Lobato, Darwin, Dec. 1975. The following account of the coup is drawn principally from the Portuguese account, Rogério Lobato's account, the UDT cables sent to Darwin, and interviews with the *Macdili*'s Captain Fred Dagger. These comprehensive accounts, from different views of the coup, tally in most factual respects, if not in the political conclusions they draw from events. The UDT cables were reprinted in the *Northern Territory News* at the time.
3. 'Three Dead in Timor Fighting', the *Sydney Morning Herald*, 15 Aug. 1975.
4. (Transl.) 'Text of the Proclamation of General Armed Insurrection Against the Traitors of the Homeland and for the Genuine Liberation of the Maubere people', *Timor Leste* (extra), 4 Dec. 1975.
5. The three journalists were the *Age*'s Michael Richardson, Peter Munckton of the Australian Broadcasting Commission and Colin McIntyre of *AAP*–Reuters. Richardson reported the incident in full in 'Our Man Banned from Flying to Portuguese Timor', the *Age*, 21 Aug. 1975.
6. Jolliffe, Interview with Major Francisco Mota.
7. (Transl.) 'Communication from the Armed Forces at the Command in Aileu and the Light Infantry Company No. 10 in Maubisse', reprinted in *Timor Leste*.
8. Jolliffe, Interview with Major Francisco Mota.
9. Jolliffe, Interview with Major Francisco Mota.
10. (Transl.) 'The Beginning of the End ... Revolutionary Front of East Timor: Communique, 18 Aug. 1975', reprinted in *Timor Leste*.
11. 'Communication from the Armed Forces at the Command in Aileu'.
12. (Transl.) 'August 20: The Dili Garrison in Arms', *Timor Leste*. The last two sentences appear in the original as: '*Palapaço rendido. Presos politicos libertados*', which is interpreted here as 'Palapaço surrendered, political prisoners freed'. However, all accounts suggest that UDT held Palapaço for some days after and that the prisoners were not freed until 26 August. Possibly the tense is ambiguous due to the telegraphic language of the radio communication.
13. Jill Jolliffe, Interview with Rui Fernandes, Loes River, 27 Nov. 1975.
14. This account is drawn from an interview with Nicolau Lobato and UNETIM delegate Hamis Bassarewan. It was later confirmed by António

Coelho, a Portuguese student who was imprisoned by FRETILIN as a UDT suspect. According to Coelho, fellow-prisoners in the Aileu gaol were involved in the UNETIM killings.

15. Tribalism in East Timor was a contentious question in the period of the UDT coup, with some commentators denying its existence and others treating it as an explanation of political events.

It is not a problem confined to the liberation movement in East Timor: manifestations of acute tribal rivalry have been common to most Portuguese colonies, especially when the national process is in motion.

The late penetration of the interior of the African colonies and Timor meant that authority was initially exerted through the skilful balance of the vying political claims of various kingships. Before they were effectively a settler power, the Portuguese quelled insurrections by means of expeditions into the interior with Portuguese forces accompanied by columns of Timorese. After the late nineteenth century 'pacification' wars the practice of using Timorese troops was continued; ethnic divisions were now reinforced in the hinterland by restrictions on travel and the use of troops from neighbouring regions for police actions. Abílio de Araújo (*Timorese Elites*) has documented the betrayal of Boaventura by *liurais* loyal to the Portuguese. After 1912, the Maubisse massacre witnessed by Australians during the second world war was put down in like fashion and Dunn has reported that the Uatolári people were used to put down the 1959 rebellion. The similarity with the procedure used in Angola is striking:

> Whenever large raids or looting parties were in hand ... the governor could also call on a 'second line' army, known as the *guerra preta* ('black army'), consisting of a larger number of African warriors. These were raised on a vassal basis by chiefs of the coastal belt whom the Portuguese had terrified, corrupted or otherwise persuaded into cooperation ... . Two persistent features of the system had thus appeared. White soldiers ran the colony at all decisive points, civil as well as military; and their feeble power was buttressed by black mercenaries or conscripts. (Davidson, *Eye of the Storm*, p.109.)

It follows too, that if traditional divisions were used in the establishment of colonial rule and decolonisation is directed to a nationalist conclusion, tribalism and resistance to change by those who benefited from it will surface during the breakdown of colonial structures.

Thus much FRETILIN work is devoted to combating 'divisionism' —tribalism and regionalism:

> One of the variations of tribalism is the division of the population into '*Loro Mono*' and '*Loro Sae*', into '*Kaladis*' and '*Firakus*', ['easterners' and 'westerners' in two Timorese languages] and the belief that some groups are superior than the others. Still, today, in spite of a year of clarification, we frequently hear our friends saying that 'the *Firakus* are better than the *Kaladis*' or that 'the *Loro Mono* are no good, the *Loro Sae* are the ones that are good'. These ideas ... in no ways help our struggle ... FRETILIN wants the unity of the people and this is only possible by eradicating the false ideas which come

from a colonial and traditional society. (Mau Lear, (Transl.) 'The Establishment of New Relationships in East Timor', *Timor Leste* 2, 4 Oct. 1975.

Again, the African comparison is worth making. An MPLA cadre discusses local differences with Basil Davidson:

> 'We had to learn about these eastern peoples, we had to learn their languages, we had to find out how they think about each other, even what we should call them'.
>
> ... Petrov thinks as an Angolan and reproves me gently for inquiring into ethnic identities. 'It's tribal talk, it's greatly harmed our people' (*Eye of the Storm*, p.24).

16. Although Australian newspapers ran conflicting reports from refugee sources of, on the one hand, FRETILIN mortaring the harbour and, on the other, of UDT mortar attacks, both the Portuguese in the harbour area and the Australians in the Hotel Dili were puzzled about the source of tbe bombardment.
17. Dr John Whitehall, Personal Diary, Timor, Aug. 1975.
18. Gerald Stone, 'Timor—Island of Tragedy', the *Bulletin*, 6 Sept. 1975, pp.46–49.
19. M.F. Willis, Report of Activities of ICRC Medical Team, 30 Aug.–4 Sept. 1975.

CHAPTER 5: INTERREGNUM

1. The author arrived in Dili on one of the 11 September press planes and remained in East Timor until Red Cross evacuation flights of 2 December. The material in the chapters following is drawn largely from, personal experience.
2. The Portuguese proposal for a joint peace-keeping mission quickly collapsed, partly due to its rejection by the Australian Labor government (see Chapter 9). The proposal, and Australian responses to it, is described in an August 1976 publication of the UN Decolonization Commission, *Decolonization: Issue on East Timor* 7 (Aug. 1976) (UN Dept of Political Affairs, Trusteeship and Decolonization, New York, 1976), pp.20–21.
3. Dunn, *The Timor Affair*, p.4.
4. An exception to this rule may have been in some interior areas where APODETI appeared to fight as a separate force against FRETILIN and UDT, depending on local tribal loyalties.
5. Jolliffe, Interviews with José Martins, p.4.
6. Basil Davidson, *Eye of the Storm*, describes the comparable trend within Angola's MPLA as 'the Africanisation of Marxism', invoking a rather elastic definition of Marxism.

7. FRETILIN Central Committee, 'Press Statement, 16 September 1975', in *Timor Leste* 1, 27 Sept. 1975. The conservative stress of this statement probably expresses the influence of Ramos Horta in its formulation. He was particularly conscious of the situation in Australia at this time and the need to present a moderate face to regional governments. Ramos Horta's original draft spoke of a FRETILIN commitment to defend private property but this was deleted after the Central Committee discussion. According to the press statement the meeting was convened at Ramos Horta's request.
8. Rick Collins, AAP Interview with Alarico Fernandes, 28 Sept. 1975. Unless quoted in published form, AAP interviews are from carbons of the AAP file, Dili, Sept.–Dec. 1975, in the author's possession. A duplicate is housed in the ANU Asian Studies Library, Canberra, A.C.T.
9. Dunn, *The Timor Story*, p.45.
10. Dunn, *The Timor Story*, p.51.
11. Michael Richardson, 'FRETILIN Ready for Long War of Resistance', the *Age*, 9 Dec. 1975.
12. John Edwards, 'Timor: A New Vietnam?', the *National Times*, 29 Sept.–4 Oct. 1975.
13. Dunn, *The Timor Affair*, p.7.
14. The circumstances of this mis-reporting are described in a letter from the author to the *National Times*, 3–8 Nov. 1975.

CHAPTER 6: BALIBÓ AND BEYOND

1. Rick Collins, AAP Report, Dili, 25 Sept. 1975.
2. Rick Collins, AAP Report, Dili, 8 Oct. 1975.
3. Rick Collins, AAP Report, Dili, 27 Sept. 1975.
4. Jill Jolliffe, AAP Report, Dili, 18 Oct. 1975.
5. (Transl.) Radio Kupang, 21 Oct. 1975, recording in possession of the author.
6. Roger East, 'Journalists Shot in the Back by Indonesians', the *Australian*, 10 Nov. 1975.
7. For detailed accounts of the circumstances of the Balibó deaths see Jill Jolliffe, 'How did these Australians Die?', *National Times*, 8–13 Mar. 1976 and Michael Richardson, 'The Odour of a Cover-up over the Balibo Five', the *National Times*, 3–8 May 1976. A fuller account of Australian government responses to the deaths is given in Chapter 9 of this work, and in the final chapter is a description of the attack on Balibó from Timorese who were on the Indonesian side of the border including witnesses who were located in 1977.
8. (Transl.) 'Today, Melo Antunes and Adam Malik Meet in Rome', *Timor Leste* 6, 1 Nov. 1975.
9. Minister for Foreign Affairs, Press Release: Portuguese Timor: State-

ment of Senator Willesee to the Senate, Canberra, 30 Oct. 1975.
10. J. Dunn, 'The Political Situation in East Timor', in *Report on Visit to East Timor for the ACFOA Timor Task Force*, pp.16–18.
11. Jolliffe, Interviews with Former Portuguese Administration Officials.
12. Dunn, 'The Political Situation', p.17.
13. Anonymous, The Indonesian Republic's Involvement ...
14. Adam Malik and Maj. Melo Antunes, 'Portuguese Timor: Memorandum of Understanding', Rome, 3 Nov. 1975.
15. Michael Richardson, 'Fretilin Suffers Bitter Setback', the *Age*, 5 Nov. 1975.
16. Jill Jolliffe, AAP Report, Dili, 5 Nov. 1975.

CHAPTER 7: THE FRAGILE PEACE

1. Lear, 'The Establishment of New Relationships'.
2. Jill Jolliffe, AAP Report, Dili, 4 Nov. 1975.
3. Jill Jolliffe, 'FRETILIN Survives, Functions: Dili Government Working', the *Canberra Times*, 20 Nov. 1975.
4. Anonymous, The Indonesian Republic's Involvement ...
5. Anonymous, The Indonesian Republic's Involvement ...
6. The following sample of stories published in the Australian-read press based on Antara reports gives an idea of the extent of their acceptance:
   *Bobonaro captured—*Sydney Morning Herald*, 28 Oct. 1975 ('Pro-Jakarta Unit "Kills 89 FRETILIN Soldiers"'); the *Canberra Times*, 23 Oct. 1975 ("Jakarta Prediction: Dili 'Will Fall'"); *Far Eastern Economic Review*, 31 Oct. 1975 (Dan Coggin, '"Beaten" Army Back on the Battlefield').
   *Fighting in Maubara—the *Canberra Times*, 19 Nov. 1975 ('Timor Talks Depend on FRETILIN').
   *Landing in Baucau—the *Age*, 3 Nov. 1975 ('Jakarta Takes Tough Line in Timor Talks'); the *Canberra Times*, 3 Nov. 1975 ('Renewed Fighting in Timor'); the *Sydney Morning Herald*, 29 Oct. 1975 ('Indonesia "Heavily Involved" in Timor'); the *Sydney Morning Herald*, 14 Nov. 1975 (Michael Richardson, 'The War that Indonesia Won't Declare').
   *Dili under attack–the *Sydney Morning Herald*, 4 Nov. 1975 ('Dili Under Heavy Attack'). This front-page story, which ostensibly emanated from diplomatic circles in Canberra, pre-empted by one day the trouble in Dili with the military police.
   According to Dunn, *The Timor Story*, p.64, even Moscow's *Pravda* carried some of these reports without comment.
7. Jill Jolliffe, Interview with Mari Alkatiri, Dili, 25 Nov. 1975.
8. Roger East, *'Independence or Death!': East Timor's Border War*, (Campaign for Independent East Timor, Sydney, 1976), p.8. This undated account

refers to Roger East's observation of Indonesian activity from Bobonaro in the (approximate) period of 10–28 Nov. 1975.

9. FRETILIN Central Committee, Telegram, 24 Nov. 1975.
10. (Transl.) Propaganda Leaflet, Balibó, 26 Nov. 1975, in ANU Asian Studies Library, Canberra, ACT.

CHAPTER 8: INDEPENDENCE

1. Jill Jolliffe, Interview with Alarico Fernandes, 14 Nov. 1975.
2. Jill Jolliffe, AAP Report, Dili, 30 Nov. 1975.
3. Jill Jolliffe, AAP Report, Dili, 1 Dec. 1975.
4. The author was present at one such demonstration on 11 March 1975, where estimated attendance was 15,000–20,000.
5. Xavier do Amaral, Inauguration Speech, Dili, 29 Nov. 1975.
6. (Transl.) Constitution of the Democratic Republic of East Timor, ANU Asian Studies Library, Canberra.
7. Dunn, 'The Political Situation', p.16.
8. Dunn, 'The Political Situation', p.18.
9. Jolliffe, Interviews with José Martins.
10. 'Malik Warns', the *Canberra Times*, 3 Dec. 1975.
11. Bruce Juddery, 'Warning on Danger Received Last Week', the *Canberra Times*, 27 Nov. 1975.
12. 'We Won't Meddle in Timor War, Says Former PM', the *Sydney Morning Herald*, 5 Dec. 1975.
13. 'Letter from Indonesia—Indonesian Government's Lies Exposed', *Timor Information Service*, 9/10 (Melbourne), 6 May 1976, pp.2–3.
14. Roger East, 'Timor—Flee' (Reuters News Report), 6 Dec. 1975. This was Roger East's last published communication with the outside world. It was received by Reuters in London at 1.58am—two minutes before midnight in Dili. According to Reuters staff in Darwin and Sydney, East succeeded in sending another dispatch, an hour or so after Indonesian forces had landed in Dili. Because this report was not used by Reuters, no record has been kept, but its substance was recalled as saying that Indonesian troops were in the city, that the airport had been taken and that East expected the Marconi communications centre to be taken soon. The sending of this bulletin from the Marconi centre may have cost Roger East his life.

CHAPTER 9: 'AUSTRALIA'S ROLE'

1. Jill Jolliffe, Interview with Ian Carroll (former Channel 9 producer),

Melbourne, Nov. 1976 and Michael Richardson, 'The Odour of a Cover-up'.

2. Department of Foreign Affairs, *Report Outlining Investigation into Deaths of Five Television Reporters in Balibo, East Timor*, (1), Canberra, 31 Oct. 1975.
3. Foreign Affairs, *Report Outlining Investigation* ... (2), Canberra, 2 June 1976. This letter is reproduced in full in Appendix C.
4. Foreign Affairs, *Report Outlining Investigation* ... (2).
5. Michael Richardson, 'Men We Killed Directed Fretilin, Says UDT', the *Age*, 4 Nov. 1975.
6. Foreign Affairs, *Report Outlining Investigation* ... (2).
7. Radio Kupang, 21 Oct. 1975; Jill Jolliffe, AAP Report, Dili, 27 Oct. 1975; Roger East, 'Journalists "Shot in the Back" ... '.
8. Foreign Affairs, *Report Outlining Investigation* ... (1).
9. Australia. House of Representatives, *Debates* 1975.
10. These accounts were given by Mr and Ms Rex Syddell, Mr José Martins of KOTA and Timorese refugees from Atambua in Indonesian Timor, interviewed in Portugal in early 1977 by Mr J.S. Dunn. All are discussed in the final chapter.
11. Peter Hastings, 'The Timor Problem—II: Some Australian Attitudes 1903–1941', *Australian Outlook* 29 (2), Aug. 1975, pp.180–96.
12. Callinan, *Independent Company*. p.228.
13. Hastings, 'The Timor Problem—II'.
14. Hastings, 'The Timor Problem—II'.
15. W.D. Forsyth, 'Timor—II: the World of Dr Evatt', *New Guinea* 10, May–June 1975, pp.31–38.
16. Quoted in Helen Hill, 'Australia and Portuguese Timor—Between Principles and Pragmatism', in comp., Roger Scott and J. Richardson, *The First Thousand Days of Labor*, vol.i, (Australasian Political Science Association, Canberra, 1976), pp.339–56.
17. Hill, 'Between Principles and Pragmatism'.
18. Hill, 'Between Principles and Pragmatism'.
19. 'The Prime Minister's Visit to South-East Asia', *Australian Foreign Affairs Record*, 1974, p.161.
20. Hugh Armfield, 'Canberra Aim for Timor: Go Indonesian', the *Age*, 13 Sept. 1974, quoted in Hill, 'Between Principles and Pragmatism'.
21. Michael Richardson, 'East Timor: the War Australia Might Have Prevented', the *National Times*, 19–24 July 1976.
22. Gregory Clark, 'With Australia's Blessing the "Dragon" Moves on Timor', the *National Times*, 22–27 Mar. 1976.
23. Australia. House of Representatives, *Debates* 1974, no. 91, p.3044.
24. House of Reps. *Debates*, pp.3049–50.
25. House of Reps. *Debates*, 1975, 93, p.641.
26. House of Reps. *Debates*, p.644.
27. Quoted in Hill, 'Between Principles and Pragmatism', p.17.
28. Richardson, 'East Timor: The War ... '.
29. Clark 'With Australia's Blessing'.
30. Nancy Viviani, 'Australians and the Timor Issue', *Australian Outlook* 30 (2), August 1976, pp.197–226.

31. Australia. House of Representatives, *Debates* 1975, no. 96, pp. 492, 493.
32. Australia. House of Representatives, *Debates* 1975, no. 96, pp.685, 1390.
33. 'ALP Men Concerned', the *Canberra Times*, 29 Aug. 1975.
34. Clark, 'With Australia's Blessing'.
35. Australia. Senate, *Debates* 1975, vol. 66, pp. 1609, 1610.
36. Bruce Juddery, 'Do Not Accuse Jakarta: Ambassador', the *Canberra Times*, 31 May 1976.
37. Quoted in Richardson, 'East Timor: the War ... '.
38. Peter Bowers, 'Whitlam Attacks Leaking of Timor Cable', the *Sydney Morning Herald*, 14 Aug. 1976.
39. Bruce Juddery, 'Deduced Answers on Timor', the *Canberra Times*, 6 Dec. 1975.
40. 'Peacock: Timor a Blight on Record', the *Age*, Fri. 28 Nov. 1975.
41. 'One Voice on Timor', the *Age*, 2 Dec. 1975.

CHAPTER 10: AFTERMATH

1. (Transl.) Radio Dili, 8 Dec. 1975, recording in possession of the author.
2. 'Fighting Tragic, Says Peacock' and 'Our Troops Will Leave, Says Malik', the *Age*, 8 Dec. and 9 Dec. 1975.
3. UN Decolonization Commission, *Decolonization*, pp.64–66.
4. 'String of Timor Coastal Towns Hit', the *Sydney Morning Herald*, 13 Dec. 1975.
5. Jolliffe, Interviews with former Portuguese Administration Officials.
6. Radio communications from FRETILIN, 2–5 Jan. 1976. The exact texts of FRETILIN radio messages to Australia from 7 Dec. 1975 to Nov. 1976 have been reproduced in the bulletin of the Melbourne-based Timor Information Service. Much of the material in this chapter is drawn from that source.
7. (Transl.) Radio Dili, Dec. 1976, recordings in possession of the author, and Jolliffe, Interviews with Portuguese Administration Officials.
8. (Transl.) Aco Manafe, 'Between Caution and High Hopes', *Sinar Harapan*, 6 Jan. 1976.
9. Tony Joyce, 'A.M.' (Australian Broadcasting Commission), 11 Jan. 1976 and Michael Richardson, 'Under the Double-talk, Timor Suffers', the *Age*, 15 Jan. 1976.
10. UN Decolonization Commission, *Decolonization*, pp.61–62.
11. Andrew Clark, 'From Canberra ... What We Knew', the *National Times*, 5–10 Jan. 1976.
12. '"Timor Death Toll 60,000": Leader', the *Age*, 14 Feb. 1976.
13. Dunn, *The Timor Story*, p. 73.
14. Hamish McDonald, 'Witnesses to Murder Held for "Protection"', the *Sydney Morning Herald*, 12 Mar. 1976 and Errol Simper, 'The Surprising Mr Syddell', the *Canberra Times*, 7 Aug. 1976.

15. Quoted from *Indonesia Times*, 26, 28 Apr. 1976, which reprinted the text of Rex Syddell's UN testimony, in 'True Story About East Timor: as Told by [R. Syddell]'.
16. Quoted in 'José Martins Defects—Does the "Provisional Government" Exist?', *Timor Information Service* 9/10, 6 May 1976, p.5.
17. Jolliffe, Interviews with José Martins, and Dunn, *The Timor Story.*
18. Richard Tanter, 'The Generals: Background', *Dissent* 36 (Autumn/Winter 1977), pp.38–39.
19. Foreign Affairs, *Report Outlining Investigation* ... (2).
20. 'Indonesia to "Crush" Timor Rebels', the *Canberra Times*, 26 July 1976.
21. Antonio de Figueiredo, 'Portugal's Premature Sell-out', *Guardian Weekly*, 29 Aug. 1976.
22. Michael Richardson, 'Quit Timor, Indons Told', 'Deadlocks Mar Summit', and 'Asean Nations Attacked' the *Age*, 19, 20, 21 Aug. 1976.
23. Michelle Grattan, 'PM Told: Call Off Indon Trip', the *Age*, 5 Oct. 1976.
24. Michelle Grattan, 'PM Tries to Shut the Timor Book', the *Age*, 11 Oct. 1976.
25. 'Recognise Takeover: Companies in Approach to Canberra', the *Age*, 23 Oct. 1976.
26. Michael Richardson, 'Indonesia's Timor Carrot', the *Australian Financial Review*, 19 Oct. 1976.
27. Michael Richardson, '"Don't Anger Jakarta": US Protecting Indon Channel for its N-Subs' and 'Indons: Two Warnings', the *Age*, 3, 4 Aug. 1976.
28. Quoted in Molly Bondan, ed., *Indonesian Current Affairs Translation Service*, Feb. 1976.
29. Anthony Goldstone, 'No Glory in the Timor Secret War', the *Guardian Weekly*, 22 Apr. 1975.
30. Notes on East Timor, document from Catholic relief sources, East Timor (undated).
31. J.S. Dunn, *The East Timor Situation: Report on Talks with Timorese Refugees in Portugal* (Parliamentary Library Legislative Research Service, Canberra, 1977), p.10.
32. Joseph Conrad, 'Heart of Darkness' in *Youth, Heart of Darkness and The End of the Tether: Three Stories by Joseph Conrad* (London, J.M. Dent and Sons, 1956), p.161. Conrad was writing of atrocities committed during Belgium's colonisation of the African Congo.

Glossary

ACFOA Australian Council for Overseas Aid

ADITLA Associação Democrática Integração Timor-Leste—Australia (Association for the Integration of East Timor and Australia)

APODETI Associação Popular Democrática Timorense (Popular Democratic Association of Timorese)

ASDT Associação Social Democrática Timor (Social Democratic Association of Timor)

ASIAT Australian Society for Inter-Country Aid (Timor)

chefe de posto administrator of *posto*, Portuguese administrative post

concelho Portuguese administrative division; province

conscientização process of developing political consciousness described by Brazilian educator Paulo Freire:

> the process in which men, not as recipients, but as knowing subjects, achieve a deepening awareness both of the socio-cultural reality which shapes their lives and of their capacity to transform that reality.
> Paulo Freire, *Cultural Action for Freedom* (Penguin, Ringwood, 1974), p. 51.

deportado Portuguese political exile

DGS Directorate General of Security, Portuguese secret police organisation, successor to PIDE

FALINTIL Forças Armadas de Libertação Nacional de Timor-Leste (National Liberation Forces of East Timor); FRETILIN army

FRELIMO Frente de Libertação de Moçambique (Mozambique Liberation Front)

FRETILIN Frente Revolucionária do Timor-Leste Independente (Revolutionary Front of Independent East Timor)

ICRC Internationale Çomité de la Rouge-Croix (International Committee of the Red Cross)

KOSTRAD Strategic Reserve Command, Indonesian Army

KOTA Klibur Oan Timur Aswain (Sons of the Mountain Warriors);

literally, in Tetum, 'Warrior-dogs'
kuda Timor pony

lipa basic Timorese garment; skirt
liurai traditional king, East Timor
loja de povo 'shop of the poor'; FRETILIN-sponsored consumer co-operative

MRAC Movimento Revolucionário Anti-Comunista (Revolutionary Anti-Communist Movement); anti-Communist movement formed by UDT and pro-integrationist parties after UDT coup of 11 August 1975
malai foreigner (Tetum)
mestiços people of mixed race
MFA Movimento das Forças Armada (Armed Forces Movement); democratic officers' movement, also known as the 'Captains' movement', which overthrew the Salazar regime in Lisbon on 25 April 1974
MPLA Movimento Popular de Libertação de Angola (Popular Movement for the Liberation of Angola)
MRPP Movimento Revolucionário do Proletariado Português (Revolutionary Movement of the Portuguese Proletariat); Portuguese Maoist party

'Operasi Komodo' Indonesian military/political operation for the incorporation of East Timor into Indonesia
OPJT Organização Popular da Juventude Timor (Popular Organisation of Timorese Youth)
OPMT Organização Popular da Mulher Timor (Popular Organisation of Timorese Women)

PAIGC Partido Africano da Independencia da Guiné e Cabo Verde (African Party for the Independence of Guinea and Cape Verde)
Panca Sila the five principles of Indonesian nationalism: faith in one God, humanity, nationalism, representative government and social justice
PKI Partai Kommunist Indonesia (Indonesian Communist Party)
Partido Trabalhista Labor Party, East Timor
PIDE Policia Internacional e de Defensa do Estado (International and State Defence Police); Portuguese secret police under the Salazar régime
posto Portuguese administrative post

raja traditional king, Indonesian Timor
retornado refugee from Portugal's colonial wars now living in Portugal

SAPT Sociedade Agrícola Pátria e Trabalho; Portuguese-sponsored agricultural company founded in 1897 by Governor Celestino da Silva, military commander of the Portuguese campaign against Dom Boaventura

TAT Transportes Aéreos Timor (Timor Air Transport); government airline under the Portuguese administration

UDT União Democrática Timorense (Democratic Union of Timorese)

APPENDIX A

Founding Political Programmes of APODETI, FRETILIN, and UDT

APODETI

MANIFESTO OF THE ASSOCIAÇÃO POPULAR DEMOCRÁTICA TIMORENSE

In view of ending the 400-year Portuguese occupation, the Portuguese Armed Forces Movement has concretely and objectively as well decided the right of overseas people to determine their own flag.

Considering that in facing the freedom to be granted, Timor will concretely have the following choice:

a) to be integrated into the Portuguese community
b) to be independent, and
c) possible autonomous integration into the Republic of Indonesia, based on international law.

In view of the first two mentioned have been taken by the União Democrática Timorense and Associação Social Democrática Timorense, both of which we highly honour, we the undersigned, herewith:

realize the failure of the Portuguese colonisation of Timor, due to the distance separating Timor;

realizing the political as well as historical situation at present, that a wrong choice will ruin the future of Timor's next generation, due to the immaturity of the economic and political conditions of Timor;

realizing that the association can be established to develop the prosperity as well as welfare of the Timorese people in the future if all Timorese people sacrifice, especially the more advanced, to immediately abandon their own interest;

realizing, at last, the existing culture of traditional mysticism of our Timorese ancestors which has been forgotten, and the unchanged Timorese geo-political situation, we have determined to develop our future.

In this respect,

After having had a long and careful discussion, and being representative of the majority of the 600,000 Timorese people to exercise their fundamental right, and according to the political as well as social conditions, to guarantee their mutual interest and peaceful co-existence with other peoples and other nations as well, we have come to an agreement to establish a political party by the name of **'Associação Popular Democrática de Timor'** (shortened to APODETI), to maintain the following rights:

1. An autonomous integration into the Republic of Indonesia in accordance with international law.
2. The teaching of the Indonesian language as a compulsory subject at all secondary schools, and the opening of elementary schools teaching Indonesian as the first language, without necessarily abolishing the present Portuguese schools.
3. The exercise of freedom and essential human rights.
4. Just distribution of wealth by the government.
5. Just employment with fixed minimum salary.
6. The exercise of labour's right to strike.
7. To enjoy the Portuguese language and civilisation as well.
8. Free education and medical treatment for all.
9. Freedom of religion with particular respect to Catholic churches, in which humane activities are always carried out, and, where necessary should be encouraged, since its doctrine has consolidated our socio-political activities.
10. Freedom of expression with a sense of responsibility.
11. Direct voting in general elections in accordance with the principle of [electoral] regulations.
12. APODETI is openly opposed to:
    a) activities which are against human interest, and the unpopular practices of government officials in obtaining labourers.
    b) racial discrimination, and
    c) corruption and all other colonial practices.
13. To be a member one should meet the following requirements:
    a) A Timorese by birth, living in or outside Timor.
    b) If not a Timorese by birth, one should accept the party's principles, or be prepared to expand APODETI.

REGARDING GUARANTEES

In accordance with [APODETI's] political evaluation of South-east Asia, APODETI can assure all members, and the people of Timor that the party will pursue:

1. a peaceful co-existence policy, and to those who wish to remain in Timor, APODETI promises to maintain their rights and wealth, so long as they do not harm the economy and political situation of Timor;
2. the right of students to study at foreign universities, especially at the universities in Indonesia and Australia as well.

FOUNDERS OF THE PARTY

Signed: José Fernando Osório Soares—Arnaldo dos Reis Araújo—Armindo Tilman—José Martins—José António Bonifácio dos Reis Araújo—Gaspar da Silva—José Soares—Abel da Costa Belo—Moisés da Costa Martins—Ermínia da Costa dos Reis de Araújo—Felisberto de Jesus Soares—João de Assunção O.C.Ximenes—João da Costa Damas—José da Costa—José Morato—Manuel Jacinto G. da C. Soares—Francisco Orlando de Fátima Soares—Basílio de Sá Moniz da Silva—José Amaral—Maharus Alkatiri—Ernesto Rebelo—João Afonso Gusmão—Ernesto Ananias Almeida da Costa—Duarte da Silva—João Soares da Silva—João Pereira da Silva—Abílio José Osório Soares—João Hermenegildo da Costa—Domingos F. Aleixo da Silva—Alexandrino Borromeu—Frederico Almeida Santos Costa.

FRETILIN

FRENTE REVOLUCIONÁRIA DE TIMOR LESTE INDEPENDENTE

As it is not possible for the existence of a liberal fascism or democratic colonialism, it becomes absurd thinking that any kind of dependency, either displayed openly or indiscreetly, can promote the progress of the colony and the liberation of the people under colonial domain.

It is a fact that 500 years of Portuguese colonialism can be translated into the following human, social, economic, cultural and political panorama, which is clearly oppressive and violating the most basic rights of the human being—

a) Ridiculous, humiliating, undignified per capita income [symptomatic of] the unbounded exploitation of man.

b) A very high rate of illiteracy, which displays the discrimination and domination of the Portuguese government's colonial policy.
c) Cancerous and degrading corruption of the political and economic superstructures that paralyses any form of development of the country and of the dominated people.
d) Obsolete and anachronistic political and administrative structure.

Thus, it is urgent, for the making of a clear, concise, vigorous and active decision ... considering the circumstances of the actual political moment and considering that our country is crossing a grave hour and decisive step of our history ...

Considering that this moment must be of action, responsibility, courage and generosity at all lengths and of a clear and formal decision; in one word, it is urgent to awake the CONSCIOUSNESS OF THE NATION ...

Considering that it is necessary and opportune to pass to a more active stage among the people of East Timor, in order to help them in their struggle for liberation and independence.

After prolonged meetings and debates, the General Assembly of ASDT, the Social Democratic party, decided to issue the following manifesto:

MANIFESTO

I

The Social Democratic Party considers itself the interpreter of the profound ideals of the people of all East Timor and, because of this reason, declares itself the only legitimate representative of the people and will now be called "Revolutionary Front of Independent East Timor"—FRETILIN.

II

The aims of FRETILIN are based essentially on those previously that of ASDT, and can now be summarised as following:—

1. FRETILIN is a forefront movement that is the incarnation of the most profound aspirations of the people, that is, the thinking, feeling and will for liberation of the people of East Timor—INDEPENDENCE.

2. FRETILIN recognises that the only way for a real liberation and progress of the people of East Timor is INDEPENDENCE, to be consolidated with the following:–

2.1 Total abolition of colonialism to be done under the following:–

a) Profound and quick transformation of the old colonialist structure implementing new forms of democracy.
b) Cultural development inspired by a new process and concept of the culture which is to be from the people, with the people and for the people.
c) Active movement against corruption and exploitation of the people.
d) Multi-racial living without discrimination of race and religion.

2.2 Strong rejection and repudiation of neo-colonialism and all forms of alienation of the country to another foreign country.

3\. FRETILIN defends strongly the right of INDEPENDENCE and declares:–
a) Immediate declaration of INDEPENDENCE *DE JURE.*
b) Immediate decolonisation. This process will be integrated in the process of the transference of power, to be done simultaneously with the transformation of the structure pointed out in no. 2.1, in order to achieve DE FACTO INDEPENDENCE.
c) Its recognition by Portugal as the only mouthpiece for discussions about the process mentioned in b), by mutual agreement.

4\. FRETILIN defends the policy of closer international co-operation with Portugal, Brazil, Guinea-Bissau and the future countries of Portuguese expression, as well as the countries of the geographic area in which Timor is integrated, safeguarding the superior interests of the people of East Timor.

5\. FRETILIN will resort to international aid and the goodwill of all nations and international organisations in order to solve the most urgent problems in the social, economic, cultural and political fields.

6\. FRETILIN will resort essentially to the United Nations for supervision, and other forms of aid, related to the process of decolonisation and transference of power in order to achieve de facto independence.

7\. FRETILIN will reserve the right to select the member countries of the United Nations that will integrate the supervision commission.

NATIONALIST MOVEMENT WANTS IMMEDIATE INDEPENDENCE

The Timorese Social Democratic party, which wants full independence for Portuguese Timor, has been hardening its policy. After a long debate by the general assembly of the party, the announcement of a new programme for more [positive] action was made through the local radio.

The party issued a manifesto and announced the formation of the REVOLUTIONARY FRONT OF INDEPENDENT EAST TIMOR (FRETILIN), headed by Francisco Xavier Amaral, 38, as General Secretary, with the support of about 50,000 members throughout the country. The manifesto was enthusiastically welcomed by the people, and everything indicates that in the very near future the REVOLUTIONARY FRONT OF INDEPENDENT EAST TIMOR will win the great majority of Timor's population.

According to the manifesto, the leaders of the movement will negotiate with the Portuguese government for the recognition of FRETILIN as the only legitimate representative of the people of East Timor, which wants immediate independence de jure.

They will apply also to the United Nations for supervision of the process of decolonisation until the country achieves full de facto independence.

The economic and political philosophy of the revolutionary front is based on a concept of social democracy, the same as the previous Timorese Social Democratic party.

It is completely false that about 70% of East Timor's population want integration in Indonesia—Ramos Horta, secretary of the new Revolutionary Front of Independent East Timor, said. Horta denies what Arnaldo Araújo, 62 years old, leader of APODETI, a tiny political party that wants integration in Indonesia, has stated.

POLITICAL PROGRAMME OF THE REVOLUTIONARY FRONT FOR THE INDEPENDENCE OF EAST TIMOR

INTRODUCTION

For more than four hundred years our land, East Timor, has lived under Portuguese colonialism. These five hundred years in the historical march of humanity have little significance or place for us. It refers to a time in which a system was introduced into Timor by force—the system of colonialism. These past five hundred years of our development are full of dramatic developments: wars of oppression and subjugation, accompanied by the exploration and the rape of the riches of the people. Our land in which we have lived during these centuries has experienced many moments of anguish when our forefathers raised their voices against Portuguese colonialism, and many times had recourse to armed struggle in defence of their legitimate rights. These various uprisings and rebellions over the long five hundred years of colonial domination registered and proved irrefutably the strong spirit and desire for independence which tied together our forefathers.

Our people fell under the domination of a foreign power by virtue of the armed superiority of the colonialist enemy. But this was not the only reason for the loss of our independence. Our forefathers' sentiment for independence was restricted by tribal feuds and by geographical divisions. This fact was able to be exploited by the Portuguese colonialists. Through intrigues and promises the new enemy was easily able to divide us, and this helped to facilitate our domination.

Through the exercise of colonial power we gradually lost our land, our women were maltreated, we were reduced to lives of slavery and obscurity, our culture stagnated, our daily lives were full of misery and hunger, leading to premature death. With our culture and lives severed at the root by COLONIALISM, we were not able to combat these evils. This form of colonialism was unable to guarantee for our people an existence imbued with liberty and progress.

FRETILIN struggles against colonialism and any form of domination of our people. We struggle for a humanitarian existence, for our development and for our lives. But this struggle cannot be conducted if the people are factionalised. We remember very well that the DISUNITY of our forefathers caused their defeat. We will not repeat the same error. We will go forward in unity.

For this, it is urgent and necessary that all people participate in the Revolutionary Front of Independent East Timor (FRETILIN).

Here is our political programme:

MINIMAL PROGRAMME

FRETILIN, in the struggle for the national independence of East Timor, proposes the following minimum programme for fulfilment, and as an outline of the process of decolonisation. It is a *sine qua non* condition for the start of the development programme.

A. NEGOTIATIONS WITH THE PORTUGUESE GOVERNMENT, IN ORDER TO CONCRETIZE THE FOLLOWING BASIC POINTS:

1. Recognition of FRETILIN as the only legitimate representative of

the people of East Timor.

2. Immediate recognition of independence *de jure* to the people that live in the territory of East Timor.
3. Co-operation of the Portuguese Government with FRETILIN within the framework of the extensive programme drawn up by FRETILIN to execute the tasks of reconstruction and development in the following sectors of our country:
   a) The total eradication of colonialism through a profound and accelerated transformation of the old colonial structures and the implementation of other structures that truly serve the people of East Timor.
   b) The rejection and energetic repudiation of neo-colonialism and all forms of alienation of the country to any potential foreign power.
4. Revision of all the accords and contracts signed by the Portuguese Government with foreign economic groups, contracts of compromise, especially those that refer to the exploration of the soil, underground exploration, exploration on the continental shelf of East Timor, as well as the occupation of agricultural land by régimes of large property, and activities developed by foreign capital or Portuguese capital.
5. Suspension of all the affirmed applications by foreign groups or Portuguese which were addressed to the Portuguese Government.

B. INTERNATIONAL RELATIONS

1. Non-alignment.
2. FRETILIN will immediately develop widespread diplomatic activity with all the countries of the world and with international organisations, in order to gain moral, diplomatic, political, technical, economic, financial and military support, with a broad view to constructing and developing the country, but always safeguarding the policy of non-alignment.
3. FRETILIN defends a good neighbour policy of no interference and co-operation with all countries of the world.
4. FRETILIN is in solidarity with all people of the world struggling for progress.

Viva FRETILIN
Viva Timor-Leste Independente

PROGRAMME OF THE REVOLUTIONARY FRONT OF EAST TIMOR

The Revolutionary Front of Independent East Timor (FRETILIN) is a fore-front movement which interprets the profoundest aspirations of the people of East Timor to be free from political, cultural and economic colonisation and other forms of domination and exploitation.

FRETILIN, being the only legitimate representative of the people of East Timor, aims to develop all efforts in order to be the only valid mouthpiece in the process of decolonisation which, to be authentic, must adhere to the following program:

I. IMMEDIATE RECOGNITION OF INDEPENDENCE *DE JURE* BY THE PORTUGUESE GOVERNMENT

FRETILIN interprets independence *de jure* as the formal recognition that the only way for the future of East Timor is *total independence*. Until this is achieved, FRETILIN will have the co-operation of the Portuguese government to implement the program of reconstruction and development of the country. FRETILIN will discuss with the Portuguese government the best form of this co-operation.

II. RECONSTRUCTION AND DEVELOPMENT OF THE COUNTRY

A. BASIC POLICIES

1. Gradual elimination of colonial relations and structures and the active struggle against the establishment of new forms of domination and exploitation.
2. Creation of new political, economic and social structures which will serve the interests of the people of East Timor.
3. Resort to the Portuguese Government, foreign governments and international organisations to obtain economic, financial and diplomatic support for the implementation of the program of reconstruction and development.
4. FRETILIN reserves the right to control and orientate the implementation of this program through the existing departments, or others to be created to guarantee its fulfilment.
5. FRETILIN also reserves the right to administer its funds independently and without interference.

B. SPECIFIC MEASURES

1. Economic reconstruction:

a) Creation of social, economic and technical structures.

b) Creation of co-operatives. The co-operatives will be the base of the economic and social life of East Timor. Co-operatives of production, distribution and consumption will be set up throughout the country.
c) Elimination of excessive dependency on foreign countries. Incentives will be given to the production of goods of basic needs through diversified agriculture. Mono agriculture will be discouraged.
d) Agrarian reform. All large farms will be expropriated and returned to the people and will be used within the co-operative system. Fertile lands not under cultivation will be distributed to the people and will be utilised in co-operatives or by state enterprises.
e) *Agricultural mechanisation*
f) Promotion of fishing and cattle.
g) Protection of all flora and fauna. Re-afforestation and introduction of new species.
h) Development of food manufacturing industries (milk, cheese, butter, canned meats, fish and fruits) by the utilisation of national resources. Also, the utilisation of forests for timber and the manufacture of timber products, including furniture and paper. Local industry, including native handicrafts and weaving, will be encouraged. Modern industry will be promoted and geared to a rapid economic and social development.
i) Commerical exploitation will be stopped, prices controlled and a new fiscal system introduced. Control of commerce.
j) Internal commerce: co-operatives will ensure the distribution of national and imported goods.
k) Exports will be organised through the central co-operative in Dili, which will receive all products and produce from the regional co-operatives for export.
l) Imports: The central co-operative will handle all imports and will distribute them to the regional co-operatives.
m) Balance of payments: Imports will be strictly controlled.
n) Introduction of a national currency.

2. *Education and Culture:*

a) Elimination of the colonialist educational system. This will be replaced by a system which will serve all people. At the same time, Timorese culture will be maintained, fostered and encouraged.
b) An extensive program will be initiated to eliminate illiteracy and ignorance among people of all ages.
c) A university and technical colleges will be established and

scholarships awarded for study in overseas countries.

d) The Portuguese language will be retained as the official language of the country.

e) A program of research and study will be made into the Tetum language, as well as other local languages. A further aim is the fostering of literature and art of the various ethnic groups through cultural exchanges for the enrichment not only of Timorese culture as a whole, but also as a contribution to universal culture.

f) Physical education and sports will be encouraged.

g) All citizens will have free choice of religion. Native religious houses, churches, mosques and temples will be protected.

3. Health:

a) Clinics and hospitals will be established throughout the country. A mobile doctor service also to be formed to serve outlying areas.

b) Immediate steps will be taken to eradicate prevalent diseases including leprosy, TB and malaria.

c) Timorese will be encouraged to train as doctors and nurses in foreign countries. Foreign doctors will be invited to work in East Timor for varying periods of time.

d) Children, invalids and the aged will be protected.

e) Free medical assistance will be given to all citizens.

f) All health services will be controlled by the state.

4. Social Justice

a) Gradual elimination of exploitation.

b) Forced labour will be abolished immediately.

c) Wages will be determined by the state on the basis of equal work, equal pay for both sexes.

d) Women workers will be paid wages during and after pregnancy.

e) Educational programs will be launched to help combat alcoholism, vagrancy, prostitution and gambling.

f) Traditional institutions of justice will be preserved and protected and improved by international law.

g) Organisations for workers, women, students and youths will be established so that every person will actively contribute to the political life of the country.

5. Internal Administration:

a) Abolition of the colonial administrative structure.

b) Division of the territory of East Timor into regions.

c) The regions to be administered by representatives from both FRETILIN and the Portuguese Government. Regional committees of FRETILIN will launch the basis for a democratic administration and will ensure the implementation of the program of reconstruction and development in each region.

6. National Defence:

a) The defence of the territories of East Timor will be guaranteed by the armed forces, which will serve the people.
b) The armed forces will protect the rights of the people.
c) The armed forces will defend the rights of the people by securing peace and order necessary for the implementation of this program.
d) Restructure of the armed forces.

III. INTERNATIONAL RELATIONS

1. Non-alignment.
2. Good neighbour policy and non-interference.
3. Co-operation with all countries in the world.

IV. PROCLAMATION OF INDEPENDENCE

FRETILIN reserves the right to decide the date of the proclamation of independence of East Timor.

Sovereign and Independent State

1. Republican, democratic, anti-colonialist and anti-imperialist Government.
2. General elections for a constitutional assembly through direct and secret universal suffrage.
3. Equality of all citizens before law.
4. Organisations and groups which support the annexation of the country to a foreign power will be forbidden to exercise political activities.
5. Protection of all citizens in foreign countries.

UDT

TIMORESE DEMOCRATIC UNION

PROVISIONAL STATUTES

Following various work sessions, it was decided recently to elaborate the Provisional Statutes of the Timorese Democratic Union.

The first section of the Statutes constitute the principal ideas for the existence of UDT, although there have been some alterations and modifications to the original wording in the section 'on organization'. However, they do not modify in essence the ideas which founded the party. On the contrary, they have translated more faithfully our thoughts, and more clearly our final objective. Which is, through our propaganda to enlighten those of the interior, and for UDT delegates to give knowledge to the Timorese people.

Article 1—The Timorese Democratic Union (UDT) is a political party whose objectives and principles are the following:

a) Accelerated promotion—proceeding in the shadow of the Portuguese flat—of the social, economic, cultural and political development of the Timorese people.
b) Self determination for the Timorese people oriented towards a federation with Portugal, with an intermediary stage for the attainment of independence.
c) Integration of the Timorese people through the use of the Portuguese language.
d) Acceptance and observance of the Universal Declaration of Human Rights.
e) Good neighbour policy.
f) Defence and enrichment of the Timorese culture.
g) Just distribution of income.
h) Active struggle against corruption.
i) Democratisation of Timorese life.
j) Rejection of the integration of Timor into any potential foreign country.

Article 2—For the diffusion of our principles and our ends, UDT stands for:

a) Sessions of clarification and propaganda.
b) Plenary sessions.
c) Elaboration of the programme in line with the preceding articles.

d) Co-operation with international organizations for technical, financial and human help for the promotion of the Timorese people.
e) Co-operation with other political parties, political and civil associations, always with the wishes of Timor foremost in our mind.
f) Active participation in Timorese life.

Dili, August 1st, 1974. By the Organizing Committee.

from Grant Evans, *Eastern (Portuguese) Timor: Independence or Oppression?* (Australian Union of Students, Melbourne, 1975).

APPENDIX B

Communique from the FRETILIN-UDT Coalition

JOINT COMMUNIQUE, ISSUED BY THE COALITION REVOLUTIONARY FRONT OF INDEPENDENT EAST TIMOR AND TIMORESE DEMOCRATIC UNION

The Revolutionary Front Of Independent East Timor (FRETILIN) and the Timorese Democratic Union (UDT) are the legitimate representatives of the people of East Timor, because of our intransigent defence of the right of the people to national independence. We insist that independence is the only possible way for real liberation of the people from exploitation and oppression of any form.

FRETILIN and UDT are interpreting the will of the overwhelming majority of the People of East Timor for National Independence, thus we reject strongly any other form of domination and our position is—INDEPENDENCE OR DEATH!

FRETILIN and UDT also reject any questioning of the right of the people to independence implied in a referendum, a so-called "act of free choice": nobody should ask a slave if he wants to be free! This means that the position of the coalition is unshakeable and we shall fight to the death for national independence, the legitimate right of all nations in the world.

Due to the economic and political limitations and with a deep sense of realities, the coalition has proposed the following program towards full independence:

1. A transitional government to be formed by a High Commissioner, representing the President of the Portuguese Republic and to consist of: equal representation of the Portuguese Government, FRETILIN and UDT. During this period a reform of all internal administrative and political structures will take place.

2. The minimum period of the transitional government will be three years; this period can be extended if this is determined by the circumstances.

3. General elections for a Constitutional Assembly will take place after the process of decolonization has been completed.

The transitional government will be responsible for the implementation of the program of Reconstruction and Development of the country.

The transitional government will endeavour to promote friendship, goodwill and cooperation with all countries of the world, but particularly with Australia and Indonesia for the peace and security of the whole region.

Dili, 18th March 1975.—
Central Committee of FRETILIN,
Francisco Xavier do Amaral
—President—
Central Committee of UDT,
Francisco Lopes da Cruz
—President—

APPENDIX C

Balibó

I. Joint Statement by leaders of APODETI, UDT and KOTA, Balibó, 22 October 1975.

STATEMENT

1. APODETI, UDT and KOTA have been requested by the Government of Republic Indonesia to perform an action of searching concerning the placement of five Australian journalists whom eventually are believed to stay inside the areas under our present control.
2. As regard to such official request of the Indonesian Government the leaders of APODETI, UDT and KOTA, namely Mr. Guilherme Maria Goncalves, Liurai of Atsabe, Mr. Francisco Lopes da Cruz, President of UDT and Mr. Jose Martins, President of KOTA went on a visit together for the purpose of inspecting the troops over the areas already taken out of FRETILIN's control by the combined forces of APODETI and UDT and as far as the request of the Indonesian Government about the five Australians is concerned the above leaders have obtained the following report:
   a. The military Commander of Balibo Mr. Tomas Goncalves has reported that some days ago there was a big fight between the forces of APODETI and UDT against the positions held at the time by FRETILIN.
   b. Referring the actions carried out by our combined forces the above mentioned Commander stated that on their way up to the Balibo fortress, suddenly, there was a counter-attack launched from a house against our forces. Therefore, it became necessary to blow out with heavy fire that house-position which became into flames afterwards. As soon as our front forces arrived to the house it was found that fifteen people were killed being among them some white people whom were previously controlling and guiding the fire of FRETILIN position against our troops.
   c. Among the 15 dead people there were several white men that

might be or not the Australian journalists questioned on the request of the Indonesian Government.

3. For the above mentioned facts we do declare that the journalists now under search are not of our responsibility and therefore their presence is to be confirmed with Australian, Portuguese and FRETILIN's sources as the responsible entities for the presence of those journalists.

Balibo, October 22, 1975.

[signed] On behalf of Presidium of APODETI
Liurai of Atsabe
D. Guilherme Maria Goncalves
On behalf of Political Committe of UDT
Francisco Xavier Lopes da Cruz
President
On behalf of KOTA—Klibur Oan Timur Aswain
Jose Martins
President

II. Statement by Francisco Lopes da Cruz, Batugadé, 27 October 1975.

Batugadé, 27th October 1975

Mr. R.K. Johnson
Third Secretary
Australian Embassy
KUPANG

Further to my previous letter and in response to your last letter dated also October 13, 1975 I do have the honour to add some more considerations to those already stated as far the searching for australian citizens is concerned.

I do have concentrated some more details, not so much positive, related to the village of Balibo after the fight erupted overthere. As trying to perform some eventual help to you here is the results of our investigations.

1. On the wall of one house in Balibó has been painting by hand the following inscription:

   First, the word AUSTRALIA
   Below, a rough drawing of the Australian flag
   Very close to these, was written in portuguese:
   "Falentil está sempre ao lado do povo maubere"

2. I do question myself whether the people of that house were journalists or not. This is a point to clarify having the inscriptions in mind.

3. According to the words written in portuguese: "Falentil está sempre ao lado do povo maubere" Fretilin must be responsible for any australian citizen present at Balibó at the time.
4. Also it must be questioned the real meaning of these inscriptions as they may seem a form of publicity to be demanded to Fretilin, as this is traditional a political tactic of the leftist groups.
5. Meanwhile, I inform you that UDT and APODETI have been requested by the Government of Jakarta to find out any possible documents of the australians. If there are any the same will be sent directly to the same government.
6. For all the regretable situation that our territory is facing this moment we are now expecting that the Australian Government take the necessary steps to stop australian citizens to come and fight side by side with Fretilin and fight and press the timorese people.

For the opportunity this is all I can supply you as information to your searching.

Yours truly
[signed]
Francisco Lopes da Cruz
President of UDT

from *Report on Investigation into Balibó Deaths* Foreign Affairs Department, Canberra, 2 June, 1976.

Index